Émile Alglave, J. Boulard

The Electric Light

Its History, Production, and Applications

Émile Alglave, J. Boulard

The Electric Light
Its History, Production, and Applications

ISBN/EAN: 9783743400641

Manufactured in Europe, USA, Canada, Australia, Japa

Cover: Foto ©ninafisch / pixelio.de

Manufactured and distributed by brebook publishing software (www.brebook.com)

Émile Alglave, J. Boulard

The Electric Light

Moorish salon in the Continental Hotel lighted by the Jablochkoff candle.

THE

ELECTRIC LIGHT:

ITS HISTORY, PRODUCTION, AND APPLICATIONS.

BY

ÉM. ALGLAVE AND J. BOULARD.

TRANSLATED FROM THE FRENCH BY

T. O'CONOR SLOANE, E. M., PH. D.

EDITED, WITH NOTES AND ADDITIONS, BY

C. M. LUNGREN, C. E.

ILLUSTRATED WITH TWO HUNDRED AND FIFTY-TWO WOODCUTS.

NEW YORK:
D. APPLETON AND COMPANY,
1, 3, AND 5 BOND STREET.
1884.

EDITOR'S PREFACE.

THOUGH there are already a number of popular expositions of the subject of electric lighting, the work of Messrs. Alglave and Boulard has been thought to have sufficiently distinctive merits to warrant its introduction to the English-reading public.

While not pretending to be an exhaustive presentation of the subject, the exposition will be found to be sufficiently full to enable the reader to understand the essential features of present electric-lighting apparatus, and to appreciate the character of the problems which had to be solved before this method of illumination could enter upon an industrial career.

In adding to the work of the authors I have made no attempt to introduce either all of the lamps and machines which have been devised, or even all of those which have passed into actual use. The additions of this kind which have been made are either later forms of the apparatus described by the authors, or those which have distinctive features of interest of their own. The chief additions which I have thought it desirable to make relate to the general aspects of the subject, rather than to special forms of apparatus. Changes have been found necessary throughout the text, either in correction of erroneous statements, or in amplification of insufficient ones, but these are in all cases inclosed in brackets, as are the additional chapters and sections, and the notes.

I have to express my indebtedness to Mr. Edison, the United States Electric Lighting, Fuller Electrical, and Brush Electric Companies, for information concerning their various systems, and cuts illustrating their apparatus.

C. M. L.

NEW YORK, *April, 1884.*

PREFACE.

TEN years ago, it was generally admitted that the *rôle* of electricity was practically confined to telegraphy and electroplating. Outside of these two uses it seemed destined to remain a costly curiosity, available at the best in those cases in which ordinary economy could be left out of account, in the presence of necessities not governed by expense, as in theatres and light-houses. But, since the invention of the Gramme machine, the rapidity of its daily progress has astonished the most sanguine. The International Exhibition at Paris was a genuine revelation to the public, and perhaps even to many savants. In spite of its scientific character, its success exceeded all expectations, and its popularity proved that the public began to understand the important *rôle* that electricity already fills in the life of society, and to divine the still greater importance reserved for it in the near future.

This exhibition, which may justly be termed educating, was principally instituted and advocated by the founders of a journal of electricity, bearing the same name as this book, "La Lumière Électrique."

The original committee comprised among others Dr. Cornelius Herz; M. Adrien Hébard, senator, and editor of the "Temps"; M. Jules Bapst, editor of the "Débats"; M. Jaques de Reinach; and M. Georges Berger, who was Commissioner-General of the Exhibition. The project, warmly supported from the beginning by the Minister of Public Works, M. Varroy, finally reached its consummation under the patronage of the Minister of Mails and Telegraphs, M. Cochery, and supported by the successor of M. Varroy in the Ministry of Public Works, M. Sadi Carnot.

The success of a large fortnightly journal, devoted exclusively to electricity, is another proof of the growing importance of this branch of physical science, which promises to be more fertile than all the others in industrial applications. Further, we must state that there exist in Paris alone one or two other periodicals also devoted to electricity and its applications.

This book is devoted entirely to that one of the applications of electricity, which, without doubt, is about to experience the most rapid practical development : we refer to artificial lighting.   But, for the economist as well as for the engineer, the use of the electric light belongs to the general applications of electricity, on account of the question of the distribution of this physical agent, which now can be utilized by the general public.   We shall never have cheap electricity until the day comes when it shall be distributed to each individual house by such a system as that used for gas, and then it will distribute power as well as light.   This marvelous result is not only possible but easy of accomplishment to-day.   The important labors of M. Marcel Deprez, detailed in the fifth book of this work, furnish a complete solution, founded upon discoveries which have greatly modified the theories generally accepted up to the present time.   The first experiments have brilliantly confirmed the previsions of the inventor, who is now preparing to reproduce them on a large scale.

The system of electrical distribution of M. Marcel Deprez has more than an industrial interest ; its importance is also great from a social point of view, for it may perhaps modify the economic development of the modern world.   The concentration of industrial processes in immense factories where the workman loses his individuality and his originality, has hitherto seemed an inevitable consequence of the domination of mechanical motors, because small heat-engines are too costly to render possible the distribution of work in the family workshops.   Electricity, on the other hand, does not suffer the same losses in being divided so as to be put at the disposition of the humblest. It can penetrate the poorest of garrets by a wire similar to a bell-wire, and then can drive the smallest sewing-machine, at almost the same cost, in proportion to the power employed, as if it were actuating the largest class of machinery. The turning of a switch suffices to give immediately, and to the full extent, the quantity of power desired, and to make it vary at will, without any loss when the work is interrupted or diminished.

Doubtless electricity, thus under perfect control, will not be able to re-establish a complete equality between the large and small producer. But the contest will become possible in many cases, and the development of the smaller industries will furnish the workman, desirous of raising himself to the rank of master, an ideal less inaccessible for him than is the proprietorship of Creusot.

In such a question as this, the initiative should be taken by the Municipal Council of Paris, because it alone can authorize and encourage effectively the general distribution of electricity in the city where such distribution can render the greatest services. To take this initiative it has only to persevere in the way it has followed for the last three years. The Universal Exhibition of 1878 showed us the advent of the electric light upon the principal streets of the capital. The Exhibition of 1881 should leave us as a souvenir a general distribution of power and light by electricity. We may hope that the Municipal Council of Paris will not hesitate in a question where the democratic spirit so happily allies itself with the scientific.

CONTENTS.

BOOK I.

HISTORY OF ARTIFICIAL LIGHTING.

BOOK II.

THE VOLTAIC ARC.

BOOK III.

THE INCANDESCENT LIGHT.

BOOK V.

DISTRIBUTION OF ELECTRICITY.

LIST OF ILLUSTRATIONS.

2

HISTORY OF ARTIFICIAL LIGHTING.

CHAPTER I.

OILS, CANDLES, AND GAS.

To acquire a real comprehension of the true *rôle* of the electric light and the changes which it can introduce both in our habits and in the industrial world, it is necessary to give succinctly the history of lighting in general, and of electric lighting in particular.

Fats and oleaginous materials were employed as a means of lighting by the most ancient peoples. But, even among the most civilized nations of antiquity, such as the Greeks and Romans, this mode of lighting had preserved nearly as barbarous a form as among the savage tribes. The lamp of a Roman emperor was not much pleasanter or less smoky than the torch of resinous wood with which the first known men lighted their abodes—those men whom history ignores, and whom geology has resuscitated during the last twenty-five years.

This lamp consisted simply of a vessel filled with oil, into which dipped a thick, twisted wick, formed of any fibrous material, wool, linen, cotton, etc. The end of this wick was raised so as to rest on the edge of the vessel, and it was there that the oil burned, creeping up through the wick by capillarity (Fig. 2).

Specimens of these apparatus can still be seen elsewhere than in museums. The peasants of other countries have preserved the classic lamp up to our days, perfecting a little the burner, or neck, to prevent the wick from falling back into the oil. As a regulator to advance this wick as fast as it was burned, the Roman matron, as well as the peasant's wife of to-day, had doubtless no better arrangement than a common hair-pin; for the pincers and hook specially made for this purpose resembled one in shape, and were but little more convenient (Figs. 1 and 3).

This thick wick, or, we should rather say, this string of tow, does not permit the air to penetrate sufficiently to burn completely the carbon of the oil. The unburned carbon escapes in a nauseous smoke, which produces a choking sensation. But the smoke of ancient times must have been much worse than that of to-day, because the oil was very impure, and was often replaced by fats full of all kinds of impurities. We give here illustrations of the lamp which figures in the most poetical stories of Greece. We may see in it the elegant lamp which the imprudent Psyche over-

Fio. 1.—Pincers   Fio. 2.—Bronze Roman lamp.   Fio. 3.—Hook
for lamp.   for lamp.

turned upon Cupid on that fatal night when she yielded to the ill-fated desire of unveiling the *incognito* of her mysterious lover. We can understand the anger of the divine child, which, in the case of the little electric burner, would be inexplicable. In this last case, even if he were to be burned, he would need no perfumes to disinfect himself.

In the sumptuous palaces of imperial Rome, as well as in the hovel of the slave situated in the remotest fields, the system of lighting was everywhere the same. It was easy to substitute for coarse earthenware precious metals for making the lamp, to give it an elegant form, and support it on candelabra, richly sculptured (Figs. 4 and 5) and designed with skill; but it is always the same lamp which we have to describe—its luxurious appearance could not modify its organization in any essential.

Many savants to-day consider fire, as well as language, to be the great characteristic of humanity. It is singular that this primordial invention, which has made man the superior of all that is highest in nature, and has taken him out of the rank of animal, has been one of the last to be perfected. Yet this is precisely what has happened. The Roman lamp, scarcely superior to the utensils of the primitive savages, remained without a rival during the greater part of the middle ages.

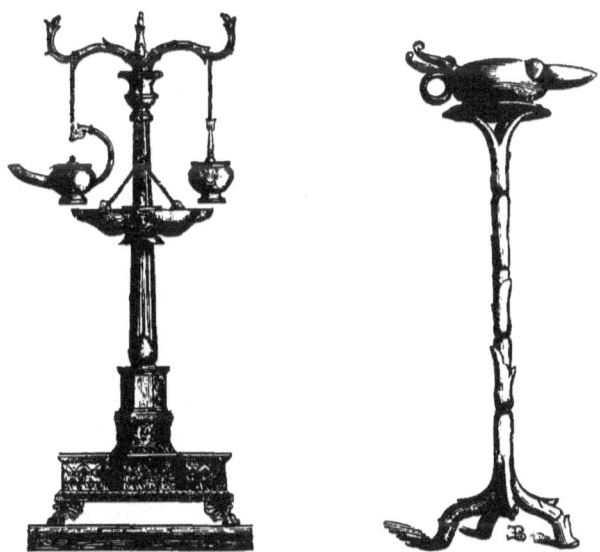

Figs. 4 and 5.—Roman candelabra in carved bronze, bearing one or more lamps.

Only at the end of the twelfth century did the great novelty dawn upon England—a light-giving solid material to replace oil. This novelty had for name the "tallow-candle"! It was made of sheep's fat, and of the well-known form which it has preserved to the present day. It may have seemed a dangerous invention, because it took a long time for its use to extend itself. It was in the reign of Charles V, at the end of the fourteenth century, that the French began to use it. I refer to the rich men of France; it was as yet too great a luxury for the commonalty to indulge in.

To our fathers it seemed a great step in advance—and for their epoch they were right—and they were contented with it for a long time. *Le roi soleil* had no other luminaries to light up at night the glories of Versailles, and the plays of Molière, of Racine, and even those of Voltaire, were produced by the light of candles of six to the pound.

For a long time, also, those traveling through the streets of the cities were most happy to be guided on their way by the light of candles placed in the corners of the windows. Lanterns for public lighting date from the middle of the seventeenth century only; and it is not until a hundred years later that we find them surmounted by a reflector, depriving the sky of their slender rays in order to cast them back upon the earth. It was then that they assumed the well-known name of reflectors (*réverbères*). Some among us, who have passed the critical time of youth, can remember them dangling from the altitude of a gallows-frame, whence they descended at the end of a cord, like a bucket into a well, when it was necessary to light or to extinguish them.

To-day the tallow-dip has developed into the candle. Thanks to the discovery of the composition of fatty bodies, made by Chevreul in 1811, it became possible to extract from tallow the best of its luminiferous components, stearic acid. M. Chevreul himself tried it in conjunction with Gay-Lussac, and the two took out in Paris a patent for the process, which, however, was never used, any more than the English patent taken out in London by Gay-Lussac under the name of Moses-Poole. We must not forget, however, that their method could not work in practice.

Another chemist, Cambacérès, took out four patents for the same object during the years 1825 and 1826. He was somewhat more fortunate than his illustrious competitors, and was the first to manufacture stearine-candles, undoubtedly very imperfect and very impure, as their yellow coloration plainly showed. These candles soiled the hands like the tallow-dips, smelled almost as bad, and burned in an inferior manner in spite of the perfecting of the wick. For these reasons their sale was very limited, and Cambacérès soon gave up the manufacture.

It was two young physicians, MM. de Milly and Matard, who took up the problem in 1829, and reached at last a satisfactory solution after two years of patient research. Thus it is in the year 1831 that the history of the manufacture of stearine-candles begins, and, as the first factory was situated near the Arc de Triomphe de l'Étoile, they were named *bougies de l'étoile* (star-candles), soon known throughout the world, which name they kept when the factory was moved away from that place.

More solid and better in appearance, as well as less greasy to the touch, and provided with a wick which needed no snuffing, because it burned itself up, burning without smoke or disagreeable odor, the stearine-candle preserved the form of the old tallow-dip, and, from the physical point of view, worked in the same manner. But it also gave more light. It is it which will hereafter be employed as a standard in comparing sources of light, a candle being taken as such standard which burns ten grammes of stearine per hour—unfortunately, a unit which varies greatly according to the greater or less purity of the stearine employed in commerce.

The "star-candles" then sold for three francs fifty centimes a kilogramme, so that the standard candle, burning ten grammes per hour, costs three and a half centimes for one hour's burning. On account of a lower price, it now costs little over two centimes. On the other hand, it is much dearer than the tallow-candle, which formerly did not bring half the price of the stearine-candle, and which to-day is worth far less, in the proportion of one franc twenty-five centimes to two francs ten centimes a kilogramme. It is true that a kilogramme of tallow gives only four fifths as much light as the same quantity of stearine. But, taking this difference into account, the expenses will be found not to exceed one centime and a half per hour and per unit of light; that is to say, hardly three quarters of the cost of the stearine-candle for the same result.

Hence the new candle has only been an advance from the point of view of comfort and luxury, but not from the standpoint of economy. The same does not apply to another invention, which has transformed the conditions under which oil is employed—we speak of the modern lamp.

The end of the eighteenth century was marked by a discovery which produced upon the public as great an effect as that of the electric light to-day. This discovery, whose name now sounds even vulgar to us on account of its very popularity, is the Argand lamp. We shall now show how it has transformed the ancient Roman lamp.

If the lamp with thick wick gives so much smoke and so little light, it is because enough air does not get access to it to supply the oxygen necessary for the complete combustion of the carbon. The light being produced by the combustion, it is much less vivid, just like the combustion itself. On the other hand, the flame, full of particles of carbon which have not found molecules of oxygen to unite with in legitimate marriage, has not enough heat to bring all to the temperature where they become luminous. It remains, then, charged with black particles—that is to say, with smoke—which obscures it and fills it with all the odors that can be produced from the oil, odors which a more complete combustion would have destroyed.

To suppress all these troubles a greater influx of oxygen upon the flame must be contrived. To do this, Argand had the idea of giving to the wick the form of a cylindrical tube,

and allowing the air to penetrate to its center. The flame no longer formed a solid cylindroid like that of a candle, but a circular plane, quite thin, and well supplied on both sides with air, so that it no longer was in want of oxygen. The reservoir of oil was placed at a certain distance from the burner, and in a somewhat more elevated position, so that the fluid would rise to the level of the wick, in accordance with the laws of equilibrium in communicating vessels. The apparatus divided thus into two parts, and united by a communicating tube, was fastened to

FIG. 6.—Quinquet's lamp hung upon a wall.

a wall (Fig. 6), or it rested on a rod or flat-footed standard of some degree of stability.

To this new disposition of parts Quinquet added a chimney of glass, which increased the draught—that is to say, increased the quantity of air supporting the flame—and he produced the complete invention under his own name in 1785. This date is of as much importance in artificial lighting as is 1789 in politics. It was the epoch, in effect, of a complete industrial revolution. Between the ancient lamps and the lamp of Quinquet there is as much difference as between the chimney of our parlors and the fireplace of our original Aryan ancestors, formed by a hole dug in the ground in the center of their cabins.

Later, Carcel excited a universal enthusiasm in adapting to Quinquet's lamps a clock-movement—replaced at a more recent period by a spring—and moving by it a piston which pressed upon the oil and forced it to rise in the wick in greater quantity. This made it possible to place the oil-reservoir below the wick, and the flame could be given a brightness which surpassed all expectations (Fig. 7). Louis XIV would have been dazzled by it.

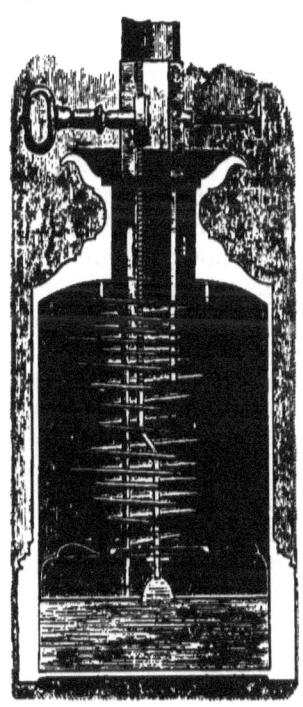

Carcel's invention, giving to the light of the lamp more regularity than the candle possessed, furnishes us with a new unit for comparing sources of light, and for measuring their illuminating power. The conditions under which the type of lamp adopted, called the Carcel, should burn, have been determined, and have been expressed in the practical directions drawn up in 1860 by MM. Dumas and Regnault for the daily tests of the illuminating power of the Paris gas. The wick should be three centimetres in diameter, and the lamps should burn forty-two grammes of purified colza-oil, with a flame four centimetres in

Fig. 7.—Lamp of the Carcel type, with moderator mechanism, and bottom oil-reservoir.

height. Compared with the different standard candles adopted elsewhere, the Carcel lamp equals seven and a half stearine-candles, those which are called "star-candles," and which are still used in France for minor illumination. For the spermaceti-candle employed in England, or "*standard candle*," a Carcel lamp is equal to seven and four-tenths candles. For the paraffine-candle used in Germany, a Carcel burner equals nine and six tenths candles.

The Light-house Board of France had adopted a somewhat lower type, burning only forty grammes of purified colza-oil per hour. But the Congress of Electricians, without arriving at an absolute decision as regards photometric standards, has expressed the desire that all experiments should be conducted upon the uniform type of forty-two grammes; in other words, with the Paris standard.

Taking the price of oil at one franc and fifty centimes a kilogramme, the expense of a Carcel lamp is six and three tenths centimes per hour, while eight candles for the same space of time would cost seventeen centimes. Lighting, therefore, is three times cheaper with the Carcel lamp than with candles. At the same time the light is whiter, more regular. and also more concentrated, so that a greater luminous intensity can be obtained. Thus the lamp appears from all points of view an advance upon the candle and tallow-dip.

The modern lamp, which we use to the present day, was a. completed invention. But, just as it took its final form, it found ready for it a rival which has rapidly replaced it for all extended uses.

Before the year 1801 the French engineer Lebon had discovered and demonstrated the powerful lighting qualities of gas produced by the distillation of bituminous coal in closed vessels. But, as often happens, the idea originating in France was at first only applied in England. In France, gas was pronounced unhealthy, just as coal itself had been for the same reason condemned a short time before. Nevertheless, it was tried in Paris in 1818, under the administration of M. de Chabrol, and its immense success immediately forced it into the public service; after having conquered the streets, the conquering hero soon penetrated also the private houses, and was accepted everywhere.

It is this light that reigns to-day, and its supremacy is due principally to its cheapness. A gas-flame equal to the Carcel lamp only costs at Paris three centimes per hour, instead of six and a half; that is to say, less than half the cost of oil. This calculation is based on a high price for gas, such as still obtains in some situations, namely, thirty centimes per cubic metre ($1.70 per 1,000 feet). But in the case of cities, which pay only fifteen centimes, the expense comes down to one quarter the cost of oil, and this is the price all consumers pay in London, as well as in most English cities.

The producers of oil believed that they had received a death-blow, and, as bituminous coal as well as oil was a home product, they could not suppress the new industry by a protective tariff. Gas gave more light for less money, could be conveniently used in all places, and did away with a lot of utensils which were always a source of trouble and uncleanliness. How could such a rival be conquered?

Natural as these pessimistic forebodings seemed, experience has proved their falsity. The oil industry is as prosperous to-day as it ever was. Its production has not diminished. By the side of the brilliant triumphs of gas, it has filled many places where the new conqueror could find no footing, and in these cases the original consumption of oil has been increased, because the eye, more exacting on account of the prodigal light of gas, is not content with the feeble light which formerly satisfied it. Thus, what the lamp has lost by competition with gas, it has gained in the competition with the candle, in spite of the transformation of the latter into a cleaner and better luminary than it was of old.

About 1860 the discovery of petroleum added still more to our resources, giving us a light at least as good as that of gas at a much lower price, yet we (the French) were the only ones who were not allowed to profit by the discovery, because of the heavy tariff which the oil had to pay on its entry into France. Again, the oil-producers, and even the gas-manufacturers, felt themselves seriously menaced. Nevertheless, gas continues to prosper, not only in France, but also in England and Germany, where petroleum costs twenty centimes a litre, and even in New York, where it hardly costs two centimes,* on account of the proximity of the Pennsylvania wells.

What has been going on for the last fifty years between oil and gas is taking place to-day between gas and electricity. Since the electric light has grown, and seems to threaten the domain of gas, all the interests there engaged are trembling, as the representatives of oil did of old. Already it has several times happened that the announcement of such or such an electrical discovery has induced real panics among the numerous stockholders of the gas companies of the world, especially those of America.

These fears are without foundation: the coming of the electric light will create new needs; without injuring con-

---

* [This price is about two cents a gallon. Petroleum suitable for burning in lamps can not be bought in New York by the barrel at less than seven times this price.]

temporaneous industries, it will cause improvements, and probably a lowering in price, by which the whole community will profit.

The consumer will spend just as much money, but will have a better light, and the producer will make his profit on

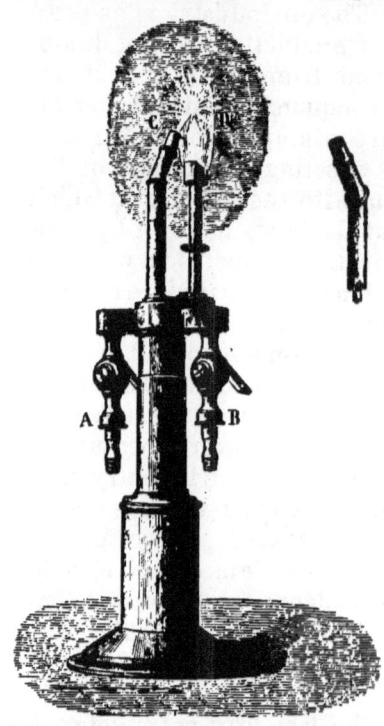

an increased sale. Of this we have already seen the proof in the improvements recently introduced in gas-burners, in which the illuminating power has been increased and the consumption of gas diminished in a ratio that four or five years ago would have seemed incredible.

As for coal, it is not at all menaced, because it is by the intermediation of the steam-engine, that is to say, by the consumption of coal, that electricity is produced. It may be that in some conditions gas-engines may be employed instead of steam-engines, so that gas will profit by the development of electricity.

Here we must speak of two other processes of lighting which are interesting, because the principle of incandescence on which they are founded is applied with success in certain recent systems of electric lighting, and because they give us very powerful lights, comparable from this point of view with the arc-electric light itself.

FIG. 8.—Lamp of M. Tessié du Motay for production of the Drummond light.

A and B, inlet-cocks for oxygen and coal gas, brought through caoutchouc tubes fitted below.
C, blow-pipe, with issuing gas-jet. The two gases only mix at the end of the jet, following separate conduits up to this point, one cylindrical, the other annular, surrounding the first as shown in the detail section on the right.
D, plate of magnesia, which becomes incandescent under the action of the lighted gaseous mixture.

The first consisted in the employment of a cylindrical cage of platinum wire brought to incandescence by the heat from a jet of hydrogen gas. This system was publicly experimented with in 1859, in some streets of Narbonne. The effect was satisfactory, but it was far too expensive.

The other system, invented by Mr. Drummond, was modified by M. Tessié du Motay, who made several trials of it from 1867 to 1872 in different localities in France, notably in the Place de l'Hôtel de Ville and the Place du Carrousel. The Drummond system, still in use for experiments, consists in heating a pencil of lime by the heat developed by the combustion of a gas-jet formed of two volumes of hydrogen and one of oxygen. M. Tessié du Motay replaced the hydrogen by ordinary coal-gas, and the lime by compressed magnesia (Fig. 8).

The same objections were made to the too great intensity and too great whiteness of the light that are made to the electric light to-day. Lamps on this system can give a light of twenty Carcel lamps, by burning about two hundred litres (seven cubic feet) of gas per hour. But the cost of production, and of the separate gas mains and pipes for the oxygen gas, raise materially the cost of this light.

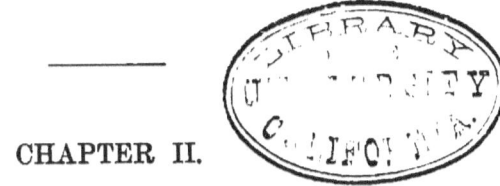

CHAPTER II.

HISTORY OF THE ELECTRIC LIGHT.

It would be going too far to trace the history of the electric light back to the Greeks of the heroic epoch, that is to say, to Thales of Miletus, considered by many savants as the first ancestor of our electricians, because he is supposed to have known the attraction developed in yellow amber by friction. But, without going so far back, mention must be made of the inventor of the first electric machine, in the latter half of the seventeenth century, the studious burgomaster of Magdeburg, Otto von Guericke, to whom also is due the first air-pump.

We know that Otto von Guericke produced electricity by rubbing a globe of sulphur with the hand (Fig. 9). He is the first who produced light from this electricity ; this was rather a faint glow, like that of phosphorus in the air, for he com-

Fig. 9.—Hawksbee experimenting with Otto von Guericke's electric machine, in England.

pares it to the light produced by rubbing pieces of sugar together in the dark. It is a long way from this insignificant and fugitive light to the immense lights of to-day which rival the sun. Yet the cause is the same : the whole question is to concentrate it sufficiently and to properly regulate it.

The glow seen by Otto von Guericke was soon noticed more clearly by Dr. Wall. He obtained electricity by rubbing a stick of amber with a linen cloth, which augments the quantities of electricity produced and makes the phenomena more sensible. Upon squeezing the amber tightly while rubbing it, he heard a prodigious number of cracklings, accompanied by flashes of light. Rubbing the amber lightly, the luminous flashes were produced alone, without any noise ; finally, if the finger was brought close to the piece of amber, a loud noise accompanied by a great flash of light was produced. It was the electric spark, perfectly characteristic, though very feeble under such circumstances.

"I have no doubt," added Dr. Wall, "that by using a larger and longer piece of amber both the noise and the light would be greatly increased. This light and noise appear to represent in a certain fashion thunder and lightning."

This comparison would seem overdrawn for a spark which seems to-day so very small. But it is none the less remarkable to see the analogy between lightning and electricity clearly presented at the commencement of electrical studies, nearly a century before Franklin, who thought himself venturesome in declaring it, and feared that he would seem ridiculous in trying to prove it; for it is known that he hid himself carefully from his friends in making his famous experiment with a kite made to ascend into a thunder-cloud (Fig. 10), the string of which kite gave sparks of electricity.

This exceeding correctness appears more remarkable in Dr. Wall, because it was joined in his mind to the wildest ideas. After he had most satisfactorily demonstrated that all electrified bodies produced light, in the same way as amber and sulphur, he called this light the cause of electricity, employed it as an infallible means of distinguishing true from false diamonds ; affirmed, moreover, that it only was produced at night, and that the most favorable period was when the sun had gone eighteen degrees below the horizon ! In spite of the moonlight, the electric light was produced then with the same brightness as characterized it in the most profound darkness—all which made him bestow upon his fantastic godchild the name of *noctiluca.*

A short time after Wall, an Englishman, named Francis Hawksbee, studied static electricity, following the track of

Fig. 10.—Franklin making the experiment with a kite, to establish the identity of lightning and electricity.

Wall, but with less visionary ideas. He also considered the electric light as a phosphorescent light, which he compared to that emitted by sugar when rubbed. But he succeeded in producing it in much greater quantity by different means, and notably by shaking mercury in a vessel of glass which he had previously exhausted of air. Dominated by his erroneous theories, he called this electric light, produced by the friction between glass and mercury, *mercurial phosphorus*. On another occasion he used melted wax to cover half the interior surface of a glass globe exhausted of air; this he moved about, applying his hand to the upper surface to electrify it. He was greatly astonished to see his hand appear within and through the wax, which in places was over an eighth of an inch in thickness.

"But the greatest electric light which Hawksbee ever produced," says Priestley, "was when he inclosed a cylinder exhausted of air within another not exhausted and when he rubbed the exterior, moving both cylinders at the same time. He found no difference in the effects whether both moved together or not. He adds that, when the outer cylinder alone moved, the light became quite strong, and extended itself over the surface of the inner vessel. But what most surprised him was this : After both vessels had been moving for some time, during which he had applied his hand to the surface of the exterior vessel, if the combined movement ceased, there was no light; but, if then he brought his hand near the surface of the exterior vessel, flashes of light like the aurora were produced within the inner vessel. It would appear that the emanations from the exterior vessel were made to impinge upon the inner vessel with more force by the simple approach of the hand."

All these facts, which disconcerted as well as astonished the old physicists, are without difficulty explained to-day, and have for us no more than an historic interest. But we see that the faint glow of Otto von Guericke had already made much progress ; it was destined to increase and attain far greater proportions in the eighteenth century, and above all to be distributed by wires, an improvement destined to increase its power tenfold.

Under the English physicist Grey, electricity was studied in an altogether new way. The territory of chimera and chance observations was abandoned in favor of the more rational course of experimental studies, which at last took possession of all the sciences. In 172? he proved, in a series of experiments made in conjunction with ████, that certain substances conducted the *electric virtue*, as it was then called,

3

so that the attractive properties of bodies electrified by friction could thus be transmitted to great distances. The metals were found particularly available. Other bodies, on the contrary, did not enjoy this property, and did not transmit the *electric virtue ;* this, for example, was the case with silk.

Electric conductivity, and in consequence the essentially mobile nature of electricity, was established by these experiments. Several other discoveries, only realized at a later period —such as electrization by induction—were foreshadowed by Grey. Had he lived a century earlier, he would probably have affirmed them without waiting ; but the experimental method prohibited men of science from advancing any theories except so far as they were able to prove the truth of their position to all by tangible facts.

After having proved metallic conductivity, Grey observed the escape of electricity from points, a manifestation which constitutes the electric taper, and he showed that the spark is due to a true movement of electricity.

He observed, in fact, that the spark, drawn from water contained in a vessel about an inch distant, produced a little mountain of water of conical form. From the summit of this mountain of water a light, perfectly visible in darkness, emanated. Next, the mountain shrank within itself, and fell back into the general mass of liquid, to which a trembling and undulatory movement was imparted. Grey even succeeded in discovering in this experiment still better evidence of mechanical transportation ; he showed that the little liquid particles flew upward with the light from the summit of the mountain, and that there was thus formed, at the top of the cone, a very minute thread of water emitting a fine spray or mist, so delicate that it could hardly be discerned.

In consequence of his experiments, Grey declared that he could by means of electricity make cold water boil, and produce from it a flame and an explosion. The great future of this flame appeared very clearly to him, for he says, "Although these effects have never been hitherto produced except on a very small scale, it is probable that with time a way will be found to accumulate a greater quantity of electric fire, and consequently to increase the potency of this force, which, from several of these experiments (*si parvas de magnis componere licet*), would seem to be of the same nature as that of thunder and lightning."

We now have reached the end of the first quarter of the eighteenth century, about 1727. It is the idea of Wall which reappeared twenty years later, but emanated from the lips of a man of higher authority, trained in the severe school of experience, and who did not trust to the chimeras of the imagination.

All this while electrical studies were extending; they became to a certain extent the fashion; the general public became interested in them, and France, supreme arbiter of opinions as well as of elegance in the eighteenth century, began to be occupied with them. A member of the Academy of Sciences at Paris, Du Fay, superintendent of the Jardin du Roi (to-day the Jardin des Plantes), repeated Grey's experiments, and made new ones. It was he who first produced a spark from a living body.

Every one knows to-day the experiment, which is reproduced in the course of physics, by placing a child on an insulating stool, and making communication between it and the electric machine. In itself, the experiment does not at all astonish us. But it then produced an extraordinary sensation, and attracted every one to the new science. The effects were varied in numberless ways, and they did not fail to exaggerate them greatly in conversations, or in the periodical literature of the subject then beginning to appear (Fig. 11).

Fig. 11.—Experiment of electrifying a woman, from an engraving of the eighteenth century.

The monks even joined the popular movement: a Scotch Benedictine, the reverend Father Gordon, increased the force of the spark until it killed little birds, and made a man trem-

ble from head to foot with its peculiar agitation. A professor
of dead languages at the University of Leipsic, abandoning
the ancient classic humanities for the study of the new science, increased still further the force of electric machines by
increasing the rapidity of rotation of the globes or cylinders
which composed them. He reached as many as six hundred
and eighty turns a minute, and obtained sparks which burned
the skin like a caustic, and made the blood in the veins gush
out, and accomplished, according to the stories of the contem-
porary savants, many other horrible things.

In 1744 a savant of Berlin, named' Ludolf, ignited ether
with the spark ; and, later, another scientist, Boze, performed
the most paradoxical experiment of all, by igniting alcohol
and spirituous liquors by a jet of water which served as conductor for the electricity.

In 1746, in a memoir read before the Royal Society of London on the 6th of February, Dr. Watson demonstrated that
the electric sparks appeared of different colors according to
the nature of the substance from which they emanated.
Bodies with roughened surfaces, such as rusty iron or oxi-
dized copper, gave redder sparks than bodies with clean surfaces.

But it was long before the full signification of this fact was
known, which should have furnished the explanation of the
true nature of the electric spark. The spark, in fact, is in-
debted for its brilliancy to the particles which it detaches
from the more or less volatilized conductors, and carries off
with itself ; its color, therefore, should vary according to the
nature of these particles—that is to say, of the conductors
whence it emanates. Watson approached very closely the
true explanation, simple as we know it to be, yet tried to find
a complicated cause for the phenomenon in the difference of
reflection of light according to the variable nature of the substances reflecting it.

Finally, it was this savant who first produced a real electric
light. By uniting in action four of the globes, which furnished him, by their rotation, with electricity, he produced
genuine jets of flame, which gave almost a continuous light,
because of their size and rapid succession. The experiment
was naturally conducted in a dark room, and light enough
was produced to show distinctly the features of the persons
present.

During this same year (1746) Muschenbroek and Cuneus discovered at Leyden, in Holland, the principles of electrical condensation. They accumulated in the famous Leyden-jars quantities of electricity which were enormous for the epoch, and which enabled them to produce electric phenomena of an

Fig. 12.—The Abbé Nollet giving a lesson in electricity.

altogether new intensity ; for example, to pass an electric discharge through the bodies of all the soldiers of a regiment. But it is only in our century that the means of rendering the light more intense, and above all more continuous, was sought for in this direction.

During the second half of the eighteenth century the labors of the following electricians—the Abbé Nollet, Franklin, Father Beccaria, Canton, Dr. Desaugiers, and of many others—did not furnish a single new element to the electric light. But the knowledge of electricity continued to develop, and apparatus was invented for measuring it (Fig. 13). It was only in 1800 that the decisive fact appeared which opened a way, entirely new, by which the electric light could be produced, not as a mere curiosity of the laboratory, as in Watson's experiment, but in the state of practical and every-

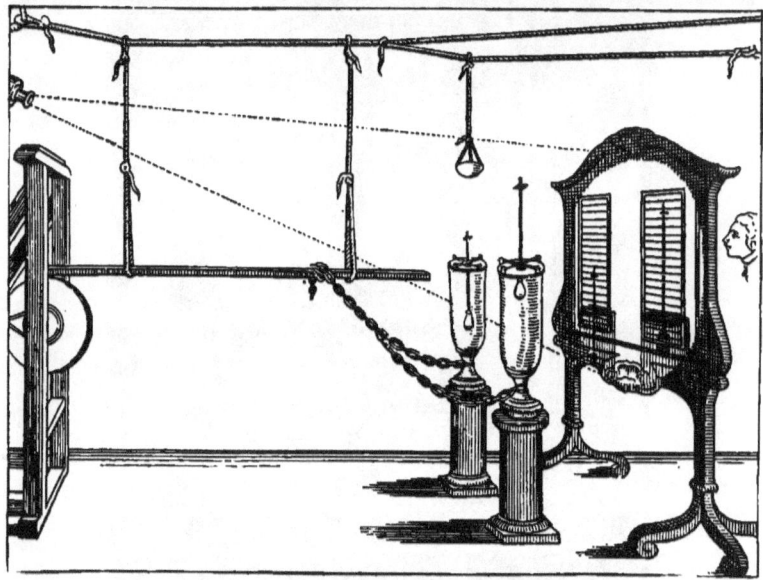

Fig. 13.—Electrometer, after the design in the Encyclopædia.

day application, as we now witness it. This achievement was the invention of the pile or battery by Volta—the discovery, in fact, of electricity in the dynamic state, or state of currents, which we shall endeavor to illustrate and explain in its movement and action in the next chapter.

The wonderful invention of Volta, inspired by the well-known experiment of Galvani, gave electrical studies at once a new direction. The ways trodden for three quarters of a century (since the experiments of Grey) were deserted, and the new territory, whose bonds of union with the old were

not as yet understood, was eagerly explored. A complete re-
vision of the old experiments had to be made, for the luminous effects as well as for the others. It was perhaps in that
direction that the most striking results were attained.

Thirteen years after the discovery of Volta, in 1813, Sir
Humphry Davy, bringing near together the terminals or
electrodes of a powerful battery, caused a jet of flame to
play between these electrodes, which was not momentary like
the electric spark, but was continuous. It was the voltaic
arc, observed for the first time in London in the laboratory of
the Royal Institution of Great Britain, which, since then, has
been the theatre for the production of so many beautiful researches in magnetism and electricity, particularly of those of
Faraday.

The battery used by Sir Humphry Davy had as many as
two thousand elements, and the active surface of all these
elements came to a sum total of eighty square metres. Over-
whelming as the production of light was, it could not cause
the enormous apparatus to be ignored, more costly even than
cumbrous, and it is hard to dream for a moment of the introduction into ordinary life of so expensive a light.

Nevertheless, the study of the electric light was prosecuted. Sir Humphry Davy had placed at the extremities of
his electrodes two carbons, which became incandescent by the
passage of the current, and which furnished the necessary
elements to render the flame brilliant. These carbons could
be drawn ten centimetres apart without extinguishing the
wonderful light which had been produced, and without even
weakening it. How did the electricity pass? and would this
open space be an obstacle to its passage? A crowd of savants
devoted themselves to these questions in England, in France,
in Switzerland, in Germany, in Italy. Sir Humphry Davy
showed that the electric light sprang through a vacuum as
through air, but with more difficulty, and the difficulty grew
with the increased vacuum. Thus, in the imperfect vacuum
of the air-pump, it passed over six times as great an interval
as that which arrested it in the more perfect Torrecellian
vacuum. But Davy persisted in believing, in spite of the objections of Father Beccaria, that the electric light could be
propagated in an absolute vacuum, if such could be produced.

Much later, in 1850, when the electric light began to enter,
if not into the domain of practice, at least into the laborato-

ries, Masson, Professor of Physics in the École Centrale des Arts et Manufactures in Paris, repeated the experiments of Sir Humphry Davy. He concluded that electricity could produce no current in an absolute vacuum, and, in consequence, no voltaic arc. In fine, the light produced by this arc appeared to have the same cause as that of the electric spark : it is due to the transport by electricity of the incandescent particles of the electrodes. These results are the more readily admitted to-day, as they have been confirmed by the researches of Matteucci, coming soon after those of Masson.

When it came to the practical applications, a host of difficulties were encountered. Nevertheless, in 1841 and 1844, two French savants, MM. Deleuil and Archereau, had conducted in Paris, on the Conti dock and Place de la Concorde, public experiments which excited the astonishment and admiration of all. They developed the electric arc in a closed vessel, exhausted of air to retard the combustion of the carbons. They already hoped to increase the power of their apparatus, so as to create little suns for the use of cities not favored by the real one. This idea dates still further back, for a professor of the University of Halle, named Meinake, had already made the same suggestion in 1821 (Colburn, "Practical Economy "). But, in 1844, as in 1821, this was but a dream without serious foundation, because everything was wanting that would be required to realize it even in part. Again, batteries strong enough to illuminate such areas of lighting could not be constructed at any price. Finally, carbons capable of giving a good light for a sufficient period were unknown.

As the carbons burned up during the passage of the electric current, and grew shorter, some means had to be found to bring them together—either good regulators or other means. This was the programme thirty years ago. We can say that it has been carried out to-day, and that every problem in it has received generally several solutions.

The first really practical application—that is to say, paid for—was in 1846, for a special object. The sun was to appear during the opera of "The Prophet." Recourse was had to electricity, and such was its success that, under the auspices of M. Dubosq, a regular service for its administration was organized.

At the end of the succeeding year (1847), W. E. Staite publicly experimented with it in England, in the large hall of a hotel of Sunderland. It was probably the first trial of ordinary lighting by electricity, because no account has reached us of a reduction to practice of the earlier patents of De Moleyns (August 21, 1841), Thomas Wright (March 10, 1845), and E. A. King (November 4, 1845), all taken out in London. This lighting of Sunderland seems to have lasted some time, and the great journal of London, the "Times," became quite enthusiastic over it. Its power, it said, was immense ; it resembled the sun, or the light of day, and made candles appear as obscure as they do by daylight (November 2, 1848).

During four years the inventor multiplied his experiments in a certain number of cities of England, and in 1852 the directors of the Liverpool docks placed a large apparatus on his system on top of a tower built expressly for the purpose. But in this year Staite died, and his idea was consigned with him to the tomb.

All this did not pass unremarked in France, and it had even been spoken of in the Academy of Sciences in Paris in the beginning of the year 1849. Two Lyonnese, MM. J. Lacassagne and Rudolphe Thiers, took up the question soon after the death of Staite. They patented, in the beginning of the year 1855, a new form of regulator, in which the lower carbon rested on a column of mercury which raised it up, in proportion to the rate of its combustion, by aid of a special mechanism.

The first public experiments took place at Lyons, in the month of June, 1855, on the quai des Celestins, and the journals of the period show no less enthusiasm than was shown by the "Times," six years before, over the system of Staite. The whole quay was flooded, they say, with refulgent rays, by which one could read at a distance of four hundred and fifty metres from the light, and the very birds, believing day had come, quitted their nests under the eaves, to fly about in the rays of the new sun ("Salut Public").

The following month the experiments were repeated at Paris, in the château Beaujon, the home of the famous marine painter, Théodore Gudin. The accounts given us are no less enthusiastic ; they tell us that the ladies had to open their parasols to protect themselves from the ardors of the mysterious star ("Gazette de France," July 5, 1855). They tried to interest the emperor in so marvelous an invention, and for this

end organized in the month of October, 1856, a grand demonstration from the summit of the Arc de Triomphe de l'Étoile.
The avenue des Champs Elysées was thus illuminated for a
space of four hours.

This year also saw experiments frequently repeated in
Paris and Lyons, notably in the Alcazar, in the Winter Garden, in the Observatory of Fourvières, etc. At the beginning
of 1857, MM. Lacassagne and R. Thiers tried to light permanently the Rue Impériale in Lyons, with only two centers of
illumination ; and in the month of March experiments were
conducted in Toulon, in the interest of the light-house service,
for the illumination of the harbor.

Little by little the subject fell into oblivion, and not much
was again heard of it until 1860. Nevertheless, during this
epoch, there were several electric illuminations on a large
scale ; but they were executed with the regulator of M. Serrin, invented in 1859. Particularly the lighting of the tile-
factories of Angers in 1863 must be cited, and, above all, the
lighting of the railroad excavations of the Northern Spanish
Railroad when crossing Gaudarrama, which lasted ten thousand hours ; then the lighting of the work of demolishing la
Samaritaine, and of various public *fêtes*.

The principal obstacle was found in the insufficiency of
the means for producing electricity. The magneto-electric
machine of Nollet, simplified by Van Malderen, was destined
to do away with this trouble. This machine, known in France
under the name of the Société l'Alliance, was used as early as
1863 to light by electricity the large light-house at Havre, soon
after that of Odessa, and several others. In 1866 a new order
of applications for it appeared, the electric lighting of vessels,
introduced for the first time on the yacht of Prince Napoleon,
the Prince Jérôme, which could thus enter at night, and without a pilot, the harbors of Gibraltar, Malta, Constantinople,
and Toulon. The trial was repeated the same year upon one
of the large transatlantic steamers, the Saint-Laurent.

Finally, the invention of the dynamo-electric machine of
Gramme in 1870 placed at the disposal of engineers as powerful a source of electricity as they could wish for; and six years
later, in 1876, the Jablochkoff candle gave them a burner so
simple in construction that it was at once accepted in every-
day practice. The first great application was the lighting of
the Avenue de l'Opéra, decreed by the Municipal Council of

Fig. 14.—The Avenue de l'Opéra in Paris lighted by Jablochkoff candles.

Paris on the occasion of the Universal Exposition of 1878, and which has been maintained to the present day (Fig. 14).

Here the history of the origin of the electric light ends. It passes now from the stage of experiment to that of industrial applications, where it had rarely made its appearance in our country (France) even after 1870.

BOOK II.

THE VOLTAIC ARC.

CHAPTER I.

HOW THE ELECTRIC LIGHT IS PRODUCED.

AT this period in our study and comparison of the different systems of electric lighting, which have multiplied greatly
in the last five years, it is necessary to examine the conditions
under which the electric light is produced, to study its nature,
and ascertain the different means offered by scientific theories
for obtaining it.

We are entirely ignorant of the nature of electricity, and
we can not even directly recognize it as we do light and heat ;
we only know it by its luminous, calorific, chemical, or mechanical effects. Yet, though electricity does not fall under
any one of our five senses, we have a sort of vague sensation
of it, as, for example, when the air is charged with electricity
on the approach of a thunder-storm. It then produces in us
a particular nervous condition, before the storm will have
manifested itself by any calorific, mechanical, or luminous
effects, and this particular nervous condition evidently corresponds to the electric state of the atmosphere. But all this
is limited to a vague sensation, which does not concentrate
itself in any special organ, as the organs of the five senses,
and thus can not become a distinctly marked perception.

On the other hand, there is no doubt that electricity is not
the only one of the properties of matter which partly evades
our perceptions. We may reasonably suspect that many
others are entirely unknown to us, even by their effects, because these effects are not among those which are perceived
by the five senses.

Long ago philosophers remarked that our knowledge of

nature was limited by the number of our senses, and would probably extend itself if these were increased or even perfected. Nothing, indeed, authorizes us to believe that the properties of nature are limited to those which affect the senses of man. Electricity furnishes a good example of a material property which we never knew directly, and whose existence is still perfectly certain, since we have for a long time studied it in its manifestations, and have succeeded in thoroughly mastering it.

Physicists who live on intimate terms with this electric agent have not succeeded any better than the ordinary observers in penetrating into the inner nature of this mysterious being, which, nevertheless, they control and direct at pleasure. But, to facilitate their explanations of it, they represent it as an invisible fluid, many million times lighter than air, and whose different forms of movement produce electricity, heat, and light.* Some savants still admit two electric fluids—not, however, deceiving themselves into believing in the objective reality of their theory, whose end is only to facilitate the exposition of facts.

Electricity, then, is, by hypothesis, a sort of fluid, formed of imponderable molecules, which travels through material bodies—more or less easily, according to the nature of these bodies, that is to say, according to their conductivity for electricity—and which accumulates on their surfaces. In any given body completely removed from exterior influences, the electric molecules, left to themselves, would evidently seek some order in which they would not further tend to change— this is what is called a state of equilibrium, and then we have to deal with electricity in repose, or in the *static* condition.

Let us next suppose that, by the action of an exterior cause, this equilibrium is destroyed at some particular point ; for example, that the density of the molecules diminishes at

---

* Some physicists may think that our assertions overstep a little the limits of actual experiment, and that we give too restricted a form to ideas, which in actual science have not such exact precision ; for, if the theory of single-fluid electricity has no opponents left, the identity of this fluid with the luminiferous ether is not formally established by any direct experiments ; but, as soon as the phenomena of electricity are explained by the single-fluid theory, the principles of scientific method force us, if nothing opposes, to confound it with the fluid that is the cause of luminous phenomena. In short, we have no right to multiply hypotheses without necessity.

this point. The effect is the same as may be produced in a gas, such as air, for example: the electric molecules of the surrounding space flow toward the point of rarefaction to re-establish the equilibrium; there will be, it may be said, a sort of electric wind, provided, be it understood, that the electric molecules can move in the body in which these actions are taking place; in other words, provided the body is a good conductor. The same thing in inverse effect will be produced if the electric density be augmented at any point: an electric wind will be produced directed away from this overburdened point toward the parts containing fewer molecules.

It is this species of electrical wind that is called a current. Electricity is no more in the static condition; it is in motion; it is *dynamic electricity*, the electricity of Volta, or of batteries, the variety that furnishes almost all the applications of electricity, and especially the electric light.

The function of the current is only to re-establish the overturned electrical equilibrium; it should then disappear as soon as this equilibrium is re-established. Consequently, if the cause which has destroyed the equilibrium is temporary in its action, the current will last only a short time; it will be a simple *discharge*. But it will be altogether different if this cause is permanent, or at least greatly prolonged—if, for example, the excess of the density of the electric molecules at a given point is maintained, in spite of the escape of this excess to neighboring points. Then a *continuous current* is formed, a true current, quite comparable to a brook, which will have its origin in a place where density is always in excess, as we may boldly say, in the electric spring, for thence it is that the current of electric molecules supports itself.

Running water, to form a stream or river, should concentrate itself in a bed which fixes its direction and makes its force sensible. It is the same for the electric current, which should follow a conductor, drawn out in form like a wire, to produce visible effects. As its end and result is to re-establish the equilibrium destroyed throughout the extent of the conducting system, the two free extremities must be united so as to form a complete circuit of any form—for it will often be made of a perfectly flexible wire—but which can be represented to our minds as a circle to facilitate our conception of the phenomenon.

Here the analogy with the stream would seem defective,

for rivers do not, at first sight, seem to form closed circuits; they fall into the seas or oceans, which form for them indefinitely large reservoirs. Nevertheless, large as they are, these reservoirs would be overflowing if the heat of the sun did not vaporize the water of the sea, and pump it up under the form of clouds which finally dissolve in rain, which rain nourishes the springs of the rivers or brooks. It is thus that the circuit closes, as perfectly, it will be seen, as in the case of an electric current; and thus also the current would cease if the sea did not vaporize so as to keep a place free for the discharge of the waters of the rivers; for in this case the springs would dry up for want of rain.

If the circuit is not closed—that is to say, if it is incomplete—the current reaching the end most remote from the spring would find no means of discharge; it would practically be dammed up, and the electric molecules would accumulate at this extremity. The power which they tend to exert in escaping is called their *potential*.

As often as the equilibrium of electric molecules is destroyed in a conducting body, or, to express it differently, when a difference of potential is established between two points of a circuit, an electric current is necessarily produced. Whatever the force may be that tends to destroy this equilibrium is the true cause of the current; it is called, in a general way, *electro-motive force*, but its particular nature may vary greatly.

The current has two distinct properties, *quantity* and *tension*—properties which play very different *rôles* in different electrical apparatus, and which must be taken into strict account in order to understand the phenomena which accompany the production of the electric light.

The electric molecules which are put into motion by the electro-motive force encounter a certain amount of resistance; to overcome it this same electromotive force must expend a certain part of its energy in giving these molecules a sufficient impulse. It is the state in which they find themselves when obeying this impulse which is called their *tension*.

It follows that the quantity of molecules put in motion by the same electro-motive force increases or diminishes inversely as the resistance which opposes their motion, or, what is the same thing, to the tension which they may possess.

The final result—that is to say, the quantity of molecules

in movement with a determined tension—is called the *intensity* of the current, an intensity which Ohm has represented by the relation between the electro-motive force and the resistance, because, in effect, the intensity of a current does not only depend on the energy of the electro-motive force, but it depends also on the resistance of the circuit in which this current is developed.

In all cases a certain minimum of tension is required to establish the current. This minimum depends upon the obstacles which the current has to overcome. If the circuit was completely closed and formed of a substance of perfect conductivity, offering no resistance to the passage of the electric molecules, these obstacles would not exist, and an infinitely small tension would suffice. But this case is rarely realized. In fact, no substance is a perfect conductor. The imperfection of this conductivity constitutes the *resistance* to the passage of the current, which thus is the inverse of the conductivity. It may be compared to the friction which the stream, or any liquid flowing in a tube or aqueduct, encounters. This resistance diminishes the living force of the current, as the friction diminishes the force of the water; but just as there are surfaces more or less favorable to the flowing of water, there are materials more resisting than others to the passage of electrical molecules.

To conceive of the production of heat and light by the passage of electric currents in conducting bodies, it is necessary to remember that all bodies of this nature are composed of molecules animated by a continual motion of vibration; that their temperature increases or decreases in inverse ratio with the amplitude and duration of these vibrations; finally, that these vibrations of the molecules of matter are reproduced by those of the ether which surrounds them, and by whose agency they produce their effects upon us.

The molecules which we call electric molecules are no other than the molecules of ether, impressed with a particular movement, and moving through bodies whose molecules bear such a relation to them that the first set of molecules pass between the second set without much loss of their own movement.

Electric conductivity, calorific conductivity, and transparency, are states of matter corresponding to those movements of ether which we call electricity, heat, and light.

4

If two conductors made of the same material be compared,
we should naturally expect the electric molecules to move
easier in the larger, just as water would run easier in a tube
of large than in one of small caliber. Resistance then diminishes as the conductor is enlarged, and Ohm has shown that
it is inversely proportional to the cross-section of the conductor—that is to say, to the surface of the cut obtained in
dividing it perpendicularly to its length. Following this
out, if the conductor diminishes the resistance increases, the
molecules squeeze closer, as it were, so as to pass without
retarding their companions; as they pass through it they rub
against the molecules of the conductor, whose vibrations thus
become more rapid; the metallic wire gets hot, which further
diminishes its conductivity; and, finally, it becomes red-hot.
If the current is intense and the resistance considerable, the
temperature rapidly rises, and the conductor becomes incandescent. Here we have reached the electric light.

Then, if the current of electricity meets no resistance, it
passes through the molecules of the conductor without dis-
turbing them, or the disturbance is so slight that the heat
resulting is quite balanced by the cooling due to radiation;
but, if at any point of the circuit any particular object presents itself which prevents the current from going freely on
its way, since it is necessary that the same number of molecules traverse in the same time all points of the circuit, a disturbance is produced at the point where the obstacle exists:
the electric molecules yield up a part of their electric force
to the molecules of the conductor, and it is the augmentation
of movement impressed on these last which creates the heat,
and in consequence the light.

This particular obstacle can be created in several ways, to
each of which one variety of the electric light corresponds.

It may happen that the circuit, properly so called, may
be interrupted, so that the current has to pass through the
air by an intermediary gaseous conductor; there is then produced between the two ends of the cut circuit, or poles, a
jet of electrical molecules which is called the *voltaic arc*. It
was the first known of the different electric lights, for Sir Humphry Davy produced it before 1813. To possess the great
brilliancy which characterizes it, the voltaic arc should contain a large number of material particles very finely divided
and brought to a white heat. These particles are torn off and

carried along by the current, on account of the enormous temperature of the severed ends of the circuit. As, among the bodies which are sufficiently good conductors, it is carbon which supports the most intense heat, and which, consequently, can furnish the most light, it is that which has been chosen to form the ends of the circuit (Fig. 15).

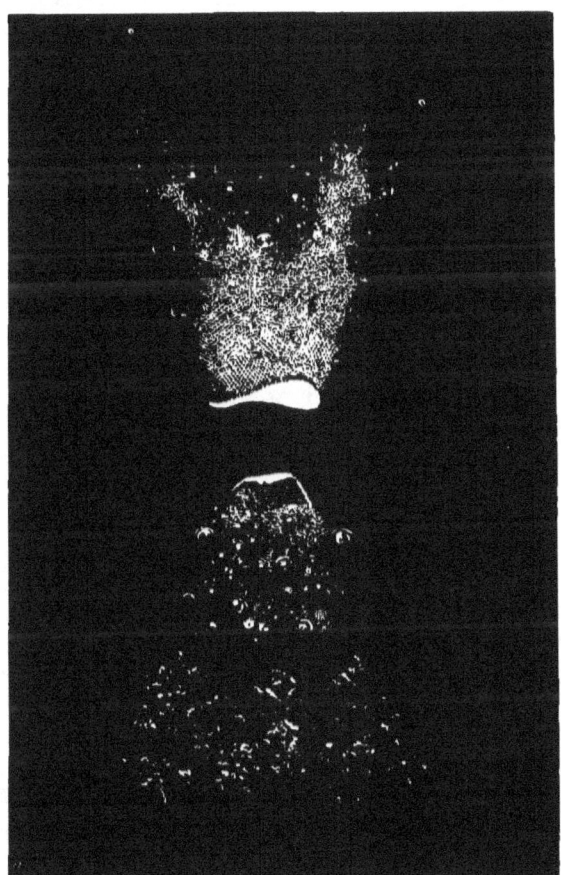

Fig. 15.—The two poles of the voltaic arc.

If the electric current succeeds in overcoming the resistance of the air, it is because the gases become better conductors as they are heated, which naturally happens from their contact with the heated electrodes. Besides this, the layer of air to be traversed must be thin. Now, the passage

of the electric current destroys quite rapidly the extremity
of the electrodes of carbon, so that, if the electrodes are not
brought together in exact proportion to this destruction, the
current will soon cease to pass, and the light will be extinguished.   To effect this approach with regularity, regulators
must be employed, and it is the perfecting of them that has
been the great problem of this kind of electric lighting.   It
may, therefore, be properly termed the "regulator system."

Instead of placing the two electrodes of carbon one above
the other, which necessitates the employment of a regulator
to bring them together, they may be placed side by side, separated by a solid insulating substance which will volatilize
at the same rate as that at which the carbons are consumed
under the action of the voltaic arc.   This is the candle system, from the name given by M. Jablochkoff to these new
apparatus because of the resemblance between the method of
using them and the consumption of a candle.

We have said that the voltaic arc was produced when the
circuit traversed by the electric current was interrupted ; this
rupture of the circuit should not be done too rapidly, or it
will only produce a spark, a species of flash very bright and
very rapid.   The two poles should separate so slowly that
heating will take place, and that a sort of chain of moving
material particles will be formed, torn from the positive and
transported to the negative pole.   The two poles reach thus
an enormous temperature, nearly 4,000° at the positive and
3,000° at the negative pole, the latter only being heated by a
secondary cause, which we shall examine.

The true sources of luminous radiation are the carbon-
points, and, above all, the points where the passage of the
electrical molecules are concentrated ; as for the arc itself,
notwithstanding its high temperature, about 4,800°, it gives
but little light, and the light which it gives is of a violet-blue.
It is this that gives to electric lighting its disagreeable reflections which have been so much criticised, and which are reduced as much as possible by diminishing its length, that is
to say, by separating the carbons only the distance that is
indispensable, and which is naturally in proportion to the
intensity of the current.

We have said that the current which springs from the
positive pole to the negative one tears off and draws with it
material molecules in the state of incandescence.   These mole-

cules, projected against the other pole, heat it doubly by the
heat which they bear with them and by the shock which results from their velocity ; but this species of bombardment of
one pole by another represents a mechanical action, and creates in consequence an electro-motive force. The enormous
difference of temperature of the two poles produces another
electro-motive force, and both working together give rise to
a counter-current, which in its turn seizes and transports particles of the negative to the positive pole. This reactionary
force is of considerable importance, because in the arc produced by a battery of forty Bunsen cells it has been found
equal to twelve cells (Latschinoff) ; with another battery of
twenty-six Bunsen cells it has been found equal to nearly ten
cells (Edlund) ; finally, M. Leroux has been able to prove its
existence, and to measure it two tenths of a second after the
rupture of the current. The total resistance of a voltaic arc
is thus composed—first, of the resistance, properly so called,
of the arc ; and, secondly, of that which is created by the
electro-motive force of the reaction.

It will be understood, from what precedes, that the positive carbon should be the brightest, because the light emitted
by an incandescent body rapidly increases with its temperature. Besides, the consumption of the two poles is very unequal, and, when they both have the same section, the positive
is consumed twice as fast as the other. Finally, numerous
experiments have shown that the resistance of the arc is less
when the positive pole is the uppermost ; it is also more luminous, and M. Niaudet has found, for the same current, a
luminous intensity of two hundred and seventy-eight Carcel
burners with the positive carbon uppermost, and two hundred
and seventeen only with the positive below. Small as the
mass of the particles transported may be, does it not seem
that their weight plays a part in this difference ?

When the arc is produced by alternately reversed currents,
the consumption is equal if the carbons are horizontal ; if
they are vertical, the upper carbon is used up a little the
quicker, in the ratio of one hundred and eight to one hundred. The current of warm air which surrounds it raises its
temperature, and probably the force of gravity assists the
separation and fall of a greater number of particles.

The resistance of the arc diminishes as its length diminishes ; but at the same time the temperature is lowered, and

the light diminishes, so that, to keep it up sufficiently, more electrical molecules must be passed through the polar carbons, or else the section of the carbons must be considerably reduced, which are then more rapidly consumed; besides, the heat spread over a great length will not give enough light.

By augmenting the dimensions of the negative carbon, its consumption is retarded; by reducing the section of the positive carbon, and by restricting, by the aid of a properly adjusted contact, the length of the incandescent portion, the heating is concentrated in this part, and enough light is produced, the more so as the solution of continuity which always exists at the point of contact of the two carbons greatly increases the resistance. It follows that the little rod of positive carbon exhausts itself at the end which rests upon the other carbon, and that it suffices to make it advance so as to keep up the contact and obtain a luminous focus, less intense, it is true, but milder and more agreeable than the voltaic arc because of its fixity and its regularity. This is what is meant by incandescence in the open air.

Another mode of using the voltaic arc consists in interposing in its passage a block of refractory material which becomes the true source of light, on account of the enormous temperature which it may attain. With this arrangement, it is especially the heat of the arc which is utilized, and the polar carbons only serve to produce it. The yellow coloration of the light thus obtained resembles to a considerable extent that which the rays of the sun give us, whence the name of *solar lamp* given to the apparatus serving for its production.

Finally, the obstacle opposed to the passage of the current can consist simply in a sudden diminution of the conductivity of the circuit, and the best mode of obtaining this sudden diminution is to diminish the conductor. This diminished part should be formed of an infusible substance of high resistance, such as a fine thread of platinum or a very thin filament of carbon. This thread becomes incandescent on account of the friction of the electric molecules as we have described above, and, if care be taken to inclose it in a globe of glass completely exhausted of air, it does not burn, and lasts a very long time. It is the system of incandescent lighting which was the great sensation of the Exhibition of Electricity at Paris—the systems of Edison, of Maxim, of Swan, and of Lane-Fox.

These different systems exact different conditions, and are not all adapted to the same needs, as we shall see further on.

CHAPTER II.

ELECTRICAL UNITS.

[BEFORE proceeding to a description of the lamps in which the current is utilized, and to the generators by which it is produced, it will be desirable to consider the relations of the electrical elements with which we have to deal, the units of measurement, and the relations these bear to the mechanical ones of force and work.

Whenever a body is moved against any force opposing its motion, *work* is done, and its amount will depend upon the intensity of the force and the distance through which it is overcome. Thus, if we lift a pound-weight up against the force of gravity, we perform a certain amount of work. If we raise two pounds the same distance, or the one pound to double the height, we shall evidently do twice as much work. Similarly, work will be done in overcoming any other force than gravity, such as the molecular forces of chemical attraction, in separating the constituent elements of a compound, or magnetic force, in drawing a piece of iron and a magnet asunder, or in rotating a closed coil of wire in front of the poles of a magnet, and the amount of this work will always be expressed by the product of the force by the distance through which it is overcome.

A body is said to possess *energy* when it is capable of doing work, either in consequence of the motion with which it is endowed or of its position. If we fire a ball upward from a rifle, it possesses the power of doing work on account of its motion. It is then said to possess moving or *kinetic* energy. As it rises against the pull of gravity, its velocity, and consequently its moving energy, constantly grows less, until at the top of its flight it has wholly disappeared. The energy of the ball has not, however, been lost, but simply transformed. The ball now has energy due to its position, and in falling to the earth again it can do the same amount of work as that done in projecting it upward. As long as the ball is supported in its elevated position, it evidently retains this power of doing work. Its energy is *potential*, and may be called upon to perform work whenever desired. The separated elements of a chemical compound just as truly possess energy of position as an elevated body. Allow them to unite, and their potential energy will pass into kinetic, and the work of separation be returned in that of chemical combination. If we consider the projected ball at any point of its passage upward, we shall see that what it has lost in kinetic energy it has gained in potential energy, and that the sum of these two is throughout its whole flight constant. Considering the universe as a whole, we shall find a like condition of things. Amid all the multifarious changes of the material universe, the sum of the energy due to position and of that due to motion remains the same. It is this fact which is expressed by the great generalization of the conservation of energy.

Work is, therefore, the measure of the expenditure of energy—that is, the transformation of energy from one form to another. Conversely, no such transformation of energy can ever take place without the performance of work. The absolute measure of a force is the velocity it can impart to a given mass of matter in a given time, but for most purposes it is convenient to determine a force by comparing it with gravity. As the weight of a body measures the intensity of this force at any given place, the magnitude of any force can therefore be expressed simply by a weight, and the amount of work by the product of a weight by a distance.

Work and power are not infrequently used as equivalent terms, though there is an important difference between them. Work has reference solely to the amount of effort necessary to accomplish a given result, and is independent of time. The same amount of work is done in lifting a pound one foot high, whether this be performed in a second or a year. Power, on the other hand, expresses the *rate* of doing work, and is evidently greater, the shorter the time in which a given amount of work is performed.

We have seen in the preceding chapter that, whenever we connect two points which are at different potentials by a conductor, a current of electricity will flow from the point of higher to the one of lower potential. A difference of potential is analogous to a difference of level of water, and just as work must be done in raising water from the lower to the higher level, so work must be done in raising electricity from the lower to the higher electrical level. The water, in falling, is able to perform the work done in lifting it; and the electricity, that done in raising it to the higher potential. The amount of this work is in each case the quantity multiplied by the height from which it fell. In the case of electricity, the difference of electrical level is expressed in terms of the force or pressure due to it. This force is termed electro-motive force.* The work done, then, by any given quantity of electricity, Q, falling through a difference of potential, E, is E Q. As the strength or intensity of the current expresses the rate at which electricity moves through a circuit—the number of units of electricity that pass a given point in a given time—the product of the strength of the current by the electro-motive force will evidently express the rate of the performance of work—that is, the power.

The intensity of the current in any electrical circuit will not depend solely upon the electro-motive force impelling it, but will also depend upon the resistance offered to its passage. There are, therefore, in any electrical circuit, three elements to be taken into consideration—the intensity of the current, the electro-motive force, and the resistance—the relation of which to each other is a very simple one, which is expressed by a formula known as Ohm's law. Denoting the intensity of the current by C, the electro-motive force by E, and the resistance by R, this formula is—

$$C = \frac{E}{R}.$$

This formula shows us that the strength of the current that will flow through any circuit will be directly in proportion to the electro-motive force, and inversely as the resistance of the circuit. In applying the formula in any particular case, it must be borne in mind that the electro-motive force and resistance refer to the same circuit, or to the same part of it—that is, that R represents the resistance of the same part of the circuit of which E represents the difference of potential.

---

* The term *electrical pressure* is coming into use as a substitute for this. It has the great advantage of expressing this electrical conception in terms of an already familiar one.

MECHANICAL UNITS.

To compare different quantities it is evident that we must have a unit in terms of which they can be expressed. The fundamental units upon which all others may be made to depend are those of mass, length, and time. Until recently there have been no units of these quantities universally agreed upon. In England and the United States the unit of weight most generally employed is the pound, that of length the foot, and that of time the second or the minute; while in France the first of these is the kilogramme (2·2 pounds), and the second the metre (39·37 inches). In the former countries the unit of work most commonly employed is the work required to raise one pound one foot, termed the foot-pound, and that of power, the horse-power, equivalent to 550 foot-pounds per second, or 33,000 foot-pounds a minute. In France the unit of work is the kilogrammetre, and that of horse-power (*force de cheval*) 75 kilogrammetres per second, equal to 542½ instead of 550 foot-pounds per second.

The need of a uniform system of units had long been felt, and such a system was finally adopted by the International Congress of Physicists, at Paris, in 1881. This system is known as the centimetre-gramme-second, or, more briefly, as the C. G. S. system, so named from the units of length, mass, and time.

In it the unit of force, termed the *dyne*, is that force which, acting upon a mass of one gramme for one second, is able to give it a velocity of one centimetre per second. This unit, it will be observed, is independent of the varying force of gravity, but it can readily be expressed in it by taking account of the amount of this force at any given place. The value of gravity usually adopted is that at Paris, which is able to impart to one gramme a velocity of 981 centimetres per second, so that a gramme is equal to 981 dynes, and a dyne to $\frac{1}{981}$ of a gramme. From what has already been said it will be readily understood that the unit of work is the dyne-centimetre—that is, the product of the dyne by a centimetre. It is termed the *erg*. Since a kilogramme is equal to 1,000 grammes, this latter to 981 dynes, and a metre to 100 centimetres, the kilogrammetre is evidently equal to (981 × 1000 × 100) 98,100,000 ergs. The foot-pound is in like manner converted into ergs by multiplying the product of the equivalent of the pound in grammes (453·6) by the equivalent of the foot in centimetres (30·48), and this by the number of dynes (981) in a gramme. It is, therefore, equal to (453·6 × 30·48 × 981) 13,563,000 ergs. The French horse-power, equivalent to 542½ foot-pounds, or 75 kilogrammetres, becomes in the new unit of work equal to 7,357,500,000, and the English horse-power, equivalent to 550 foot-pounds, or 76 kilo-grammetres, equal to 7,460,000,000 ergs per second. These are usually written 735·75 × 10⁷, and 746 × 10⁷.

HEAT UNITS.

To raise the temperature of a body—say, that of a pound of water one degree Fahrenheit—evidently requires the expenditure of energy. The amount of heat requisite gives us a unit by means of which we can compare the heat expended in any other case, but does not give us a basis for comparing the expenditure of energy in the form of heat with that in other forms. To be able to do this we must know the relation existing between heat and mechanical energy, so that the former can be expressed in terms of work. This relation was established some forty years ago by the labors of the German physician, Mayer, and the English physicist, Joule. By a series of careful experiments, Joule showed that the amount of heat necessary to raise a pound of distilled water one degree of the Fahrenheit scale, would be sufficient, if converted into mechanical energy, to raise a weight of 772 pounds one foot high. The number expressing the relation between heat and work is termed the mechanical equivalent of heat, and is frequently spoken of as Joule's equivalent. Evidently its value will vary with the units of work and temperature adopted. When the degree is that of the centigrade scale (⅑ that of the. Fahrenheit), this equivalent becomes equal to 1,390 foot-pounds; and, when the unit of work is the kilo-grammetre, and of temperature the centigrade degree, it becomes 424 kilogrammetres.

In the English-speaking world the heat unit has usually been the pound-degree, the latter being measured on the Fahrenheit scale; while in France the kilogramme-degree, the latter reckoned on the centigrade scale, was common.

The gramme as the unit of weight and the centigrade degree as the unit of temperature have for a considerable time been in use in all countries in scientific work. Their use was ratified by the Paris Congress, and the heat unit of the C.G.S. system is therefore the gramme-degree. It is termed the *calorie*, and its mechanical equivalent is equal to 42,000,000 ergs, written 4.2×10^7.

ELECTRICAL UNITS.

Electricity can be measured in two different ways, corresponding to the two different classes of electrical phenomena with which we are acquainted—those of statical and those of current electricity. The readiest way of measuring the strength of an electric current is by its magnetic effects, and the electric quantities in dynamical, or current, electricity are, therefore, measured electro-magnetically. It is this system which alone concerns us here, but, for the sake of clearness, it will be desirable to give a brief outline of the electro-static system of measurement.

As is well known, a body charged with electricity will attract another body with an unlike, and repel one with a like, charge. The amount of this attractive or repulsive force will depend upon the amount of the charge and the distance of the bodies asunder. A unit of statical electricity can, therefore, be very readily defined with reference to these conditions. It is that quantity of electricity which repels a similar and equal quantity, at a unit distance (one centimetre), with a force of one dyne.

The difference of potential between any two points is measured by the work which must be done to move a quantity of electricity from the lower to the higher. A unit difference of potential is, therefore, that difference of potential which must exist between two points in order that a unit of work will be done in conveying a unit of positive electricity from the lower to the higher. A unit of work will, of course, be performed by a unit of electricity in falling through this unit difference of potential.

A unit current in this measure is one which conveys an electro-static unit of quantity per second, and a circuit of unit resistance is one in which the number of units of quantity which pass in a second is equal to the number of units of difference of potential between its ends—that is, in the equation $R = \dfrac{E}{C}$, where R = the resistance, E the difference of potential, and C the strength of current, R is unity when E = C.

In the electro-magnetic system of measurement the units of these different quantities bear the same relation to each other—that is, the unit current will flow through a circuit having a unit difference of potential between its ends, when it has a unit resistance, and the unit quantity is the amount of electricity conveyed in a second by a unit current, but they have different absolute values.

In adopting units of current strength and quantity, we may determine either unit by reference to some particular standard, and then express the other in terms of this; just as, in the case of a current of water, we may take the unit of quantity to be a gallon, and then define a unit current as one which conveys a gallon a second; or we may adopt some given current as the unit of current, and then define the unit of quantity as the quantity delivered by this current per second. The first of these methods is followed in electro-static measurement, where the unit quantity is determined by reference to its effect upon a like quantity; the second is adopted in electro-magnetic measurements. In this system the strength of the current is defined with reference to its effect upon a magnet-pole in its vicinity. This effect will depend upon the strength of the magnet-pole, of the current, the length of the circuit, and the distance of the circuit from the pole. Evidently, to get an expression for a unit strength of current, each of these quantities must be unity. The unit of current-strength, therefore, becomes that current every centimetre of whose length acts with a force of one dyne upon a unit magnet-pole at a distance of one centimetre (a unit magnet-pole is one which will repel an equal like pole with a force of one dyne at a distance of a centimetre). This condition is realized when the wire conveying the current is bent into a circle of one centimetre radius, at the center of which is placed the unit magnet-pole. Then, when a unit current flows through the circuit, every centimetre of its length will act upon the central magnet-pole with a force of one dyne. The unit quantity, as before stated, is the quantity conveyed by this unit current in one second, and the unit electro-motive force is in this case, as in that of electro-static measure, determined by the condition that it requires the expenditure of one erg of work to raise a unit of quantity through a unit of potential. As, however, the electro-magnetic unit of quantity is much larger than the electro-static, the electro-magnetic unit of potential is correspondingly smaller. The electro-magnetic unit of resistance is determined by the same condition as that of the electro-static unit. As the unit quantity of electricity in falling through a unit difference of potential performs one erg of work, it is clear that a unit electro-motive force does a unit of work per second in a circuit of unit resistance.

One more unit remains to be noticed. This is the unit of capacity. This term denotes the ability of a body to hold a charge of electricity, and this capacity is measured by the quantity of electricity at unit potential which it can contain. When this quantity is unity, the body has unit capacity.

PRACTICAL UNITS.

Most of the above units are too small for use in practice. Another system of units, based upon them, termed practical units, has therefore been devised. In this system the unit of electro-motive force is termed the *volt*, in honor of the Italian physicist, Volta. It is equal to 100,000,000, written 10^8, C. G. S. units. The unit of resistance, termed the *ohm*, is equal to 10^9 C. G. S. units. It is equal to the resistance of a wire of pure copper one millimetre in diameter and forty-eight metres long. The unit of current adopted is the current produced in a circuit of one ohm resistance by a difference of potential of one volt. Its value is evidently $\frac{1}{10}$ that of the C. G. S. unit, since $C = \dfrac{E}{R}$, and the practical units of E and R are $E \times 10^8$ and $R \times 10^9$. It is written 10^{-1}. It was, previous to the Paris Congress, denoted in England and this country by the name *weber*. A unit, $\frac{1}{10}$, of this was in use in Germany under the same name. The congress, therefore, in order to avoid confusion, substituted for this name that of *ampère*. The unit of quantity, which is the quantity conveyed by a current of one ampère in a second, is termed the *coulomb*. Its value is evidently $\frac{1}{10}$ of the C. G. S. unit. The practical unit of work is, therefore, the volt-coulomb, and of power, the volt-ampère. The former is equal to $10^8 \times 10^{-1} = 10^7$ ergs, and the latter to 10^7 ergs per second.

Since the English horse-power is equal to 746×10^7 ergs per second, a volt-ampère is equal to $\frac{1}{746}$ of it, and to $\frac{1}{731.75}$ of a *force de cheval*, and the horse-power developed by any number of ampères, C, falling through a difference of potential, E, is therefore $\dfrac{E\,C}{746}$ in English, and $\dfrac{E\,C}{735\cdot75}$ in French measure. The equivalent of a horse-power in electrical measure (746 or 735·75 volt-ampères) is commonly spoken of as an "electrical horse-power," or a "horse-power of current." In his presidential address in 1882, before the British Association, Sir William Siemens proposed that the practical unit of power, the volt-ampère, be termed the *watt*, in honor of James Watt, and this suggestion has been very generally acted upon. He also proposed the name of Joule to designate the heat produced in one second by a current of one ampère in a circuit of a resistance of an ohm. This unit, it will be seen, is equivalent to the volt-coulomb, since this latter is the work done in one second, in a circuit of one ohm resistance, by a current of one ampère, and the whole of the work done by the current in this case is spent in the production of heat. Its value is, therefore, 10^7 ergs, and, since a heat unit is equal to $4\cdot2 \times 10^7$ ergs, it is equal to $\frac{1}{42} = \cdot24$ of a calorie.

The unit of capacity is termed the *farad*, in honor of Faraday. Since the capacity is determined by dividing the quantity of the charge by its potential, this unit is equal to $\dfrac{Q}{E} = \dfrac{10^{-1}}{10^8} = 10^{-9}$, or $\dfrac{1}{10^9}$ of the C. G. S. unit of capacity. As this unit is very large, the one-millionth part of it, the *microfarad*, is commonly used in practice. It is equal to 10^{-6} farad, and 10^{-15} C. G. S. units.

The following summary of these units will facilitate reference to them, and help the comprehension of their relations:

Unit of force = dyne.

Unit of work = erg, = dyne × centimetre.

Unit of heat = calorie = $4\cdot2 \times 10^7$ ergs.

Volt = practical unit of electro-motive force = 10^8 C. G. S. units.

Ohm = practical unit of resistance = 10^9 C.G.S. units.

Ampère = practical unit of intensity of current = 10^{-1} C. G. S. units.

Coulomb = practical unit of quantity = 10^{-1} C. G. S. units.

Farad = practical unit of capacity = 10^{-9} C. G. S. units.

Joule = electrical unit of work = volt-coulomb = 10^7 ergs = ·24 calorie.

Watt = electrical unit of power = volt-ampère = $\frac{1}{746}$ horse-power = 10^7 ergs per second.

English horse-power = 550 foot-pounds = 746 × 10⁷ ergs per second = 746 watts.

French horse-power = 542½ foot-pounds = 735·75 × 10⁷ ergs per second = 735·75 watts.]

CHAPTER III.

THE ARC-LAMP CARBONS.

THE first condition to be fulfilled in making the voltaic arc a good source of light, is to make it play between two electrodes, capable of furnishing to this arc the minute incandescent particles which give it its immense brilliancy. Carbon only seems adapted for this end, and it was, in fact, with electrodes of carbon that Sir Humphry Davy produced the first voltaic arc. But there are many kinds of carbons, and the choice of this material is not the least difficult of the questions that have arisen in electric lighting, because the two electrodes should combine qualities that are different and often even opposite ones.

After his famous experiment in 1813, Sir Humphry Davy employed pieces of wood-charcoal quenched in water or in mercury. But these pencils of soft carbon were too rapidly consumed to afford a light of any definite duration, even in operating in a closed vessel, almost completely exhausted by the air-pump, as Davy attempted to do, in spite of the inconvenience of this arrangement. Carbons were elsewhere sought for that would be more compact and consequently more durable, and which were also capable of being formed into pencils without breaking or going into powder.

Foucault, one of the greatest French physicists of this century, first had the idea of using the carbon which is deposited on the sides of gas-retorts. This carbon, slowly formed, is more durable than all the others, and burns much more slowly, so that Foucault succeeded in obtaining a voltaic arc of much longer duration.

But gas-carbon was anything but perfect, especially from not being homogeneous. It was mixed with earthy substances, particularly silica, which melted and often made the carbon sparkle by causing minor variations in the light, which already was too unsteady. Sometimes, too, the silicious matter volatilized and projected jets of vapor which were better conductors of electricity than the air, even when hot; in this case the electric discharge followed by preference these vapors, and passed into obscurity, as no solid particles were present to produce incandescence. It was so much loss of light.

There are, without doubt, in these carbonaceous deposits some parts more homogeneous than others, and to-day the locality of these superior parts can be found with greater certainty than formerly, and the pencils for electrodes can be taken thence. But, in spite of everything, it is very hard to avoid all traces of silica. Besides, it takes so long to form carbon in the gas-retorts that it would be impossible to procure enough from that source to give to the voltaic-arc system of illumination the development that has been anticipated for it.

An artificial carbon, therefore, must be made to supplement the deficient supply of gas-carbon. Bunsen was the first to make it in 1838 or 1840, although for another purpose. He was in search of a suitable material of which to form the cylinder of carbon that constitutes an essential feature of his nitric-acid cell.

Among other trials he thought of agglomerating with glue dry bituminous coal finely pulverized, and of baking in a furnace the blocks thus obtained. But these blocks split. To increase their solidity he conceived the idea of immersing them in a sugar-sirup which would fill all the cracks, and then of baking them a second time. The sugar was carbonized in this second baking, and completely filled all the pores, so as to furnish as compact a carbon as the gas-carbon, but purer and much more homogeneous. If necessary, they could be heated a third time after a third immersion, to complete the effect of the second one.

In 1846 two Englishmen, Staite and Edwards, patented a mode of manufacture analogous to that of Bunsen, but they specified particularly that they wished to obtain carbons for the electric light. Soon other improvements were effected. In 1849 Le Moult added coal-tar to the sugar-sirup, and used different kinds of powdered carbon which he heated for thirty hours, and then purified by immersion in acids. In 1852 Watson and Slater preferred twigs of wood purified by lime, sev-

5

eral times heated, after having been dipped first in alum, and then in molasses.

Later on, in 1857, Lacassagne and Thiers returned to gas-carbon; but they purified it by a number of successive operations which re-moved its silicious and other impurities. The light was not so unsteady; unfortunately, the carbon, whose compactness was destroyed by this laborious purification, permitted sparks and even cinders to escape.

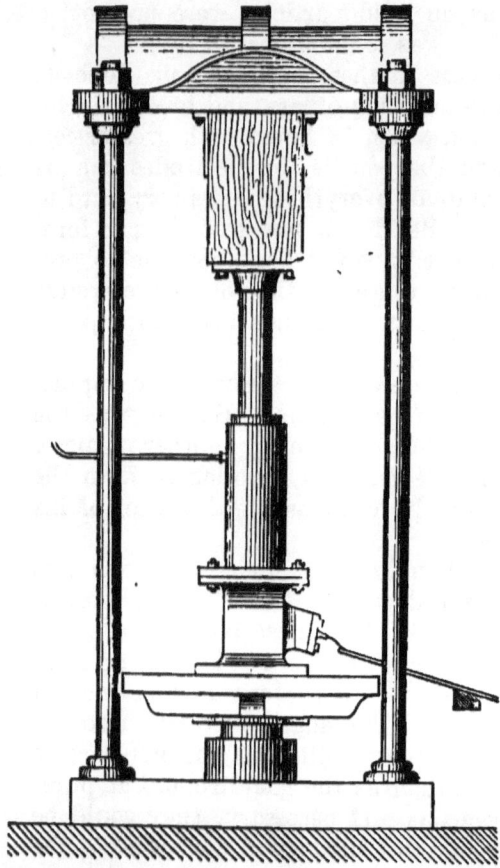

FIG. 16.—Draw-plate, with hydraulic press, for making artificial carbons.

About the same time, an old chemist of the École Centrale, M. Jacquelain, made a very pure artificial carbon with the tar derived from the distillation of coal or of schist; the intensity of light these carbons gave was one quarter greater than that afforded by the others; but the blocks thus made had to be cut up, a long and costly operation, on account of the hardness of the carbon. A little later M. Archereau obtained also excellent results in mixing magnesia with carbon-dust. He first conceived the idea of compressing the paste by passing it through a draw-plate such as is used for wire-making, a process followed to-day by all manufacturers.

Toward 1876, M. F. Carré introduced important improvements into this manufacture, notably the use, for driving the paste through the draw-plate, of a very powerful hydraulic press (Fig. 16). The carbon-paste was composed of fifteen parts of very pure coke, reduced to extremely fine powder, five parts of calcined lamp-black, and seven or eight parts of sugar-sirup mixed with a little gum. The whole was ground up with exactly the right quantity of water to form a paste of the desired consistency, and intimately mixed by machinery. After the passage through the draw-plate, which was facilitated by heating the body of the press, the pencils were arranged on grooved tablets covered with charcoal-dust, and these tablets were introduced into a furnace where they were maintained for about five hours at a cherry-red heat. The pencils were next plunged into a sirup of boiling caramel, dried, and reheated in crucibles, but at a higher temperature : this was called nourishing them. These two operations were repeated until the pencils had acquired the necessary density and hardness, and they were finally dried in a stove.

M. E. Carré, who worked under his brother's patents, succeeded in making continuously pencils of more than a metre in length, and of all sizes. In some the diameter was reduced to a millimetre. They were perfectly straight and of remarkable solidity. The results he obtained have done much to contribute to the success of electric lighting.

In 1877 M. Gaudoin also succeeded in furnishing carbons of excellent quality, which many engineers prefer even to Carré's carbons, although the last are most widely used in France, and are exported abroad, especially to England.

In Germany, carbons made by the house of Siemens are principally used, which are exported also to other countries. They give very good results, especially as regards fixity of the light ; but their composition and mode of manufacture are kept secret.

The last improvements introduced in France are due to M. Napoli, who especially had in view pencils destined for open-air incandescent burners of the Reynier-Werdermann type. His principal object was to obtain a carbon that would burn more slowly than the Carré or Gaudoin carbons, so that the lighting could last for a longer period without renewal of the carbon-pencils. He succeeded, in fact, in decreasing the consumption of the carbons to only five centimetres per hour of lighting, while the Carré carbons burned five times faster under the same conditions, that is to say, consumed twenty five centimetres of length, or one and a half metres per one evening's lighting of six hours' duration.

This result was due to the materials employed and to the means used to unite them intimately.

M. Napoli attributed the rapidity of consumption of the

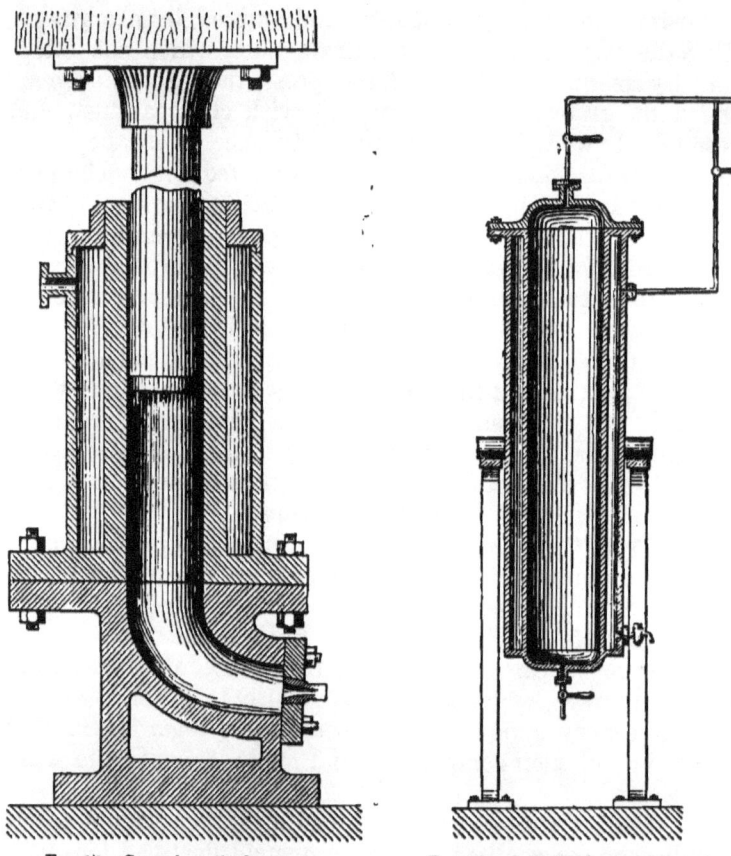

FIG. 17.—Curved nozzle draw-press of M. Napoli (vertical section).

FIG. 18.—Cylinder for nourishment of the carbons under pressure, by M. Napoli's method.

carbons to the original difference between its constituent elements, namely, the agglomerating liquid and the solid matter it was to agglomerate ; a difference which did not disappear at all during the fabrication, and which thus prevented the perfect homogeneity of the carbon-pencil obtained. He chose accordingly, for agglomerating and solid material, two substances of identical origin—for one, the tar of bituminous coal; for the other, the coke left as residue from the distillation of this tar at a low red-heat, which coke, before using, was reduced into very fine powder, which was carefully sifted.

The paste employed consists of three parts of coke and only one of tar. M. Napoli strove to reduce, as far as possible, the proportion of agglomerant to avoid the shrinkage during ignition of the rods, which often caused cracks. This paste was but slightly fluid, so that he had to employ a drawing-machine of curved shape (Fig. 17) for forming his pencils.

To still further nourish the carbons in spite of the considerable density they already possessed, he placed them in a special cylinder (Fig. 18), where alternately a vacuum could be produced or the pressure of a steam-boiler admitted. This cylinder was itself surrounded by a double jacket, into which steam was introduced to heat it to a proper temperature during the operation. When the carbons had been placed in the cylinder, a vacuum was produced there which caused the air condensed in their pores to be expelled; then the nourishing liquid was introduced, on which steam-pressure was made to act which drove it into the pores exhausted of air; finally, when the liquid nourisher had run out, a jet of steam driven through the bundle of rods wiped off their surface just like a moistened rag in the hands of a dish-washer.

The *tout ensemble* of the operations may be seen in Fig. 19, which shows the temporary workshop of M. Napoli, Rue des Martyrs, Paris. In front, the grooved tablets are spread out, holding the carbon-rods; on the left appear the reverberatory furnaces where they are reheated; then the drawing-machine, with the hydraulic press that forms them, and, further back, the cylinder which nourishes them under pressure. At a distance is seen the receptacle in which the mixture of substances is made, by the side of the engine which furnishes steam and drives the whole machinery of the workshop.

To indicate the importance of a good choice of carbons, it is enough to give the result of several comparative experiments. The source of electricity which could furnish a light equal to one hundred and three Carcel lamps, with retort or gas-carbon pencils, gives one hundred and twenty Carcels

FIG. 19.—Workshop of M. Napoli, showing the different operations of manufacturing electric-light carbons.

with Archereau's carbons, and one hundred and eighty with Carré's carbons. It is claimed that Gaudoin's carbons will go still further, and will give as much as two hundred or two hundred and ten Carcels, or double that which retort-carbon gives under the same conditions.

If artificial carbon possesses the qualities necessary for the production of the electric light, it has the inconvenience of being a very poor conductor; for equal dimensions its resistance is much greater than that of pure copper, and it is very important not to introduce into the circuit more length of carbon than is strictly necessary, even if its resistance diminishes when heated.

An idea of the factors of this problem can be obtained from the following figures, resulting from the experiments of M. Joubert with Carré's carbons:

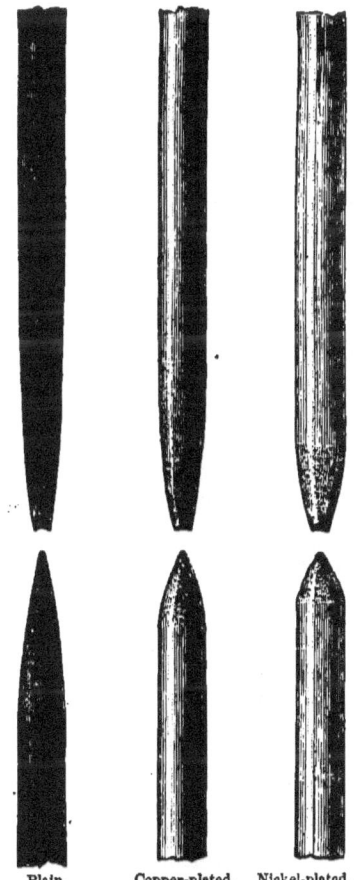

Diameters in millimetres.	Resistances in ohms at 20° centigrade.	Equivalent length in copper wire of four millimetres diameter.
1	50·000	20,000 metres.
2	12·500	5,000 "
3	5·550	2,222 "
4	3·125	1,250 "
5	2·000	800 "
6	1·390	555 "

Between 32° and 212° the resistance diminishes $\frac{1}{3442}$ for each degree; at 1,832° it is reduced to one third.

Plain. Copper-plated. Nickel-plated.

Figs. 20, 21, 22.—Points of a pair of carbons, plain, and coated with metal.

Gas-carbon pencils are about seventy times more resisting; those of M. Gaudoin would be about 2·16 times more resisting than those of M. Carré.

We have said that the electric light is principally produced by the incandescence of polar carbons, and that it is the points whence the current flows that reach the highest temperature ; for the light to be fixed, these points must displace themselves as little as possible in operation, and this is quite hard to realize because of the invincible tendency of the current to choose always the shortest path—a path which the wearing away of the carbons is continually changing, as may be seen in examining the image of a voltaic arc magnified and projected on a screen. The displacement of the points of emission is one of the principal causes of the oscillations continually objected to in the electric light. The light would unquestionably be more fixed and more intense with thinner carbons, but then a greater part of their length would grow red-hot, and would be burned through back of the points by slow oxidation by the air.

To prevent this waste and diminish the resistance of the carbons, M. Reynier conceived, in 1875, the idea of preventing the contact of the air by covering the carbons with a metallic pellicle, copper or nickel, galvanically deposited. With a very thin deposit of metal, excellent results were obtained. M. Tchikoleff, of St. Petersburg, has proved, in fact, that a layer of copper $\frac{1}{800}$ millimetres thick increases the conductivity four and a half times its normal amount ; with a $\frac{1}{80}$ coating, it increases one hundred and eleven times ; the duration of the carbon can be at the same time increased fourteen per cent, as is proved by experiments made by M. Lemonnier with a Gramme machine with continuous current (Figs. 20, 21, 22) :

Diameter of pencils in millimetres.	State of surface.	Consumption per hour in millimetres.			Intensity of the light in Carcels.
		Positive.	Negative.	Total.	
7	Plain............	166	68	234	947
	Copper-plated..	146	40	186	
	Nickel-plated ..	106	38	144	
9	Plain............	104	50	154	528
	Copper-plated..	98	34	132	
	Nickel-plated...	68	36	104	

Using alternate currents, the two carbons form symmetrical points, and it is quite easy to secure steadiness. With continuous currents the metallic coating does not become dissipated quickly enough from the negative carbon, and often forms a barricade which hides part of the light ; the best plan is to employ metallic plating only for the positive carbon.

Trying in another direction to secure the steadiness of the light, M. Carré thought of constructing the polar carbons with a very fine central rod of carbon inclosed in a tube of carbon which it exactly filled, and which would serve to support it; the combustion resembled exactly that of a candle-wick and the wax surrounding it. The two parts of the carbon naturally are made of different composition appropriate for the different *rôles* they have to fill.

By using these carbons, and by properly reducing the section of the negative carbon, not only is a remarkable steadiness attained, but the peculiar hissing noise that too often accompanies the voltaic arc is suppressed, a hissing that must not be confounded with the peculiar rustling inseparable from the employment of alternating currents, but which does not exist when continuous currents are employed.

CHAPTER IV.

SINGLE-LIGHT REGULATORS.

THE electric lamp for production of the voltaic arc is composed essentially of two rods of carbon, shaped at the ends like pencils, and placed in the prolongation of their mutual axis ; between these electrodes the current passes, and forms the voltaic arc. We have already explained, in the preceding chapter, the nature of the carbons employed, and the cause of the brilliant light produced. It remains to be shown how this light can continue long enough and in a sufficiently regular manner to constitute a practical system.

When the current is to be made to pass from one of the carbons to the other—that is to say, when the lamp is to be lighted—the carbons must be put in contact, end to end, because the electric current is incapable of overcoming the resistance which the almost non-conductivity of cold air offers to its passage. The ends of the carbon-rods, sharpened to a point, soon grow red, because of the crowding of the electric molecules in this choked passage. The air becomes heated by these incandescent points, and thus becomes capable of conducting a little electricity. The carbon-rods must then be separated from each other a certain distance, to cause the development of the voltaic arc in all its powerful brilliancy.

We now have the lamp lighted. Unfortunately, it threatens to go out very soon. In fact, the carbon, brought to in-candescence, burns quite rapidly, however compact it may be. The rods, or electrodes, continually grow short, so that the distance which the electricity has to traverse in air aug-ments every moment. As air even when heated is a poor conductor, the current experiences an increasing resistance before it, which it soon is unable to overcome. Then the voltaic arc disappears, and the lamp goes out.

To add to the trouble, the two carbons burn unevenly be-cause of the difference of their physical condition, and be-cause of the transportation of particles of incandescent car-bon from one pole to the other under the effect of the current. The positive pole burns twice as rapidly as the negative one, which is the cause of several· in-conveniences. Thus, the center of radiation, which evidently cor-responds to the center of the vol-taic arc, or center of the inter-val between the two electrodes, is displaced by receding from the positive pole. Furthermore, the poles themselves change their form, and do not any longer re-semble each other in shape (see *ante*, Fig. 15, page 33, and Figs. 20–22, page 53).

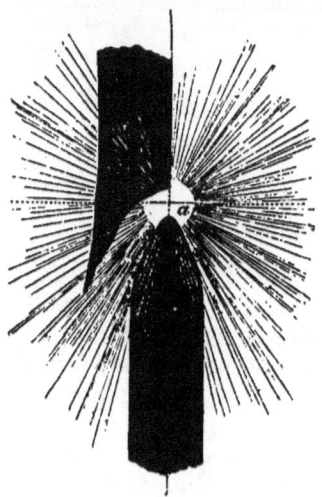

Fig. 23.—One-sided position of the car-bons, for the purpose of causing the light to be of greater intensity in one direction.

While the negative pole grows more pointed, the positive pole hollows out into the shape of a little crucible, facing the oppo-site carbon. This hollow is called the crater. The light becomes brighter there than in other parts of the voltaic arc, which increases still further the variations in light pro-duced by the other causes. From an early period, when this light was only employed for scientific projections, M. Duboscq had shown that the defect could be partly cured, and more light could be obtained by placing one carbon, the nega-tive one, a little in front of the other (Fig. 23). This artifice is employed at the present day in the powerful lights of light-houses, where continuous currents are employed. MM. Fontaine and Lemonnier in France, and Messrs. Tyndall and Douglass in England, have made many experiments on this subject, which prove that the intensity is thus increased fifty per cent in the line in which the radiation is directed.

But, for most applications, it is necessary above all to have an equal distribution of light, so that anything which tends to diminish it becomes a grave fault, which fault is avoided where alternating currents are employed.

If the lamp after being lighted is left to itself, it begins to burn for some minutes with a very variable intensity, then it suddenly grows weak and goes out. To prevent this extinction from taking place, the carbons must be continually brought together, so that their distance apart shall remain substantially the same. The ideal would be to cause them to advance both together with a continuous and regular movement in exact proportion to their consumption. This is the

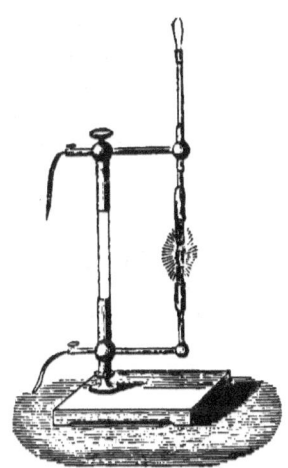

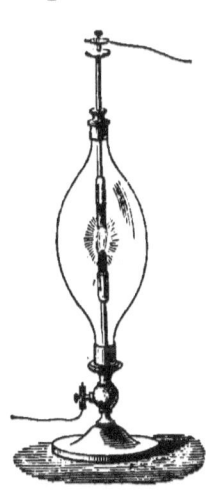

Fig. 24.—Carbon-holder regulated by hand, for the production of the electric light.

Fig. 25.—Primitive carbon-holder, for production of the electric light in a vacuum.

principal trouble with electric lamps; it is on this point that almost all inventors have concentrated their efforts, and it is in this particular that most electric lights differ, except the incandescent systems, which solve the problem in another way.

At first, the operation was conducted by hand. The carbons were fixed to metallic rods, one of which worked by

friction in a fixed ring. The movement was by the hand of
the operator: the movable rod was pushed down to light the
lamp, it was drawn up a little to extend the arc, then from
time to time it was slightly advanced as the brightness of the
arc diminished sufficiently to call attention to it. As it was
necessary to be very close to the lamp in working this rod,
there is no need of mentioning the dangers encountered by
the eyes of the unfortunate being in charge of this work (Figs.
24 and 25). It was thus that Sir Humphry Davy operated in
1813, sometimes in the open air, sometimes
in a vacuum. Imperfect as this method
was, it was thus that thirty years later Léon
Foucault worked in his first researches, and
that Deleuil, in his public experiments in
lighting in Paris, operated on the Place de
la Concorde and in front of La Monnaie.

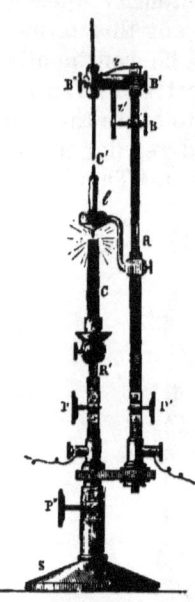

This process, crude in a double sense,
which we have all of us seen followed in
experiments in courses of physics, governs
the light, as is evident, in a very imperfect
manner by fits and starts. It is seldom
employed now even for the use of labora-

C, lower carbon.

R', rack by which it was raised or lowered by aid of the pinion P.

C', upper carbon.

e, guide, which can be displaced at pleasure. When there is
used, as shown in the figure, a long and thin rod of carbon,
whose resistance is great, the guide is placed on the bar R.
It supports the carbon and facilitates the passage of the current, and limits the length of the incandescent portion.

R, rack worked by the pinion P' for the upper carbon-holder.

B, B', buttons for bringing the point of the upper carbon into
position.

Fig. 26.—Hand-regulator
of M. Boudreaux, with
vertical carbon-hold-
ers, for magic lanterns
and other experiments
with electric light.

r, r', contact springs.

B'', button for holding the upper carbon.

P'', button for working the third rack, serving to raise or lower
the luminous center.

S, foot of the lamp.

tories. It is almost everywhere replaced by the hand-regulator of M. Boudreaux (Fig. 26), which works much better.

If, for so many years, no better method was sought for, it
is because the light was as yet but a simple curiosity of the
laboratory, and a curiosity rarely exhibited because of its
great expense, and of the endless variety of trouble entailed
in its preparation. The batteries then at the disposal of the

physicist were very weak, so that it was necessary to unite a multitude of elements to obtain the strong currents necessary for the electric light. Sir Humphry Davy, as has been seen, never employed less than two thousand. Even in the best laboratories this involved an expense and trouble that no one would dream of encountering to-day.

The discovery of the Bunsen battery, which was published in 1840, changed the state of affairs by placing at the disposal of all a battery much more powerful, and relatively less cumbrous, and at the same time less costly. Thus it is since the year 1844 that the electric light has been seriously studied, and all at once a means of regulating it was searched for that would effect mechanically the approach of the carbons.

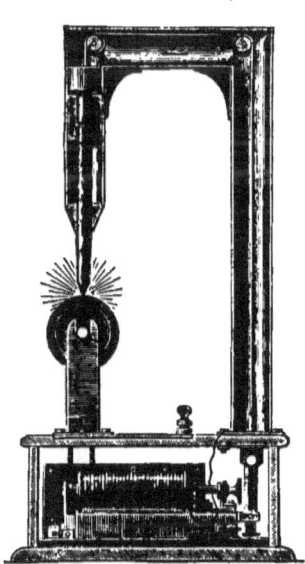

The first trial which gave any results dates from 1845. It is due to an Englishman named Thomas Wright, who conceived the idea of replacing the cylindrical carbon-rods by disks beveled on their peripheries, and turned by a special mechanism, which kept them at a constant distance. The voltaic arc played between these disks. The attempt of Thomas Wright passed almost without notice; and almost the same may be said of an analogous experiment of a French physicist, Le Molt, known also by his experiments on artificial carbons. He patented in 1849 an apparatus capable of acting automatically,

FIG. 27.—Harrison's regulator (1857). The lower carbon consists of a disk rotating on its axis. The upper carbon is kept at a suitable distance by a cord running over pulleys, and governed by the armature of an electromagnet placed below.

according to his accounts, for twenty or thirty hours, without the need of any intervention by the hand of the operator. Nevertheless, the idea was taken up later (1857), with some modifications, by Mr. Harrison (Fig. 27); and the recent apparatus of M. Reynier presents many analogies with this system, originally unsuccessful.

But two or three years later, about 1848, Messrs. Staite

and Petrie in England, and Léon Foucault in France, worked at the same problem in an altogether different way.

To them is due the first serious solution—even if as yet it is not practical in all its details—of this difficult problem, and it is in the road opened up by their labors that inventors are now marching.

I. Regulators with Electro-Magnets.

How may the problem be summed up? The burning up of the carbons under the effect of the heat increases the distance between them, and for a continuous light they must be brought together; but this must be done at the proper moment. Suppose it is done too soon, the voltaic arc is shortened until it disappears; if done too late, on the contrary, it grows weaker, and perhaps is extinguished. How, then, can the exact moment of action be chosen?

No one can know this exact moment or feel it better than does the current itself. If the distance of the carbons increases, the current has more difficulty in traversing the elongated aërial conductor; if, on the other hand, the distance diminishes too much, the current knows it very well, for then it passes more readily. Like a well-trained sentinel, it is not satisfied to remark the occurrence, it wishes to notify us of it; for, in the first case, its intensity becomes less on account of the greater resistance it encounters, and in the second case, on the contrary, its intensity increases from the reciprocal cause.

All this can easily be proved with a galvanometer, but that is not enough. After having been notified by the current itself, the same current must be made to work, and by its own efforts prevent the evil it has been demonstrating. This is achieved by forcing the current to pass, before going to the carbons, through the magnetizing helix of an electro-magnet, whose armature has the office of regulating the movements of the mechanism which advances the carbons.

The strength of this electro-magnet varies with the intensity of the current, and the armature is in turn attracted and released at the precise moments where its intervention is necessary to regulate the approach of the carbons.

This is the very simple principle upon which the regulator of Foucault works, so simple that one asks why it was not at

once thóught of as soon as the researches of Oersted and Ampère had revealed the laws of electro-magnetism. But, if
attention was not earlier turned in this direction—in other
words, before 1847, the date of the first labors of Foucault—
the art of making small, easily-worked electro-magnets was
not known. For it would not do to introduce into these delicate pieces of apparatus parts weighing a quintal or half a
quintal, like those hitherto employed. It is thus that all
scientific progress advances, and it often happens that very
slight improvements in a given point of construction, even in
a secondary one, carry with them a considerable progress in a
number of other more important points.

This has all happened with the regulator of Foucault,
whose mechanical complication was in other respects very
great. Thus he himself describes it in a summary manner:
"The two carbon-holders are pressed together by springs;
but they can not come in contact without moving a train of
wheels, the last of which is controlled by a detent. It is here
that electro-magnetism is used. The current which causes the
illumination passes through the spirals of an electro-magnet,
whose energy varies with the intensity of the current; this
electro-magnet acts upon an armature of soft iron, drawn
away from it again by a counteracting spring. Upon this
movable armature is fastened the detent which locks the train
or releases it as the current dictates, and the motion of the
detent is such that it presses upon the wheel when the current grows strong, or lets it go when the current grows weak.
Now, just as the current grows strong or weakens, as the interpolar distance diminishes or increases, it will be understood
that the carbons have the liberty of approaching at the moment when the distance between them tends to increase, and
that this approaching can not bring them in contact, because
the increased electro-magnetic action resulting therefrom offers an insurmountable obstacle, which disappears of its own
accord as the interpolar distance again increases."

It appears, then, that the motion of the carbon in this
apparatus is intermittent; but, as the periods of repose and
advancing should follow each other with great rapidity, and
last but a short space of time for each one, Foucault supposed
that this in practice would amount to the continuous movement of progression necessary for the fixity of the light.

Nevertheless, the regulator had more than one fault, and

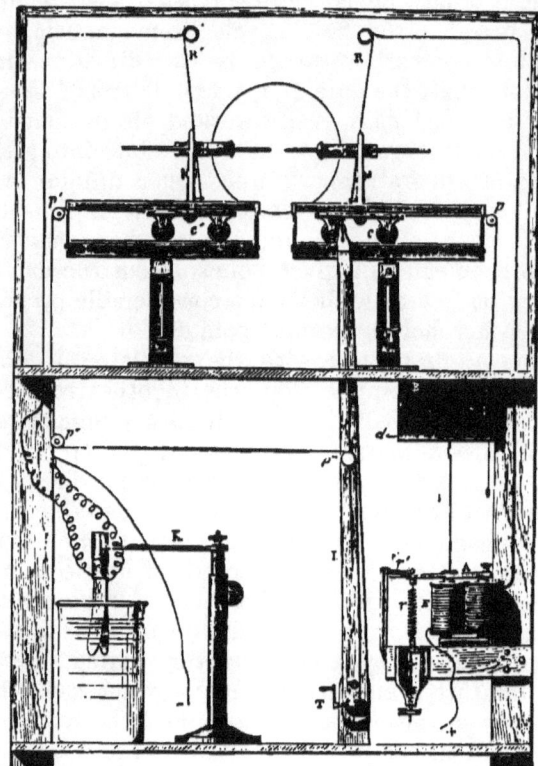

Fɪɢ. 28.—First regulator of the electric light of Foucault (1849).

c, positive carbon-holder car.   c', negative carbon-holder car.

R, R', springs which push the cars together and conduct the current.

L, large lever which forces the cars to move simultaneously, causing, by the attachment of the return cord p', p'', p''' to the lever, the car c' to move slower than the other.

T, little windlass, serving to regulate the position of car c'.

M, clock-work, to which the car c is attached by the cord p, and whose scape-wheel, held by a detent, can not move.

E, electro-magnet with thick wire, through which the current passes.

A, armature of the electro-magnet, pivoted at r' to a Robert Houdin lever.

D, rod of the detent mounted on the armature. When the current grows strong, the armature is drawn down, the detent presses upon the wheel, and the cars cease to move. When the current grows weak, the detent releases the wheel, and the cars approach each other.

r, counteracting spring drawing back the armature.   d, hand-lever for stopping.

K, regulator of the current, whose use is rendered necessary by the battery which produces the electricity ; it is made of two plates of platinum, arranged parallel to each other, one millimetre apart, and insulated from one another. The current passes from one to the other through the conducting fluid (sulphate of potash solution), into which they are plunged to a greater or less depth in proportion to the intensity of the current.

was not entirely automatic, because it required the aid of an operator's hand to light the lamp at the beginning by separating the carbons. Foucault was obliged to further complicate it to overcome this imperfection.

The new machine had two distinct clock-movements—one to bring the carbons together, the other to separate them. An electro-magnet placed in the circuit unlocked and put one or the other of these movements into action by means of a lever fastened to its armature. This is attracted in one direction by an electro-magnet, and in another by an opposing spring, whose tension is regulated in proportion to the intensity of the current employed. The inconvenience of such a spring, which the variations of the current can not influence, and which has to be adjusted by hand in proportion to the power of the electro-magnet opposed to it, can be easily understood.

M. Duboscq, who had been the collaborator of Foucault, introduced several other improvements in this apparatus (Fig. 29), which is used in this form in all laboratories, and at all the lectures in which M. Duboscq so often gives his assistance.

It is also with this regulator that he has introduced the electric light into the opera, and it is always it that is used when it is necessary to introduce the sun upon the scene, as when grand effects of light should mingle with the expressive dances of the ballet.

Fig. 29.—Regulator of J. Duboscq.

These two regulators of Foucault and Duboscq have served as types for their followers, which differ from them in the most diverse mechanical combinations, but which resemble them in their physical principles. We will only examine those more widely used; but many others exist which present almost analogous arrangements.

In the year 1859 M. Serrin constructed a regulator realizing the different conditions of the problem by new and very ingenious arrangements. The clock-work is done away with,

6

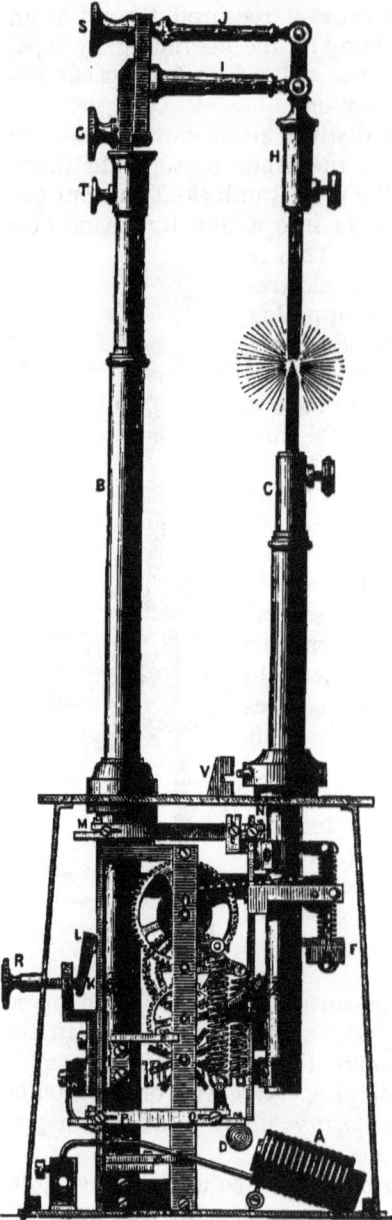

FIG. 30.—Serrin's regulator (1859).

H, upper carbon-holder (positive).

J, movable intervening piece, which is advanced or drawn back by means of the button S.

G, button terminating in a small eccentric. The two buttons, S and G, permit the upper carbon to be moved in two directions, to keep the points well opposed to each other.

B, stationary tube serving as guide to the rod of the upper carbon-holder. This rod is provided with a rack on its lower end, and serves by its weight as motor for the whole apparatus.

C, lower carbon-holder (negative).

M, N, P, Q, jointed parallelogram, or oscillating system, serving to govern the advance of the carbons.

O, series of cog-wheels, the first of which engages with the rack of the upper carbon-holder, and transmits the movement to the lower carbon-holder by means of a small fusee-chain, whose extremity is fastened to the stud F. The last axle carries a rachet, on which acts an abutment fixed on one of the sides of the parallelogram.

E, springs: one is fixed, and balances the weight of the movable pieces fastened to the oscillating system; the other serves as opposing spring against the action of the electro-magnet on its armature.

D, armature of soft iron fixed to the oscillating system. A, electro-magnet.

K, L, lever regulating the tension of the opposing spring. If the electric current does not circulate, the electro-magnet is inactive; the oscillating system is kept up by the springs; the rachet is free, and, under the influence of the weight of the upper carbon-holder, the wheels turn and the carbons approach each other. If the current is now turned on, it passes through the rod B H, through the carbons which are in contact, descends the rod C, and, by the intermediation of the corrugated plate which is seen behind, reaches the electro-magnet, and returns to the generator. The electro-magnet, put into motion by this passage of the current through its helices, attracts its armature; the oscillating system drops down, the lower carbon descends, the stop-piece catches in the rachet, the wheel-work becomes motionless, and the descent of the upper carbon is arrested. The two carbons separate, and the arc is started. Each time that the increased length of the arc weakens the current, the electro-magnet releases its armature, and the same movements of approach and then of separation are repeated.

and the carbons are advanced simply by the weight of the upper carbon-holder. The rod of the lower carbon-holder is carried by an oscillating parallelogram sustained by two springs, one of which is fixed, and keeps an equilibrium between the weights of the movable pieces, while the other is governed by hand by means of a button (Fig. 30).

An electro-magnet, worked by the current of the lamp, also governs the movement of the apparatus; but its armature, fastened to the oscillating parallelogram, fills a double *rôle:* at the time it stops at the proper moment the approach of the carbons, by acting on a rachet-wheel, it causes the formation of a voltaic arc by attracting the lower carbon-holder, and producing thus between the points of carbon the necessary distance, so that the lamp lights of its own accord when it receives the current. It is the second spring that has to furnish the force necessary to draw back this armature of the electro-magnet when the latter is weakened through diminution of the strength of the current.

On account of the exactness of its movements the carbons progress with absolute steadiness and regularity. It is the apparatus adopted since 1863 for light-house illumination in France and England; it has

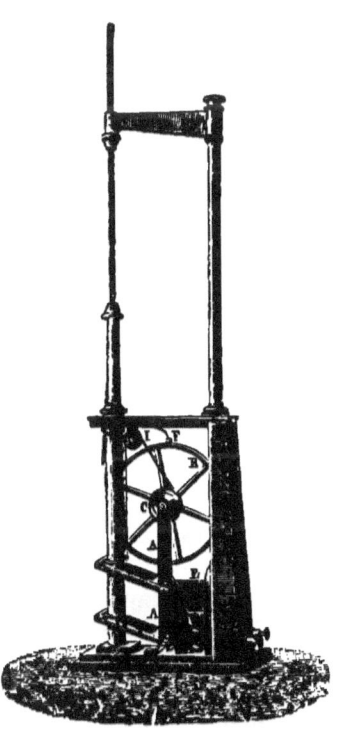

FIG. 31.—Bürgin's regulator.

been for a long time the principal reliance of electricians, and has contributed largely to the success of electric lighting.

In the Bürgin lamp, now antiquated, the movement of the

moving carbon (or of both carbons in another model) is governed by a spring-brake, only it is not the brake which is
displaced, but the fly-wheel on which it acts. This wheel is
fastened to the armature of an electro-magnet with thick
wire, and moves with it. When the current passes with full
energy the armature is attracted; the wheel is raised up, and
presses upon the brake, which stops it from turning. When
the current begins to grow weak, the armature and wheel fall
down, and the carbon can descend. The slight displacement
of the armature is transmitted to the lower carbon by a cord,
and suffices to produce the separation. This apparatus (Fig.
31) is arranged for only one light, but it can easily be changed
so as to act for several luminous centers, according to principles which will be explained in the next chapter.

The Gulcher lamp is also a single-light lamp of great simplicity. The rod of the upper carbon-holder is of iron, its
descent is regulated by the attraction of a straight electro-
magnet, mounted on trunnions like a cannon, and which oscillates perpendicularly before it. The farther end of this electro-magnet is placed under a block of iron, which attracts and
balances it. The other end raises the rod of the positive carbon and produces the separation. The reverse takes place
every time the current weakens. The two carbon-holders are
united by a connecting cord, and their movements are coincident.

Finally, the lamp of M. Girouard must be cited, invented
in the beginning of 1876, because it shows a disposition of
parts which is peculiar to it. The apparatus is divided into
two distinct parts: one the lamp, properly so called, with
clock-work for approaching and separating the carbons; and,
second, the regulator in the form of a relay, which can be
placed at a distance from the lamp, and which works by
means of a small special battery.

In this apparatus, then, there are two distinct currents.
The first, which comes from the dynamo-electric machine, is
very intense, and serves for the production of the electric
light, having, however, first passed through the bobbin of an
electro-magnet fixed to the relay. The second current, which
comes from the battery, is very feeble, and has nothing to do
but to start the clock-work, which advances or draws back
the carbons. A very complicated mechanism permits the
electro-magnet of the relay to act upon the lamp. This sys-

tem has only one advantage : that it permits the operator to govern from a distance the movements of the apparatus, something that in many cases is very convenient.

II. Solenoid Regulators.

While Foucault worked at his regulator, founded on the action of electro-magnets, another French savant, Archereau, invented an apparatus founded on the action of solenoids, and which, differing from that of Foucault, is distinguished by great simplicity.

A solenoid is a spiral, or helix—a sort of corkscrew, if you please—through which a current passes. When an iron rod is passed through the opening in a solenoid, as if in a sheath, its tendency is to place itself symmetrically with respect to the two ends of the solenoid ; consequently it is attracted by it, and that with more or less force according as the current passing through the solenoid is of greater or less intensity. This is the principle of Archereau's regulator.

In this apparatus the positive carbon placed above is stationary. As for the negative carbon, placed below, it is attached to a rod of iron, situated in the middle of the solenoid, and balanced by a counterpoise by means of a cord passing over a pulley. The current of the voltaic arc passes through the solenoid wire, and it is at once clear that its variations

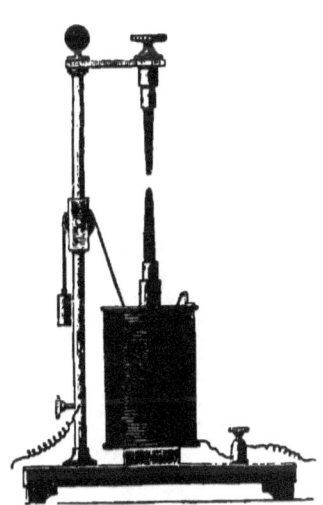

Fig. 32.—Archereau's regulator, type of solenoid regulators.

will bring about the rise or fall of the negative carbon at the right time if all the parts of the apparatus are properly proportioned.

Archereau's regulator has no clock-work. It is a true marvel of simplicity ; so much so, that the first model constructed only cost seventeen francs, and, notwithstanding, does actually work, if not always perfectly. But, as it is not the positive carbon that moves, the negative carbon must rise to follow its

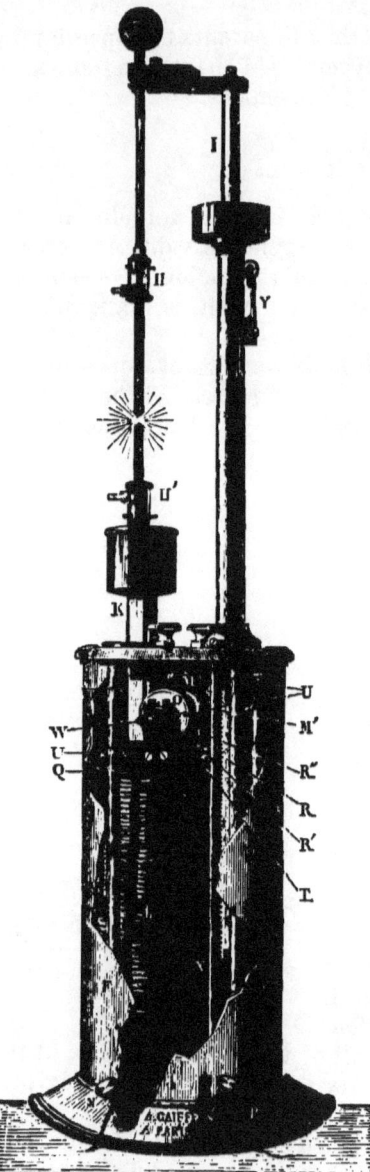

FIG. 33.—Gaiffe's regulator.

II, II', carbon-holders, upper and lower.
I, rod of the carbon-holder II, provided at its lower extremity with a rack.
K, rod of the lower carbon-holder; it is of soft iron and of quadrangular section. The upper part is provided with a rack; the lower enters into the interior of the bobbin L.
M, M', cog-wheels turning freely on the axle W, and separated one from the other by an ivory wheel; their diameters are in the ratio of 1 to 2. The larger engages with the rod I, and the smaller with the rod K. The distances traversed by these rods are thus proportional to the consumption of the carbons.
O, barrel containing a spring which tends constantly to bring the rods together, and, consequently, the carbons.
W, extremity of the arbor, terminated by a square shank for receiving the key with which the tension of the spring is adjusted.
R, R', R'', reverse motion-pinions. They can be displaced in parallelism with themselves, and act upon the rods I and K when both carbons are to be raised or lowered without stopping the working of the apparatus. The axle of these pinions carries for this purpose a square shank to receive a key. A spring placed on the same axle takes them out of engagement when the key is no longer turned.
L, hollow electro-magnetic bobbin, whose helix increases in thickness from top to bottom.
X, vertical rod for the passage of the current from the binding-screw P to the column J.
Y, contact-key, penetrating by an opening through the tube J, and bearing against the rod I by a spring, to insure the contact necessary for the passage of the current.
U, guides serving to direct the rods I and K, and prevent them from turning. As long as the current does not pass, the carbons are kept in contact by the barrel and spring; but, as soon as it is passed into the apparatus, the bobbin attracts the rod K, and, as the two rods are connected, the carbons separate, and the arc is established. Its length is regulated by the tension of the spring, which should be in equilibrium with the attractive force of the bobbin. While the increased length of the arc diminishes the force of contact, the spring overcomes the attraction of the bobbin, and the carbons approach until equilibrium is re-established.

waste, so that the luminous center is continually shifting, in the exact ratio that the positive carbon burns away—an inconvenience that does not exist in the Foucault regulator.

As derivatives of the

A, rod of positive carbon-holder. A guide, placed at the lower part of this rod, prevents it from turning, and keeps the carbons opposite one another.

B, iron rod of the negative carbon-holder. These two rods are united by two small cords to the rim of two pulleys, which work together, and of which one has twice the diameter of the other, so that the rod A descends twice as fast as the rod B rises.

C, solenoid with coarse wire, through whose interior the rod B descends.

D, small cylinder filled with mercury.

L, stem fastened to the rod B, and ending below in a little piston, which plunges into the cylinder D, but with enough clearance for the mercury to pass it.

F, counter-weight sliding on a horizontal lever, fastened by a cord to a third pulley, which works in unison with the other two. It acts in the opposite direction to the motor rod A.

K, button by which the weight F is brought nearer, or pushed away, according as it is desirable to augment or diminish its action, and regulate thus the quickness of progression of the carbons according to the intensity of the current.

E, counterpoise fastened between the arms of the first pulley, and serving to balance the variations in the attraction of the solenoid on the rod B. As the pulley turns, the action of the weight diminishes at the same time that the attraction of the solenoid diminishes, by the deeper penetration of the rod B.

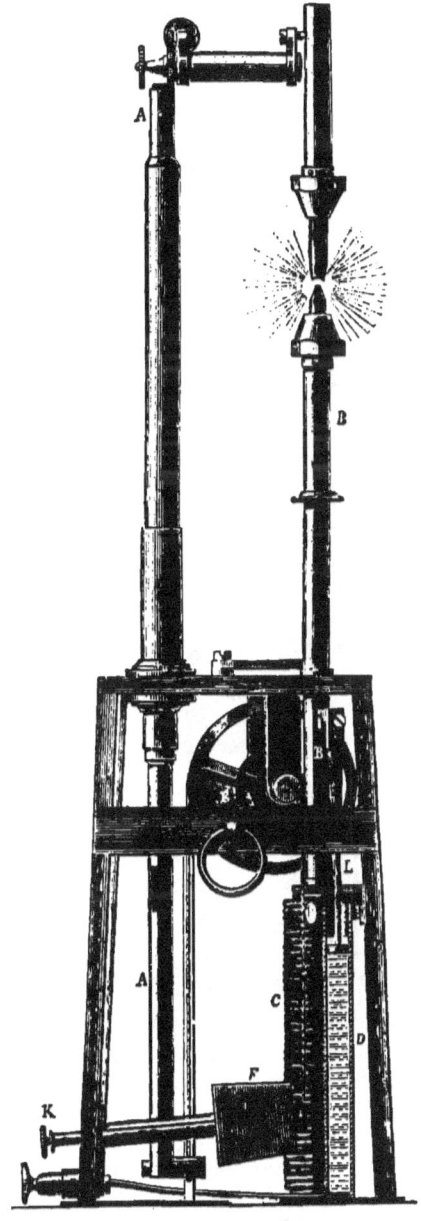

Fig. 34.—Jaspar's regulator.

Archereau type, the regulators of MM. Gaiffe and Jaspar must be cited.   In the regulator of M. Gaiffe the motor is a spring inclosed in a barrel.   This spring is wound up by the same movement of separation of the carbon-holders that is needed to put the carbons in place, and in position for acting.   The solenoid is formed by a helix whose turns increase from top to bottom, so that a stronger and stronger attraction is continually exerted on the iron rod which terminates the lower carbon-holder. Thus the necessary length of movement is obtained (Fig. 33).

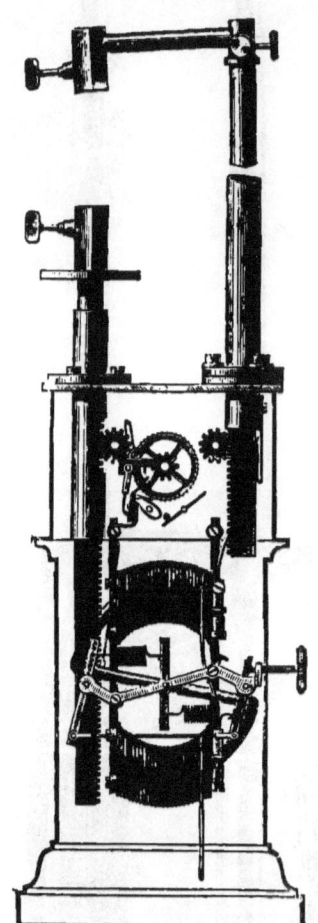

FIG. 35.—F. Carré's regulator.

This apparatus is supplied with an arrangement which permits the two carbons to be raised or lowered at will and simultaneously, without extinguishing the arc.   This condition is indispensable when the luminous center has to be kept in the focus of optical apparatus, such as magic-lanterns and light-house apparatus.

The regulator of M. Jaspar (Fig. 34) is very simple in construction. The movable rod of the upper carbon-holder is the motor, and, by its weight, causes in its descent the elevation of the lower carbon-holder to which it is united by a small cord passing over a pulley. The separation is effected by the action of a solenoid which attracts the iron rod of the lower carbon-holder; as this action is much more powerful at the beginning of the course, it is balanced by the aid of a counter-weight fixed upon the transmission-wheel, and turning with it, so that the lever-arm of this counterpoise varies inversely with the action of the solenoid. A second counterpoise, whose position is regulated by hand, permits of the adjustment of the apparatus in accordance with the intensity of the current to be regulated.

The iron cores attracted by the solenoids have not, as in the case of the armatures of electro-magnets, a sharply-limited course. To limit their oscillations, a little rod of iron is used, fastened to the lower carbon-holder, and plunging into a cylinder filled with mercury ; the resistance which the mercury offers to the displacement of the iron rod checks and regulates the movement, and, in consequence, that of the carbons themselves. On account of this disposition, the passage of the current takes place under excellent conditions. The regulator of M. Jaspar is remarkable for the regularity and certainty of its operation.

In this same category may be placed the regulator of M. F. Carré, whose movement is regulated by two solenoids, curved in the arc of a circle. The armature which moves in their interior is of S-shape, and oscillates at its center on a fixed point. The wire is wound on the bobbins so that both branches of the armature are attracted in the same direction. Thus, the attractive effect is doubled.

CHAPTER V.

MULTIPLE LIGHT, OR DIVISION, REGULATORS.

ALL the apparatus which we have studied have a common defect, derived from this very mode of regulation by the current, whose discovery was so important a progress. By using the whole current the light was in the first place subject to all the reactions due to the work done by the current every time it actuates the electro-magnet, while in the second place an almost insurmountable obstacle is created in the way of using simultaneously several lamps upon the same circuit. To appreciate this it is enough to study that which takes place when two apparatus only are to be placed in the same circuit ; if they are regulated for the same length of arc, it is necessary, in order that the approaching of the car-

bon shall take place in each lamp in similar amount and in
the same time, that their respective carbons shall be consumed
with exactly the same speed, which is impossible. Thus in a
short time one lamp is sure to present a wider opening than
the other. Now, as the electro-magnets work with the same
current and symmetrically, they tend to work almost together; in the apparatus where the carbons are most widely
separated they will return to the normal state, in the second
apparatus they will at once come in contact. If, on the contrary, they are arrested together, the distance between the
carbons will adjust itself, and one lamp will go out; the circuit will be interrupted and the second will also go out, until,
both carbons coming in contact, both will light up for a new
start. This would be still worse if more than two burners
were to be employed. For this reason these apparatus are
designated to-day by the name of *monophotes*.

There will be no difficulty in understanding that, when
success was achieved in producing electric currents in all
imaginable conditions, inventors applied themselves with
ardor to seek the solution of this problem so inappropriately
named the divisibility of the electric light. It has been solved
by the employment of the *derived current.*

I. Derived-Current, or Shunt-Circuit, Lamps.

When a current finds two paths open to it, it acts like
a stream of water; it divides itself between the two paths
directly proportional to the facility of passage, or inversely
to the resistance. Thus, if the resistance increases on one
branch of the circuit, the current will pass in larger quantity
by the other wire. In the polyphote regulators the current
is thus divided into two portions, one of which goes to the
voltaic arc, the other goes to the electro-magnet charged with
regulating the movement of the apparatus. The wire with
which this electro-magnet is wound is much finer than the
rest of the circuit; it causes, therefore, high resistance, and
ordinarily only suffices for the passage of a small derived
current, insufficient to make it active. But when the resistance of the voltaic arc increases, the derived current in the
electro-magnet increases in intensity, and this, by the aid of a
mechanism analogous to those which we have already described, releases the carbons, which approach each other,

diminish the resistance of the arc, and re-establish the preceding state of affairs. It is necessary, as will appear evident, to properly proportion the relative resistances of the arc circuit and electro-magnet circuit. With this distribution of current the regulation of the lamps is effected in an independent manner, because the same quantity of electricity will always pass from one lamp to another, however this passage be effected. In the experiments made by the jury of the Universal Exhibition of 1878, twelve regulators were made to work upon a single circuit of an alternating-current dynamo.

The first employment of a derived current for regulating the advance of the carbons was made in 1855 by MM. Lacassagne and Thiers; it was also combined with the main current of the lamp so as to utilize the differential action, as we shall see further on.

In 1877 the Lontin company again employed it in the Serrin regulators with which they experimented in lighting the station of the Paris, Lyons and Mediterranean Railroad. The apparatus has been modified thus: the electro-magnet with coarse wire of the

Fig. 36.—Serrin regulator modified for derived current by the Lontin company.

ordinary model is replaced by an electro-magnet with fine wire A, placed vertically. The armature B placed below is attracted when the derived current has sufficient intensity ; in obeying this attraction it releases the rachet and permits the carbons to approach ; it permits also the lower carbon to slightly advance. When the passage of the lighting current through the carbons is re-established, the armature is released, checks the movement, and moves the lower carbon enough to produce the arc.

Using derived-current regulators, the number of lamps that can work upon the same circuit is only limited by the tension of the current at disposal; thus this system is in use to-day in a great number of regulators, and we shall show that it is easily adopted in former systems of lamps. We shall only describe one of the most recent of such apparatus; we refer to that of M. Gramme.

In this the upper carbon is the only one that moves, and the rod which sustains it turns, by means of a rack, a series of wheels, the axle of the last of which carries a rachet, or scape-wheel, with long teeth. The electro-magnet with fine wire operates an armature that arrests the motion of this wheel, which is arranged in a peculiar manner. It carries an interrupter which cuts off the derived current every time the armature is attracted and has released one tooth of the scape-wheel. The action of the spring opposed to it is thus much facilitated, and the armature forms a species of vibrator or escapement which only permits the scape-wheel to turn tooth by tooth. An electro-magnet with thick wire placed on top of the apparatus lowers by its armature the frame carrying the lower carbon, when it is necessary to produce the first separation for lighting the lamp.

Improvements succeeded each other rapidly; but, when we pass from the laboratory into the domain of actual practice, difficulties show themselves at every step. In their first attempts a new trouble was encountered; the polar carbons are consumed quite rapidly, and yet, as they are only held by one extremity, it is difficult to use long and fragile rods, and to direct them end to end with accuracy. They must be frequently renewed, which is very inconvenient because the lamps, on account of their power, are generally placed very high up. It is a cause of trouble that in many cases is inadmissible.

To avoid this objection M. de Mersannes invented a new mode of moving the carbons which permits the employment of rods of all sizes, yet only introducing into the circuit the absolutely necessary length. This system consists in passing the carbons between grooved wheels which turn by the action of a spring, and in turning advance the carbons.

The apparatus contains two electro-magnets with fine wire placed in the same derived circuit. One of them serves to govern the movement of the motor, and, in consequence, the

C, upper cross-piece acting as armature for the electro-magnet A A.

A A, electro-magnet with thick wire traversed by the light current.

R, R, counteracting springs, fastened at X, Y to the bars E, E of the movable frame.

D, upper carbon-rod; it is provided with a rack, and actuates by its weight a train of wheels, the last of which is an escapement-wheel.

B, electro-magnet with fine wire traversed by a derived current.

F, attachment of the derived circuit to the rod E. The other extremity of the circuit is attached to the spring N.

I, armature of the derived-current magnet carried by a lever L, whose other end carries a plate S designed to catch in the scape-wheel.

L, lever pivoted at V.

M, contact-screw, which causes, by the movements which the armature I gives to the lever L, an intermittent contact with the spring N.

K, bridge-piece carrying the lever L.

U, spring opposing the action of the armature I.

When there is no current passing through the lamp the springs R, R keep the movable frame and lower carbon raised up; the armature I is also held up by its spring U, and the plate S stops the movement of the scape-wheel. The carbons are now separated. This break of continuity forces the current, when it is turned into the apparatus, to pass into the derived circuit instead of going through the carbons. The electro-magnet B becomes active, attracts its armature, the lever L swings over, and the plate S releases the scape-wheel. The rod D descends, the carbons approach, and the passage of the current is established. At this moment the electro-magnet A becomes active, and attracts its armature C; the lower carbon descends, but at the same instant the electro-magnet B becomes inactive. The lever L swings back the other way and the scape-wheel is caught. The checking of the motion of the upper carbon and the lowering of the lower carbon have produced the necessary separation for the establishment of the arc. The screw M is then in contact with the spring N, so that, as soon as the main current weakens, the derived current starts, and the same movements are reproduced; but this derived current is also interrupted, because the swinging of the lever separates this screw from the spring and breaks the circuit; it follows that the counteracting spring acts more readily, and the releasing is less prolonged. The approach of the carbons takes place by fractions of millimetres, and the arc has very few variations.

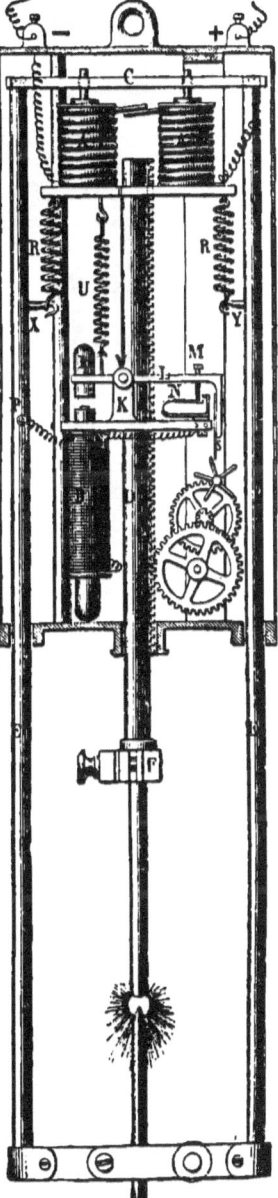

Fig. 37.—M. Gramme's derived-current regulator.

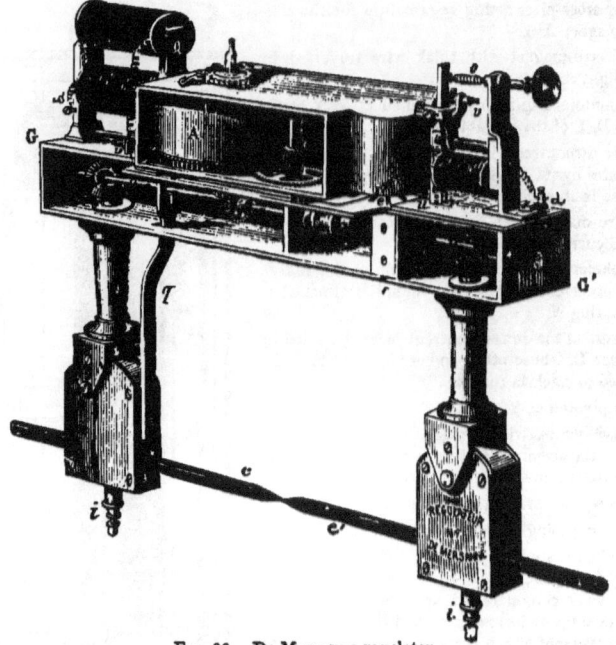

FIG. 38.—De Mersanne regulator.

A, barrel-spring actuating the longitudinal arbor a a.

a a, arbor which transmits the movement to the two arbors b, b of the carbon-holders; it is divided into two unequal parts united by Cardan's sleeves, electrically insulated.

G G', rectangular box containing the arbor a; the part G is also mounted at s on hard caout-chouc and ivory, so that all the pieces of one of the carbon-holders are insulated electrically.

b, b, arbors of the carbon-holders driving the small arbors d, d.

d, d, transverse arbors which transmit the movement by the wheels e, e, e to the feeding-guides (Fig. 39).

g, g, feeding-wheels which advance the carbons c and c one toward the other in proportion to the waste due to the combustion (Fig. 39).

h, h, contact-guides acting to insure the contact between the carbons and the feeding-wheels; they are carried by a small lever, on the bearings of which presses a spiral spring whose action is regulated by the spring i i (Fig. 39).

e, ratchet-wheel placed horizontally.

B, electro-magnet, hollow, and with fine wire helix; the two extremities of this wire are connected respectively to the two carbon-holders, that is to say, to the two poles of the main current, so that it is only traversed by a desired portion of the current. When the separation between the polar carbons increases, and consequently the resistance of the arc to the passage of the principal current, the derived current which circulates in the magnetizing helix of the electro-magnet immediately increases and develops in it a sufficiently powerful magnetization for it to attract its armature n.

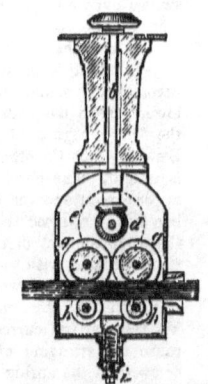

FIG. 39.—Section of the carbon-carrier of the De Mersanne regulator.

n, armature provided with a detent against which the teeth of the scape-wheel or ratchet strike; when it is attracted, these teeth escape, the carbons begin to move, and approach each other. When the arc has attained its normal length, and when, in consequence, the passage of the principal current is re-established, the derived current almost ceases from passing, and the electro-magnet, becomes almost inert, abandons its armature, which a spring, *o*, draws forward; the scape-wheel is caught by the detent, and the movement ceases, to start anew each time that the same conditions prevail.

o, spring operating the armature *a*.

V, limiting-screw serving to regulate the position of the armature according to the attractive force developed in the electro-magnet by the derived current.

r, screw serving to regulate the detent without the necessity of touching the screw *v*, and without deranging the regulation of the armature.

C, electro-magnet whose helices are in the same derived circuit as that of the electro-magnet B.

q, rod fixed upon one of the carbon-holders and carrying on its upper extremity the armature of the electro-magnet *c*.

s, opposing-spring of the armature *q*. The action of this spring is governed in such a way that the armature can not be attracted except when the current attains its maximum intensity, either because the arc is not yet formed, or because it has been broken by too great separation of the carbons. It follows that, at the moment when the current is turned into the apparatus, the armature is attracted, and the carbon-holder corresponding, drawn by the rod *q*, moves like a scale-beam; it remains in this position until the moment when the carbons come in contact; then the passage of the principal current is re-established, the derived current disappears altogether, the armature is set free and is drawn along by its spring with the carbon-holder; thus there is produced between the points of the carbons, a slight separation which immediately induces the formation of the arc.

progression of the carbons. The *rôle* of the other is to produce between the carbons the separation necessary to cause the voltaic arc to play between them; for this purpose it is given a slightly greater resistance, and does not act until the carbons come into contact.

Like all the apparatus with derived current, M. de Mersanne's regulator is polyphote. Fig. 38 shows the horizontal type, and Fig. 39 the sectional view of one of the carbon-holders.

With this regulator, the duration of the period of light-

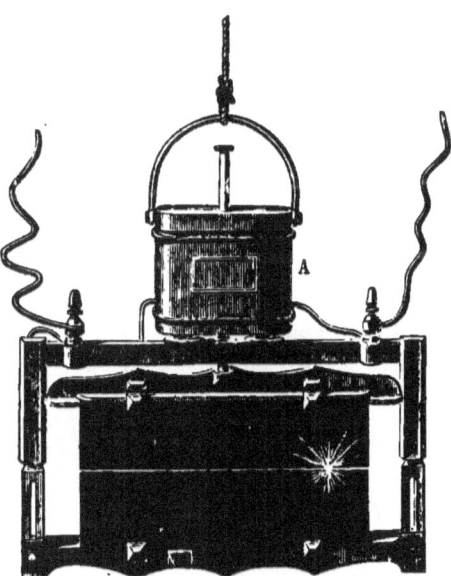

Fig. 40.—The Wallace lamp.

ing is no longer limited, because the carbons made by M. Carré are a metre or more in length ; they can last through the longest nights of winter, about eighteen hours, without any necessity of renewing them—they could even burn longer.

Mr. Wallace has thought of another mode of prolonging the duration of the period of lighting, which we will describe *en passant*, although his apparatus does not come in the category of lamps with derived current. He produces the voltaic arc between two rectangular plates of carbon placed vertically one above the other (Fig. 40). The lower plate is fixed ; the upper plate is movable and supported by the armature of an electro-magnet inclosed in the box A. While the current does not pass through the apparatus, the two plates touch ; as soon as the circuit is established the electro-magnet raises the upper carbon and the arc is established ; as their borders are never rigorously parallel, it starts at the point of least resistance, and then travels along the entire length ; when the distance becomes slightly increased by the combustion, the upper plate descends, the arc begins again to travel the other way, until both plates are quite used up—that is to say, in about a hundred hours. This regulator is very simple; but the incandescence of the carbons never reaches its full power, and the results attained in the production of light are not very good.

II. Differential Lamps.

All this was not enough, for there always was retained the opposing armature-spring, a spring whose inconvenience we have already noted, and which must be suppressed to avoid the hand-regulating required each time the intensity of the current is modified, either by the changes in the number of lamps working on the circuit, or by the variations in the working of the generators.

Thus, as we have said before, it is MM. Lacassagne and Thiers who first employed an electro-magnet with derived current to replace the opposing spring of the armature of an electro-magnet with thick wire, so that the movement of this armature was due to the differential action of the two currents.

In their apparatus the lower carbon was alone movable, the rod which carried it being fastened to a piston raised progressively by mercury. The admission of this mercury into the iron cylinder which contained the piston was regulated by the greater or less compression of the India-rubber tube through which it passed. This compression was exercised by an armature subjected at the same time to the actions of two electro-magnets, one with thick and one with thin wire. Its sensibility was such that the armature remained in one position, permitting a fine stream of mercury always to pass, so that the approaching of the carbons takes place in a continuous and uninterrupted manner.

On the same principle Dr. Siemens arranged his differential lamp (Fig. 41), in which the principal current and the

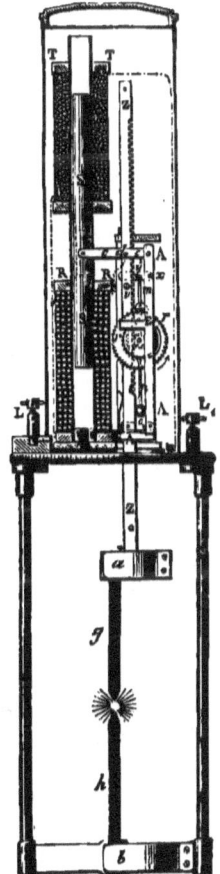

FIG. 41.—Siemens differential lamp.

h, stationary lower carbon held by the clamp *b* on the lower cross-bar of the frame.

g, movable upper carbon, held by clamp *a* on the bar Z.

Z, upper carbon-holder, serving as motor to the system. The upper part of this rod is made into a rack.

r, ratchet-wheel, driven by a small pinion, which itself works into the rack on the rod Z.

m, p, small pendulum provided with an escapement which prevents the wheel turning except a half-tooth at each oscillation. It is this pendulum which governs the escapement.

c c, A A, *c³*, jointed parallelogram whose upper arm *c c* is fastened to the bar of soft iron S S.

T T, fine wire solenoid.

R R, thick wire solenoid. Both act together on the bar S S, which moves freely in their interior.

x y, small lever pivoted at *x* to the vertical member A A of the parallelogram. This lever has at *y* an indentation which receives the end of the pendulum-rod *m p*.

L, L, binding-screws where the current enters and leaves the lamp.

When the arc is started and is of proper length, it is the action of the solenoid R R under the influence of the main current that predominates; the bar S S is attracted toward the base, and changes the shape of the parallelogram; the lever *y x* descends and locks upon the pendulum-rod *m p*, which it prevents from working.

When the current becomes weak by the lengthening of the arc, the derived current which passes through the solenoid T T increases, the bar S S is attracted upward toward the top, and the parallelogram tends to reassume its original shape. The lever *x y* rises, the pendulum *m p*, disengaged from its lock, begins to oscillate and permits the ratchet to turn. The bar Z descends, and brings the upper carbon down toward the fixed carbon.

The parallelogram is connected to a little air-pump or dash-pot which governs its movements. In case of extinction or breakage of the carbons, the derived current, grown more intense, gives the solenoid T T very great power; the bar S S is strongly attracted, and operates a safety contact of platinum, which throws the lamp out of circuit, until the rack Z has descended enough for the arc to be re-established between the carbons, or until new carbons have been introduced.

7

derived current act simultaneously in two opposite directions, so that the difference between their relative effects regulates the apparatus.

As in the Archereau model, only one of the carbons moves. The electro-magnetic regulator is composed of two solenoids, placed one in prolongation of the other and oppositely wound, the lower one having a short and thick wire, the upper one having a long and fine wire whose resistance is nearly a hundred times greater than that of the principal current. They contain a soft iron tube which can move freely up and down, and whose weight is balanced by that of the other movable pieces of the apparatus. Upon this tube and in the middle of the space which separates the solenoids is articulated a lever which controls the movements of the movable carbon. As is evident, the tube is attracted by two opposed forces, and the equilibrium depends only on the relation of the resistances, a relation which remains the same, whatever be the variations in intensity of the current. A small piston, which compresses the air in a cylinder, insures the steadiness of its movements. By this system ten lamps can be placed on the same circuit, and independence of action be maintained.

Differential lamps represent the last phase of progress in regulators, and we have only to note, as a final improvement, the location of the arc below the machinery, which makes it possible to suspend the lamp and better utilize its light. The use of a single movable carbon has been returned to, because it has been recognized that the fixed position of the luminous center in space was not really indispensable except for optical apparatus or mathematical reflectors. In ordinary lighting, the displacement of this center, due to the consumption of the fixed carbon, is much the less appreciable to the eye, as the lamps are generally at a considerable distance ; in the case of lighting by reflection on stages it is of no importance. In simplifying the mechanism, the certainty of working is increased, and the price of the apparatus is diminished, and this is to-day the principal question to be solved in electric lighting.

Inventors have availed themselves of all these successive improvements, and excellent pieces of apparatus were to be found at the Exhibition of Electricity, giving a reasonably uniform light, as long as the current supplying them experienced no extreme changes. We shall cite, among others,

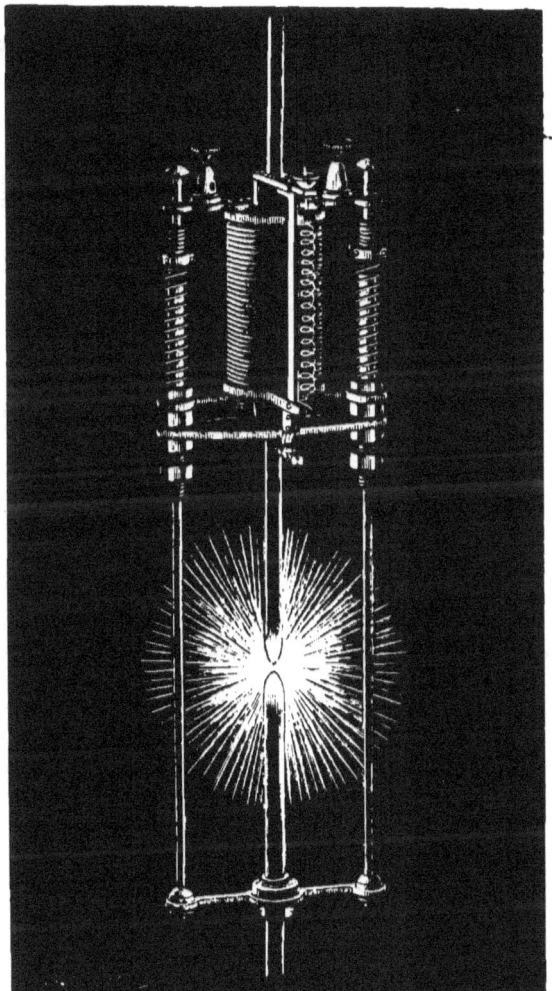

Fig. 42.—Gérard lamp.

the Crompton, Pilsen (Piette and Krizik), Gérard, Brush, and Weston lamps.

The Crompton lamp is somewhat of the Siemens type, but the wheel-work is simplified by the employment of an endless screw ; this screw is regulated by a spring brake, upon which act in opposite directions two electro-magnets—one with thick, and the other with thin wire.

The Pilsen lamp also resembles the Siemens type; it contains two superimposed solenoids, one with thick wire, the other with fine wire. The upper positive carbon is the movable one, but the lower carbon receives a slight lifting movement destined to produce the separation when it drops again. The plunging armature is of peculiar shape; it is formed of two elongated cones united at their bases so as to form a species of spindle. M. Krizik has found that with an armature of this shape the attraction exercised by a solenoid remains equal for all positions of the armature.

In the Gérard lamp (Fig. 42) the upper carbon traverses a tubular electro-magnet placed above the apparatus, and descends freely by its own weight; but its descent is governed by a screw acting as a brake and placed at the end of an articulated lever whose other end carries the armature on which the electro-magnet acts. An opposing spring draws back this screw and sets free the carbon, when the derived current grows weaker.

Between the uprights of the frame which carries the lower carbon, and immediately below the electro-magnet, is secured a transverse bar of insulated iron which constitutes a second armature. At starting, the carbons are separated; the derived current actuates the electro-magnet which draws together the two armatures; one sets free the upper carbon which descends, and the other raises the lower carbon; the points touch; when the current passes, the electro-magnet grows weaker, and the two armatures are drawn back by their respective springs. One presses the brake-screw upon the upper carbon and holds it; the other descends, drawing with it the lower carbon; the resulting separation creates the arc, and the movements thus continue.

The Brush lamp has a lower fixed carbon; it has only one solenoid, on which two wires, a thick and thin one, are wound in two layers, but in opposite directions. The upper carbon freely descends, but the rod which sustains it passes through a metal ring which only permits the descent when it is horizontal. When it is raised obliquely, it binds upon it, and not only stops the descent, but raises the carbon the necessary distance to make the separation and produce the arc. The solenoid contains a soft iron tube, provided with a hook, which effects this lifting at the proper time, under the differential action of the attraction exercised by the derived current (Fig. 43).

To prevent the sudden descent of the carbon-holder, and to cause it, on the contrary, while it is free, to descend with a continuous and slow motion, the upper part of the rod is hollow, and the tube thus formed is filled with glycerine (Fig.

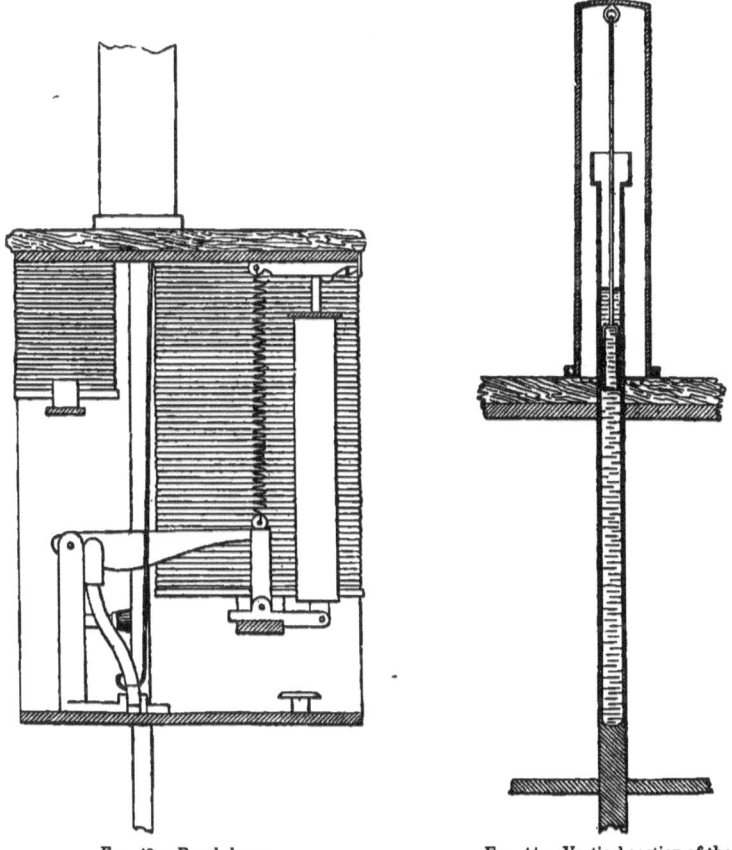

FIG. 43.—Brush lamp.

FIG. 44.—Vertical section of the upper carbon-rod.

44). From the top of the chimney which covers it a rod descends, carrying a small copper bell forming a piston, and only leaving a slight annular passage for the liquid ; the resistance due to the narrowness of the passage regulates the movement.

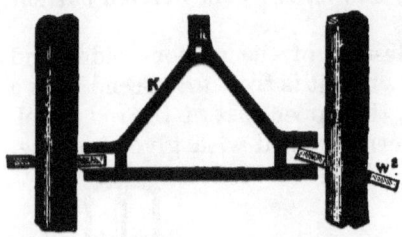

FIG. 45.—Relation of the two carbon-rods to each other in the double lamp.

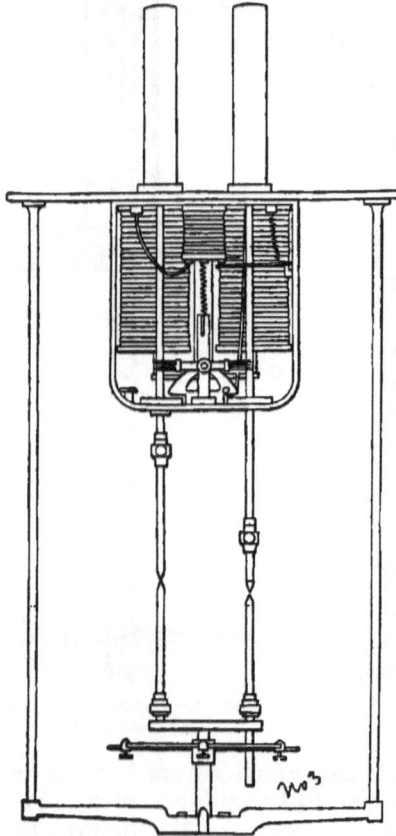

FIG. 46.—Brush double lamp.

The same means is employed to make the movements of the plunging armature of the solenoid easy, and the little cylinder filled with glycerine to which this is connected may be seen in front of the bobbin (Fig. 43).

A third smaller bobbin, visible in front of the mechanism, is placed in the same circuit of derivation. It offers a slightly increased resistance, and only comes into action to close a safety contact in case a too prolonged interruption of the voltaic arc would expose the derived-circuit wire to the danger of being burned by too great an increase of current.

For lights of long duration the Brush lamp contains two pairs of carbons very ingeniously arranged. The second pair, governed by the same mechanism, do not act until the first are in operation, and that in the simplest possible manner, by means of the distance maintained between them by the difference of height existing between the two hooks which raise the rings (Fig. 45). It follows that only one of the carbons is raised ; the arc

Fig. 47.—A street of New York lighted by Brush lamps.

plays between the carbons thus separated, and is maintained there until they are used up.

The complete double lamp is shown in Fig. 46.

This apparatus has worked several years in America. It

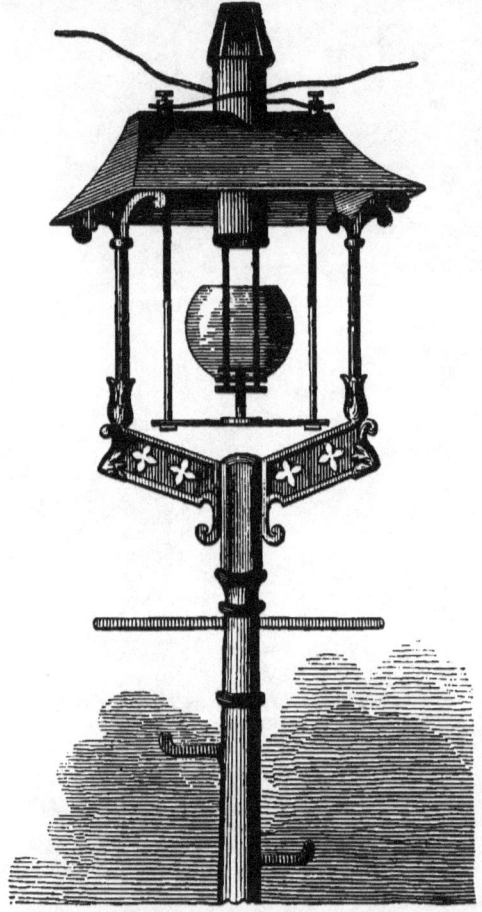

Fig. 48.—Brush street-lamp.

lights notably several streets of New York (Fig. 47). Fig. 48 shows the establishment of a double lamp upon one of the pillars.

The Weston lamp (Figs. 49 and 50) works on the same principles; the movable ring is replaced by a lever pierced with a

hole for the carbon to pass through. This lever constitutes
one part of an articulated parallelogram, one of whose sides is
of iron, and acts as armature. This is actuated by an electro-
magnet, whose branches are wound alternately with thick and
thin wire, so that it is still the differential action of the two
currents which governs the movements
of the armature, and consequently the
movement of the apparatus. A small
plunger, moving in a cylinder filled with
glycerine, serves as moderator.

[In the lamp now used by Mr. Weston the magnets are not differentially
wound, but the main and shunt magnets are arranged so as to mutually oppose the effect of each other in moving
the upper carbon-rod. The mechanism
of this lamp is shown in Fig. 52, and
the mode of action more clearly in the
section in Fig. 53. The carbon-rod R
is gripped by a clutch, shown in section
in Fig. 54, operated by the iron cores
of the main circuit magnet A, and the
shunt or fine-wire magnet B, through
the medium of the lever L. This lever
is raised by the core of the main magnet, when a current is sent through the
lamp, causing the piece I to bind against
the rod R, which is then carried upward
by the further movement of the core.
As the arc lengthens, the shunt-magnet
B becomes strong enough to check the
movement of the lever L, the two magnets being in equilibrium when the arc
is of normal length. With the elonga-
ting of the arc due to consumption of
the carbons, the power of the magnet B

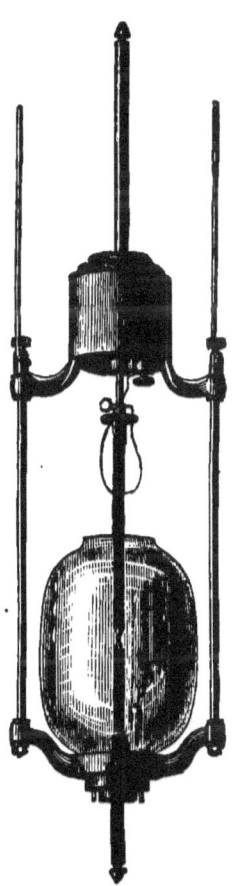

Fig. 49.—Weston lamp.

increases and draws up its end of the
lever L and carries down the carbon-rod. When this reaches
a position in which the piece I ceases to bind on the rod,
this is allowed to slip downward, and the carbon feeds. A
dash-pot, D, serves to prevent too sudden movements of the
lever L.

A lamp of the same class is that of the Fuller Company, designed by Mr. J. J. Wood. Its construction is shown in Fig.

R R, rod of the upper carbon-holder.
C C C, curved lever pierced with a hole through which the rod R R passes.
A A, armature which is fastened to the lever C C. The springs O, N, which sustain it, only
    permit vertical movements.
S, opposing-spring which has its tension regulated by a screw acting on an elbow-lever.
M M, electro-magnet whose branches are wound alternately by a thick and a thin wire (Fig.

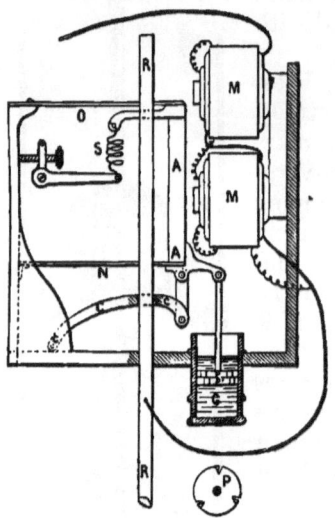

51).   These wires are wound in reverse directions, one from the other,
and the action of the electro-magnet
depends on the differential action of
the two currents which traverse them,
the main current in the thick, and the
derived current in the thin wire.

G, movable piston working in a small
cylinder filled with glycerine; the rod
of this piston is fastened to the armature A A.

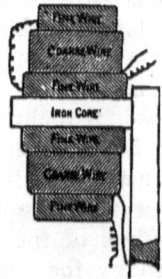

FIG. 50.—Details of the mechanism of the
         Weston lamp.

FIG. 51.—Section of one of the differ-
         ential magnets of the Weston lamp.

P, plan view of the round plates which form the piston G; there are two, one fixed on the
    piston-rod and the other movable. Each has three triangular notches, and, by turning
    the movable plate, the size of the openings is regulated. The resistance which the piston
    offers to displacement through the glycerine prevents the too sudden movements of the
    armature.
    As long as the apparatus is in normal action, the action of the main current is in the
    ascendant; the lever C C is raised up by the armature, the rod R R binds in the hole, and
    remains immovable. If the main current grows weak, the derived current increases,
    and produces the reverse action; the armature left free is drawn back by its spring S; the
    lever C C lowers, and the rod R R is allowed to descend. Under the differential action
    of the two currents, the lever C C takes a permanent intermediary position, which per-
    mits the carbon-holder to slide slowly in a continuous manner. It does not descend en-
    tirely except when the voltaic arc is entirely broken; in this case the rising up of the lever
    C C draws the rod back sufficiently to produce the separation necessary for relighting.

55, and the relation of the various parts in the diagram, Fig.
56.   The connection of the controlling mechanism with the
upper carbon-holder is effected by gearing instead of by

means of a clutch, as in the lamps of Brush and Weston. This carbon-holder is a toothed bar or rack, into which gears a pinion connected with a train of wheel-work. It moves downward by its weight, this movement being governed through the intermediation of a pawl acting on one of the wheels of the train by the electro-magnetic apparatus shown. In Fig. 56, $f f$ are the main magnets placed in the arc circuit and wound with coarse wire. The fine-wire magnets h, h are placed in a shunt-circuit, and oppose by their action the effect of the main magnets. The current enters at a, passes down by the holder e e, through the arc, around the main magnets, and out to the next lamp at a'. A rocking lever, j, carrying the armature i, serves to control the descent of the upper carbon. The carbons being together, the magnets $f f$ are excited on the passage of the current and attracts the armature i. This movement separates the carbons and establishes the arc. The winding of the shunt and main circuit magnets is such that the strength of these magnets is the same when the arc is of normal length. When the arc exceeds this length, the attraction of the shunt magnets becomes greater than the main ones, and the armature i is attracted, allowing the lamp to feed.

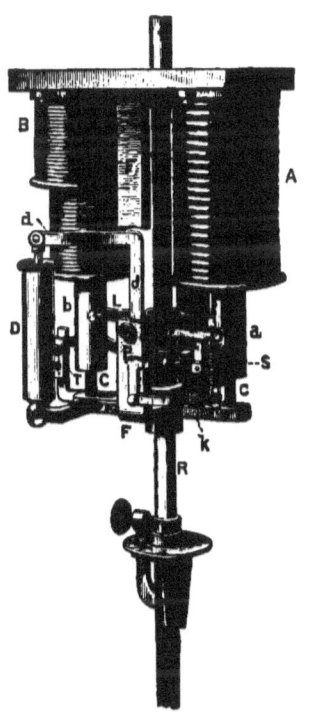

Fig. 52.—Mechanism of the Weston lamp.

The switch b enables the lamp to be turned out by hand when desired, by throwing its end over so as to make contact with o, the current then passing directly from a to a' through the contact o and lever b. This switch is operated by turning the key b (Fig. 55).

The ordinary form of the single-carbon lamp is shown in Fig. 57.

The single-carbon lamp is converted into a double-carbon one for all-night operation in a very simple manner. It is also

constructed for use in reflectors. In this case both carbons
are moved toward each other in proportion to the waste,
the upper one moving at twice the rate of the lower. As

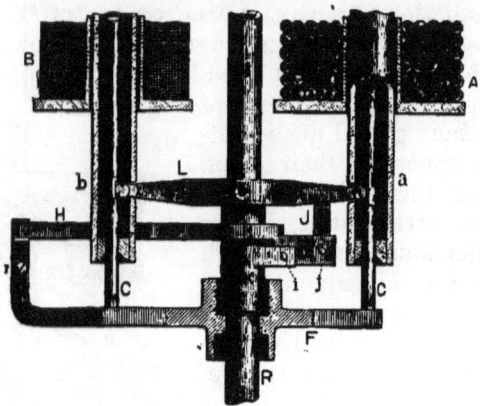

Fig. 53.—Vertical section of operating parts of the Weston lamp.

both carbons are positively controlled, this lamp can be
used in situations where it will be subjected to constant
jars, such as in the head-light of a locomotive.]

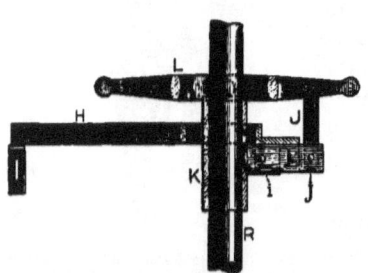

Fig. 54.—Clutch of the Weston lamp.

Here we shall stop this
enumeration; it would re-
quire a volume to describe
all the apparatus which can
give a good light. The Electrical Exhibition contained
eighty - six different types,
among which we must cite
still the Berjot and Cance
lamps. Unfortunately, the
regulation and maintenance
need special workmen, very
skillful and very careful; besides, the original cost, with the
indispensable accessories, is always quite high; for this reason
the use of regulators has great difficulty in becoming general.

III. Automatic Safety Apparatus.

In lamps with derived circuit, and in differential lamps,
the employment of a fine wire for the derived circuit requires

the addition of a safety contact, which, in case of accident to the mechanism or to the carbons, opens a passage for the current. In effect, while the principal current is interrupted by a prolonged cessation of the voltaic arc, the current finds only one way to pass, namely, the derived current circuit, and can not pass in sufficient quantity to supply the other apparatus upon the same circuit; besides, if this passage of

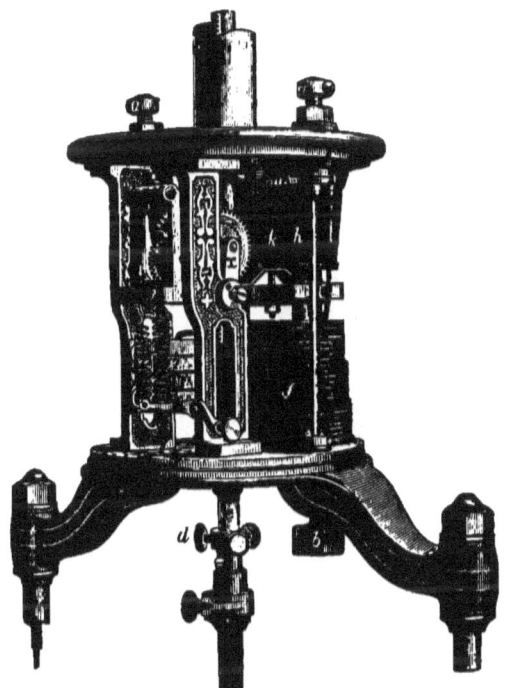

Fig. 55.—Mechanism of the Wood lamp.

an intense current in a wire of too high resistance were to last too long a time, the wire would heat and might even be destroyed.

To prevent variations in the intensity of the current from causing general extinction, the extinguished lamp must be replaced by a resistance equivalent to that which it represents, with the maximum length of arc admitted by its regulator.

To satisfy all the exigencies of electric lighting, a certain number of supplementary apparatus have been invented, of all which we shall only examine the automatic device of Gérard, and Mersanne's safety-box. The automatic lighter of Reynier comes also in this category, but, as it is designed for another system of lighting, we shall study it at the same time with the lamps in connection with which it was designed to operate.

Gérard's automatic apparatus has for its object the cutting out, in case of accident, of the lamp to which it is appended,

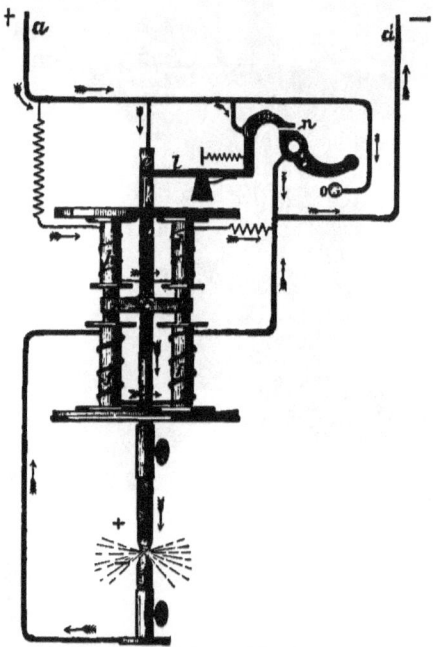

Fig. 56.—Diagram of the working parts of the Wood lamp.

and the opening of a direct passage to the current, so quickly that the other lamps on the same circuit shall not be affected. It consists of a straight electro-magnet whose bobbin, wound with fine wire, has a higher resistance than the lamp; of a sliding piece with two rods sliding through insulating rings in two cups containing mercury; of a jointed square frame, carrying on one side the armature of the electro-magnet, on the other the hook which holds the suspended sliding piece.

If the lamp becomes extinguished, the current passes through the electro-magnet; the armature is attracted and the hook releases the slider; the rods fall into the mercury-cups, and the current, leaving the electro-magnet, passes directly through the mercury and the rods; by pressing on a vertical rod placed below the slider, the former circuit is re-established and the lamp is lighted; a second rod, resting on the armature, permits the unlocking to be done by hand, so that the apparatus can be used as a switch. There is need, of course, of one for each lamp.

The safety-box of M. de Mersanne goes much further in its surveillance; in case of accident tending to interrupt the voltaic arc for a long enough time to expose the derived current wire to the danger of being burned, such as the breakage of a carbon, for example, it so substitutes itself for the lamp as to protect the derived circuit parts without interrupting their action. It follows that, if at the end of a certain number of hours the lamp is again ready to operate, it assumes once more its place in the circuit, and the safety-box ceases to act, and is then in condition to again work whenever it may be necessary.

This apparatus is composed (Fig. 59) of an electro-magnet, one of whose arms is wound with thick and the other with thin wire. This last forms a second derived circuit which does not act until the principal current, being broken, flows in

Fig. 57.—Wood single lamp.

excess into the derived current wire of the regulator. In this case the electro-magnet of the safety-box becomes active, and its armature brings about the contact between

FIG. 58.—Gérard automatic cut-out.

two blocks of graphite; these open for the principal current a new passage through a resistance-coil which is inclosed in the safety-box, and which represents exactly the resistance of the arc with the maximum separation of the carbons that is caused by the regulator. The choice among equivalent resistances is not an indifferent one ; that which

P P', electro-magnet whose arm P' is wound with thick wire, and placed in the voltaic arc circuit. The arm P is wound with fine wire and placed in the derived circuit.

C, armature working between contact-points.

T, support of the armature.

S, bent copper wire connecting the armature C to the support T, and insuring the passage of the current.

L, corrugated plate of copper, of sufficient section for the passage of the current; it insures, by its flexibility, a perfect contact at E', and absorbs the vibrations which might be produced in the armature C by the use of alternating currents.

K K', blocks of graphite between which the safety-contact takes place. The graphite is used here because it does not oxidize at high temperatures, and better resists the breakage-sparks which appear between the two blocks each time they are separated. It is quite a good conductor especially when heated.

S S', supporting-rings of the graphite blocks.

r, spring opposing the armature.

a d, binding-screws for the regulator-wires.

m m, points of attachment of the thick wire of the arm P'.

R, auxiliary resistance-coil.

b c, points of attachment of the wire of the resistance-coil.

E', safety contact.

v, screw serving to limit the motions of the armature C.

G G', metal plates replacing the wood of the apparatus in places where it might be burned by the graphite blocks heating.

J, wooden support of the electro-magnet.

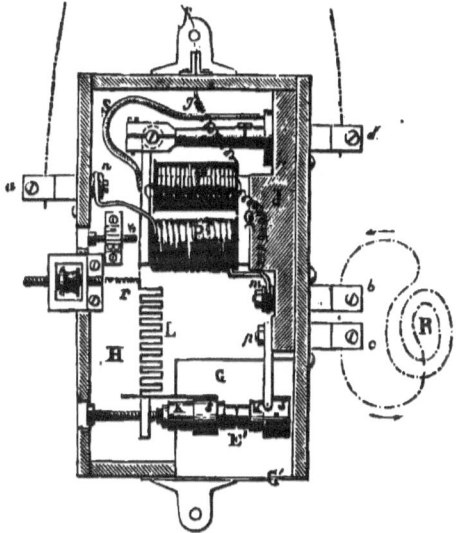

Fig. 59.—Safety-box of M. de Mersanne.

The derived circuit of the safety-box has higher resistance than that which actuates the electro-magnets of the regulator; it only permits the current to pass if, in consequence of prolonged interruption of the voltaic arc, the current flows in excess through the last; then the two circuits act together; one actuates the safety-box; the other continues to actuate the regulator. The passage of the main current through the thick wire of the arm P is only established after contact at E between the graphite blocks takes place; it has for end to reinforce the attraction of the armature C, and insure a better contact.

produces the least heating should be preferred. M. de Mersanne has observed that the best condition was to give the wire of the resistance-coil the same length and thickness as

8

that of the induction-wire in which the current is originally produced.

Graphite is used here just as mercury was in the preceding apparatus, because metallic contact-pieces would be burned and even soldered together by the powerful spark which is produced each time the auxiliary circuit is broken by the play of the apparatus itself.

The arm of the electro-magnet that is wound with thick wire is placed upon the auxiliary circuit, and has for object the re-enforcement of the attraction of the armature and the rendering of the contact of the graphite blocks better and more certain.

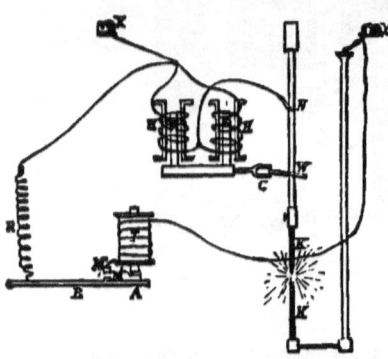

These safety-boxes can be placed anywhere, no matter how far from the lamps, in the locality of the machines for example; they then serve to control the general lighting. It follows of itself that the resistance-coil can be suppressed, which reduces the safety-box to an automatic regulator.*

FIG. 60.—Diagram of Brush lamp connections and cut-out.

[The Brush *automatic cut-out* is shown in the diagram (Fig. 60). The normal course of the lighting current is from the terminal x, through the coarse-wire helix of the regulating magnet H, H, through the carbons and out by the terminal y. When, however, from any cause the path through the carbons ceases to be available, the current is diverted around the arc through the path formed by the spiral R, the lever B, and coil T. This is accomplished by means of the electro-magnet T, which is wound with a thick and fine wire coil, both in the same direction. The fine wire is in the same circuit as the fine-wire differential helices of the regulating

* [All the successful modern lamps are provided with a safety apparatus. This is termed in this country an *automatic cut-out;* it serves simply to automatically provide a path around a defective lamp, and does not introduce a resistance equal to that of the lamp switched out, or otherwise regulate the current traversing the circuit. This is done by apparatus acting upon the generating dynamo.]

magnet H, H. When the arc greatly elongates, the magnet T is sufficiently excited to attract its armature A on the end of the lever B. This brings together the two contact-pieces M and M', and the current then has a path between the two terminals x and y, through the thick-wire coil of the magnet T. This path will remain closed as long as that through the arc is interrupted, as the attraction of the magnet T keeps the contacts M, M', together.

The Weston cut-out is shown in Fig. 61. It consists of an electro-magnet in the main or arc circuit, arranged so as to allow its armature to drop down and short-circuit the lamp, when it ceases to be active, owing to abnormal lengthening of the arc. A coarse coil in a shunt-circuit, wound over the main coil and in the same direction, serves to cause the electro-magnet to act more quickly in opening the short circuit when the lamp is started. The apparatus, which is in a very compact form, is usually placed on the upper frame of the lamp.

The cut-out of the Wood lamp is shown in Fig. 56. It consists of a lever, l, arranged so as to trip the curved lever m and close the circuit at n, when its end is raised by the pin k. This pin is carried by the armature i, and stands vertically in

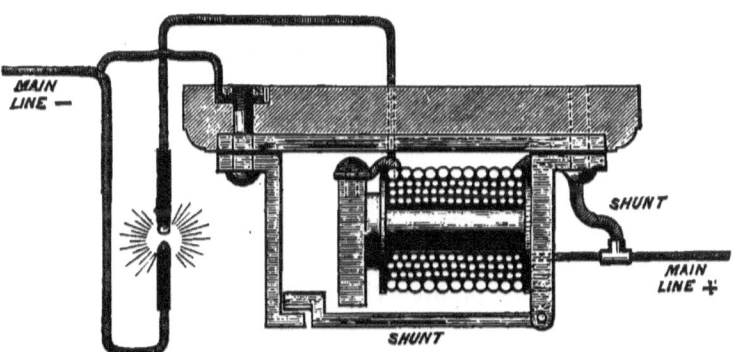

Fig. 61.—Weston automatic cut-out.

front of the carbon-rod e. The armature i is attached to the rocking lever j (Fig 55), so that it has a vertical play. As explained in describing the lamp, the shunt-magnets $h\ h$ grow stronger as the arc lengthens and attract the armature i. The rocking lever j follows their movement, and, by doing so, allows the lamp to feed. Stops on this lever prevent it going upward more than a determined distance, but, on account of the vertical play of the armature *i*, this can continue to move upward under the attraction of the magnets *h h*. When, therefore, the arc becomes of abnormal length, the armature *i* is drawn clear up, and the lamp short-circuited through *n*.]

CHAPTER VI.

THE JABLOCHKOFF CANDLE.

ONE of the principal reasons which for a long time retarded the progress of the electric light was the necessity of employing mechanical regulators for bringing together progressively the carbon rods between which the voltaic arc played. We have seen in the preceding chapter that these regulators have been successively improved and at the same time simplified. But they always present a complication which most people regard with distrust. Things were in this state some five years ago, when, in 1876, a Russian officer, M. Jablochkoff, found a way of entirely obviating these troubles, and thus put the electric light on the footing of daily practical use.

The great merit of this invention is its perfect simplicity, which has impressed every one, and silenced those who wished to see in the electric light only a complicated curiosity, needing the presence of a professional electrician. Instead of placing the carbons point to point, M. Jablochkoff placed them parallel, side by side, which gave the simple apparatus the shape of a candle, and suggested its name.

The two rods of carbon were separated, as is understood, by a band of insulating material that the arc could not pierce, and so could only be produced between the two points. There was no longer any necessity of arranging for the approach of the carbons to each other; they remained always at the same distance as they burned, and it was enough to choose an insulating material that would burn away and disappear along with the carbons so as not to form an obstacle in the path of the voltaic arc; at first the material used for this purpose was that out of which china is made, kaolin.

The apparatus thus constructed could be placed on any

kind of a chandelier, by inserting it in a socket just as would
be done with an ordinary candle ; the only requirement is
that metallic parts, arranged conveniently, so as to produce a
contact, should bring the electric current that penetrates by
means of wires in the standard of the chandelier.

The lighting of the candle is still to be provided for—that
is to say, the starting of the voltaic arc, which is done in regulators by causing the two points to approach until in contact
with each other. Such approach is here impossible, because
of the interposition of the solid insulating material. To effect
the lighting, M. Jablochkoff reunites the two points of the
electrode rods by a very small slip of carbon which the passage of the current brings to a red heat, and which serves as
a leader for the voltaic arc.

Nevertheless, the apparatus such as we have described it
is subject to one great difficulty. We have seen already that
the wasting of the two carbons in the voltaic arc is unequal.
At the end of a very short time the two carbon-points would
no longer be opposite each other, and this distance increasing,
would soon render impossible the passage of the current.

To obviate this, M. Jablochkoff tried giving the positive
rod of carbon a double thickness ; this compensated very well
for its greater rapidity of consumption, but it produced
another inconvenience. The thinner negative carbon, offering more resistance to the current, grew red for a considerable
part of its length, and burned up rapidly.

M. Jablochkoff then had an idea of as remarkable simplicity as the principle of the whole system : it was to change
frequently the direction of the current, so that each rod of
carbon would become alternately a positive and a negative
pole ; then the consumption on both sides should be equal.
The method of accomplishing it consisted simply in the use
of alternating currents, and there was no trouble in getting
them, because the magneto-electric machine then in most extensive use and the most powerful, produced currents of this
description.

The apparatus once arranged, all its parts were studied,
so as to be perfected as much as possible. At first it was
surrounded by a coating of insulating material, covered in
its turn by asbestus, to restrain as far as possible the capri-
cious course which the voltaic arc might choose to follow
(Fig. 62) ; but this same fitful arc showed itself wiser than

was allowed for, and this thick envelope, found useless by experience, was dispensed with (Fig. 63).

The insulating material placed between the two carbons (called in a general manner the "colombin") was also changed.

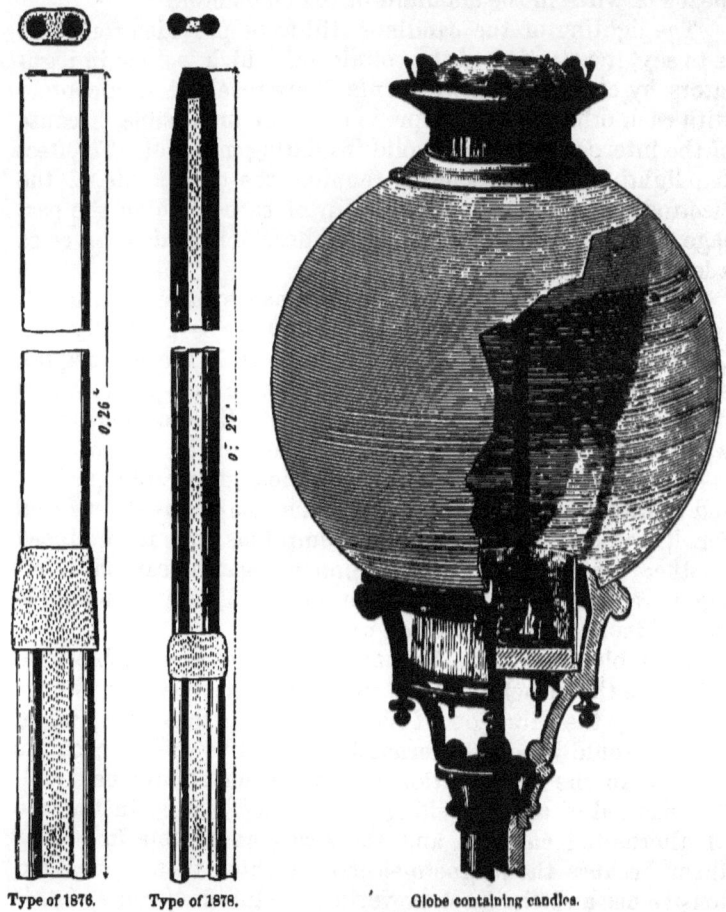

Type of 1876.   Type of 1878.   Globe containing candles.

Figs. 62, 63, and 64.—Jablochkoff candle.

The kaolin originally employed melted at the end under the influence of the voltaic arc, and thus created between the points of carbon a little liquid conductor which gave a passage to the current. A voltaic arc, properly so called, was no longer formed, because the electricity no longer traversed the air ; already, so to say, an incandescent light was produced. Unfortunately, this arrangement of kaolin, favorable in itself, entailed a considerable absorption of heat, and, in consequence, a considerable increase in cost of maintaining each lamp.

To-day the kaolin has been replaced by a mixture of two parts of sulphate of lime and one of sulphate of baryta. This mixture is not melted by the current ; it volatilizes immediately, and thus furnishes incandescent particles which increase the brightness of the light produced. Besides, it is easier to manufacture than kaolin ; it can be molded or drawn out as easily as plaster, so that two workmen can make nearly fifteen thousand insulating plates per day.

A Jablochkoff candle, then, is actually composed of the following parts : Of two carbons, four millimetres thick and twenty-five to thirty centimetres long, always cut from the same stick, so that they will always have the same composition ; of a colombin, three millimetres wide and two millimetres thick, whose composition we have already given ; of two little copper tubes, fifty-five millimetres long, split parallel to their axis : these tubes, into which the carbons penetrate fifteen millimetres, have for object the insuring a perfect contact between the carbons and the jaws of the candle-socket ; they are themselves joined by means of an insulator four centimetres long, of the same form as the colombin, but made of more solid paste so as to resist the pressure of the jaws. The whole is bound together at the junction of the colombin and the lower insulator with a paste of silicate of potash base. The upper ends of the carbons are sharpened to points on an emery-wheel, then plunged into a composition of three parts of coke in fine powder and two parts of plumbago rubbed up with gum-water ; this species of cap serves to produce the lighting.

The most important point to be insured in the manufacture of the candle is the perfect adherence between the carbons and colombin and the solidity of the latter. If it breaks during the burning, or if a piece falls from it, or if it is more quickly consumed than the carbons, the points remaining project above it and the arc descends into the cavity thus formed ; the temperature of the points lowers, and the light produces those reddish tints which have been found so objectionable.

Each candle is carried in a metallic pincers, whose two jaws are properly insulated; one of these jaws, A (Fig. 65), is hinged and is pressed by a spring strong enough to insure good contact; they have semi-cylindrical grooves in which the brass tubes are received. The fixed jaws are united to the same support and connect with a single return wire, R R.

At the end of two hours the exhausted candle must be replaced, and, to facilitate the operation, the lamp-posts have several candles arranged to succeed each other. The globes of the Avenue de l'Opéra contain four. When the first candle goes out, a commutator, hidden in the foot of the lamp-post, protected from interference on the part of unauthorized persons, allows the current to be passed into the second, then into the third and into the fourth. The light can thus be kept going for nearly eight hours.

Several automatic arrangements for making the current itself produce the change of candles have been thought of, among others a mercury commutator, which we will describe further on; the duration of the light can then be much greater if there are enough candles provided; and a period of eighteen successive hours, without the candlebra re-

Fig. 65.—Sockets of Jablochkoff candles and switch for lighting the candles successively by hand.

quiring any attention, has been attained in a Belgian factory.

It is the Jablochkoff candle that has brought the electric light into prominence and given it a genuine popularity. An influential company was formed to introduce the new system ; the press followed the exchanges in its attention to it, telling wonders about it, so that every one wished to see it, and public experiments multiplied on all sides.

For three years the Avenue de l'Opéra has been lighted by electric candles, the large stores have adopted it as a means of advertising, and the large hotels for a sign ; it is a feature of all the public *fêtes* in the great cities of Europe as well as in Paris ; and to-day there are not less than twenty-five hundred in use in the two hemispheres, especially in large workshops, railroad-stations, public halls and squares, warehouses, theatres, such as the Hippodrome in Paris (Fig. 66), and in several palaces. One of the most beautiful examples of this mode of lighting is that of the Moorish saloon of the Continental Hotel in Paris, shown in the frontispiece of this volume.

Within four years these wonderful little candles have found means, not only of spreading through France, Belgium, and England, and Russia, the country of the inventor, but also have succeeded in penetrating into Greece, Portugal, Brazil, La Plata, Mexico, and even into those places where there would be the least expectation of finding improved machinery, such as the palace of the Shah of Persia, of the King of Cambodia, and the residence of the fierce King of Burmah who massacred nearly all his family.

Its extended success could not well be greater, although it is far from combining all the qualities indispensable to a good light. The light of the electric candle is fluctuating, and its variations in intensity are magnified by flashes of different colors which often mingle with its light. Those who frequent the Avenue de l'Opéra may have remarked that accidental extinctions, from whatever cause, are sufficiently numerous to render the exclusive employment of the lights of this system in the public service very dangerous. In exhibitions and experiments, where great care has been bestowed upon the establishment and maintenance of the apparatus, they seem to work a little better. But they never have been able to compete with regulators of the best systems, espe-

Fig. 66.—The Hippodrome of Paris lighted by Jablochkoff candles.

cially differential lamps, not to mention the systems of open-air incandescence which supply also strong centers of light much more agreeable to the eye.

———

CHAPTER VII.

LAMPS WITHOUT MECHANISM.

THE invention of the Jablochkoff candle in 1876, and the immediate impulse given by this discovery to the use of the electric light, has brought out during the last five years a number of new inventions. These inventions are for the most part designed to obviate the necessity of using the tyrannical mechanical regulators, which still meet with public distrust, in spite of all recent improvements, since M. Jablochkoff has in a practical way shown how they can be dispensed with. While all inventors agree upon the result to be reached, they seek to attain it by two very different ways. One way is to change the nature of the luminous center by substituting as the source of light for the voltaic arc the incandescence of a body which this arc will heat, whether carbon electrodes, as in the Reynier-Werdeman lamps, or another substance introduced into the path of the arc, as in the *sun-lamp;* the other way is to preserve the regular voltaic arc, but to regulate the approach of the carbons without the use of mechanical apparatus properly so called.

I. LAMPS WITH CONVERGING CARBONS.

The first lamp invented in the second method spoken of above, like the electric candle, is due to a Russian. M. Rapieff invented it in 1878. This idea is of still greater simplicity than that of M. Jablochkoff. Imagine two rods of carbon placed point to point like the two lines of a V, and kept in this position by small pulleys or rollers, so as to move down by their individual weight. It is clear that as these rods become consumed they will to the last remain pressed one against the other, and always in the same place (Fig. 67). Because they touch, the voltaic arc can not play between them. But there is nothing to prevent us from arranging below them two other

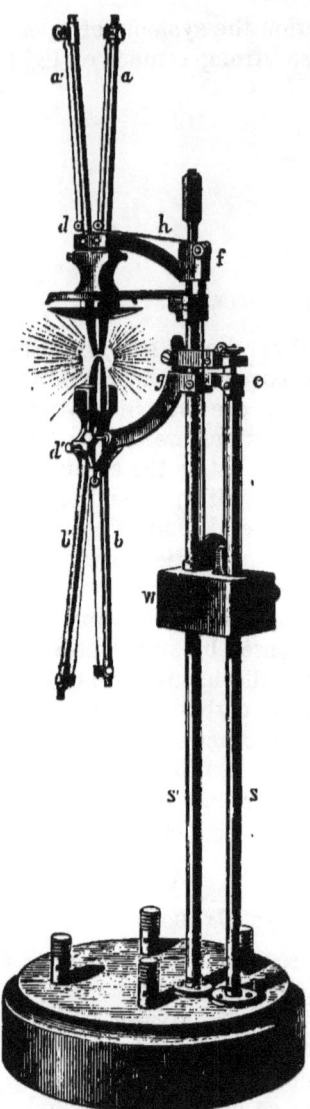

FIG. 67.—Rapieff arc lamp.

a, a', upper carbons forming an acute angle whose apex is the positive pole of the lamp.

b, b', lower carbons arranged in the same way, with their points opposed to those of the upper carbons.

d, d', carbon-holders.

h, cord connecting the carbons to the motor-weight W.

f, g, e, pulleys carrying the cord h, so placed as to preserve the oblique direction of the carbons. The lower pulleys establish the contact for the passage of the current, and limit the length of carbons that enters into the circuit.

S, S', rods supporting the carbon-holders. The rod S' and the positive carbon-holder are insulated. The rod S contains a rod connected with the armature of an electro-magnet placed in the base of the lamp, and designed to maintain the necessary separation between the two pairs of carbons when the current passes.

W, counterpoise, which constantly acts to bring the two pairs of carbons in contact; on account of their obliquity they stop reciprocally as soon as they touch. The cord, in passing around the pulley of the counterpoise, causes it to act incessantly on both pairs of carbons in proportion to their consumption, so that the light-center shall not change its place; this arrangement permits the use of direct or alternating currents.

The lamp relights itself, and can be placed on the same circuit with as many apparatus as the tension of the current will admit of.

rods forming a reversed letter V. These, of course, do not tend to press against each other by their own weight, but the same movement is produced by using a cord attached to them and passing it over pulleys to a counterpoise heavier than the rods. The voltaic arc will then play between the points of the two V's placed at a proper distance from each other—only, each pole will be formed of two rods instead of one.

To light the lamp—in other words, to make the current pass for the first time—it is necessary that the two V's touch each other for an instant. This manœuvre is executed by the apparatus itself by means of an electro-magnet arranged so as to push one of the V's in advance of the other ; this electro-magnet is worked by a derived current from the main current that produces the voltaic arc. As soon as the arc is formed, this current returns to its natural course ; it abandons almost entirely the electro-magnet, which becomes inactive and abandons the movable V ; this reassumes its regular position, which it retains as long as the lamp continues to burn.

M. Rapieff's system, like that of M. Jablochkoff, admits of placing five or six, or more, lights upon the same circuit. It has given good results in England, where it has lighted, among other places, the press-room of the printing-house of the largest journal in the world, the London "Times." The Rapieff lamp burns seven consecutive hours without change of carbons, and in case of accidental extinction lights itself. It is superior in these two points to the Jablochkoff candle, and can rival it in luminous intensity.

M. Rapieff had his predecessors, for as early as 1846 an Englishman, Edward Staite, invented an analogous combination ; and in 1875 a Frenchman, M. Reynier, constructed also a regulator with oblique carbons, which he soon abandoned, to seek in incandescence another solution of the problem. In his turn M. Rapieff was imitated, in the year after his invention—that is to say, in 1879—by a Parisian engineer, M. Anatole Gérard.

The principle of his apparatus is exactly the same as that of M. Rapieff ; but the two V's, instead of being placed one under the other, are placed beside each other in two planes intersecting each other like the two opposite faces of a pyramid. The rods of carbon represent in some sort the four edges of a pyramid, except that they do not come quite together at the summit (Figs. 68, 69). It must be understood that the pyramid is inverted, the rods of carbon having their points directed downward, so that all the parts capable of casting a shadow are situated above the luminous center.

In addition to this M. Gérard establishes between the carbons a sort of *magnetic wind*, which serves to repel the flame toward the end of the rods, and thus prevent it from rising. This magnetic wind is formed by an electro-magnet, whose poles exercise a repulsive action on the flames, by virtue of the well-known laws of electro-magnetic action, as they are manifested upon a magnetic needle.

In the Rapieff and Gérard lamps, as in the candles, alternating currents are usually employed, because of the unequal consumption of the positive and negative carbons.   In conse-

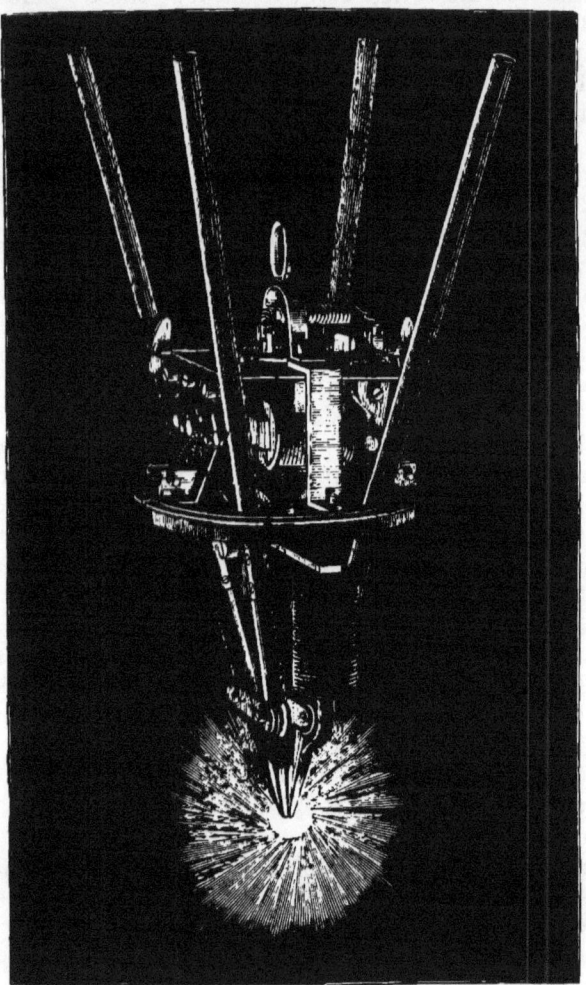

Fig. 68.—Gérard lamp.   General appearance.

quence of their mode of production these currents are always accompanied by a peculiar noise, more intense than the hissing of the voltaic arc, to which it is added, thus constituting

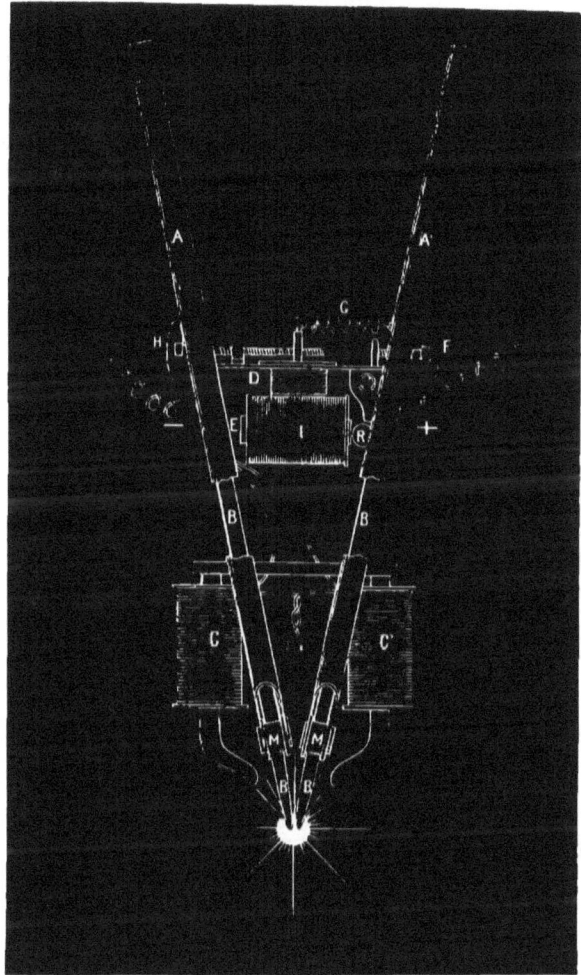

Fig. 69.—Vertical section of Gérard lamp.

A, A', tubular carbon-holders, forming together a quadrangular pyramid.

B, B', carbon-rods.

D, plate supporting the tubes; the tube A is fastened to the plate, from which it is insulated by an ivory plate; the tube B' is pivoted by means of a hinge to the support D.

F, screw serving to regulate the distance of the carbons, and keep the length of the arc proportional to the tension of the current.

G, spring serving to maintain the separation.

H, screw serving to regulate the tension of the spring G.

I, electro-magnet with fine wire, excited by a derived current from the main circuit.

R, armature of the electro-magnet I. It is fastened to the movable tube A'.

M, M', bronze rings serving at the same time to guide the carbons and establish the passage of the current; they also enable one to limit the length of carbons comprised in the circuit.

C C', electro-magnet with thick wire, through which the main current passes; its poles are prolonged and curved inward so as to exercise upon the current which forms the arc a sufficient influence to keep it between the points of the carbons.

On starting, the points of the carbons are separated; the main current not having any way of passing, the derived current starts into action. The armature R is attracted, brings the carbons in contact, and opens a passage for the main current. The electromagnet I becomes inactive, the spring G draws the carbons back the proper distance, regulated beforehand by the screw E, and the arc begins to play. This burner lights itself automatically, and admits of the current being divided among several lamps. The length of the carbon-rods being of any desired length, they may be made to last twelve hours or more without renewal.

a real inconvenience in most cases. It may be for this reason that M. Gérard, abandoning this apparatus, very interesting from its certainty of action, returned to regulators, and has invented, since then, in this field, so crowded already, a new combination, of which we have spoken in the preceding chapter.

But lamps with converging carbons can work very well with continuous currents. It is only necessary in this case to give the positive carbons a greater length than that of the negative carbons, to compensate for their more rapid consumption. This arrangement ordinarily is free from any objection.

II. RECENT CANDLES.

While engaged in inventing the lamp with oblique pencils, M. Rapieff was also busy perfecting the Jablochkoff candle, and he made known his type of burner in the same year, 1878. This type greatly resembles that of M. Wilde, published almost at the same time, which started one of those battles for precedence so frequent where a large number of ardent inventors are exploiting the same field. M. Wilde is generally thought to have first reached the goal, and it is his candle which we shall here describe at greatest length.

Wilde's Candle.

Several of the inconveniences of the Jablochkoff candle seem due to the "colombin," or solid insulating material placed between the two carbons. It is this which prevented the approach of the two points, necessary for automatic lighting. M. Wilde started by omitting the "colombin." His candle is composed of two parallel rods of carbon, four millimetres in diameter, analogous to those of Jablochkoff, but separated only a space of three millimetres. These carbon rods are fastened by pincers to metallic supports, and one of these supports is pivoted so as to permit the rod to incline a little to come in contact with its neighbor.

This is its natural position, that which it occupies of itself when the apparatus is out of action. When the current is sent through, it passes easily from one point to the other, and lights the lamp.

It is next necessary for the rod to be drawn back to produce the voltaic arc. This it does with great quickness, under the influence of an electro-magnet, which acts upon its lower end, and thus turns it upon

A, A, A, A, supports on which the movable carbons are maintained by the springs r; each of these carries at right angles a plate armature for the electromagnets a, a, a.

R, central support on which the stationary carbons of the four candles are held by a spring S.

a, a, a, a, electro-magnets with thick wire traversed by the current, and keeping the carbons separated as long as the current passes.

If the passage of the current is interrupted, the weight of the supports A makes them overbalance, and bring the movable carbon in contact with the stationary one, so that relighting takes place.

Fig. 70.—Wilde's candle. Four-candle holder.

its pivot. This electro-magnet is operated by the current itself; it is therefore inactive when the current is not passing, and only acts when the current reaches it, or when the lamp is lighted. If the candle becomes extinguished by any accident whatever, the current no longer passes through the voltaic arc nor through the electro-magnet; this becomes then inactive; it releases the movable rod which leans over toward the point of its neighbor, and re-establishes the circuit. Thus the lamp lights itself; all is done so quickly that the extinction is hardly perceptible.

9

Superior to the Jablochkoff candle on account of its automatic lighting and relighting, the Wilde lamp also excels it
in the duration of its period of illumination. The Jablochkoff
candles last only one hour and a half, and it is with great
trouble that they can be made to last two hours by lengthening them. In the Wilde burner there is no limit to the length
of the carbon except the fear of too frequent breakage, because
the carbons can be carried down into the foot of the apparatus.
They have been made sixty-five centimetres long, which represents about five hours' burning, at the rate of twelve centimetres per hour.

If the foot of the candle remained fixed, as in the Jablochkoff system, the luminous point would descend thus sixty-five
centimetres during its period of illumination. Such a displacement would be entirely inadmissible. To prevent this it
sufficed to return to the old form of kitchen candlesticks or
hotel candelabra, in which the candle rests upon a small socket
sliding in the tube, and which can be lifted up little by little
so to keep the end of the candle constantly at the same elevation. In a like manner the Wilde candle is operated after
one or two hours' burning.

Where the lighting is to last more than five hours, M. Wilde
arranges a series of candles in a circle or crown on a round
frame, which can be turned by hand or automatically; the arrangement resembles quite closely that of the Jablochkoff
candles, because in this case it is not possible to make the carbons so long.

M. Wilde's candle can be turned upside down and work
in that position, which avoids the casting of shadows by the
different parts of the apparatus. But the arc then is in
danger of abandoning from time to time the points, and of
causing by these oscillations the production of the reddish
flashes, which are one of the disagreeable features of the Jablochkoff candle.

The Jamin Candle.

The Wilde candle belongs to 1878. The following year, in
1879, another appeared, that of M. Jamin, which was modified
frequently, and which finally borrowed from the Wilde candle
its most characteristic feature. M. Jamin, professor of the
Sorbonne, and also of the Institute, had been retained by the
Jablochkoff company from its beginning as consulting en-

A, clay plate acting as support for the carbon-holders and directing-frame.

B, directing-frame, in the form of a flattened groove, in which the copper wire which is traversed by the current before it reaches the carbons, is wound.

C, upper portion of the frame, constructed of soft iron, which becomes magnetized under the influence of the current. This part constitutes the electro-magnet that operates the carbons.

D, plate of iron, pivoted to the three movable branches of the carbon-holders, to which they impart the same movement. As soon as the current passes into the apparatus the part C, or the frame, becomes magnetized, attracts this plate, and keeps the carbon separated. As soon as the current ceases to pass the plate falls back, and, by its weight, forces the movable carbons to approach the others. As the three pairs of carbons are of unequal lengths, it is only the longest that come in contact, and only one candle lights.

a, a, a, movable carbons in the plane of the directing-frame.

b, b, b, movable carbons in planes perpendicular to that of the directing-frame.

H, plates pressed each by a spring and resting on the carbon-holders b, b, b.

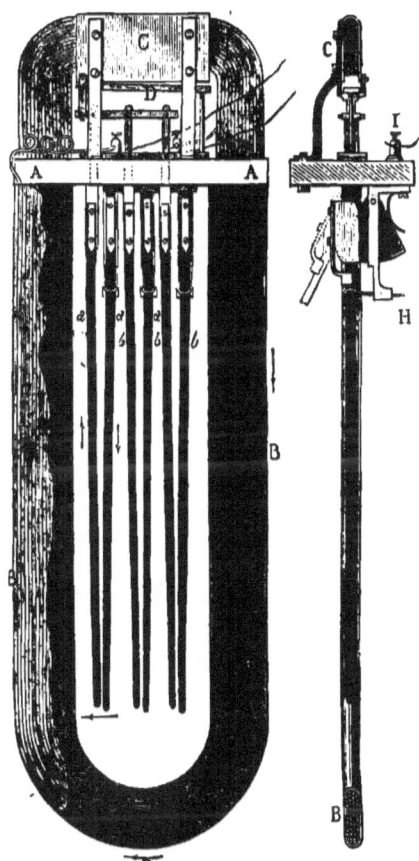

Fig. 71.—Jamin candle.

The action of these plates is restrained by a brass wire, one of whose ends is kept secured in a small plate, and whose other end, bent into a curve, sustains the carbon-holder b. When the carbons are used up, the heat of the voltaic arc melts the wire; the spring acts and draws the carbon-holders to one side, so that the passage of the current can not be re-established between the ends of the stationary carbons.

I, binding-screws for entrance and exit of the current.

The arrows indicate the course of the current, which traverses the directing circuit, reaches the three movable carbons at the same moment, passes through those which are in contact, and lights them. It may be seen by the direction which it follows in the two branches of the directing-frame, and in the two carbons of the candle, that each portion of the circuit tends to make the arc descend and remain between the points; with this burner no switch is required, and one single conductor answers for all the candles in the same circuit. But the wire that is wound in the frame introduces an important resistance, which makes a current of higher tension necessary; the dimensions which the frame ought to have, for efficacious action, does not allow the introduction of more than three candles.

gineer. He resigned finally, for the purpose of devoting all his time to the improvement of candles. His principal idea apparently was to make the light fixed, by preventing it from leaving the points, so that he could turn the apparatus upside down, something which certainly could be done with the Wilde candle, but without any certainty in this case of sufficient stability.

To reduce this idea to practice, he surrounded the candle with a certain number of turns of the wire conveying the electric current. This current acts upon the electric light as it would on a magnetized needle, and it is easily understood from a consideration of Ampère's law that the four sides of the frame exercise an accumulative action (Fig. 71). At first M. Jamin only used six turns of wire, then he ran up to forty, to obtain a more energetic action. But it costs a great deal to obtain this action, for it requires a current of higher tension, and thus increases to a certain extent the cost of maintaining the lamp. The frame, too, produces a disagreeable effect. Finally, it gives shadows which do away with all the advantage obtained by reversing the candle.

In other respects M. Jamin preserved the arrangements of M. Wilde for doing away with the insulating "colombin" and the automatic reillumination. Later on he added a particular mechanism for the purpose of communicating to the carbons an oscillating movement, synchronous with the pulses of the current. According to him, this vibratory movement should enable him to better utilize the current. This, however, has not proved true in practice; experience has only made the quite intense noise produced by these vibrations more remarked, something which makes the use of these burners in a room very disagreeable.

To sum up, the Jamin candle is the most unstable of all, and its light costs more than that of others.

Debrun Candle.

Finally, we must speak of a quite recent candle, as its first invention is only a few months old (December, 1880); it is the candle of M. Debrun. This is a provincial production; it first saw the light in Bordeaux, where M. Debrun, *Preparateur à la Faculté des Sciences*, was commissioned by the Jablochkoff Company to arrange for an introduction of its system of lighting. Having been struck, like all others, with the changes in color of these candles, he tried to overcome the difficulty, and saw at once that he would have to do away with the insulating "colombin," as M. Wilde had already done.

The Debrun candle lights itself automatically, as does that of M. Wilde, but by a different process. In place of inclining one of the carbon rods so as to touch the other rod with its point, M. Debrun unites them by a transverse priming, which touches them at their bases, and starts the voltaic arc. By making the contact at the base it is possible to relight the carbons, even when they are very short, at the moment of their accidental extinction; and it appears that the voltaic arc tends to fly to the points without any need of the directing frame with which M. Jamin surrounds his candle. The lighting contact is actuated, as in the Wilde candle, by an electro-magnet; but here this electro-magnet is placed in a shunt circuit, instead of in the main circuit of the voltaic arc, and by the details of construction all loss of energy is prevented.

The Debrun candles have also the advantage of lasting much longer than the Jablochkoff or Jamin candles. They are of two different lengths. One lasts three hours and a half and costs thirty-five centimes in the stores, the others last six hours and cost sixty centimes.

This is cheaper than the last prices of the Jablochkoff candles, for these only last two hours, according to the declaration of those most interested. Without doubt, the cost of establishing the electric light includes many other elements than this one; yet it is worthy of notice here.

Although still in its infancy, the Debrun candle is already introduced in the Grand Theatre of Bordeaux, its place of birth, in several *cafés*, or important hotels, and several studios. It has lighted several public *fêtes*, especially the National Fête of July 14, 1881, at Bordeaux, and the district agricultural fair of Alençon. It appears that it will soon light the Place des Quinconces, also in Bordeaux.

A final judgment can not be pronounced upon it without having followed its success for some time in the public experiments; it seems, indeed, very liable to vacillate, yet less than the Jamin candle.

BOOK III

THE INCANDESCENT LIGHT.

CHAPTER I.

HISTORY OF INCANDESCENCE.

THERE are two very different modes of transforming electricity into light, one could almost say two distinct species of electric light: the light of the voltaic arc—which is that of all the systems with regulators, and of all the candles—and the incandescent light of a solid refractory conductor, which can itself be produced under two separate conditions quite distinct, either in the open air, or in a closed vessel exhausted of air.

In the first case the incandescent body burns more or less rapidly, and this combustion helps to produce the light. In the second case the incandescent body, placed out of the influence of all oxygen, can not burn, and ought, in consequence, to last, if not forever, at least very long ; this is termed true incandescence, because in this kind of lighting no accessory phenomenon helps in the production of light.

I. THE DÉBUT OF PLATINUM.

It is with simple incandescence, out of contact with the air, that these researches commenced, and they date back a long time. The experiment of raising to incandescence a wire of platinum, by passing an electric current through it, has long been well known, as also how to vary at will all the conditions of the experiment, for it was enough for the purpose of augmenting the intensity of the light to diminish the diameter of the metallic wire, or to make it of another metal which was a poorer conductor of electricity.

This principle was applied in 1841, now forty years ago,

by an Englishman of Cheltenham named Frederick de Moleyns, who used a platinum-wire for his experiments. Eight
years later another Englishman, named Petrie, replaced the
platinum by iridium, either pure or alloyed with other metals,
and patented in England his method of preparation of the
iridium-wires destined for electric lighting.

These first attempts passed almost unnoticed, and it is
doubtful if they even were remembered nine years after, in
1858, when M. de Changy published his process of lighting
with an incandescent platinum-wire rolled in a spiral, analogous to that which Mr. Edison used again, for a short time,
in the first period of his experiments. Mr. Jobard, director
of the Industrial Museum at Brussels, cited no precedent in
announcing on February 27, 1858, to the Academy of Sciences
at Paris, that M. de Changy had succeeded in resolving the
problem of the divisibility of the electric light. This was the
end which had been long sought for, with the more ardor because the way which had been followed seemed to lead to no
solution.

The invention of M. de Changy made a great noise at once ;
but the noise soon ceased in presence of the undeniable inconveniences, which made the system almost impossible in
practice. The principal one of these inconveniences is the
ease with which platinum melts if the temperature at which
it furnishes a good white light be exceeded. A slight variation in the intensity of the electric current is sufficient to produce this injurious heating, and as yet they were unable to
regulate, even in an approximate manner, the force of the current employed.

The platinum-wire lamp was condemned to remain at relatively low temperatures, so as not to risk its melting all at
once and disappearing. Now at these low temperatures platinum gives naturally a decidedly colored light, yellow, or
sometimes red, and, worse yet, not bright enough for the
needs of practice even the least exacting. A red-hot wire can
not be called a lamp, and all the cooks would prefer, without
hesitation, the poorest of candles of six to the pound.

II. The Début of Carbon.

A substance less fusible than the metals then had to be
sought for, so that the temperature could be raised without

fear.   Such were not wanting; but the most of them could
not be reduced to fine wires, and almost all of them burned
readily, which was worse yet than melting.   In producing incandescence in a vacuum the danger of combustion can be
avoided.   On this basis, difficult as it was to realize at this
time, carbon engaged the attention of inventors almost at the
same time as platinum, for the first patent in this direction
was taken out in 1845 by an American named King, four years
after the first experiments with incandescent platinum tried
by the Englishman Frederick de Moleyns.

The origin of the incandescent-carbon lamp is surrounded
by a sad mystery.   We are at liberty to believe that the true
inventor was a scientist of Cincinnati, named J. W. Starr,
and whose work to-day is forgotten even in America.

Like all true philosophers, J. W. Starr was poor.   But he
made the acquaintance of the great philanthropist Peabody,
the founder of several great scientific institutions of the
United States, and whose name is as celebrated on this side
of the Atlantic as in the New World.   Peabody showed himself generous, as usual, and gave the inventor all the money
he required to submit his processes to the great savans of
England.   At this time the young American showed himself
a submissive and devoted disciple of science, and did not follow the custom of this day, in believing that he had the right
to consecrate to himself alone his great discoveries.

J. W. Starr sailed then for the Old World, bringing with
him as agent a man more accustomed to business affairs, and
provided with a smaller quantity of philosophic naïveté, who
would not let the natives of perfidious Albion get the better
of him ; this business man was King.

When he arrived in England J. W. Starr set to work to
prepare a great public demonstration.   He set up a great candelabra of twenty-six lights, to symbolize the twenty-six
united States of North America, which have since then increased greatly in number.   The great physicist, Faraday,
assisted at these experiments, admired them greatly, and prom-
ised him success.

These experiments terminated, Starr and King re-embarked
for the United States, without doubt to report to Peabody the
sanction of European science, and ask of him pecuniary means
to realize the invention on a large scale, and enable it to enter
the industrial domain.   But the day after they embarked,

Starr was found dead in his berth, and it was never known exactly how he came to his death.

King had taken out a patent in his own name. He then declared that gas-carbon gave better results than others, and referred to the necessity of placing it in a vessel exhausted of air to avoid its combustion. King also remarked that several apparatus of this kind could be placed upon the same circuit, as Starr without doubt had done in his experiments before Faraday, and that this circuit could receive its electricity either from a battery or from a magneto-electric machine, types of which were then known, it is true, but the machines were very weak.

A year after the American King, in 1846, two Englishmen, Greener and Staite, who may have had little knowledge of the experiments of J. W. King in London, also took out a patent for a lamp with incandescent carbon analogous to that of King. They added to it, however, a new process : the employment of *aqua regia* (nitro-muriatic acid) to free the carbon of its impurities, and to give thus more regularity to the light and at the same time a greater solidity to the filament.

In spite of a beginning that seemed to promise a great deal, the whole affair fell into oblivion for thirty years. It is probable that Peabody did not wish to continue conferring upon King the favors he reserved for Starr, and that King did not find others to supply funds to carry on an enterprise very hazardous at this epoch, even in the eyes of Americans. With King reduced to impotence, the idea now disappeared from view under other preoccupations, for the public soon cease to think over an enterprise which does not succeed at the first attempt, when general opinion does not run in the same direction.

III. THE RUSSIAN LAMPS.

It was in Russia, about 1873, that the light by incandescent carbon came at last out of the oblivion in which it had slept for twenty-seven years. A Russian physician, M. Lodyguine, invented a lamp founded on this principle, and which won him one of the grand prizes of the Academy of Sciences of St. Petersburg.

In describing M. Lodyguine's labors, M. Wilde, member of the academy, charged with the report, very well expressed all the advantages which result from the employment of carbon

instead of platinum for the production of the incandescent light.

Carbon, at the same temperature, possesses a much higher radiating power than platinum ; the calorific capacity of carbon is much less, so that the same quantity of heat brings the carbon pencil to a higher temperature than it would do in the case of a platinum wire.* Besides, the electric resistance of the carbon is about 250 times greater than that of platinum, so that the carbon pencil can be much thicker, and yet reach the same temperature as the metal. Finally, carbon is infusible, and its temperature can be raised freely without danger of melting.

M. Lodyguine's lamp was formed of small needles ending in prisms, and made of retort-carbon, fastened between two insulated pincers, which placed them in contact with the two branches of the circuit, almost the same as is done with the Jablochkoff candle. For preventing them from burning, they first used to close them up in vessels exhausted of air ; but, as the removal of air by means of an air-pump was a quite costly operation for practical manufacture in the conditions under which they then worked, they generally left the apparatus full of air, carefully sealing it hermetically, so as to prevent oxygen from renewing itself after having disappeared by combining with the carbon.

But there may be produced a sort of combustion with the imprisoned oxygen, and it was without doubt one of the causes that made the carbon-rods break very frequently. These ruptures caused long interruptions, for it was not easy to replace the broken carbons. It seems that quite a satisfactory light could be produced from four lamps of this kind placed on one electric circuit supplied by one of the strong machines with alternate currents of the *Compagnic l'Alliance*.

M. Kosloff, of St. Petersburg, to whom was intrusted the importation and introduction into France of the Lodyguine lamp, improved it in certain points ; for instance, by employing a new metal for the metallic supports holding the carbon pencils, which supports melted very often in the earlier type. M. Konn, in 1875, and M. Bouliguine, in 1876, invented other lamps founded on the same principles, with different arrange-

* [Calorific capacity ceases to be an element to be taken into account when the permanent temperature is attained.]

ment of parts and of better working capacity.   Figure 73 will suffice to give an idea of these apparatus.

But all these Russian lamps, of which several, it is true, were invented in Paris, had a common defect, and a capital one at that : the carbon-rods placed between two larger pieces

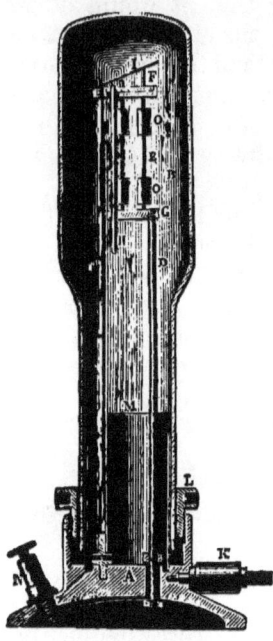

FIG. 73. — Incandescent lamp of Konn, in a closed vessel.

A, copper socket on which are fixed two binding-screws N, one of which is insulated, for attachment of the conductors.

K, small cylindrical box containing a safety - valve, which only opens from within to without. It is provided with a nipple for receiving the tube leading to the air-pump, when a vacuum is created in the bell B.

B, globe enlarged at its upper part, and held upon its base by a brass screw-collar, abutting against an India-rubber ring.

D, vertical rod, electrically insulated, and provided at its upper end with a small horizontal plate G. This plate contains five small cavities to receive the copper ends of the carbon-holders.

C, bar composed of a tube fastened to the base, and of a copper rod, split for a part of its length so that it can, with a slight effort, be forced down into the tube. This rod is supplied with a horizontal plate at its top, pierced with five holes.

E, carbons placed between the two plates. They are fastened into small blocks of carbon O O ; the bottom blocks have small rods of copper of equal length, by which they rest upon the lower plate ; the upper blocks are also provided with rods which pass through the holes in the upper plate ; as they are of unequal length, the lever I only rests upon a single one of them.

I, lever pivoted on the top of the rod C. It rests successively upon the rods of different blocks, and determines the direction of the current.

II, copper rod on which the lever rests when all the carbons are burned, and which permits the current to pass to the other lamps.

M, copper tube receiving the *débris* of burned carbons.

The five carbons are placed between the plates, and the lever I is lowered, which rests upon the longest one ; the globe is pumped out and the vacuum formed. The current is then passed into the lamp ; the little carbon E reddens, whitens, and becomes luminous ; it is consumed little by little, the rod breaks, and the light disappears. At once the lever I drops down upon another rod and the light is re-established almost immediately with the next carbon. This continues until the five carbons are used up.

were disintegrated sooner or later by an action which was not combustion, for it took place without oxygen. The pencil grew thin in the center and gradually ended by breaking ; it then had to be replaced, and this substitution had become the principal problem placed before the inventors of incandescent lamps.

CHAPTER II.

INCANDESCENCE IN THE OPEN AIR.

WE have now seen in the preceding chapter the difficulties under which the incandescent lamps up to 1874 labored. The filament of carbon always broke very soon at its center, and, in spite of the efforts of inventors, there was no means found of preventing it.

M. Emile Reynier was, in 1877, one of those who sought the solution. After having tried different means, he was led to think that if the pencil touched with its end a heavy carbon, the waste would not take place in the middle of the incandescent part but at the point of contact, which was an imperfect contact, and where the temperature ought to be the highest.

Experiments verified this theoretical view. The benefit was double, for another difficulty of the problem, that of the vacuum in the interior of the lamp, was solved, or rather avoided, at the same time with the conservation of the carbons. As the consumption of carbon took place gradually at its extremity, it became useless to retard this combustion by employing a closed vessel; the carbon had only to be pushed forward as fast as used, as the candles in carriage-lanterns are.

Still further, the slow combustion of the incandescent carbon in the air was a favorable circumstance, because it raised the temperature, and consequently augmented the luminous intensity.* It should therefore be preserved as a useful accessory.

I. THE REYNIER LAMP.

The system of incandescence in open air was thus conceived. It now had to be realized in a practical manner. M. Emile Reynier immediately devoted himself to it.

In November and December, 1877, he began the construction of his first apparatus in the laboratory of M. Breguet; on

---

* [This statement is very frequently made, but it does not seem to be warranted, as the combustion of such a minute quantity of carbon could not increase the temperature sufficiently to have any perceptible influence on the light. The cooling of the incandescent carbon by the air would, moreover, much more than counterbalance any gain from combustion.]

February 19, 1878, he applied for a patent, and on May 13 he described his system in a note addressed to the Academy of Sciences at Paris, in which he gave a *résumé* of the principle. Fig. 74.

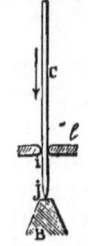

If a thin rod of carbon, C, pressed laterally by an elastic contact-piece, *l*, and pushed in the line of its axis upon a fixed contact-piece, B, is traversed by a sufficiently powerful current between these two contacts, it becomes incandescent at this part of its length, *i j*, and burns continuously, growing attenuated toward its extremity. As the end becomes used up, the rod, continuously pushed onward, advances, rubbing against the elastic contact-piece, so as always to rest upon the stationary contact-piece. The heat developed by the current in the carbon-rod is greatly increased by the combustion of the carbon.

Fig. 74.— Principle of incandescence in the open air.

M. Reynier was not slow to recognize the fact that the fixed immovable carbon, acting as contact-piece for the incandescent rod, was for several reasons inconvenient. The ash accumulated there, and interfered with the production of the light. To overcome this trouble he made the piece movable, and gave it the form of a disk turning around its axis, analogous to that which had been employed in 1845 for the voltaic arc by an Englishman named Thomas Wright. On starting out, M. Reynier, for turning the carbon disk, used a mechanism turning by the weight of the upper carbon-holder (Fig. 75). But he was not slow in simplifying his apparatus in a most ingenious manner, producing the rotation of the disk by the descent of the carbon-rod itself. This is the final form he adopted for his lamp.

The carbon-rod is pushed toward the base by its weight, and that of the carbon-holder, directed by rollers. This rod rests on a carbon-disk, a little in front of the vertical through the center

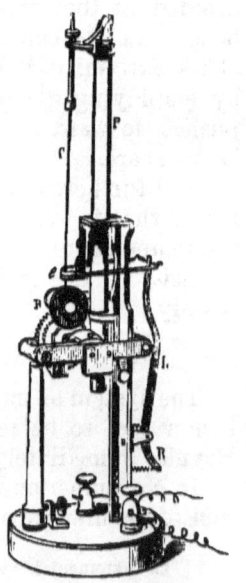

Fig. 75.—Reynier incandescent lamp; first arrangement with rotating electrode.

of the disk. The descent of the pencil, resulting from its consumption, thus turns the disk without any mechanism. The rod is supported at a short distance from its end by a sleeve, and below this comes in contact with another carbon contact-piece, which determines the length of its incandescent portion.

By a very simple arrangement the pressure exercised by the rod upon the disk is transmitted to and produces an automatic brake action upon the movable carbon-holder; it follows that its weight is effectually sustained, as long as the carbon is long enough to bear down upon the disk, and that this weight is on the contrary released when the lower support is wanting on account of the consumption of the point.

Fig. 76.—Magnified image of the incandescent portion of the Reynier lamp.

As is seen in the image of the luminous part of this lamp, magnified and projected upon a screen, the temperature is highest at the lower contact-point; the carbon, grown thin by slow combustion in the air, sharpens itself toward its base, which the shape and motion of the pencil facilitates.

Finally, to prevent the incandescence from rising too far upward on the pencil, and to prevent the luminous portion being thus extended, it is touched at a certain distance by another carbon, much larger, which brings the current. The incandescent part varies thus from four to eight millimetres, according to the quantity of light which it is proposed to obtain, and which can attain five to twenty Carcel lamps, provided, of course, that the current be strong enough.

II. THE WERDERMANN LAMP.

While M. Reynier was occupied in France in perfecting his incandescent lamp, an Englishman, Mr. Richard Werdermann, was working in London upon the same problem, and he there took out, August 23, 1878, a patent founded on the same principles, which gave rise to very energetic discussions between the two engineers. These discussions had only a theoretical interest for them, because the Jablochkoff Company, owner of the Werdermann patents, bought the Reynier patents, and it is this company which has especially contributed to fix upon the incandescent lamps the name of Werdermann lamps, although the principle at least, if not the actual arrangements, belong probably to M. Reynier.

One of the innovations introduced by Mr. Werdermann consisted in the inversion of the apparatus. The large disk placed at the base of his apparatus by M. Reynier cast disagreeable shadows. Mr. Werdermann placed it above, and pushes up his carbon-rod by means of a counterpoise (Fig. 77).

In the Reynier-Werdermann lamp it is less a true incandescence that is produced than a sort of voltaic arc, very short, combined with incandescence of the electrodes, and Mr. Werdermann has noted in his experiments some very curious deformations of electrodes of different sizes under the effect of the voltaic arc.

Fig. 77.—Werdermann lamp.

C, disk of carbon supported by the arm D.
T, tube serving to guide the carbon rod B.
R, spring, with regulating screw for limiting the action of the counterpoise.
E, counterpoise acting through the medium of a cord passing over pulleys to advance the rod B.

When the voltaic arc is produced between two carbons of the same section, the changes of their polar extremities are produced in the manner already known ; the positive electrode, heated to a white heat, takes the shape of a mushroom, hollows itself into a cup, and is used up twice as rapidly as the negative electrode. The latter, which is only heated to redness by the current, is slowly formed into a point, and the length of the arc is in proportion to the tension of the current.

The result is altogether different if different sections be given to the two electrodes. When the section of the positive electrode is gradually diminished, and that of the negative electrode is increased, the red heat observable at the end of the latter is gradually diminished, while the heat of the positive electrode increases in proportion to the reduction of its section. The electric current does not pass across the space intervening between the electrodes with the same facility, and to succeed in maintaining the voltaic arc the electrodes must be brought closer together, so that the current can pass over the diminished distance between them.

At this point a strange phenomenon becomes manifest : the end of the positive electrode increases considerably in size, and the current shows a tendency to equalize the two surfaces—that is to say, to give to the positive electrode, as far as may be, the same section as that of the negative. The greater the difference between the sections of the electrodes, the smaller must the distance between them be, and to avoid too great an increase in the size of the positive electrode the tension of the current must be somewhat reduced, which is easily managed by employing a Gramme machine, with which the tension of the current is proportional to its velocity, the resistance of its armature remaining constant.

A limit is thus reached when the distance between the electrodes becomes infinitely small—that is to say, when the electrodes are in contact. It is when their sections are in the ratio of 1 to 64 ; then the negative electrode is hardly heated at all, and consequently is not consumed. In these conditions the positive electrode only is the one that burns, producing a beautiful light, absolutely fixed, and lasting as long as close contact between it and the negative electrode is maintained. In reality, then, it is an incandescent light, increased by the presence of an infinitely small voltaic arc, which keeps the consumption of the carbon confined to its point. If the pressure is strong enough to make the contact too complete, the combustion will be retarded a little, the carbon will be detached in fragments, and the light will no longer possess the steadiness which is its most desirable quality.

When the operation is reversed—that is to say, when, instead of diminishing the section of the positive electrode, the section of the negative electrode is diminished step by step, and that of the positive electrode is at the same time increased, the light of the latter is diminished little by little, and the temperature of the negative electrode increased.

10

When the sections of the electrodes are in the ratio of 1 to 64, and when they can be brought into contact, no light is emitted by the positive electrode, but only by the negative. What is curious is that when a voltaic arc is started between the two carbons, the smaller electrode always becomes pointed, whether positive or negative.

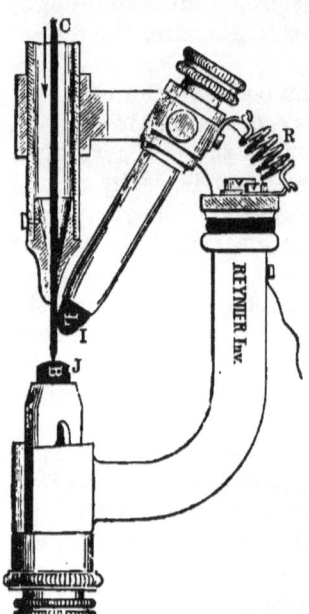

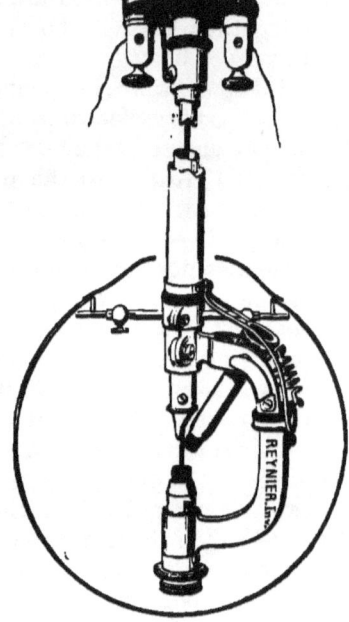

FIG. 78.—Burner of the Reynier lamp.

FIG. 79.—Reynier's incandescent lamp with globe.

C, movable rod of carbon.
B, contact block of graphite.
L, lateral contact piece made of a block of graphite fastened into a tube pivoted into the supporting arm.
R, spring maintaining the lateral contact pressure.
I J, luminous part.

III. THE ACTUAL REYNIER-WERDERMANN LAMPS.

During nearly two years in which it has been operated the Reynier-Werdermann lamp has undergone several changes in its accessory parts, especially in those which press the rod of incandescent carbon against the abutting disk. M. Trouvé, M. Ducretet, M. Tommasi, have suggested various modifications, some of which already figure in the work of M. Reynier.;

and M. Napoli, engineer of the company owning the Reynier-Werdermann lamp, inspired by the inventor's ideas, has given to the apparatus the general arrangement of parts that it possessed as exhibited in the Electrical Exhibition at Paris.

M. Reynier himself has succeeded in further simplifying his former arrangements so as to obtain better contacts, and to

Fig. 80.—Chandelier of Werdermann lamps.

diminish shadows, thanks to the substitution of graphite for carbon as contact-pieces.   To-day he uses a new burner, whose construction is shown in Fig. 78.   This burner can easily be contained within a globe, and constitutes a very simple lamp, like that shown in Fig. 79.

The rods actually employed have a diameter of two millimetres and a half, and are one metre long. They last six
hours.

Eleven of these lamps, in use in a cloth-bleaching establishment at Lisieux, and supplied by a Gramme machine,
work-shop type (*type d'atelier*), required three horse power.

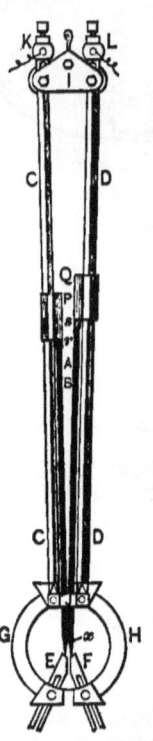

Each burner had an intensity varying from
eight to twelve Carcels, according to the speed
of the machine.

The English Joël lamp is not essentially dif-
fferent from the Reynier-Werdermann lamps.

Continuous currents are used for this kind
of incandescent lighting, and the lamps can
work not only with dynamo-electric machines
but also with batteries; eight Bunsen elements
are enough to give a light of about four Carcels, which is an invaluable feature as regards
laboratory work.

For equal production of light, incandescent
lighting in open air costs certainly more than
voltaic-arc illumination; but it makes possible the subdivision of the light into centers of
smaller intensity, while the regulator voltaic-
arc lights must be much stronger to give good
results.

This subdivision permits us to distribute in
a much more even manner, and consequently
to better utilize, the light produced, while the
great lights illuminate too strongly objects in
their immediate vicinity, and not enough at the
limiting distance of their action. Moreover,
these powerful lights need protecting opaline

Fig. 81.—Reynier's latest form of in-candescent lamp.

globes, which often cut off a third of the light
produced, and sometimes more. Finally, the
incandescent light is milder than the voltaic-
arc light; it has no bluish tints, due to little flames of carbonic oxide, which give so cold an aspect to regulators as
well as to candles; its rays, slightly yellow, do not offend the
eye, and do not subject it to the influence of rays of colors it
is unaccustomed to.

It is also the only one which not only permits extinction
and relighting of the light at will, like regulators, but also

the varying of intensity to a great extent, by introducing into the circuit suitable resistances.

The Reynier-Werdermann lamps to-day can be used almost to as great advantage as vacuum incandescent burners in the decorative fixtures of rooms. They construct especially with them lusters of ten jets (Fig. 80), which light up large saloons with as much effulgence as immense candle-chandeliers, but with much higher luminous intensity.

For all these reasons, the success of open-air incandescent lamps has been very great, especially in London, and all

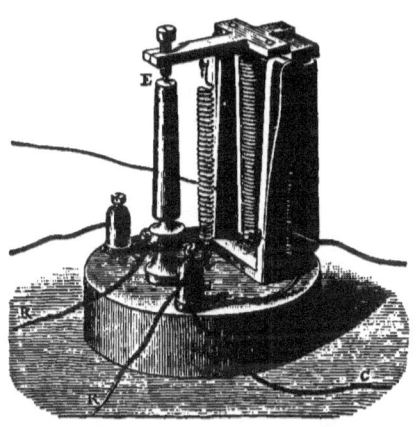

Fig. 82.—Reynier automatic lighter.

believe that their use will be continued although they have been little employed in Paris up to the present day.

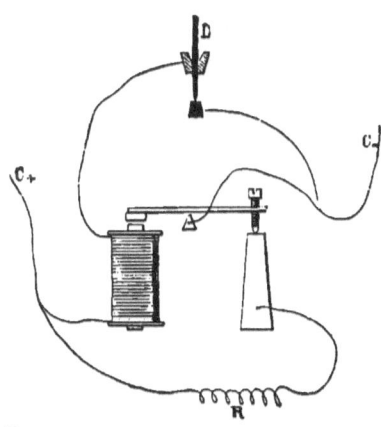

Fig. 83.—Arrangement of parts and electrical connection of the automatic lighter.

[Quite recently M. Reynier has devised another form of open-air incandescent lamp which is free from the objections to the above lamp, and which is, if anything, simpler in construction. In the lamp described, the contact which formed the upper limit to the incandescence of the pencil lowered the economy of the lamp by conducting away a part of the heat, and the feeding of the pencil through this contact was not wholly satisfactory. In the later lamp, two carbon pencils are used, slightly inclined to each other, so that they touch at a short distance from their points, which rest upon small abutments

of copper.   The relation of the parts is shown in Fig. 81.
The carbons A, B, are pressed downward by the weights
P, Q, sliding upon the metallic guides C, D.   The points of
these carbons rest upon the copper abutments E, F, attached
to the curved metallic bars G, H.   The current enters at the
terminal K, follows the rod C, the arm G, and abutment E,
to the point of the carbon resting upon it.   It then passes up
this carbon to the point x, at which the two carbon-rods
touch, then across to the other carbon and downward, out to

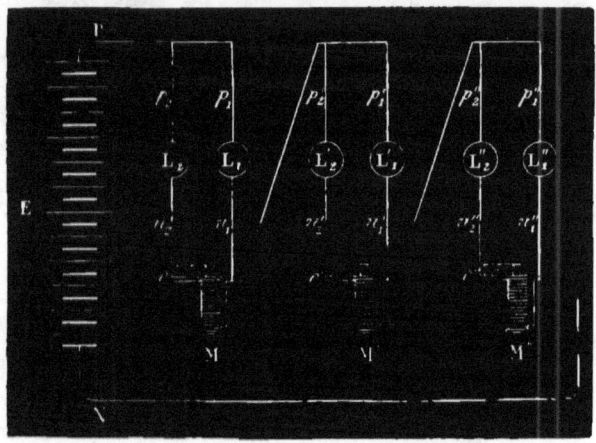

Fig. 84.—Reynier system of distribution.

the terminal L, by a similar route taken on entering.   The
contact limiting the incandescence, it will be seen, is a hot
contact, and hence this arrangement should be a more economical one than that of the former lamp.]

IV. Installation of Reynier-Werdermann Lamps.

For lamps of this system M. Reynier has invented his automatic lighter (Figs. 82, 83), which performs almost the same
office as the safety-box of M. de Mersanne does for regulators.

The most usual system of distribution consists in placing
the lamps one after the other on the same circuit; but then if
one of them goes out on account of the breakage or exhaustion of a carbon, all the others will go out at the same time.
This the lighter is designed to prevent, by substituting for

the extinguished lamp a resistance which is ordinarily formed by a wire of German silver. ·

The apparatus is provided with an electro-magnet placed in the main circuit C C (Fig. 83); while the lamp is working, the armature is attracted, and the auxiliary resistance-coil R is cut out of the circuit; when the lamp goes out, the electro-magnet becomes inactive, the armature drops back under the influence of its spring, and effects a contact, at E (Fig. 82), between the two ends of the auxiliary circuit. The current passes through the resistance-coil R, and as this represents exactly the value of a lamp burning, the other apparatus on the same circuit are not affected. As soon as the lamp is restored to its normal working condition, the current again passes in its regular course, everything resumes its place and the lighter returns to duty. Of course there must be a lighter for each lamp; but the resistance-coil can be replaced by a second lamp which burns as long as the first one is extinguished, so that the service experiences neither interruption nor diminution. Fig. 84 explains how a series of lamps can be arranged. Three lamps, L_1, L_1', L_1'', are mounted in series on the circuit, Pp Nn, of a battery, E; they are respectively in connection with three automatic lighters, M, M', M'', whose contacts are at c c' c''. Each lamp has a second resistance or a second lamp, L_2 L_2' L_2''.

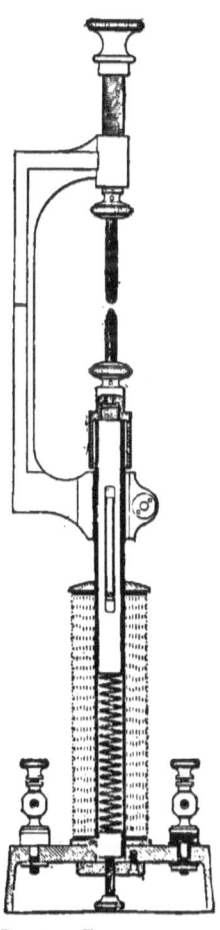

Fig. 85.—Temporary regulator of Reynier, serving as a safety-lamp, in electric installations.

To replace the German-silver coil, and as substitute for these lamps, M. Reynier sometimes uses a little regulator, which will work long enough to permit the lamp to be resupplied with carbon, without interrupting the lighting. This very simple apparatus is composed of a solenoid (Fig. 85), a soft iron rod, and a spring. The upper carbon is fixed; the lower carbon is carried by the rod of soft iron and follows its movements. The spring is adjusted to balance the attraction of the solenoid in all positions of the rod, as long as the current possesses normal intensity. If the intensity increases, the rod is attracted ; if it diminishes, the spring acts ; the length of the arc remains constant. Although supplied with a button to regulate the tension of the spring, this lamp can only work within very narrow limits of intensity of the current. It is only a safety lamp.

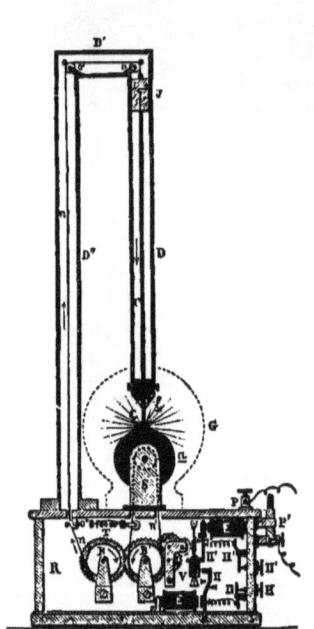

Fig. 86.—Incandescent lamp with rotating electrode, of M. Ducretet.

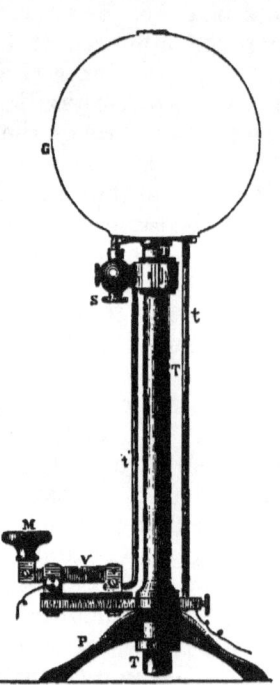

Fig. 87.—Incandescent lamp of M. Ducretet.

V. Various Lamps.

The labors of M. Reynier have produced several models of lamps which it is interesting to study, although they may not have entered the domain of every-day use.

M. Ducretet has taken up again Harrison's lamp, and has adapted to it a mechanism which at the same time regulates the descent of the carbon-rod and the rotation of the abutting-disk. In Fig. 86 it will be seen that the rod is pressed from above downward by a weight, J, and that toward the base it passes through another block, l, which acts as guide, and also limits the length of the incandescent part. The descent is restrained by a cord, u, wound upon a small drum; a second cord transmits to the disk a movement of rotation. Two small electro-magnets with fine wire are placed in derived circuit; one, E', acts to regulate the movement of the

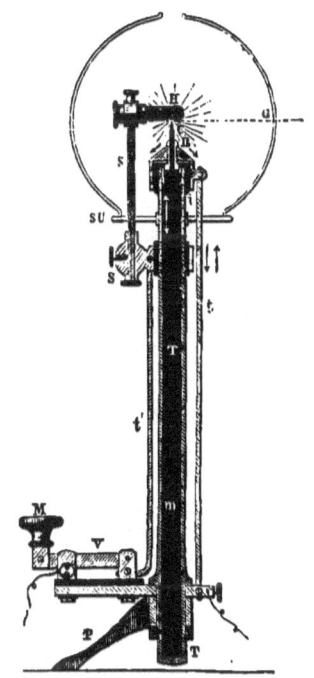

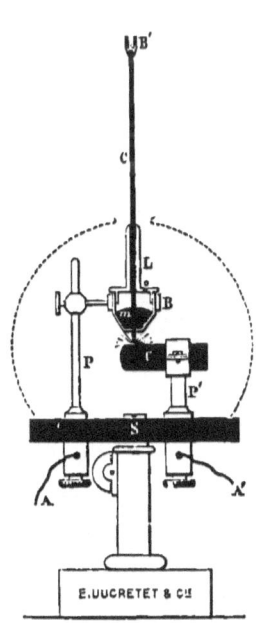

Fig. 88.—Section of M. Ducretet's lamp.   Fig. 89.—M. Clamond's incandescent lamp.

machinery; the other, E, to arrest it completely when the carbon-rod is used up.

By this apparatus the contact can be modified at will, and even can be suppressed entirely by maintaining constantly a small distance between the carbon and the disk. Six Bunsen elements are enough to give a voltaic arc.

In another model M. Ducretet has put into practice an idea formerly enunciated by M. Reynier. The carbon-rod is pushed from above downward by the hydrostatic pressure of a column of mercury sealed up in an iron tube which acts as standard for the lamp. Figs. 87 and 88 show the exterior view and vertical section of this lamp. They are so easy to understand as to need no explanation.

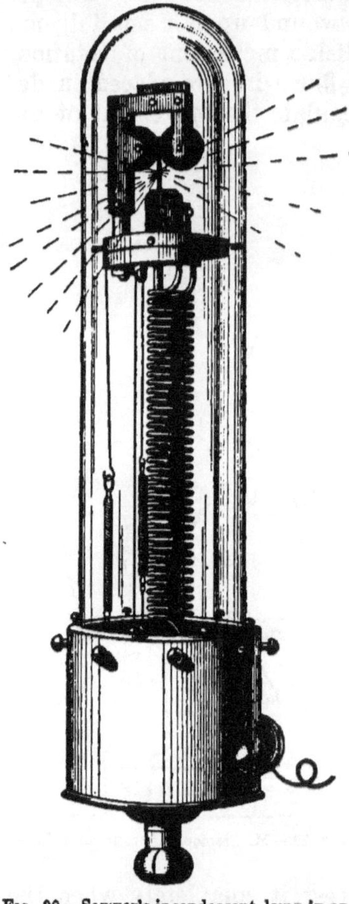

M. Clamond has invented a small incandescent lamp (Fig. 89), in which the rod of carbon, C, descends freely through a hollow iron guide, B, containing a little mercury, m. The rod fills the hole closely enough to prevent the mercury from running out; it also secures a good contact for the passage of the current. This would seem to be a very convenient apparatus for laboratory use.

[A lamp of the same type as the Reynier-Werdermann, but in which the incandescence takes place in an atmosphere of nitrogen, was constructed in the United States by Sawyer and Mann. One form of it is shown in Fig. 90. The pencil is fed upward, through an elastic contact, to a pair of grooved rollers which form the abutment. The mechanism of the lamp is inclosed in a glass bell, joined to a metal base, from which the air has been exhausted and replaced with pure nitrogen. In the latest form of this lamp the abutment is a block of carbon instead of the rollers, and a mechanism operated by a coiled spring is substituted for the electro-magnetic device previously used.]

FIG. 90.—Sawyer's incandescent lamp in an atmosphere of nitrogen.

CHAPTER III.

THE SUN-LAMP.

In the classification of electric lamps, the sun-lamp occupies an altogether separate position, and a very difficult one to define in a word. It is a voltaic-arc lamp, and yet the voltaic arc, being only utilized as a source of heat, has not the usual inconveniences ; it is also an incandescent lamp, because the light comes from an incandescent, solid, refractory substance ; but this material does not act in any sense as conductor for the electric current ; the voltaic arc heats it, and thus make it luminous.

Finally, it must be remarked that, above all it is a lamp without mechanism, the same as candles and incandescent lamps for open air or in sealed vessels.

I.

The Jablochkoff candle was the starting-point in the invention of the sun-lamp. The earlier of the two inventors of this lamp, M. Clerc, was engineer of the Jablochkoff Company, and as such had to follow day by day the practical working of all the parts of the candle. Like many others, he had doubts of the true office and utility of the colombin which separated the two carbon-rods. It was, moreover, at this period an insulating rod of kaolin, which, it was said, while preventing all passage of electricity while cold, became to some extent a conductor when heated between the two points, and thus permitted the formation of a derived current through the length of this layer of melted porcelain.

But from the moment when plaster was substituted for porcelain in the construction of the insulating colombin, this explanation could not hold, because this new colombin did not melt, and was a non-conductor when cold. To ascertain its true function, M. Clerc tried candles without a colombin, and found that they were subject to still more frequent extinctions. What was the reason of these extinctions ?

Examining these candles without a colombin, it was seen that the arc oscillated between the points, often left them and

descended toward the base of the cones, where the distance between the carbonaceous rods was less, and where the disintegration of the carbon caused the accumulation of some dust,
which seemed to attract it.

The arc seemed to lick this dust, and thus maintain itself
for more or less time at the base of the cones. If it only
deserted the points for one or two seconds there was no
extinction ; if it was longer absent, extinction was certain, the cold points offering then too great a resistance
to the formation of the arc when this tended to mount
upward again toward them. Hence it is evident that it is
necessary to keep the points warm, if extinctions are to be
avoided.

The *rôle* of the colombin becomes, then, easy to explain.
It opposes the descent of the arc and prevents it from abandoning the points for any length of time, and thus prevents
extinctions. We have seen that in the ordinary candles, if
the arc hollows out in any way the colombin, it may abandon
the points, and that then extinction becomes probable.

The Jablochkoff candle, then, has in itself a cause of extinction, which is but the exaggeration of that which produces the excessive variations in the light, and, to overcome
this cause of extinction, it is necessary to employ a material
not only refractory at ordinary heat, but also capable of withstanding the strains due to the voltaic arc.

Having gone so far, M. Clerc might have found in the researches of M. Leroux, tutor at the École Polytechnique, which
researches he may not have been familiar with, the indications
of the way to pursue to find the solution.

In 1868, long before the Jablochkoff candle, M. Leroux
had noticed the advantages of a refractory material in such
cases. He announced that if there was placed in the neigh-
borhood of the arc, on the side opposite to that where the
light was to be utilized, a body capable of returning in the
form of light the enormous flow of calorific radiations which
the carbons and arc set free, these radiations would be better
utilized than by any other process. At the same time the
arc would be protected by a sort of screen which would
annul in almost a complete hemisphere all the causes of derangement produced by the incessant shiftings of the arc,
whose point of departure is very uncertain.

To fulfill this function, it became necessary to choose a

body at once a poor conductor of heat, and of light radiating power—conditions which lime, magnesia, and in general the earthy oxides, fulfill to a high degree.

M. Leroux first tried experiments with cylinders of magnesia, compressed according to Carron's system and manufactured for oxyhydic illumination. If we place the base of one of these cylinders, whose diameter is about eight millimetres, at a very small distance from the carbon-points of an electric lamp, so that the magnesia will be, as it were, licked by the voltaic arc, this will become incandescent to a degree comparable to that of the most luminous part of the carbons.

At the same time the light acquires a remarkable constancy, due to the fixity of the arc. M. Leroux could even give to the latter more length than was usual, because the mass of magnesia acted as a screen and maintained in this location the elevation of temperature, so that the danger of rupture of the arc became much reduced.

The magnesia can also be kept in the voltaic arc for more than an hour before the surface will become sufficiently changed to vary the conditions of the experiment; during the first few moments its surface will be hollowed out, but if the pencil of magnesia is kept stationary, the action of the arc growing weaker at a short distance it ceases to waste away. It undergoes, it is true, an alteration of another kind: it absorbs the silicious vapors which the voltaic arc carries, and forms with them a sort of glass, slightly green when cold and very hard. This circumstance is attended with the inconvenience of greatly diminishing the radiating power of the magnesia, and this new experiment shows again how necessary it is to have an industrial manufacture of pure carbon in a proper condition for the production of the electric light.

"The voltaic arc," said M. Leroux, in describing his experiments, "playing between two pencils of pure carbon in the recess of a cavity of magnesia or other alkaline earth, would certainly be one of the most beautiful sources of light that it is possible to realize."

But M. Leroux did not try to practically utilize the result that theory had made him foresee, and it was no less than eleven years later that M. Clerc was logically brought to the same conclusion again by the line of research that we have just described.

II.

M. Clerc made the two rods of carbon, that formed essentially the Jablochkoff candle, abut upon a block of lime, and the arc playing across this block was not extinguished.

But the arc shifted about, and gave always a flickering light. To fix it, M. Clerc conceived the idea of placing against the carbons, and perpendicularly to the block, two thin plates of lime, provided only with a small slit through which the arc could pass. The arc was guided, in fact, and in consequence the light became absolutely fixed.

Nevertheless, it was far from perfect, for it had still the violet tints due to the presence of carbonic oxide vapors, which tints the radiation from the block of lime could not whiten because it was not yet hot enough. By enclosing the two points in a block of refractory material provided with two slits destined for the passage of the voltaic arc, M. Clerc succeeded in concentrating the heat of the carbon-poles, and while diminishing their consumption in raising still higher the temperature of the block ; the light also changed its color and assumed a slightly golden tint, like that of the sun, which gave the lamp the name it has to-day.

In spite of the importance of these results, the sun-lamp was lacking in a condition more indispensable than all the others. However beautiful it might be, its light did not last. At the end of an hour the voltaic arc became buried in the refractory material, and the light was lost along with it in the cavern it had cut out. Other materials tried in place of lime resisted no better, and the misfortune seemed irreparable. Its cause was this :

When the voltaic arc is started between two carbon-points, horizontal or inclined one toward the other, it bends and takes, under the influence of the ascending currents of air, the curved form that gave it its name. If the refractory block, which is cold, be brought near it, the arc is then repelled, and is bent in the opposite direction ; but the material soon grows hot, and, at the end of a certain period, the arc reassumes its original curved form, cutting a passage for itself in the block of refractory material. The light disappears then almost entirely.

Some arrangement must be sought for that will prevent it burying itself in this cavity. M. Clerc removed the trouble by sliding the two carbon-rods through two holes, bored through the middle of the refractory mass, so that only their points project. The voltaic arc is produced between these two points, licks the face of the material with its interior face, instead of its exterior face as before, and the chrysalis was at full liberty to develop itself into a butterfly.

At the same time the heat of the blue carbon monoxide vapor was utilized in heating the refractory material, where it produced a vitrified surface, such as that described by M. Leroux. Finally, the apparatus which formerly faced upward, now cast its light downward, generally the only part to be lighted ; in all these cases it threw it entirely in a single direction, which of course could be changed at will.

A proper refractory material now had to be chosen, which required a large number of experiments and different trials. To execute them, M. Clerc, who was engaged in establishing electric lights on

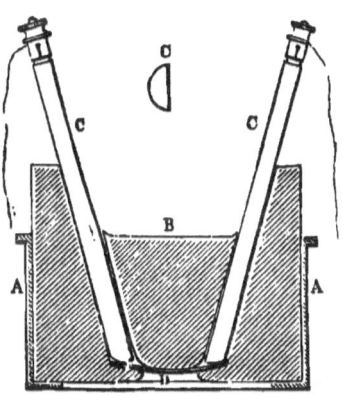

Fig. 91.—Vertical section of the lamp-soleil.

C, C, carbon-rods receiving the current by the wires shown—above, at C, the shape of the cross-section is given.

B, block of marble or compressed magnesia, the lower face of which becomes incandescent.

A, A, cast-iron box holding the pieces of refractory stone which form the protecting screen of the lamp.

D, small strip of plumbago or carbon connecting the tips of the carbon-rods, to light the lamp.

the candle system in several cities of Belgium, associated with himself one of his friends, M. Bureau, engineer of the construction works of M. Carels, at Gand, who eventually gave the lamp a final practical form and arrangement.

III.

At the beginning of the year 1880, then, the sun-lamp was essentially completed in all its parts, as we see it to-day (Fig. 91). It would be difficult to find anything simpler and less delicate.

It comprises two semi-cylindrical rods of carbon, two

centimetres in diameter, inclined at an angle of about 15°
toward each other, and separated by a small block of compressed magnesia or of marble, into which they are forced
down to a small cavity made in the lower face of the block—
a cavity in which the voltaic arc is produced. Pieces of refractory stone inclosed in a cast-iron box form a protecting
screen around the whole apparatus, and may be as large as
desired, as they can cause no imaginable inconvenience since
they cast no shadow below. Finally, a strip of plumbago
unites the two points of the carbon-rods to cause the first passage of the current and consequent lighting of the lamp.

The steadiness which is the great object sought for in voltaic lamps was here attained almost in perfection. In a word,
the principal cause of the variations of the electric light is
the instability of the arc, which at every instant changes the
point where it leaves, or springs from the carbon electrodes,
and consequently its path through the air. Hence come the
alternations of light and weakened intensity, as well as the
changes in color from red to blue. In the sun-lamp the arc
can change just as freely its point of departure from the carbons; but it has to pass through the only path that is open
to it through the refractory material. This gives it an absolutely fixed and invariable position.

A second cause of fixity is due to the fact that the greater
part of the light is due to a refractory body in a state of incandescence under the influence of the enormous temperature
of the arc. For, if the intensity of the current varies for any
reason, these variations do not manifest themselves rapidly
nor in a very sensible manner, for the temperature of the incandescent medium can not vary quickly, and it is this incandescence which produces the light. It constitutes as it were
a fly-wheel, to borrow a mechanical metaphor, and regulates
the emission of light by the quantity of heat which it keeps
stored up ready to be restored to the arc at the proper moment. From another point of view, in all the arc systems the
light is given by the points of the carbons, and it contains
many blue and violet rays. It is these rays, and the continual
and sudden variations in intensity, which are the cause of its
injurious action on the eye—an action so often and sometimes
so justly complained of in the electric light. In the sun-lamps,
the carbons being completely hidden in the midst of the refractory material, their points are invisible.

Finally, the block as it is used drops a certain amount of dust, which, after a certain time, soils the globe of the lamp, and constitutes its principal defect. This defect would disappear in the most natural manner if the glass globe were suppressed, which is all that shows the trouble, and in many cases this can be done.

The luminous center, instead of being reduced to a dazzling point, has a certain volume ; the light possesses a fixity

FIG. 92.—Lamp-soleil suspended, perspective view.

almost absolute, and a yellow tinge very agreeable to the retina, which is, on the contrary, so sensitive to the violet rays ; there need, then, be no fear for the eye, even when in the presence of the most intense lights. This can serve as additional proof of what the ophthalmologists have long ago

11

stated, that the artificial lights which we are discussing, always weaker than that of the sun, do us no injury by their intensity, but only by their particular nature.

The working of the sun-lamp is as simple as possible. Generally it is suspended, and the two carbons, placed vertically, descend by their weight alone just as fast as they are consumed. A flexible wire conducts the electrical currents, and follows them up without difficulty in their movement of descent (Fig. 92). When one wishes to incline or reverse the position of the lamp, the carbons are pushed by ordinary helical springs, or else by counter-weights.

The carbons, too, are of very ordinary quality, do not need much purity, and, because of their size, burn very slowly—only a centimetre an hour when they are hard, like retort-carbons, at the most double that when they are soft. Thus there is no trouble in putting in the apparatus carbons long enough to burn fifteen or sixteen hours—that is to say, more than is ever required in practice. The lamp, all prepared, only costs five francs, which gives some idea of its simplicity.

As in the candle systems, alternating currents are used for lighting, so that the two rods of carbon are used equally. The rustling inseparable from this kind of current is quite disagreeable. It is almost entirely suppressed or concealed now by placing the lamp in a closed lantern, the inconvenience of which we have already seen. But this trouble can be avoided, on the other hand, by using continuous currents.

From the point of view of its electrical working, the sun-lamp can be subjected to great variations in current without the fixity and coloration of its light being sensibly affected, and it resists to a very high degree the causes of extinction. None of the systems of regulator lighting can be compared to it in these respects ; as it is also superior from this point of view to open-air incandescent lamps, of which we have spoken in the preceding chapter.

If, in consequence of a variation of the dynamo speed caused by a slipping belt, for instance, or by any other cause, the intensity of the current diminishes, the luminous intensity alone will diminish. To produce extinction of the light, it will be necessary for the current to fall more than one half, and to remain at this degree of weakness for nearly a minute.

A sudden increase in intensity of current will present still less inconvenience, even after it will have reached such a degree as would constitute a serious danger for many other systems. The sun-lamp endures, for instance, without the least trouble, a current three or four times stronger than the normal current, which is entirely beyond any variations which can be expected. The only result that follows is the sudden raising to a value of five hundred carcels the lamp which formerly only was giving the quarter of it. But all soon returns to regular order, without any part of the apparatus being disorganized.

This exceptional power of resistance to electrical variations is especially due to the action of the incandescent refractory substance, which stores up and restores heat as we have explained above.

Nevertheless, as an extinction can be produced all the same, it is provided for by placing two lamps in the same circuit. Only one should work, the second is simply designed to replace the first in case of accident. The thing is done instantaneously, without need of any personal aid, by means of an automatic switch, which turns the current from one lamp into the other. This switch is governed by a small electro-magnet placed in a derived circuit. If the working lamp goes out, the principal current, suddenly stopped, is forced into the derived circuit, and augments enormously the force of the small electro-magnet, which thus becomes capable of moving the switch.

It would, without doubt, be simpler to relight the same lamp, as it is always ready in spite of its temporary extinction. For this the points of the carbons must be brought together so as to re-establish the voltaic arc. MM. Clerc and Bureau have combined with the lamp a little regulator, with derived-current solenoid, which produces this result automatically. But, simple as this arrangement is, it complicates the apparatus a little, and takes away from it in part its character of perfect simplicity which makes it so remarkably free from derangement.

IV.

According to experiments made in Brussels, in the month of September, 1880, by M. Desguin, for the International Congress of Commerce and of Industry, the sun-lamp needs no more motive power than the best regulator systems, and its carbons cost much less. But, before pronouncing upon these

different points finally, it is necessary to wait for prolonged practical experiments on a large scale.

These experiments the sun-lamp is still too recent to have furnished, although it has already been produced in public in Brussels, its native country, in London, and in Paris. In Brussels it has lighted for a long time one of the large coffee-houses of the city.

At Paris it has been in use for a month in the entrance to the passage Jouffroy (Fig. 93) and in the mayoralty-house in the Rue Drouot, where it produced a very good impression; it participated brilliantly in the national *fête* of July 14th, 1881, in the Place de Château d'Eau. Soon it will be seen under more difficult conditions.

M. Ch. Garnier proposes, in fact, to choose it for trying, at the same time with the Edison light, the electric lighting of the grand lobby of the Opera, where the gas is in a fair way to destroy the beautiful pictures of Baudry. The Edison light is to fill all the lusters, and the sun-lamp, hidden in the ornaments of bronze, will cast upon the platform floods of light whose origin can not be seen by the spectators. This new light, which produces hardly any heat, will permit soon a useful effectual cleaning of the works of Baudry, so badly blackened by the pestiferous exhalations of gas.

At London twenty-four sun-lamps have been established since the month of July, 1881, in the Westminster panorama, where it appears that they have won the suffrages of all. No one, in fact, can deny that they are not far superior to the regulator lamps for the lighting up of pictures. All could see this at the Electrical Exposition at Paris, where they occupied a room entirely furnished with cloths of all kinds, which were not all very bright in tone nor easy to be lighted up. It is certain that the colors underwent no alteration, and perhaps, indeed, the electric light made the designs come out better than does the daylight.

The effect is more complete still when the lamps are screened by a cloth on the side of the observer, as the picture-merchants always do who wish to display their merchandise. It is thus, for instance, that they are arranged in London at the Westminster panorama, and the arrangement adopted in Paris, in the grand lobby of the Opera, is equivalent to this, as the luminous centers are not visible.

CHAPTER IV.

THE EDISON LAMP.

AMERICAN as he is, Edison has no need of introduction to the European public. His name has already won everywhere the celebrity of great inventors by a crowd of discoveries, mostly relating to electricity ; it is enough to cite the phonograph and carbon-telephone, which has almost everywhere replaced the telephone of Graham Bell.

It was in 1878 that Edison began to be occupied with the electric light. His project was conceived during a voyage to the Rocky Mountains, in company with Draper, whose many scientific works, translated into all the languages of the Old World, have made his name as popular in Europe as in America. On his return he set to work immediately, with the promptitude of resolution which characterizes his compatriots.

His laboratory, in Menlo Park, was already full of telephones or of phonographs of all kinds, and of materials and apparatus designed to perfect them. In the twinkling of an eye all these were sent to the storehouse, to give place to a new order of work, corresponding to a different character of studies, even if electricity was still the base of work.

I. HIS FIRST RESEARCHES.

In this territory, already well worked over during several years, Edison "took the bull by the horns" by placing before himself the problem in its full extent and under the most extreme difficulties. He sought for a complete solution ; to make it do everything which gas could do—in furnishing a light of constant intensity, easily manageable, capable of being placed everywhere in small amounts like our actual gas-jets, corresponding to eight or sixteen candles—that is, to one or to two carcels ; but he was to make it do all this better than gas, in giving a light deprived of all odor, which would not transform salons into furnaces, and would emit no vapor injurious to the health of man, destructive to furniture or to delicate pictures, multiplied around us. This is the problem corresponding at once to the fixity and divisibility of the electric light. It remains to see to what extent and at what price this programme has been carried out.

Thomas. A. Edison.

Fɪɢ. 94.

Edison naturally began with the voltaic arc * used now in most of the known systems. This voltaic arc, whose luminous working has been explained in a preceding chapter, did not give a steady light, which is principally due to two causes :

First, the electric current which flows from one carbon-pole to the other is less a true current than a very rapid succession of instantaneous currents or sparks ; this electrical discontinuity creates a sort of luminous flickering very painful to the eye, and accompanied besides very often by a sonorous hissing. Finally, the carbon-poles, which appear to us very thin, are in reality very large compared to the electrical molecules ; now, the current passes from one pole to the other, following the line of the warmest particles of air, because the heating renders them better conductors, and this line can not always be the same in air disturbed by currents. Then each electric discharge from a pole starts from the part of the pole where the tension is greatest, and this point also will vary.

On account of these and still other circumstances, the voltaic arc which oscillates from right to left and left to right, at the same time oscillates also in a certain sense from above downward and the reverse, because it is formed by distinct successive discharges. Here was a double obstacle to overcome to obtain a light of constant intensity such as Edison wanted.

Seeing no good practical means of attaining this end, he at once abandoned the voltaic arc and its troubles, and, without further delay, turned to the other method of developing electric light : the incandescence of a conductor traversed by a strong current, whose molecules, finding no longer a sufficient free passage, rub one against the other, come in contact with the material molecules, and heat this insufficient passage up to a high temperature.

The idea was not new in itself, for it went back at least a third of a century—that is to say, to 1845—as we have seen in a preceding chapter. More recently, in 1873, a Russian physicist, M. Lodyguine, took up the idea of Starr, and had been followed in his turn by several others. Unfortunately, he came in contact with a decisive obstacle, from the industrial

* [Mr. Edison worked from the first on an incandescent lamp. Later he experimented with the arc-light with a view to rendering it steady, and for this purpose patented a lamp in which one or both of the carbon electrodes were given a rapid rotary motion.]

point of view, though it may seem of little account in the eyes of the savant : this obstacle is the cost of production.

Incandescence is not subject to two causes of trouble that affect the voltaic arc ; it can, then, if it avoids the perils of another sort, furnish a perfectly steady light. But the incandescent body presents a cooling surface much larger, and radiates heat more easily, than the particles of air heated by the voltaic arc. It loses, then, much more energy without useful result—that is to say, without corresponding light. In other terms, the economical return of the system is very small ; with the same source of electricity the incandescent system furnishes much less light than the voltaic arc ; in consequence, this light costs more. Now, a light that is too costly, whatever be its other good qualities, is in practice a Utopia.

The weak point of the system, it will be seen, resides in the matter that is made incandescent. If the defects of the substance in question could be suppressed or at least restrained to a sufficient extent, the rest could be arranged. It is, then, on the class of material, and the disposition to be made of it, that all his care was to be expended, as this was the root of the whole matter. Edison was not wanting. To attain his end, he was obliged to display marvels of tenacity and patience, and use at the same time the immense means of action which American capitalists gladly place at the service of inventors.

This incandescent material also, like the valet of the comedy, should unite many qualities in itself which are very difficult to find. In the first place, it should remain incandescent without burning, otherwise the apparatus would be consumed immediately, and would be unable to afford any real service. In the second place, it should offer to the passage of the current a resistance precisely such as would bring about the increase of heating which produces incandescence. In the third place, it should be infusible under the influence of this high degree of heat, so as not to disappear as quickly as if it burned. In the fourth place, it should also not be oxidizable, which would bring about its destruction the same as if by an ordinary combustion.

In the fifth place, as it should, for increasing the resistance to the current, be reducible to fine filaments like a woman's hair, it should be capable of preserving a rigid form even at this state of ideal thinness. In the sixth place, it should be arranged to diminish as much as possible the conductivity of its middle section, for electricity, and, above all, for heat, so as to avoid the chilling which would carry with it a considerable loss of energy—a loss which constitutes the principal trouble of the system.   In the seventh place—but the enumeration is not nearly ended, and enough is presented here to illustrate the difficulties of the subject.   What substance would be worthy of being the valet of so exacting a master ?

II. Platinum-Wire Lamps.

Edison first tried platinum and the very rare metals which are called metals of the platinum group, as they are usually found associated with it in the same minerals.   Platinum

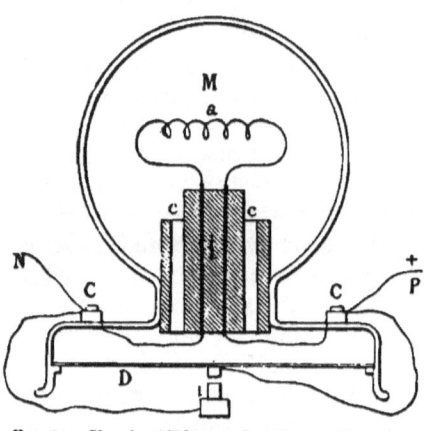

Fig. 95.—Sketch of Edison's first lamp.   From his French patent.

is easily reduced to as thin wire as can be desired, even to the point of being invisible; even in this state of fineness it retains enough consistence to keep the shape that is given to it, and its flexibility suffers it to be rolled in all conceivable directions without breaking.   Edison made with it a small spiral, which he inclosed in a vessel of glass as large as a small apple.

This vessel, which really had the shape of an apple, was closed at its base by a mass of plaster which the metallic conductors passed through, conducting the current through the platinum spiral destined to illuminate by incandescence (Fig. 95).

Here was the Edison lamp, in its first design, perfectly independent in its movements, and capable of assuming all forms and all shapes that could be desired.   It sufficed, in fact, to make the apparatus work, to place the metallic conductors in contact with any wires bringing the electric current, perhaps, from a great distance, and these electrical wires would be susceptible of gliding into all corners, like the wires of electric

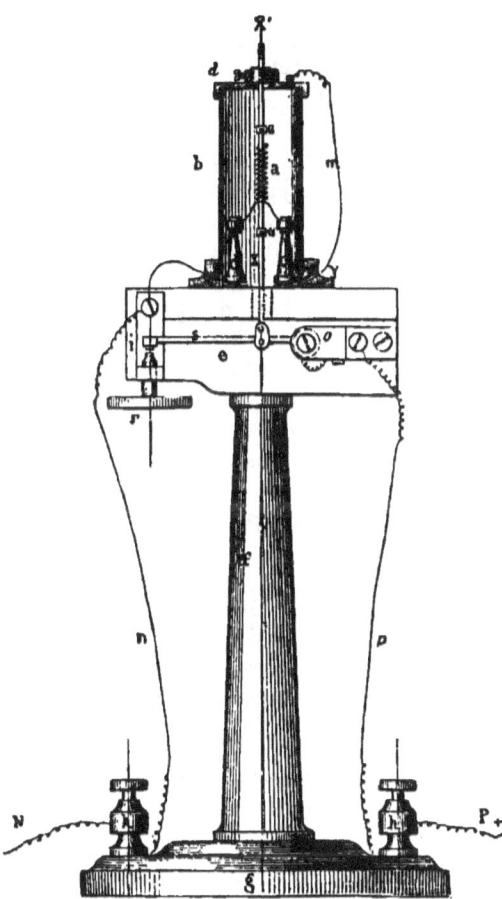

a, spiral of platinum, to be rendered incandescent. It is attached to two binding-posts. That on the right is connected by the wire *m* with the top plate *d*; the other is attached by a wire *z* to the piece *i*, and the outgoing wire *n*.

b, glass cylinder containing the spiral *a*, in which a vacuum can be produced. Mr. Edison indicates also the employment of two concentric cylinders, the annular space between which may contain certain liquids, such as the sulphate of quinine.

d, top plate of cylinder *b*.

x x′, small metallic rod passing through the center of the spiral *a*, and descending so as to rest upon the lever *s*, which it forces down whenever it is elongated by the expansion due to the heat developed in it by the passage of the current, and by the radiation from the incandescent spiral.

s, lever pivoted at *o*, and insulated. When it

Fig. 96.—Edison lamp with incandescent platinum spiral, provided with safety apparatus. (French patent, 1879).

is pressed down by the rod x x′, it forms a contact at its extremity with the piece *i*, and provides a passage for a part of the current flowing through the spiral.

i, piece carrying the safety contact and its regulating screw *r*.

P, N, *p*, *n*, *h*, *k*, wires and binding-posts for the entrance and departure of the current.

y, base of the cylinder *b*.

e, *f*, *g*, foot of the lamp.

The current arrives at P, passes through P, N, S, x x′, *d*, *m*, *c*, *a*, *c′*, *i*, *n*, *k*, N. The shunt is established through S, *i*, *n*. It is evident that this arrangement causes an intermittent action, which renders it very difficult to obtain uniformity of light in the spiral *a*.

bells now universally used. Nothing can be imagined more simple in its general aspect; we shall see that this apparent simplicity hid many real complications (Fig. 96).

[Another form of this lamp, and the one which Mr. Edison designed using before he succeeded with carbon, is shown in Fig. 97. The platinum wire is coiled upon a spool of lime or similar infusible material, *d*, which is supported by a stick, *e*, of the same material. The terminal wires, *f*, *g*, of the coil are sealed into the glass of the inclosing envelope, B, in which a vacuum is produced. The glass, B, is placed within another, *c*, which is closed by a base-piece containing an aneroid chamber, *n*, operated by the expansion of the air between the two glasses. When, on account of too much current passing through the platinum spiral, this air is abnormally heated, the lower surface of the chamber, *n*, becomes distended, and, through the medium of the post, *o*, depresses the lever, *p*, and breaks the circuit at R. This remains interrupted until the contraction of the air allows the lever to move upward and again make contact. A regulating screw serves to adjust the frame carrying the lever, and hence the expansion necessary to break the circuit.]

In the small glass globe, where the light spiral of platinum was horizontally extended, a vacuum had to be maintained for several reasons: first, to diminish the loss of electricity, and, above all, of heat; finally, to prevent the oxidation of the platinum, facilitated by its high temperature.

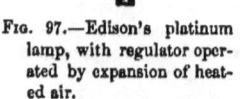

Fig. 97.—Edison's platinum lamp, with regulator operated by expansion of heated air.

When a vacuum was produced by some of the highly perfected processes, which we shall presently describe, the different gases retained in the pores of the platinum escaped. Thereupon, under the action of the passage of the current, the metal presented entirely new physical properties, so that some physicists supposed it to be a new metal. It became hard like steel, became as susceptible of polish as silver, and acquired a very high degree of elasticity, which facilitated greatly the fantastic twistings to which it was subjected. But, above all, it acquired a much greater calorific capacity, and only fused at a very high temperature, so that it could be made much more luminous. Edison even states that he succeeded in thus obtaining a light equal to eight candles with a wire that under ordinary circumstances could only have given a light of one candle.

The spiral shape given to the platinum wire was designed to diminish the loss of heat due to radiation. Every turn of the spiral or helix radiated heat upon the other spirals, so that a part of the heat radiated is utilized in a mutual reheating of the spirals one by the other. To further diminish the loss of heat the wire was covered, by means of a brush, with a thin coating of a metallic oxide ; a number of oxides were tried, those of the alkaline earth metals, and a great number of others from magnesia, lime, and zinc oxide, up to the oxides of the rarer metals, of glycenium, zirconium, and even of thorium.

In spite of all his efforts, Edison was forced, like many others before him, to abandon platinum and its related metals. The wires melt when the current acquires too high an intensity, or, if it does not melt, it disintegrates, and is thus rapidly rendered useless.

III. Lamps with Paper Carbon.

Having abandoned platinum, Edison turned his attention to carbon, which assumes in nature so many different forms. Already, in 1877, before studying the electric light, while still working on the telephone, he had several times made observations which would lead him in this direction. It was in repeating, with slight variation, the experiment known under the name of the electric cascade. A sphere of glass filled with mercury is so arranged as to empty itself through a little hole at the same time that a current of electricity traverses the mercurial cascade, which it fills with marvelous effects of light. Edison conceived the idea of placing in the glass sphere a rod of carbon for the current to pass through. This rod became incandescent without burning, because it was not surrounded by air, but with mercury, or at least a mercurial atmosphere. The incandescence appeared much more vivid than in air.

It was also under analogous conditions that the first experimenters with the electric light by incandescence, in 1845,
had worked: we refer to King and Starr. But they produced
their vacuums by means of a common air-pump, which removed the air very imperfectly, so that the vacuum left by a
removal of mercury (barometric or Torricellian vacuum, as it
is usually called) is far more complete.*

Edison would then have at once experimented with carbon
if he had not been stopped by the difficulty of obtaining filaments of carbon as fine as those of platinum, flexible enough
to permit of bending without breaking, and at the same time
firm enough to keep the form which might be given them.†
Nevertheless, one day, when lighting his cigar with a rolled
paper-lighter, he noticed that this allumette, once extinguished and freed of its ashes, left in his hand a thin spiral,
fragile without doubt, but which lasted for some time. This
spiral, in brief, was composed of vegetable carbon. A means
had now to be found to consolidate it, for, as it was, it could
not carry the smallest current, and, above all, it was necessary,
according to the method of complete enumeration, to examine
the properties and applicability of all the forms of carbon in
nature.

The work began with a mixture of graphite and pitch,
made in the form of a pencil, and carbonized with exclusion
of air in a pistol-barrel. But this did not work well. Edison
returned again to paper. He experimented successively with
all kinds of paper used in all countries, even with special
papers which he had made expressly for himself; for example, with one made from a silky cotton, very high-priced,
which he gathered in certain islands near Charleston.

[One of the earliest forms of the carbon lamp was that
shown in Fig. 99, in which the carbon filament was given a
spiral form, and joined to the leading wires by means of plastic carbon.]

* [Starr used a Torricellian vacuum, but this was far from being perfect enough
to prevent the waste of the carbon.]

† [Mr. Edison's first experiments with carbon were made with the imperfect
vacuum of a mechanical air-pump. He, therefore, did not think that carbon
could be made to stand; but, after finding platinum unsatisfactory, he returned
to carbon, using the vacuum obtainable with the mercury air-pump. He experienced no difficulty in obtaining carbon in a flexible condition, as one of the
earliest forms used was that obtained by carbonizing a cotton thread.]

This last paper gave a carbon almost absolutely free from ash—that is to say, of a homogeneity which seemed almost perfect—an indispensable condition for the regular flow of the current, and consequently for the steadiness of the light. Nevertheless, the current did not circulate with sufficient regularity in the filament of carbonized paper, and the cause of this was next determined.

In brief, paper consists of cotton fibers, pressed in disorder, one on top of the other, so as to form a sort of felting. In this felting the current finds no continuous fibers which it can follow; it finds fibers placed across its track, and has to jump from fiber to fiber, like a man crossing a brook on stepping-stones.

Now, each of these leaps constitutes a very small voltaic arc, which, quite invisible to our eyes, none the less changes the nature of the current, which ceases to be a continuous one. Moreover, these small interior sparks destroy the paper.

The discovery was important: it led him to discard all artificial products—for, necessarily, it would present this irregular felting, the cause of all the trouble —only natural fibers, produced by an exceedingly slow work of natural growth, could present the perfect homogeneity necessary for the regular passage of the current. Decidedly, the works of nature were

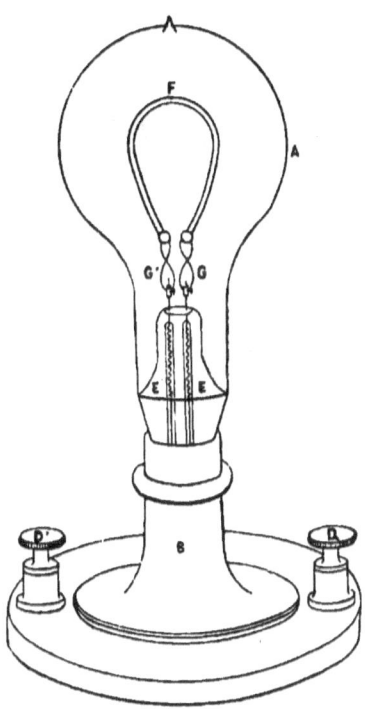

Fig. 98.—Edison lamp with Bristol-board carbon, according to his French patent of May 28, 1879.

This lamp consists of a glass globe A, in which a vacuum is created.

This globe is supported by a wooden foot B, provided with binding-screws D, D, to receive the electric wires which pass into the interior of the globe through a conical piece of insulating material E E, and terminates in two platinum plates G, G, twisted into figure eight forms.

The extremities of these platinum plates are fastened to the two ends of the carbon horseshoe.

still good for something ; even an American, and certainly no ordinary one, had to recognize the fact that human mechanism could not do everything.

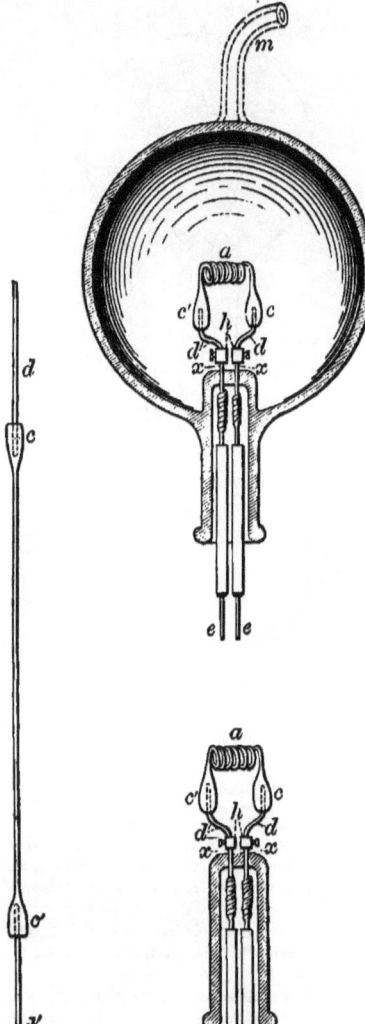

IV. Bamboo-Carbon Lamps.

He then set to work to collect all the woods or natural fibers of all countries that seemed available. Special agents were sent to China and Japan. A botanist named Ségrador, went through the south of the United States, then went to Havana, where he died, of yellow fever, when on the point of embarking, after having a short time before escaped mercurial poisoning in the Menlo Park laboratory. A fourth, named Brennan, who had already accompanied Louis Agassiz, some years before, in his great scientific voyage to Brazil, went there again to collect plants of all kinds, and he fortunately fared very well.

Soon a great variety of woods and plants began to accumulate in Menlo Park. Only three plants withstood the tests, and of these bamboo was chosen as the most perfect. But there are many varieties of bamboo to be chosen from, and nothing must be left to chance. A

Fig. 99.—Edison's carbon lamp with spiral filament. (American patent, Jan. 27, 1880.)

reliable agent, Mr. Moore, was sent to China to visit all the workshops where bamboo products were produced—all the plantations, all the localities where the plant may have suffered a modification ; he even thought of trying old pieces of bamboo that came from structures several hundred years old. The variety which proved superior to all the others was a species of Japanese bamboo, which, moreover, was found in considerable quantity, so that there was no danger of its supply running short, even when the new lamps would have everywhere replaced the old methods of illumination.

The qualities which had most to do in determining this choice were the regularity of the fibers, and, above all, the facility of division. The threads, in short, should only be one fifth of a millimetre in thickness. At first they were made round ; now they are flattened, and still thinner, for their thickness does not exceed two tenths of a millimetre, and their width three and a half tenths (Fig. 100).

This work of dividing the filaments is now done mechanically, with perfect regularity, marvelous promptitude, and remarkable economy, qualities most of all to be valued in a good manufacturing process.

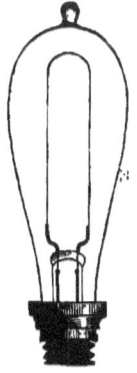

Instead of the spiral form of the former platinum wires, to-day the carbon threads have the shape of a more or less prolonged horseshoe, because the bamboo carbon does not submit to as tortuous shapes as platinum wire can assume.

Fig. 100.—Lamp with horse-shoe filament.

Finally, the most troublesome part of the fabrication of lamps is the extraction of the air, by a mercury-pump. Existing forms of pumps were first employed, such as Sprengel's and Geisler's. But the mercury had to be poured by hand, a difficult and dangerous operation, which almost poisoned Edison and his principal collaborators, notably Messrs. Batchelor and Moses, who afterward represented him in Paris, and poor Ségrador, who died from another cause, in Havana.

[The Geisler pump consists of a glass bulb of considerable size on the upper end of a vertical glass tube of large bore (from three to five eighths inch in diameter). To the lower end of this tube a reservoir of mercury (usually a glass bulb holding from thirty to forty pounds) is connected by a flexible rubber

12

tube. The former bulb is placed so as to be more than thirty inches above the level of the mercury in the reservoir. By raising this latter the upper bulb can be filled with mercury,

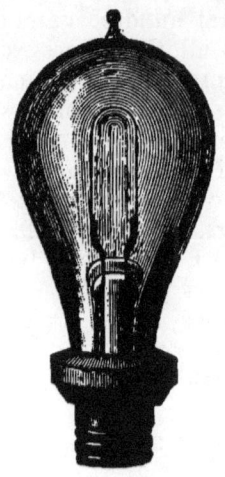

Eight-candle lamp with single filament.

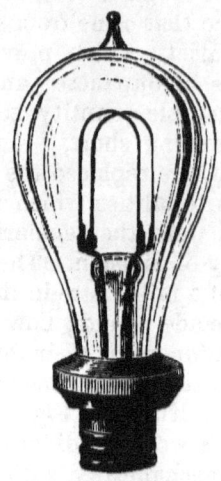

Lamp with double filament in the form of a cross, of sixteen candles.

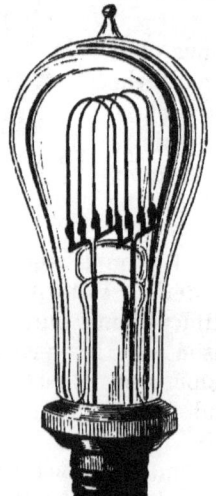

Thirty-two-candle lamp with four parallel filaments.

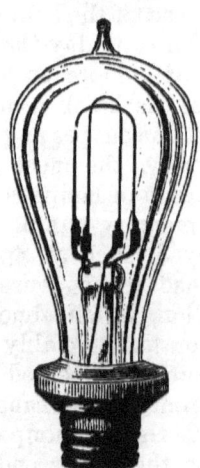

Sixteen-candle lamp with double parallel filaments.

FIGS. 101, 102, 103, 104.—The actual Edison lamps.

and its air displaced. Leading from the top of this bulb is a tube to which the lamps to be exhausted are attached. By means of a two-way cock, communication with the lamps can be shut off while the air is being driven out of the bulb, and opened when the mercury recedes into the reservoir. To ob-tain a high vacuum with this pump the mercury has to be lifted a great number of times, so that its operation by hand

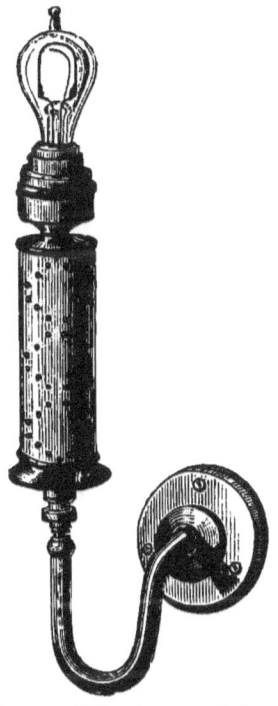

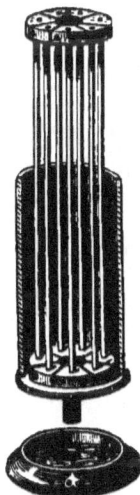

Fig. 105.—Edison lamp provided with regulator of intensity.

Fig. 106.—Carbon-rod rheostat of the regulator of intensity.

is very tiresome. When it is used in the manufacture of in-candescent lamps it is operated by power. The neck of the reservoir is usually closed by a tuft of cotton, so that there are no mercurial fumes from the pump.

The Sprengel pump, in its simplest form, consists of a fine-bore barometer-tube, through which a stream of mercury con-stantly falls from a reservoir placed above. This tube is somewhat enlarged at its upper end, from which extends a tube leading to the lamps to be exhausted. The mercury is discharged into the barometer-tube from a fine spout entering this enlarged portion. This falling stream draws the air with

it and discharges it below into a mercury-cup, into which the fall-tube, as it is called, dips. The action of this pump is very slow, but the best vacuum can be obtained with it. The mercury has to be from time to time removed from the lower receptacle and poured back into the reservoir, an operation that subjects the attendant to hurtful mercurial fumes. When this pump is used in manufacturing, the mercury is raised by power, the operation being a continuous one. It is then free from vapors, as the mercury moves in a closed channel. A combination of these two pumps is frequently employed.]

To-day the pumps, like the rest of the apparatus, are simplified, but after a hundred different trials. There are now five hundred at Menlo Park, which work automatically, without mercurial emanations, without dangerous or disagreeable manipulation, without revealing their presence otherwise than by a peculiar noise resembling a perpetual hail-storm. The perfection of the vacuum is, too, one of the principal qualities of the apparatus, for a thread of carbon which would give an intensity of ten candles in the vacuum of an ordinary air-pump would give sixteen candles in the vacuum of a mercury-pump.

Fig. 107.—Sixteen-candle lamp (three-quarter size).

Fig. 108.—Crystal chandelier of Edison lamps, used at the Paris Exposition of Electricity.

V. The Lamps actually Employed.

The exterior form of the lamp has been several times changed, on account of the several changes in shape of the incandescent filament. To-day it resembles a moderate-sized pear, about the size of the fist of a child of six or eight years old (Figs. 101, 102, 103, and 104). They are, moreover, of two dimensions. These differ not only in their exterior size, but also in the length of the carbon horsehoe-thread, which is almost twelve centimetres long in the larger—those called whole lamps—and is only about half as long in the half lamps.

The luminous intensity naturally varies with the intensity of the electric current which passes through the lamps. In good condition it reaches sixteen candles —that is to say, about two carcels for the larger lamps, and half that for the smaller lamps. Nothing prevents their being made as feeble as wanted ; all that is necessary is to shorten the horseshoe, which amounts to diminishing the extent of the incandescent luminous surface. If necessary, the lamp can thus be reduced to the proportions of a taper.

Fig. 109.—Edison lamp with shade.

Its power, on the other hand, can be increased, by the introduction of several parallel or crossed filaments of carbon (Fig. 103) instead of a single one, thus creating lights capable, perhaps, of rivaling the voltaic arc.

Not only can lamps of very varying intensity be thus made, but also, by means of a particular construction, the intensity of any given lamp can be made to vary at will through a considerable range. Edison effects this by placing under the lamp a regulator of intensity.

It is a cylindrical rheostat, containing five rods of carbon (Figs. 105 and 106), which can at will be interposed in the lamp circuit by rotating the foot which supports them. These carbon-rods, of varying size, produce a resistance which diminishes more or less the intensity of the current passing through the lamp. The result thus obtained can be compared with that produced in an oil-lamp by turning the wick up or down.

The lamp, successively improved in all its parts, is to-day more substantial than would have been deemed possible. Some are in existence that have furnished light for seven or eight hundred hours or more. For the rest, the loss of a lamp is an accident of little more moment than the break-age of the chimney of an oil-lamp, for the Edison lamp costs only twice the price of the fragile glasses which to-day break so often in our houses. They are sold in New York for thirty-five cents * (or one franc seventy-five centimes), and it seems that they can be produced at one franc twenty-five centimes, on account of economies introduced in their manu-facture. But it must be understood that this price does not include the patentee's license, which must be paid in addition, if the light be privately produced.

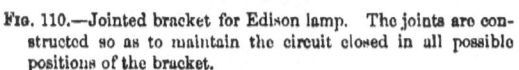

Fig. 110.—Jointed bracket for Edison lamp. The joints are con-structed so as to maintain the circuit closed in all possible positions of the bracket.

The principal accident which can happen to the incandes-cent lamp during manufacture is the breakage of the glass. After having blown it by the usual processes, it is reheated so as to anneal it, which makes it strong. [The work of sealing the filament into the globe is done before the blow-pipe. The pear-shaped envelopes are made in quantity at a factory, and are frequently blown in a mold. The glass-

* [The Edison lamps are furnished to consumers without charge. To pur-chasers of either the lamps, or of a complete isolated plant, they are sold at a dollar each.]

blower takes one of these and attaches to its top a small glass tube, which serves to connect the lamp to the pump for exhaustion. The glass stem forming the base of the lamp, with the platinum leading wires sealed into it, and the filament mounted upon them, is then introduced into the neck of the globe and united to it by fusion. With German glass it is usually necessary to blacken the exterior of the

FIG. 111.—Edison three-light chandelier.

globe after sealing, to prevent cracking by too rapid cooling. This is usually not necessary with American glass, that commonly used in this country for this work. After exhaustion the lamp is removed from the pump by fusing the glass attachment-tube, leaving the small nipple shown in the figures.] The thread of carbon also becomes hard, on account of being subjected to the passage of the current during the exhaustion of the air, which action produces on it the same effect as on platinum.

Another accident, equally to be feared, is the rupture of the carbon-thread at its points of attachment. To avoid it as far as possible, particular precautions are followed in the mode of attachment of the thread.

The two ends of the horseshoe-filament are enlarged a little, and are held in little platinum pincers,* which form the ends of the platinum wires, serving as part of the circuit of the electric current passing through the carbon horseshoe. The whole is united by a plating of copper.†

The platinum wires are naturally much larger than the carbon-thread, so they are not heated to redness. But they do heat, nevertheless, and consequently expand when the lamp is working. When it is extinguished, they return to their natural size, growing smaller as they cool. Now, these platinum wires traverse the mass of plaster which closes the lamp at its bottom. Their successive dilatations and contractions are liable to cause the formation, around them and through this mass, of a little tubular passage, through which the atmospheric air will finally insinuate itself little by little into the interior of the lamp, and destroy the vacuum. Some special process of sealing has to be devised to meet this danger.‡

This, then, is the actual Edison lamp, the latest form of which is shown in Fig. 107. It ends below in a screw-thread, by which it can be fastened on any kind of a foot, chandelier, candelabrum, bracket, etc., and it is enough to turn a key placed in the candelabrum to start it into action or to stop it. The manœuvre resembles exactly that of the operation of a gas-cock.

* [These are no longer used, the carbon filament being attached directly to copper wire, flattened and bent so as to form a sort of clamp.]

† [To render this joint an enduring one, the surface of contact between the carbon and the platinum must be cool. This is effected by increasing the amount of carbon at this point, either by enlarging the ends of the filament, moulding about it a plastic carbon, or forming a carbon deposit from a carbonaceous gas or liquid.]

‡ [In the Edison, as in all the other modern incandescent lamps, the leading wires are sealed into the glass envelope by fusion of the glass around the wires. No other mode of sealing has been found to answer, as the in-leakage of a very small quantity of air would be sufficient to destroy the carbon-filament. The plaster at the base of the lamp is merely for the purpose of attaching the glass to the threaded metal cap, by which it is held in an electrolier or bracket.]

Fig. 112.—Parlor in New York lighted with Edison lamps.

Thus constructed, the Edison lamps are adapted to all decorative appliances which we have been in the habit of using in our houses; they can be arranged on lusters (Fig. 108) as well as candles; porcelain shades can be placed over them (Fig. 109); they can be mounted on long, jointed brackets

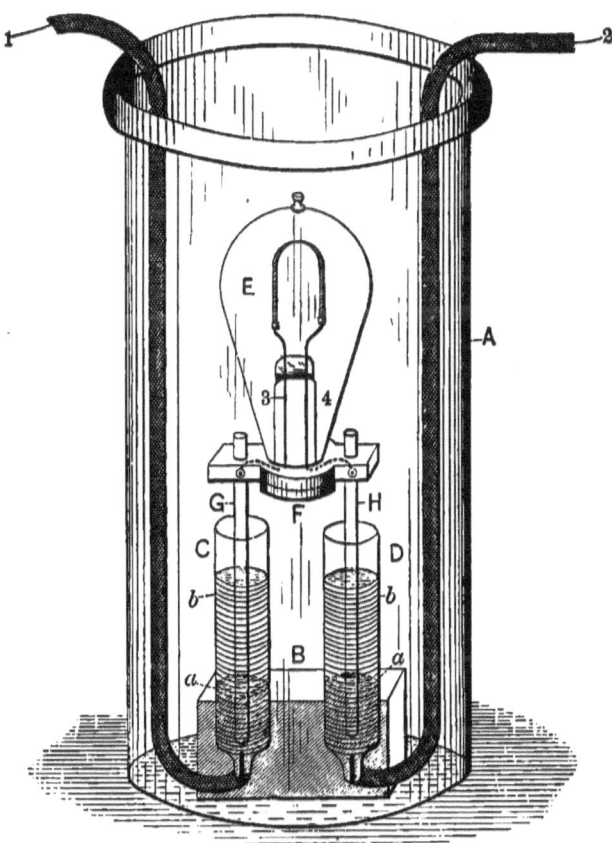

Fig. 113.—Edison mining-lamp.

like gas-brackets (Fig. 110); they can be arranged for the work of a study (Fig. 111), or the lighting of a luxurious parlor (Fig. 112).

It is even easy to place them in bronze vases or artistically designed pieces of *faïence*, imitating oil-lamps, and when surrounded by a globe the illusion is perfect. It is true that then a little light is lost. [The lamp has also been adapted to use in dangerous mines. The construction for this purpose is shown in Fig. 113. The circuit is made and broken under mercury a, a, contained in the glass tubes C, D, secured to the block B. The mercury is covered with a layer of water b, b, and the whole apparatus placed in the glass jar A.]

Mr. Edison's system of lighting is completed by special dynamo-electric machines, of which we shall speak later, in the fourth book, and by an electrical distribution, which will be explained in the fifth book. This distribution has been long experimented with at Menlo Park, in the village where the inventor resides, and he is about establishing it in New York, in the first district of the city. [This station was put in operation in September, 1882.]

CHAPTER V.

THE SWAN, MAXIM AND LANE-FOX LAMPS.

THE Edison lamp is not the only one using a carbon-filament in a vacuum. It has sisters resembling it greatly, and forms with them a distinctly characterized family. It is far from rash to suppose that this family will increase by the addition of new members in a time more or less remote. At the present moment there are at least three other lamps which ought to attract our attention by their ingenious arrangement of parts, and the extensive use which they have attained outside of France. These are the Swan, Lane-Fox, and Maxim lamps—the first two English in origin ; the last, like that of Edison, American in origin.

I. THE SWAN LAMP.

While giving above the history of incandescence, we indicated the rock upon which the first lamps with carbon-pencils, invented by the Russian savants, between 1873 and 1876, stranded. The carbon-strip, which had to be cut very thin to "strangle" the current, grew thin toward its middle, by the action of the current, and soon ended by breaking. The inventors directed all their efforts toward the discovery of

an unbreakable pencil, and it was in the midst of these experiments and laborious researches that the open-air incandescent lamp was invented in France, by M. Reynier.

Among those who studied the same problem in England
was a merchant of Newcastle, known already by several meri-
torious works on chemistry, Mr. Swan. He had already tried,
fifteen years before, to construct an incandescent lamp with a
small spiral of carbonized paper, which he placed between the
two blocks of carbon, in the interior of a glass tube, where he
had created a vacuum by pumping out the air, using the
crude means then at the experimenter's disposal. The carbon
grew red, but did not reach the elevated temperature of white
heat, which alone can convert it into a true source of light;
but it none the less was disintegrated, casting upon the walls
of the glass tube carbonaceous particles which soon obscured
them.

The principal cause of this want of success was the imperfect vacuum obtained. But, in 1877, the wonderful experiments of Mr. Crookes upon light in a vacuum showed that
much more efficacious action could be obtained with a Sprengel mercury-pump. Mr. Swan took up his studies anew, in
collaboration with Mr. Stearns, of Birkenhead, almost at the
same time that Mr. Edison attacked the same problem in
America with that energy which the Yankees bring into all
their work.

Thanks to the Sprengel pump, the vacuum was more perfect, and the lamp did better, without working perfectly by
any means, because the carbon soon became disintegrated.
We have seen that this was due to the fact that carbon,
like most other bodies, and even more than others, occluded
in its pores a considerable quantity of air and of other gases,
which the disturbance produced by the current slowly set at
liberty. A double inconvenience resulted from this: the more
perfect the vacuum that was obtained, the more the cohesion
of the carbon was injured by these internal gaseous ebullitions.

The remedy was perfectly clear: it was to bring the carbon
to incandescence while the vacuum was being produced, and
to repeat the operation several times, to completely free it of
all its gaseous guests. The filaments of carbon subjected to
this prolonged treatment became greatly modified; they grew
very much harder, and acquired an elasticity that they would
hardly have been deemed capable of.

An analogous fact had already been proved by Mr. Edison in the case of platinum. It may be supposed that his experiments, already known to the world, had shown Mr. Swan the road to be followed in his studies of carbon.

It was only at the end of the year 1880 that Mr. Swan succeeded in giving his carbon-thread the solidity that characterizes it to-day, and on October 20th he presented his lamp to the Philosophic and Literary Society of Newcastle. The carbon-filament is now made out of cotton thread, which is bent into a horseshoe-shape with a spiral turn in its middle. These cotton tresses are subjected to numerous operations before being used in the lamps.

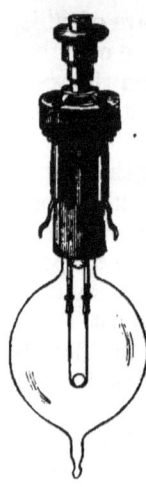

They are first plunged into sulphuric acid, diluted with one third part of water, which makes them hard like parchment; they are then placed in charcoal-dust, which is heated to orange heat. Leaving this, they are placed in the lamp—a simple bulb of transparent glass, of eight centimetres in diameter—and a vacuum is produced in this lamp with a Sprengel mercury-pump, while the electric current is kept passing through the filaments of carbonized cotton for a full half-hour. Finally, the lamp, which has a stem six centimetres long, traversed by the two platinum wires that carry the current to the carbon-filaments, is sealed (Fig. 114).

FIG. 114.—Swan incandescent lamp.

Nothing further is necessary but to force the stem of the lamp into a candlestick, as is done with a candle, when it will at once be ready for action. This candlestick receives the electric current by wires, which do not, however, prevent it from being moved, within a certain radius, with much more facility than a gas-lamp with its caoutchouc tube (Fig. 115).

Instead of being held by a candlestick, incandescent lamps can be placed in candelabra, lusters, brackets, or in ordinary lamps in place of an oil-burner. They all have more than double the intensity of an ordinary Carcel lamp, and it is easy to have them weaker if it be desired. For this the length of the incandescent filament must be diminished, or the intensity of the current reduced; but this second means is not so easy, while with the first there is no difficulty in

having at the one time lamps of all degrees of intensity, like
gas-burners, colza or petroleum lamps, candles, and tapers.

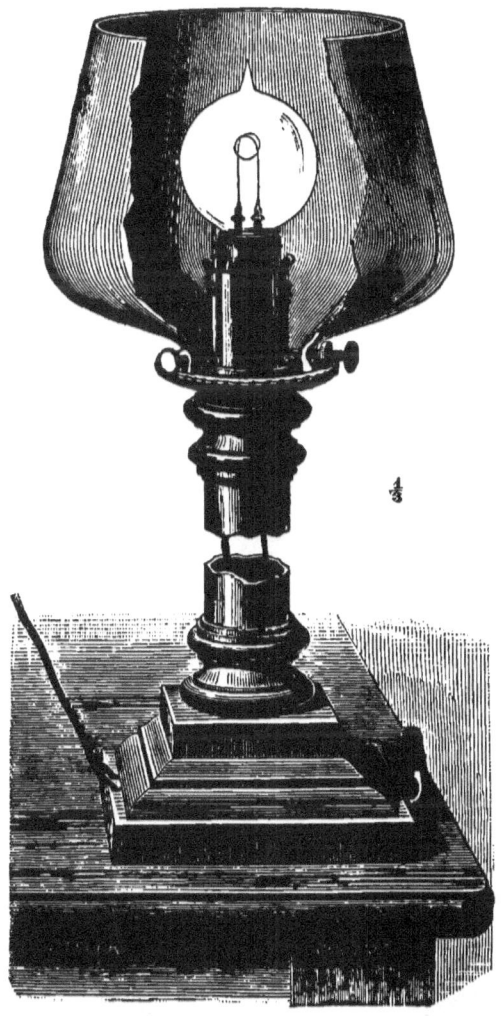

Fig. 115.—Swan table lamp.

To light or extinguish the lamp, it is enough to turn a little
electrical cock—that is to say, a key placed in the base of the
apparatus (Fig. 116), and which opens or closes the circuit.

[In the later form of this lamp the bulb is reduced in size and the neck much shortened. The mounting is elastic and of extreme simplicity (Figs. 117 and 118). The outer ends of the

platinum leading wires, a, a', are bent so as to form eyes into which hook the ends of the circuit wires, b, b'. A stout spiral spring, R, insures a perfect contact between them while allowing considerable freedom of movement.]

This system, it will be seen, also furnishes a complete solution of the problem of domestic lighting, and can supplant gas or oil in almost all their accustomed places, provided always that there

Fig. 116.—Under side of the foot of the lamp, showing the electrical connections.

be established in the streets a distributing system of electricity similar to that used at the present day for gas.

Fig. 117.—Swan lamp. Later form.

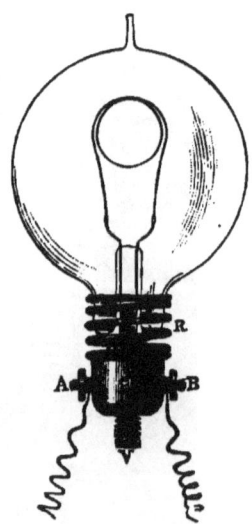

Fig. 118.—Swan lamp in socket.

Mr. Swan has not touched upon this question; herein his system is less complete than that of Mr. Edison, who has

FIG. 119.—Philosophical instrument establishment of Mr. Swan, at Newcastle, lighted by his incandescent lamps.

13

provided for everything. Mr. Swan has not yet had time to design dynamo-electric machines specially adapted to supply his lamps. He has no preference for any particular form of generator.

Nevertheless, the lamp of Mr. Swan is now used in England in a great many places. In Newcastle, the home of the inventor (Fig. 119), it lights several streets. Mr. William Spottiswoode, President of the Royal Society of London, has

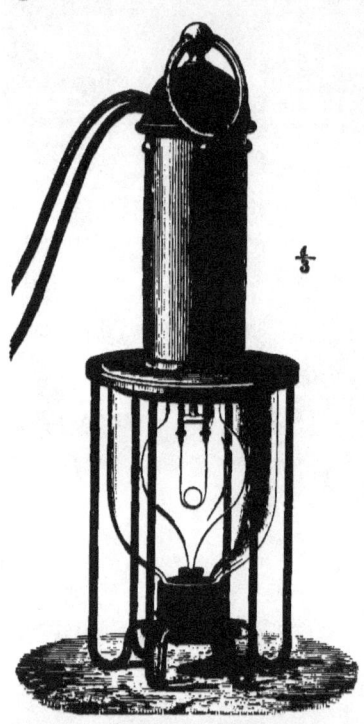

placed it, along with Jablochkoff candles, in his large residence of Coombes-Bank; and the great metal-worker, Sir William Armstrong, has also established it in his house.

One of the railroad companies of England employs it to light its cars, to the great satisfaction of travelers, who can read with pleasure. It has also been successfully tried in mines, with a special model surrounded with water, and therefore incapable of igniting the fire-damp, even in case of breakage of the apparatus (Fig. 120). Finally, it has been used in submarine operations with sounding apparatus.

We cite these different examples as proof of the many applications already in use. Many others can be added, because, at the present time,

FIG. 120.—Swan mining-lamp.

the Swan lamp is the most used of all incandescent lamps in actual practice—that is to say, in paying operation.

The thread of incandescent carbon is a little thicker in the Swan lamps than in Edison's, and consequently their luminous power is a little greater when they receive a current of sufficient intensity; but it is well understood that they need more of it to attain the same degree of luminosity, that of white heat. The inventor hoped to guarantee an illuminating power of twenty English candles, which is more than two Carcel lamps, and he affirms that under these conditions one horse-power would suffice for ten lamps.

II. THE LANE-FOX LAMP.

The lamp of Mr. Lane-Fox (Fig. 121), of English origin, like that of Mr. Swan, resembles it a great deal in its exterior form and dimensions. It is also formed of a very thin carbon-filament, bent into the shape of an elongated horseshoe, but without a central spiral; this thread is in the same manner placed in a glass bulb, where the best vacuum possible is made. Nevertheless, the lamp of Mr. Lane-Fox differs from that of his compatriot by two principal points, and those quite important, which we shall examine in succession.

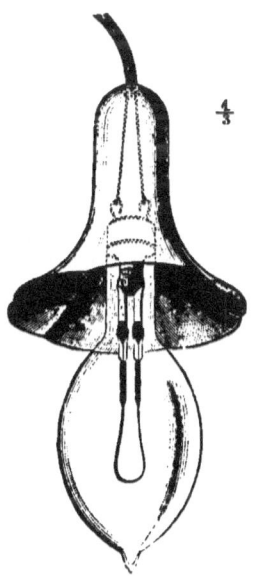

The thread of carbon, destined to become incandescent, has neither the same origin nor the same nature. Generally it is a fiber of couch-grass, carbonized with special precautions. The carbon becomes just as hard as that of Mr. Swan, and is, in the same way, deprived of the air hidden in its pores, thanks to the same precaution; it is kept incandescent while the vacuum is forming.

Instead of creating the vacuum by aid of the Sprengel pump, Mr. Lane-Fox prefers a method analogous to that which is in use in France by M.

Fig. 121.—Lane-Fox incandescent lamp.

Alvergniat, for the manufacture of Geissler tubes, in which light produces such beautiful effects in different gases. This method consists, briefly, in obtaining the same vacuum as exists above the mercury in a barometer, in what is called the barometric chamber. But ingeniously devised precautions are taken to keep the atmosphere free from mercury-vapor, which ordinarily would fill this chamber.

Mr. Lane-Fox's lamp is further characterized by the manner in which the thread of incandescent carbon is attached to

the metallic wires which conduct the electric current to it.
Instead of being thickened as it approaches the points of contact, like the filament of Mr. Swan, the filament of Mr. Lane-
Fox preserves the same diameter. But the two extremities
are fastened in the axis of two small plumbago cylinders,
where they join platinum wires relatively large, which at
their other ends are attached
to the ordinary copper conducting wire.

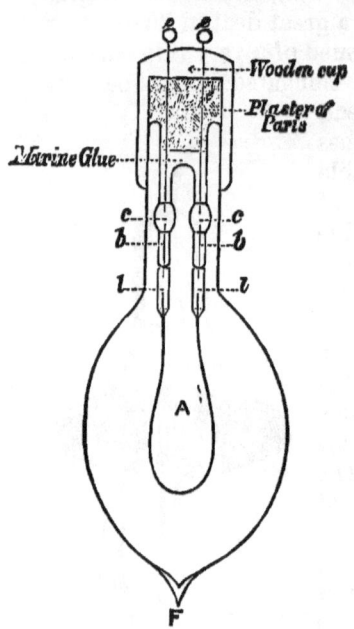

FIG. 122.—Section of Lane-Fox lamp.

[To prevent undue heating
of the leading-wires, these latter are fused into small pillars of glass, the lower ends
of which are expanded into
small globes containing mercury. The platinum wires dip
into these, as also the copper
leads which serve to make
electrical connection with the
circuit upon which the lamp
is placed. The mercury is retained in place by a filling of
marine glue, and over this a
plug of plaster. The disposition of parts is shown in
Fig. 122, in which $c\,c$ are the
mercury reservoirs, and $b\,b$
the glass pillars in which the
platinum leads are sealed.
The globe and this stem, with
the wires mounted in it, are joined together at the base of the
neck of the former by fusion, as in the case of the two previous lamps.]

Mr. Lane-Fox, like Mr. Swan, has arranged no system for
distribution or production of electricity. But he has invented
an apparatus which automatically regulates the intensity of
the current, and keeps it almost constant at the wished-for
point, or at least restrains its variations within certain limits,
without the necessity of any attention.

This automatic regulator works under the action of the
same current that goes through the lamps, like the regulator
of voltaic-arc lamps, and it is mounted on a special derived

circuit ; only, instead of bringing the carbon-rods together, it interposes in the path of the current, at the right moment and in proper quantity, resistance apparatus, which increase the resistance of the circuit, and consequently diminish the force of the current which finally passes through it.

The lamps of the Lane-Fox system are less employed here (in France) than the other incandescent lamps, and we know of no applications of them of sufficient importance to be worth describing. The truth is, that no company has been organized to introduce them.

III. THE MAXIM LAMP.

[The lamp of Mr. Hiram S. Maxim has the same general features of those above described. The filamentary con- ductors are stamped from paper, and have the form of the letter M, instead of a simple loop. They are carbonized between sheets of paper in iron molds, and are after- ward subjected to a treat- ment to render them as ho- mogeneous as possible. Mr. Edison abandoned paper as a material for his incandes- cent filaments because of the difficulty of getting it homogeneous. Mr. Maxim endeavored to overcome this defect by heating the fila- ments to incandescence in a carbonaceous atmosphere. The gas is decomposed by the heat of the filament, and the liberated carbon deposited upon it, those parts which are thinnest, and consequently hottest, receiving the heaviest de- posit.

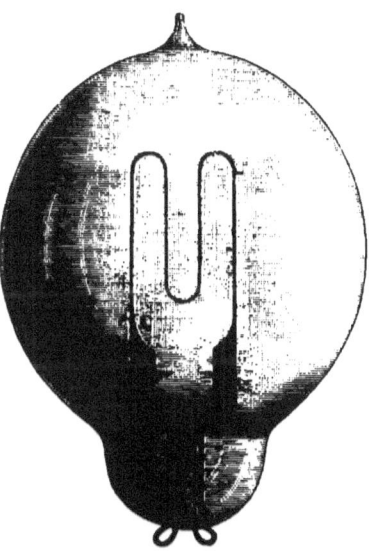

Fig. 123.—Maxim incandescent lamp. (Full size.)

Filaments of very uniform conductivity can be produced in this manner, and any form of carbon can be so treated. A rarefied atmosphere of gasoline-vapor is that usually employed, and the deposit is commonly made in a separate vessel before the filament is mounted for sealing in the final globe, though it can be readily effected while the lamps are on the mercury-pump before the final exhaustion is completed. This method of equalizing the resistance of a filament is also used by Lane-Fox, and an analogous one was employed by Sawyer and Mann.

The platinum leading wires are attached to the filament by a species of clamp. The ends of the filament are enlarged, as are also, those of the leading wires. The two are then clamped together by means of a minute bolt provided with a nut passing through each— a remarkably expensive mode of attachment. The leading wires are sealed into the glass of the globe, as in the other lamps of this kind. The appearance of the complete lamp is shown in Fig. 123, and the lamp mounted in its socket, in Fig. 124.]

Fig. 124.—Maxim incandescent lamp and socket.
(Full size).

IV. New Lamps.

[Lamps of the same general character as these, but differing from each other in the mode of manufacture of the filament, of mounting it upon the leading wires, and of sealing these latter into the inclosing globe, have been designed by various other inventors, but they do not call for a description here.

Two new lamps have, however, recently been brought to public notice which deserve mention. One is of American origin, the invention of Mr. Alexander Bernstein; and the other is an Italian invention, devised by Signor Antonio Cruto. In the first of these the light-giving portion consists of a small tube of carbon, instead of the fine carbon wire of the lamps described above. It is mounted upon platinum leading wires, and inclosed in an exhausted glass globe, as in other incandescent lamps. The carbon cylinders were first made by carbonizing straws, and later by depositing carbon upon a metallic wire and afterward dissolving the metal out. Both of these methods were finally aban-

doned, and the tubes produced by rolling paper about a metal mandrel, the successive layers of paper being made to adhere by means of gum or paste. The whole was then carbon- ized in a mold from which the air was excluded. The shrinkage of these paper tubes during carbonization was very great, and paper was therefore replaced by finely woven cotton or silk fabric. The earlier carbons were made straight, but it has been found possible to produce the tubes in the form of an arch, and the present lamp is therefore constructed with a curved carbon. It is represented in Fig. 125. These carbon tubes are said to be ex- tremely elastic, so much so that they can be drawn out nearly straight, and

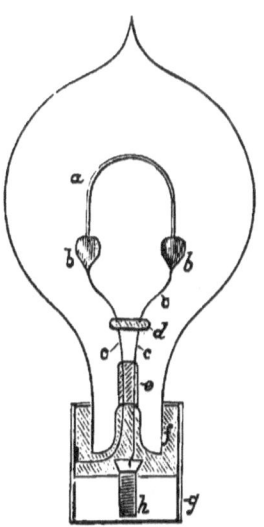

Fig. 125.—The Bernstein lamp.

will spring back to their normal shape. The lamp differs from those previously made in being of very low resistance. It is therefore not suitable for distribution on a large scale, but will answer well enough for separate installation, such as those of a shop or store.

In the first descriptions of the lamp of Signor Cruto, the incandescent organ was said to be a fine carbon tube, formed by depositing carbon upon a platinum wire heated to incan- descence while immersed in oil, and then dissolving out the platinum. It, however, appears from later descriptions that the platinum is not removed, so that the light-giving portion is really a compound filament, consisting of a platinum core and carbon exterior. This lamp was exhibited at the Munich Exhibition in 1882, and that at Vienna last year, but has not yet made its appearance in this country.]

CHAPTER VI.

MEASUREMENT OF INCANDESCENT LAMPS.

[To measure an electic lamp two quantities must be determined—the electrical work done per second to maintain the light, and the candle-power. The first of these is equal to E C, the product of the difference of potential between the terminals of the lamp, by the intensity of the current flowing through it. The difference of potential is generally measured directly, but the current can be more accurately determined by measuring the resistance, and then calculating it from the equation $C = \dfrac{E}{R}$, which is the method pursued in the case of small currents such as those through incandescent lamps. This resistance must be measured while the lamp is burning at the desired candle-power, as it changes with the temperature, becoming less in the case of carbon and greater in that of metals, as the temperature is raised. It will not be necessary to enter here upon a consideration of the details of the methods and instruments of electrical measurements, but only to indicate, in a general way, how the electro-motive force and resistance are determined. To measure resistance an arrangement termed a

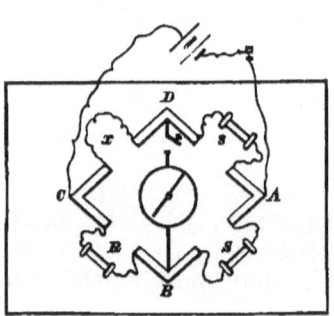

Fig. 126.—Wheatstone's bridge.

Wheatstone bridge (shown in Fig. 126) is generally used. Its action depends upon the regularity of the fall of potential throughout a circuit. If the two ends of a wire are at different potential, a point at the center of the wire will be at a potential equal to half that of the ends, and generally a point anywhere between the two ends will have a potential depending on its position. Further, a current will only flow through a wire when there is a difference of potential between its ends. In the figure the current enters at A, and divides between the two circuits A D C and A B C. If these be joined by a cross-wire, no current will flow through this wire when its ends are at the same potential. This will be the case when the resistance x is to the resistance R as the resistance s is to S.

From this we have the unknown resistance $x = R\dfrac{s}{S}$. A galvanometer placed in this cross-circuit indicates the presence of a current through it by the deflection of its needle. In the practical form of this apparatus the resistances s and S are taken of such values that the ratio $\dfrac{s}{S}$ may vary from $\frac{1}{100}$ of an ohm up to 100 ohms. When this ratio equals 1, the resistance to be measured, x, is evidently equal to the adjustable resistance R.

The most accurate way of determining a difference of potential is by the use of a condenser—an apparatus consisting of a number of sheets of tin-foil, separated from each other by means of paraffined paper, or mica, of which a familiar example is the Leyden-jar. The charge of electricity received by a condenser will be proportional to the electro-motive force of the charging current. To use it in measuring the electro-motive force of an electric lamp, it is first charged by a source of electricity of known electro-motive force, such as a standard cell, and then discharged through

FIG. 127.—Bunsen photometer.

a galvanometer and the deflection of the needle noted. The terminal wires are then connected with the terminals of the lamp, and again discharged through the galvanometer. This second deflection will then give the electro-motive force of the lamp-current in terms of the standard, and if this, as is usually the case, is unity, directly in volts.

The intensity of any light is determined by comparing it

to a standard candle. A number of different photometers, as
the instruments for making this comparison are called, have
been devised, but that most largely used is the one invented
by Bunsen. The operation depends upon the action of transmitted and reflected light. If a grease spot be made on a
sheet of paper, the spot will appear darker than the surrounding surface when the light is in front of the paper, and lighter

Fig. 128.—Method of using the Bunsen photometer.

when behind it. If the paper be equally illuminated on both
sides, the spot will be indistinguishable from the rest of the
sheet. In the actual instrument the paper is mounted in a
dark box, generally sheet-iron painted black, being placed
across the length of the box, through each end of which the
rays from the lights enter. Two inclined mirrors are placed
so that they meet at the back edge of the paper disk, as

shown in Fig. 127. The eye of the observer is placed in front, so that the reflection of the spot in .the mirrors is seen. When the reflections disappear, the two sides of the paper disk are equally illuminated, and the relative intensities of the lights are to each other as the squares of their distances from the disk. The dark box is mounted upon rollers, so that it can be readily moved between the two lights along a track, which is commonly graduated to give at once the intensity of the light being measured. Two candles are generally used as a standard instead of one. The whole apparatus is inclosed in a dark chamber, as shown in Fig. 128.

A great many tests of the performance of incandescent lamps have been made in the past few years, but it will suffice to give here the results obtained by the committees at the International Exhibition at Paris in 1881, and at Munich in 1882. The lamps examined by the Paris committee were those of Edison, Maxim, Swan, and Lane-Fox. They were measured at sixteen and thirty-two candles, with the results given in the following tables :

At Sixteen Candles.

LAMPS.	Edison.	Swan.	Lane-Fox.	Maxim.
Candles...................................	15·38	16·61	16·36	15·96
Ohms....................................	137·4	32·78	27·40	41·11
Volts...................	89·11	47·30	43·63	56·49
Ampères..................................	0·651	1·471	1·593	1·380
Volt-ampères..............................	57·98	60·24	69·53	78·05
Kilogramme-metres........................	5·911	7·059	7·089	7·939
Lamps per horse-power....................	12·73	10·71	10·61	9·48
Candles per horse-power...................	196·4	177·92	173·58	151·27
Lamps of sixteen candles per horse-power......	12·28	11·12	10·85	9·45

At Thirty-two Candles.

LAMPS.	Edison.	Swan.	Lane-Fox.	Maxim.
Candles..............................	31·11	33·21	32·71	31·93
Ohms.....................................	130·03	31·75	26·59	39·60
Volts..	98·39	54·21	48·22	62·27
Ampères	0·7585	1·758	1·815	1·578
Volt-ampères	74·62	94·88	87·65	98·41
Kilogramme-metres.....	7·604	9·67	8·936	10·03
Lamps per horse-power....................	9·88	7·90	8·47	7·50
Candles per horse-power................	307·25	262·49	276·89	239·41
Lamps of thirty-two candles per horse-power....	9·60	8·20	8·65	7·48

The lamps examined by the Munich committee were the Edison, Maxim, Swan, Siemens, and Cruto. The results are given in the following table:

Results of the Munich Committee.

LAMPS.	Mean spherical luminous intensity in normal candles.	Resistance when hot, in ohms.	Difference of potential, in volts.	Current in ampères.	ELECTRICAL WORK IN		Mean spherical intensity per horse-power.	Number of lamps per horse-power.
					Volt-ampères.	Horse-power.		
Edison B........	11·69	67·68	55·78	0·825	46·02	0·0625	186·90	23·36 (8 candles)
" A.......	15·32	139·60	103·05	0·755	77·80	0·1057	144·88	9·05 (16 ")
Maxim........	13·34	47·01	65·07	1·384	90·06	0·1224	108·98	3·89 (28 ")
Swan A........	10·95	31·91	38·38	1·222	46·90	0·0637	171·78	17·18 (10 ")
" B........	37·17	87·03	118·02	1·282	151·30	0·2056	180·75	4·52 (40 ")
Siemens	14·90	104·72	95·74	0·915	87·60	0·1191	125·14	7·82 (16 ")
Müller A	18·43	58·62	74·04	1·263	93·51	0·1271	145·01	7·26 (20 ")
" B	43·08	59·52	105·22	1·779	187·19	0·2544	169·33	3·39 (50 ")
" C........	102·35	65·41	155·15	2·367	367·24	0·4991	205·05	2·05 (100 ")
Cruto..........	8·47	8·16	22·15	2·715	60·14	0·0817	103·58	10·36 (10 ")

In each of these tables the results are expressed in French horse-power, which, it will be remembered, is equal to 735·75 volt-ampères or watts. To obtain the number of lamps in English horse-power, it is necessary to divide 746 by the volt-ampères in the table.

These two sets of measurements are not directly comparable, as the candle-power in the first is obtained by a horizontal measurement at an angle of 45° to the plane of the loop, and in the second it is averaged so as to be the same in all directions.

This latter method of expressing the candle-power places the incandescent lamp at a disadvantage with gas, the illuminant with which it is directly compared in all discussions of its use in general lighting, while it does not possess any advantage in the matter of accuracy. It would seem to be better to adhere to the established practice in gas measurements, which is to measure the flat flame horizontally, at right angles to its plane.

The Munich report is, moreover, obviously erroneous in the method of obtaining the number of lamps per horse-power. For instance, the table exhibits a great discrepancy between the economy of the Edison eight and sixteen candle lamps.

The reason of this is, however, readily apparent on finding that the eight candle lamp was measured at 11·69 candles, a much more economical incandescence than its normal one, while the sixteen candle lamp was measured at 15·32 candles, a somewhat less economical incandescence than the normal.   In several other cases lamps are measured at an incandescence considerably above or below the standard to which it is reduced in the last column.   The consideration adduced in Chapter VII of this book will enable the reader to understand why such a procedure is not permissible.

Neither of these tests, moreover, shows the performance of the latest lamps.   The carbon-filament has been steadily improved, and the present lamps are consequently more economical.   No official tests have, however, been made of these.]

CHAPTER VII.

CONDITIONS OF EFFICIENCY IN THE INCANDESCENT LAMP.

[IF a current of electricity be passed through a wire which offers resistance to its passage, the energy of the current will be converted into heat, and the temperature of the wire will rise.   The limit to the increase of its temperature will evidently be the point at which the loss of heat per second is equal to the supply.   Otherwise the temperature would decrease if the loss were at a greater rate than the supply, and continue increasing if it were at a less rate.   It might at first be supposed that the specific heat of a body should be taken into account.   But a moment's consideration will show us that this only enters as an element in determining the temperatures to which the same weights of different substances will be elevated by a definite quantity of heat.   If the supply of heat be continued until a constant temperature is attained, then calorific capacity ceases to have any influence, and the amount of heat lost per second must be equal to that supplied.

A hot wire exposed freely to the air will lose heat in three ways: 1, by radiation ; 2, by conduction through the supports ; and 3, by convection, through the medium of the enveloping air, the successive particles of which become heated by contact with the wire, and rising give place to others. In the case of an incandescent lamp, the filament of which is placed in an exhausted vessel, this latter source of loss is avoided. It will therefore lose heat only by radiation and conduction. The loss of heat by the latter means will depend upon the temperature of the wire and its cross-section, while the loss by radiation will depend upon the temperature and the surface exposed. Neglecting for the moment the loss by conduction, it is evident that, to maintain two wires at the same temperature by the same expenditure of heat per second, these wires must have equal surfaces, which will be the case when the lengths of the wires are to each other inversely as their diameters. So far as radiation is concerned, then, a short, thick wire is as economical for the purpose of incandescence as a long, thin one. But since the loss of heat by conduction through the supports will increase with the cross-section of the wire, economy demands that the wire be as thin as possible, that this loss may be reduced to a minimum.

In a wire so circumstanced, what will be the relation of its size to the temperature to which it will be raised by a given amount of heat? Let us take two wires of the same material and length, but of different diameters, d and d_1, and generate in them the same amount of heat per second—that is, let $C^2R = C_1^2R_1$.

To maintain the wires at constant temperatures the heat generated in each per second per unit of area must be, as stated above, the same as that radiated. By Newton's law of cooling, the rates at which the wires will lose heat will be directly proportional to the excess of their temperatures above that of the inclosing vessel. But the radiation per second from unit surface—which is the rate of cooling—in the two wires, will be inversely as the diameters of the wires, and we shall therefore have $t : t' = d_1 : d$, in which t and t' are the temperatures above those of the inclosing vessels, to which the wires will be raised. This law is, however, accurate only when the temperature of the wire is but slightly in excess of that of the inclosing vessel. Dulong and Petit, experimenting through a range of temperature of from 20° to 240° centigrade, found that the rate of cooling was not directly proportional to the excess of temperature, but that it was greater at high than at low temperatures. They found that it could be expressed by a formula of the form,

$$H - h = m \left(a^\theta - a^{\theta^1} \right),^*$$

in which H is the total loss of heat from unit area of the radiating body per second, and θ its temperature, while θ^1 is the temperature of the inclosure, and h the amount of heat received from it on each unit of area of the radiating body; m is a constant, depending upon the substance and the nature of its surface, and a a constant, the value of which is 1.0077, when the temperature is reckoned on the centigrade scale. This formula may evidently be written,

$$H - h = m a^{\theta^1} \left(a^{\theta - \theta^1} - 1 \right).$$

The exponent $\theta - \theta^1$ is the excess of temperature of the radiating body over that of the inclosure. Denoting this by θ_1, the second term of the equation becomes $m a^{\theta^1} \left(a^{\theta_1} - 1 \right)$. Developing a^{θ_1} into a series, we have,

$$a^{\theta_1} = 1 + \theta_1 \log a + \tfrac{1}{2} \left(\theta_1 \log a \right)^2 + \tfrac{1}{6} \left(\theta_1 \log a \right)^3 + \text{etc.,}$$

which becomes, on substituting the numerical value of $\log a$,

$$1 + .0077 \theta_1 + \tfrac{1}{2} \left(.0077 \theta_1 \right)^2 + \tfrac{1}{6} \left(.0077 \theta_1 \right)^3 + \text{etc., and}$$

$$m a^{\theta^1} \left(a^{\theta_1} - 1 \right) = m \, 1.0077^{\theta^1} \left\{ 1 + \tfrac{1}{2} \left(.0077 \theta_1 \right) + \tfrac{1}{6} \left(.0077 \theta_1 \right)^2 + \text{etc.} \right\}.$$

This shows us that the radiation from unit area, instead of being directly proportional to the temperature θ_1, is proportional to the temperature multiplied by a factor depending on it. When the temperature is such that $.0077 \theta_1$ may be neglected in comparison with unity, this factor becomes practically constant, and the formula agrees with Newton's law.†

In the case of the two wires, then, instead of having the temperatures inversely as the diameter of the wires, we shall have them in a less ratio, depending upon the values of these factors. Though the law of Dulong and Petit was experimentally proved through only a small range of temperature, it may, however, be taken as expressing the fact that the higher the temperature the more rapid the radiation of heat. From this it results that the temperature does not increase at the same rate as the generation of heat necessary to maintain it. Doubling the heat-expenditure will, therefore, not double the temperature, and as this latter is increased a larger and larger proportional quantity of heat is necessary to sustain it.

* Maxwell's " Theory of Heat."
† Deschanel's "Physics," sixth edition. New York, 1883.

In our example of the wires, if we take them of diameters as one to two, by Newton's law we shall have the smaller wire at twice the temperature of the larger, but it will have only one half the surface of the latter. By the law of Dulong and Petit the temperature of the smaller wire will not be twice that of the larger, but something less. It would seem, therefore, that there is no advantage in maintaining a small wire at a high, over a larger one at a lower, temperature. And this would be true, if the light emitted by an incandescent body was directly proportional to its temperature. But this is far from being the case.

A body heated below 977° Fahr. emits only obscure rays which affect us as heat, but are incapable of exciting vision. With an increase of temperature luminous rays begin to make their appearance, and increase both in intensity and amount as the temperature is carried up. This increase is, moreover, extremely rapid. At first a considerable augmentation of temperature is necessary to perceptibly increase the light, but soon slight additions to the temperature produce large increase of the light emitted. Experimenting with platinum raised to incandescence by means of the electric current, Dr. John W. Draper found that the light emitted and the temperature were related to each other as follows:

Temperature of the Platinum.	Intensity of Light.
980° Fahr.	0·00
1,900	·34
2,015	·62
2,130	1·73
2,245	2·92
2,360	4·40
2,475	7·24
2,590	12·34

From which it appears that the light emitted at 2,590° was somewhat more than thirty-six times that emitted at a temperature of 1,900°. The law of the increase of the light with the temperature has never been formulated, and I am not aware that experiments have been carried on at higher temperatures than those used by Dr. Draper. The melting-point of platinum placed a limit to the temperature which he could obtain, but with the incandescent carbon-lamp this limit is so greatly removed, that it would seem to offer an excellent experimental means of pursuing this investigation through a sufficient range of temperature to enable the relation to be definitely formulated. The results, however, could at best be only approximate, owing to the great difficulty of measuring high temperatures with accuracy.

While it is difficult to establish the direct relation between the temperature of a body and the light emitted by it, it is comparatively easy to determine the precise relation between the light emitted and the factor upon which the temperature depends — the heat-expenditure. It is possible to measure accurately both the heat generated in an incandescent filament per second ($C^2 R$ or $E C$), and the candle-power, and, by doing this through a sufficient range, to detect the law of their relation. That this relation should be a general one, and not simply one applicable to a particular case, the supply of heat must be expressed in terms of some definite standard. This is to be found in the rate of the generation of heat per unit surface. We can, for instance, determine the amounts of heat which must be generated per second per unit of surface to give one, two, three, etc., candles for the same surface ; or we can assume a unit rate of heat-generation per unit of surface, and measure the candle-powers corresponding to any number of such units. In either case we have a definite relation between the heat-expenditure and the light, independent of the diameter or length of the incandescent body, provided, of course, that the body is so circumstanced that it loses heat only by radiation, or that the loss by other means is calculable.

Though we have no experimental determination of this relation through any wide range, we yet have some data, in the results obtained in the measurement of incandescent lamps, which give us an idea of its character. Referring to the measurements of the Paris committee (page 185), it will be seen that, to double the light, the current energy ($E C$) was increased, for the Maxim and Lane-Fox lamps, twenty-six per cent ; for the Edison, twenty-eight per cent ; and for the Swan, thirty-seven per cent. Taking the first of these we see that, while the candle-powers were to each other as one to two, the expenditures of energy to maintain them were as one hundred to one hundred and twenty-six ; that is, the candle-powers were to each other as the cubes of the current energy. Assuming this relation to hold, up to the point where the current energy is doubled, we should have the candle-power in

14

the latter case eight times that in the former, or would get sixty-four candles instead of sixteen, with the same expenditure of energy. Since the two measurements were those of the same filament, this ratio of the expenditures of energy is, it will be seen, that of the rates of the generation of heat per unit of surface. It can hardly be supposed that the relation between the heat-expenditure and the light would be as simple a one as this, through a wide range of temperature. Doubling the energy required to maintain a lamp at thirty-two candles would probably increase the light more than eight times, while doubling that necessary to produce one candle would show a much less gain in light. The real relation would be a varying one—probably one in which the light would increase slowly at first, then with great rapidity, and, finally, more slowly again.

However this may be, the important point to be noted is that, within attainable experimental limits, the light emitted by an incandescent body increases very rapidly as the temperature is raised, and that, therefore, economy demands the maintaining the filament of an incandescent lamp at the highest possible temperature. The practical limit to the temperature attainable in an incandescent filament is that imposed by the ability of the filament to stand the strain to which it is then subjected. In the arc-lamp the incandescent material is constantly renewed, and hence it may be raised to a much higher temperature than a filament whose continuity must be preserved. We accordingly get much more light for a given expenditure of current energy in the former than in the latter case. If it were possible to maintain a filament at the same temperature as the carbon-points of the arc, we should get — with the same surface exposed —not only as good but a superior result, as the filament would be free from loss of heat by exposure to the air, and there would be a smaller loss by conduction. We are, however, very far from this condition in present incandescent lamps, and can not hope to ever reach it, though we may reasonably expect to approach it much more nearly than has yet been done. All incandescent lamps are run at comparatively low temperatures, but improvements are constantly being made in the filaments, which will better fit them for economical working.

Even at the low temperatures at which it is at present run,

the incandescent lamp is still a vastly more efficient instrument for converting heat into light than a gas-flame. Taking
the measurement of the Edison lamp, made by the Paris committee, we find the expenditure of energy in maintaining the
filament at sixteen candles to be 60·16 watts, or ·08 horse-
power, and the expenditure per candle 3·76 watts. To arrive
at similar figures for gas it is only necessary to calculate the
mechanical equivalent of the heat produced by the combustion of the requisite amount of gas. Ordinary coal-gas giving
a sixteen-candle light, with a consumption of five feet an
hour, may be taken as measuring thirty-five cubic feet to the
pound, and this amount as evolving by its combustion 12,500
pound-degree (centigrade) units of heat. Five feet will therefore evolve 1,785 such units, which are equal to 810,000 calories, since the centigrade pound-degree equals 453·6 gramme-
degrees. As this is the expenditure per hour, that per second
will be (810,000 ÷ 3,600) 225 calories, equal to 945 joules, since
one calorie equals 4·2 joules. As a joule per second is one
watt, we have energy expended in a five-foot gas-flame at the
rate of 945 watts, or 1·26 horse-power. The expenditure per
candle is therefore (945 ÷ 16) 59 watts, as against 3·76 in the
Edison incandescent lamp. This latter is consequently over
fifteen times more efficient than a gas-flame as a light-pro-
ducer. Even allowing this amount of heat-energy to represent twenty candles with gas, the incandescent lamp is still
twelve times as efficient.

This great superiority of the incandescent lamp has hardly
received the attention it deserves. Comparison has usually
been made between it and the arc-lamp, and its comparative
inefficiency chiefly dwelt upon. Yet it surpasses gas far more
in this respect than the arc-lamp does it, for, by the tests made
at Paris, the comparative efficiency of these two is as one to
seven.

The considerations presented in this chapter indicate very
clearly the direction to be taken by efforts to improve the incandescent lamp. It has unquestionably taken its final form
—that of a strip of resisting material inclosed in an exhausted glass envelope — a form of such extreme simplicity that
nothing more remains to be done in this respect. Attention
must hereafter be concentrated upon the incandescing strip
itself, as on its improvement depends whatever gain in economy is to be obtained. Methods of constructing this incan-

descent portion must be sought for which will give it increased
ability to withstand the disintegrating effects of high temperatures, and the disrupting action of the current. The problem is, therefore, but partly electrical; it is mainly one concerned with a consideration of the structural characteristics
of bodies upon which their power of withstanding strains of
such character depends.]

BOOK IV.

PRODUCTION OF ELECTRIC CURRENTS.

The production of electric currents by chemical action
goes back to the discovery of Volta in 1800, and it is the form
which he adopted for one of his first apparatus that gave
them the name of *Voltaic Piles*, which is applied to all those
which are used for the same purpose.* They are called
hydro-electric batteries to distinguish them from *thermo-electric* batteries, in which currents are produced by the direct action of heat upon two metals. The first batteries used were
too weak, and were of no service except for laboratory experiments, which were very costly. Bunsen's battery, much
more powerful, answered in some exceptional cases; but it
was only after the invention of the machines founded on the
discoveries of Ampère, of Arago, and of Faraday, that it was
possible to seriously think of the industrial applications of
electricity, especially of the production of the light for economic uses. Since that time the hydro-electric batteries have
been almost entirely put aside, and the recent progress effected in the transmission of electricity will soon succeed in dis-
couraging the few inventors who are still striving and now
hoping to perfect them. We have little need of occupying
ourselves with them; but, side by side with these ordinary
batteries there exist others, which have to play a very important part, and which have, moreover, under their last form,
made a very brilliant entry upon the industrial stage; these
are the *secondary batteries*, invented in 1859 by M. Planté,
and proposed to-day to serve for the storage and transportation of electricity. We believe it will be useful to study

* This is true only in French. In English the name *battery* is almost universally used at the present day.—Translator.

briefly both types of battery, so as to give an estimate of the resources they may be hoped to furnish.

The thermo-electric batteries are so much the more interesting, as they represent the simplest mode of producing electricity. Nothing but heat; no machines, no complications; a large heater, which is to be heated regularly—this is the solution of the problem, which an inventor, M. Clamond, seemed to have nearly attained two years ago, and yet no model of it appeared at the Electrical Exhibition of Paris. We will study this apparatus, because we are in hopes that it will reappear soon, *in propria persona*, or another of the same family, which, perhaps, reserves for us some unexpected surprise.

We will examine, finally, the machines which to-day are our principal resource, and which have certainly not yet reached their limit.

CHAPTER I.

HYDRO-ELECTRIC BATTERIES.

We have seen already that an electric current can only be produced when the equilibrium of the molecules is disturbed by some particular force, called electro-motive force. This force can be obtained by chemical, calorific, or mechanical .action. It is also probable that these different actions are always accompanied by electrical manifestations, but it is only in certain particular cases, and with special dispositions, that it is possible to collect this electricity in utilizable form.

The chemical action is effected by the well-known apparatus known as an electric battery, an apparatus in which two substances are placed in each other's presence, one of which is attacked by the other, and becomes the seat of an electro-motive force.

When a plate of pure zinc is plunged into water acidulated with sulphuric acid, a chemical action is produced: the zinc changes its state; a new body is formed by its combination with the acid, and the electric molecules which were inclosed in the metal dart through the water. If they have no way of escape, which is generally the case, because the vessels employed are not good conductors, they accumulate until a new equilibrium is produced, and the electro-motive force ceases to act. But if there is placed in the liquid, by the side of the plate of zinc, a second plate formed of a body that is a conductor, and, be it understood, unattackable by the acid—a plate of carbon, for example—the electric molecules will accumulate there. This plate will then be charged in excess, while the plate of zinc will be robbed of a corresponding quantity; the accumulation on one side, and the impoverishment on the other, will attain a power proportional to the energy of the electro-motive force which has produced them, and which maintains them without going any further; but, as soon as the two plates shall have been connected one with the other by a conducting wire, the molecules will follow the way which is open to them, and will rush from the carbon plate toward the zinc plate, where they will receive from the electro-motive force, set free, a new impulse, and will recommence the same round as long as this force will suffice to keep up their movement. The electric current will be established.

The two plates are called electrodes. The plate of carbon represents the pole of accumulation, or *positive* pole, and the plate of zinc the pole of rarefaction, or *negative* pole. In the external circuit the current always goes toward the negative from the positive pole, while in the interior of the battery it goes from the zinc to the carbon plate. The first one, then, is positive with respect to the second; it follows, and it is something which must not be forgotten, that the negative pole of the external circuit is situated on the positive electrode, and that the positive pole of the same circuit is on the negative electrode.

To the resistances encountered by the current in the external circuit a new one must be added—that of the liquid —which it must traverse to pass through the space which separates the two plates; this is called the interior resistance. The two resistances must be added together, to give the total resistance, to which, as we have seen, a corresponding tension is the equivalent. The molecules, which have acquired this total tension under the influence of the electro-motive force, must exhaust a part of it in overcoming the interior resistance; and for the useful work, to produce which the current is established, to be as great as possible, this first expenditure should be equal to one half of what they possess: in effect, if they expend a greater quantity in the first circuit, they will not have enough in the exterior circuit; if they expend less, they will have an excess of useless tension, and the electro-motive force will be wasted. From this it will be concluded that the interior and exterior resistances should be equal. Now, the interior resistance has a definite value, imposed by the nature of the battery, and generally insufficient to fulfill this condition ; there must be some means provided for increasing it, and for this it is enough to add a new element by the side of the first, by connecting the carbon plate of the first to the zinc plate of the second. The molecules coming from the first element find themselves in presence of the electro-motive force of the second, which will give a new impulse in addition to that which they have already received ; they will have a double tension. The second plate of carbon will become the positive pole of the battery.

It will be seen that in arranging in a series, one after the other, the necessary number of elements, a sum of interior resistances is finally reached equal to the exterior resistance. This is called connecting a battery for *tension*.

If, on the other hand, on one side all the zincs are connected, and on the other side all the carbons, the interior resistance will not change, because it will be the same at each instant in all the elements. What happens is the accumulation of the quantities of molecules displaced in each of the elements, and a consequent increase of the total quantity. The battery is connected for *quantity*.

The number of elements necessary to obtain a current of a determinate intensity naturally varies with the nature of the substance acting in it, and the energy of the resulting chemical action ; with those in which the interior resistance is considerable, the chemical action is more prolonged; but the electro-motive force can only displace a very few electrical molecules, and the current will have a high tension. It is often impossible to use them, because to furnish the necessary quantity of electricity the current would attain an exaggerated tension.

As the electro-motive force which results from the chemical actions is usually quite feeble, it is necessary to unite many elements, and, when it is necessary to have a current of considerable intensity, the bulk of the battery becomes very troublesome. This is a serious inconvenience; unfortunately, it is not the only one.

Chemically pure zinc is of high cost, and the zinc of commerce has to be used. This contains foreign bodies which permits the formation in the electrode of a number of small local circuits; not only is the electricity thus disengaged lost, but, as this action is continuous, even when the exterior circuit is open, the zincs are consumed without producing any useful effect.

To remedy this evil they have to be amalgamated—that is to say, a layer of mercury has to be spread upon their surface which combines with the zinc; thanks to this species of varnish, the chemical action only exists while the circuit is closed, and the zincs are preserved. But as the layer of amalgam is easily detached and drops to the bottom of the cups, the operation has to be repeated whenever the battery is to be used.

The chemical action does more than attack the zinc; at the same time it decomposes the water, one of whose constituent parts, the oxygen, combines with the zinc, but whose other part, the hydrogen, remaining free in the liquid, is carried along by the electrical molecules and stops on the surface of the carbon. This is soon covered with a layer of gas, a very bad conductor; the electric molecules can not pass any longer, and the electro-motive force ceases to act. This state of the carbon plates is denoted by saying that it is *polarized;* we will further explain this expression.

To overcome this polarization, the constant batteries have been invented, in which is placed a substance capable of absorbing the hydrogen as fast as it is deposited on the negative electrode. Becquerel was the first who suggested, in the year 1829, this mode of effecting this end. The best method consists in adding to the liquid a metallic salt in solution, of the same nature as the negative electrode; instead of gaseous hydrogen the battery deposits on this electrode a layer of the same metal, and there is no polarization. This is the arrangement adopted by Daniell in 1836, in the sulphate-of-copper battery which bears his name.

To prevent these two liquids, saturated solution of sulphate of copper and acidulated water, from mixing too rapidly, the first is inclosed with its electrode in a porous cup, through which it slowly passes, and keeps the passage free for the electrical molecules (Fig. 129).

In 1839 Grove tried nitric acid, very rich in oxygen, and easily decomposed. The polarizing hydrogen combines with part of the oxygen of the acid; unfortunately, this last is thus decomposed into binoxide of nitrogen, and this, coming in contact with the air, disengages suffocating fumes of hyponitric acid, as all know too well who have worked either with Grove's or Bunsen's battery, which only differ in the substitution of gas-carbon for platinum as negative electrode (Fig. 131).

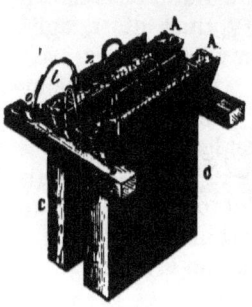

Fig. 129.—Daniell battery.

There are many other combinations; we shall only recall the employment, as depolarizer, of a solution of bichromate of potash in sulphuric acid, although this system of battery, invented by M. Poggendorf, is only available for experiments of short duration.

Another trouble remains: the liquids, whose quantity is limited, change their composition little by little; the acidulated water becomes saturated with sulphate of zinc; the nitric acid is replaced by water; the electromotive force progressively weakens, and in proportion to the quantity of electricity supplied by it. The constancy of these batteries, therefore, is only relative; it never exceeds a few hours when they are used for the electric light. If they have to be used for a

Fig. 130.—Reynier battery.

longer period the liquids must be renewed, and that so as not to change the intensity of the current. To overcome these troubles a number of combinations have been suggested, of which the most interesting, from the point of view of our studies, we shall here describe.

As the Daniell battery is more constant than the Bunsen battery, and also disengages no fumes, M. Carré invented in 1868 an arrangement which permitted him to use it for producing the electric light. The trouble was in the internal resistance of the Daniell battery; to diminish this resistance M. Carré gave to the electrodes a very large surface, and replaced the porcelain cup by a paper vessel, previously treated with sulphuric acid, called parchment-paper.

With this arrangement five Daniell cups could be substituted for three Bunsen cups, and a battery of sixty elements has worked for two hundred successive hours without weakening; it sufficed to replace every twenty-four hours by pure water a part of the sulphate of zinc formed. The light obtained cost one franc per hour.

Fig. 131.—Bunsen battery.

Following out another order of ideas, M. Tommasi has arranged the Bunsen pile so as to renew constantly the acidlated water, by which the action is kept more regular, and which diminishes a little the work of depolarization, because the bubbles of hydrogen are in part carried off by the water. Besides, the porous cups are enameled over their lower surface, which serves to retain the necessary quantity of nitric acid. A block of porcelain causes, by displacement, the acid to rise into the upper part of the cup, which part is still porous. Porcelain stoppers close these vessels hermetically and prevent the disengagement of hyponitric acid; there is some fear that at the same time they prevent the depolarization from being as completely effected; it appears also that these batteries have a little more electro-motive force, and less interior resistance than the Bunsen battery of the usual model.

A more important modification (Figs. 130 and 132) has been applied by M. Reynier to the Daniell battery, to increase its

electro-motive force and diminish its interior resistance. The
porous cup is made of parchment-paper, as M. Carré had
already made it; but an ingenious way of folding the parchment made the execution of it very easy. The negative electrode is of copper and the depolarizing liquid is a solution
of sulphate of copper. The positive electrode is always of
zinc, which need not be amalgamated; but the acidulated
water is replaced by caustic soda. The natural resistance of
these two liquids is diminished by the addition of appropriate salts. This new couple is more energetic than the other
piles, Bunsen or Daniell, and its
interior resistance much less. It
has the additional advantage of
emitting no fumes, and the invent-
or hopes to succeed in regenerating almost completely the products used by passing through the
exhausted solutions a quantity of
electricity slightly in excess of that
which the bat-
tery has emit-
ted; the cop-
per deposited
on the negative
electrode will
be dissolved,

FIG. 132.—Small model of the circular form of the Reynier battery.

and the dis-
solved zinc reduced to the metallic state. This, then, would
constitute a fluid for the storage of electricity.

Other inventors have sought for such combinations that
the battery residues—that is to say, the substances produced
after the electricity had been developed at the expense of the
original materials—would have a value in commerce, so as to
diminish the cost of such development; some have even declared that they should cost nothing. We know of no practical result due to these researches, without doubt perfectly
justifiable, but which are so complicated by the commercial
conditions that they have hitherto been fruitless.

SECONDARY OR STORAGE BATTERIES.

This name is given to batteries in which two substances in
presence of a liquid, after having been subjected to a first

transformation under the influence of the passage of an electric current, return to their first state, disengaging in this
second transformation a certain quantity of electricity. The
currents thus produced are called *secondary currents*. It is
thus that in an ordinary battery, when the negative electrode
is covered with hydrogen, the latter, which has a high affinity
for oxygen, tends to create a secondary current opposed to
the principal current. The negative electrode becomes in part
positive in its turn, and for that reason is said to be polarized.
Secondary batteries, properly so called, are those in which,
instead of the prevention of *polarization*, its development is
sought after, to re-obtain from it subsequently the work it
will have stored up ; it is one of the remarkable applications
of the reciprocity or reversibility which accompanies the production of electricity. Although these phenomena were first
observed by Gautherot in 1801, it was only in 1859 that M.
Planté took up the study again and invented the battery
composed of plates of lead so well known to-day. These plates
are rolled up parallel to each other in a spiral, and are separated by bands of caoutchouc ; they thus have a very large
surface in a small volume, and the interior resistance is low
on account of their proximity. They are contained in a jar
of insulating material, ordinarily of glass, and this jar is filled
with water acidulated with one-tenth part of sulphuric acid.
To make them capable of storing electricity, it is necessary to
form them, by causing an electric current from an external
source to pass a number of times through the cell, first in one
direction then in the other. At each passage of the current
the oxygen attacks one plate, producing on it a coating of peroxide of lead ; the hydrogen goes to the other plate where it
escapes. When the coating of peroxide is thick enough, the
pile is formed, and then it is necessary to be careful to always
charge it in the same direction.* Ordinarily several elements
are combined by means of a switch, which admits of their
being connected in quantity for charging and in tension for
discharging. The duration of this discharge is proportional
to the resistance which it encounters. Two Bunsen elements
suffice to charge twenty secondary elements, and, according to
M. Planté, the return is equal to nine tenths of the electricity

* [The object of the "forming" is to render the lead plates spongy so as to
get as large a surface as possible, with a given weight of material, on which to
deposit the active oxide.]

received.   The current can be preserved for a long time ; it is
undiminished at the end of eight days, and can furnish currents even at the end of a month.

The Planté battery had received already numerous applications, when quite recently M. Faure, impressed with the
services which it could render, and perhaps thinking a little
of those which it might render him, introduced an interesting
modification.   To make the coating thicker and more rapidly,
he covers each one of the plates with minium or other insoluble oxide of lead, and this minium is retained by a piece of
felt riveted on the plate of lead.   This battery is formed,
like the first, by passing through it an electric current which
brings the minium to the state of peroxide on the positive
electrode, and to the state of metallic lead on the negative
electrode ; when it is discharged the reduced lead oxidizes,
and the peroxide is reduced.   The layers within which these
reactions take place being thicker, the storage capacity is increased, but to an amount that is a subject of dispute : the inventor says forty times ; several experimenters say one and a
half times.   It is probable that, in attributing to the Faure
accumulator a power three times that of the Planté battery,
all is said for it that is warranted.

At the Electrical Exposition in Paris the Faure accumulators served every day, for five or six hours, to supply the
incandescent Swan lamps, which lighted the restaurant in the
first story and the Judges' Hall.   They were charged during
the day, in three or four hours, with currents from a Siemens
machine.

We have nothing to say in reference to the projects for
transporting electricity by the use of this apparatus ; it is a
false combination, in which, among other fallacies, it does not
appear how the purchaser can know whether the battery
which is brought to him is completely charged, and whether
that which is removed is completely exhausted.*

Meanwhile, although somewhat dear—one hundred and
twenty-five francs for an element of eight kilos, representing
one kilogrammetre for eight hours—these batteries can be of
very great service, and it is easy to use them by charging
them with Thomson batteries, four elements for a secondary

* [Though this mode of supplying storage batteries to consumers has been
suggested, more especially at the time of revival of interest in them several years
ago, I am not aware of its having been seriously advocated by any one.]

Faure element. The Thomson battery is inodorous, and quite constant; it can work day and night without any interruption, and needs no other care than the addition periodically of some crystals of sulphate of copper and replacement by pure water of a part of the solution of sulphate of zinc, as it becomes saturated.

They might even now be employed to replace the six or eight Bunsen elements, which have found a last asylum on the ground-floor of the Opéra, and which repay this hospitality by corroding a large part of the western façade.

Before M. Faure, Messrs. Houston and Thomson had invented in America a secondary battery, formed of two plates of copper, immersed in a solution of sulphate of zinc. [The charging current is sent through the battery from the upper to the lower plate, when the upper plate dissolves, forming sulphate of copper, which floats on the sulphate of zinc; metallic zinc is deposited upon the lower plate. The battery when charged is therefore simply a gravity Daniel. M. d'Arsonval modified this by using for one electrode lead or carbon covered with lead shot, and for the other, zinc.] As soon as attention was directed to these batteries, new ones sprang up on all sides, such as those of MM. d'Arsonval, Rousse, Maiche, etc. Evidently secondary batteries are destined to play an important *rôle* in the distribution of electricity as regulators; but we must observe that the name of accumulators of electricity does not at all suit them, because they do not in any sense store up electric currents. That which they do store up is the work of chemical decomposition between certain substances whose recombination gives back, under the form of an electric current, a part of this work. In any case the attention excited by them in these latter days will not be useless; it will lead, doubtless, to new combinations more powerful and more advantageous.

[Various other batteries have been designed, the objects in each case being to reduce the weight of the material as much as possible in relation to its storing power, and increase the efficiency. In the cell of M. de Meritens the lead plates are constructed of thin, overlapping laminæ, arranged in a manner similar to the slats of Venetian blinds. In the Sellon-Volckmar, the lead plates consist of a lattice-work, into the open spaces of which the red oxide is forced, this construction giving a much greater amount of oxide per pound of lead than when this is on the surface merely. M. de Kabath has obtained increased surface by the use of corrugated plates. A number of patents have been taken out by Mr. C. F. Brush, whose arc-lamp has been previously described, on improved modes of constructing the plates so as to render them more durable and of increased storage capacity. Much has been claimed for this battery, but, as it has not been subjected to tests by unbiased experts, nothing is known of its performance. A form of battery, claimed by its inventor to be superior to any of the above, has been designed by Mr. Henry Sutton. It consists of a positive electrode of amalgamated lead and a negative one of copper, immersed in a solution of sulphate of copper. The chemical changes in this cell, when a current is sent through it, consist in the combination of the oxygen of the decomposed solution with the lead, forming a coating of the insoluble peroxide, and the replacement of the copper in the solution by the disengaged hydrogen, the copper being deposited on the negative plate. In discharging, the copper is dissolved in the solution, and the lead plate reduced, the cell returning to its original chemical condition.

Many tests of the efficiency of the storage-battery have been made, but the results of different experimenters are discordant. Tests of the Faure, at the Conservatoire des Arts et Métiers, showed that this accumulator absorbed forty per cent of the electrical work that would otherwise have been available in the lamps through which the discharge was made. Sir William Thomson placed the loss at twenty-five per cent, while Professor W. E. Ayrton·has stated that it need not exceed eighteen per cent. In his report on the Sellon-Volckmar battery, Professor Henry Morton states that the loss does not exceed this percentage of the electrical work spent in charging. He found that one cell, weighing eighty pounds, including that of the box and liquid, was capable of yielding a current of 32·5 ampères at the beginning, and 31·2 ampères at the close of a continuous discharge for nine hours. The electromotive force is two volts, so that there would be required ten pounds of battery per Edison sixteen-candle lamp for each hour of burning ; while with the Faure battery, examined at the Paris Conservatoire, more than double this weight would be required.

The expectations entertained at the time of Faure's improvement, of the value of the secondary battery in the industrial applications of electricity, have so far failed of realization. It has been found that in practical operation it is open to many objections. The first cost is considerable, it greatly deteriorates with use, and its efficiency is low. Despite the claims which have been made for the various batteries as they were brought to public attention, the battery still remains a laboratory apparatus, in which much improvement must be made before it can become of commercial utility. For a thoroughly satisfactory battery there is doubtless a considerable field of usefulness, but its value in electric lighting has been greatly overestimated. The feasibility of operating incandescent lamps directly from the dynamo is no longer doubtful, and the employment of the storage-battery in an extended distribution presents no advantage, while it is certain to materially enhance the cost of plant.]

CHAPTER II.

THERMO-ELECTRIC BATTERIES.

If, after having soldered together by one of their extremities two bars of different metals, this soldered part is heated, the difference of the effects produced by the heat in each one of them destroys the equilibrium of the electric molecules which they contain ; and when the two free extremities are reunited by a conductor, a current is produced, going from the heated part to the cold part, in that one of the two metals which is the best conductor, finally traversing the whole of the exterior circuit and returning to its point of departure through the second bar, which it passes through in opposite direction. By thus soldering in a series, side by side, a number of bars differing alternately, and arranged so that the solderings of the even row can be heated all at the same time, and the solderings of the uneven row can be at the same time cooled, a current will be obtained whose strength will increase with the number of solderings and the difference of their temperatures. The electro-motive force, due to these effects, seems above all to depend on the variations in electrical conductivity, which the changes of temperature produce in the metals and minerals employed. When the resistance of one

15

of them increases with the heat quicker than that of the
other, it ends by producing a reversal of the direction of the
current. This is what actually happens with iron-copper and
silver-zinc couples.

This apparatus is the *thermo-electric* pile, invented in 1821
by Seebeck. For a long time it was only an excellent laboratory appliance, under the form given it by Nobili. In 1827
the elder Becquerel, to whom is due excellent work in this
branch, had constructed one with artificial sulphide of copper
and German-silver; it was composed of sixty elements, arranged at pleasure in one single or two parallel series. The
solderings were heated by gas, and the current was intense
enough to redden a short piece of fine iron wire.

Toward 1870 M. Clamond took up again the study of
thermo-electric piles, and, after having constructed a certain
number of apparatus, heated by gas, which gave excellent results, he attempted the construction of more powerful piles,
designed to produce the electric light. He seemed to have
succeeded; for we have seen, in 1879, a pile arranged like a
radiator, about two metres high and one metre in diameter,
supply two lamps with Serrin regulators (Fig. 133); each
lamp gave a light of about thirty carcels, and the expense was
nine to ten kilogrammes of coke per hour. We do not know
why these piles have been abandoned, as they did not appear
on the catalogue of the Electrical Exhibition in Paris except
as a laboratory apparatus.

M. Clamond used iron for the electro-positive plates, and
for the others an alloy composed of two parts, by weight, of
antimony, and one part of zinc. Molds, very well arranged,
admitted of a large number of couples being made at one
casting, which by that operation were joined in tension, and
formed a flexible chain easily arranged. These chains were
compressed between two frames, termed by the inventor the
collector and the diffuser, care being taken to isolate them
with asbestos. The collector was composed of several concentric iron cylinders joined together by ribs running lengthwise, so as to form a series of flues between the cylinders for
the circulation of the warm gases from the source of heat; it
also acted by its mass as a regulator of the temperature. The
diffuser was designed to facilitate the cooling, and for that purpose was formed of plates of copper, presenting a large surface for radiation. Thus the difference of temperatures, and

consequently the intensity of the currents, could be kept constant.

Thermo-electric piles are simple, economical, and easy of application. The current is very constant, but its tension is slight. As yet, experiments have not gone far enough to ad-

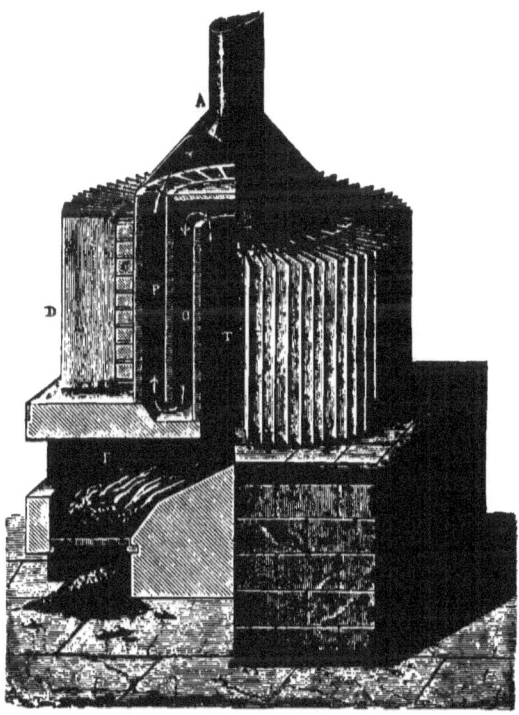

Fig. 133.—Thermo-electric pile of Clamond.

F, fireplace, with ordinary grate for coke.
T T, central cylindrical chamber.
O, P, collector, consisting of two annular concentric cylinders, joined by ribs, in which the heat is equally diffused by its movement from above downward in the space O.
C, chain of thermo-electric elements.
D, diffusers of heat.

mit of our estimating the action of the heat on the duration of the couples. The models now in use generally experience a considerable increase of internal resistance, due to the oxidation of the heated solderings—an oxidation which can, nevertheless, be resisted by inclosing them in a metallic capsule, as in the thermo-electric pile of Noé, much used in Austria.

As an example of the reversibility of electric phenomena it may be remarked that the inverse effect of the thermo-electric pile exists in Peltier's experiment. When a current passes through the soldering of two metals, the solder is heated or cooled, according as the current is directed in the reverse direction or in the same direction as the thermo-electric current which is obtained in heating this same soldering.

Although in these piles the heat disengaged by combustion is utilized without intermediary apparatus, it is but incompletely used, and the warm gases leave the apparatus at a considerable temperature. It is true that this heat can be utilized to a certain extent by making the pile serve both for heating and lighting.

Many have thought of utilizing, in a more direct fashion, the combustion of carbon by collecting the electricity which it disengages. In the year 1855 M. Becquerel obtained electric currents with a pile in which the carbon in combustion replaced the zinc of ordinary batteries, and he called the currents *pyro-electric*, to distinguish them from thermo-electric currents. This is how he himself describes his experiment: "If we fasten to one of the extremities of the wire of a galvanometer a crucible of platinum filled with nitrate or chlorate of potash in fusion, and if we attach to the other extremity a piece of retort-carbon whose end has first been brought to a red heat, then, on plunging this incandescent carbon into the bath in fusion, an energetic electric current is obtained flowing in the direction that would make the carbon negative, and the nitrate of potash positive. This effect is due to the vivid combustion of the carbon at the expense of the oxygen of the bath of fused nitrate."

For the experiment to succeed, it is necessary to sustain the piece of carbon so that it will not touch the walls of the crucible.

In 1878 M. Jablochkoff, who doubtless feared that the complication inseparable from machines would be an obstacle to the success of his candles, thought also of collecting directly the electricity which is disengaged in combustion; probably without knowing it he reproduced the experiment of Becquerel. He melted nitrate of soda in a small crucible of cast-iron; the incandescent carbon dipped into this bath is burned up at the expense of the oxygen of the nitrate, and plays the *rôle* of positive electrode ; the cast-iron is not attacked, and represents the conductor, or negative electrode—that is to say, the positive pole of the external circuit.

In his "Treatise on the Electric Pile," M. Niaudet judiciously remarks the curious phenomenon of inversion which this experiment presents. If, instead of nitrate of soda in fusion, this nitrate is used in solution in water at the ordinary temperature, the same electrodes play opposite *rôles ;* the iron is attacked and becomes the generator electrode, while the carbon will be the conductor electrode, as is the case in all the batteries where we have seen it employed.

CHAPTER III.

ELECTRICAL INDUCTION.

THE production of electric currents by machines rests upon a number of discoveries, which we shall briefly describe, to make the mode of operation of these machines understood. In July, 1820, Œrstedt, a Danish physicist, observed the deviation which the approach of a magnet, or closed circuit through which a current was passing, produced upon a magnetic needle. The analogy between magnetism and electricity was then established. On the 11th of September next following, the experiment of Œrstedt was repeated before the Academy of Sciences by M. de la Rive, and some days after, on the 20th of September, Ampère discovered the mutual action which two currents exercised upon each other ; he also proved the action of currents upon magnets and their absolute reciprocity, so important to be considered in all the applications of electricity. On the 25th of September Arago discovered that currents have the property of transforming a bar of iron or steel into a magnet ; he invented the *electro-magnet* at the same time that Ampère established the theory of magnetism, basing it upon the analogous properties possessed by magnets and solenoids. Here the discoveries of reciprocity stopped short, and it was only ten years later, in 1830, that Faraday discovered *induction*—that is to say, the property possessed by magnets of causing electric currents to arise in

a metallic circuit. It is, above all, to the use made of this last
and magnificent discovery that electricity owes the extraordinary progress of which the Electrical Exhibition in Paris in
1881 furnished us such varied proofs.

The two figures annexed illustrate the experiments, to-day
classic, which Faraday performed, both with a magnet and a
bobbin of copper wire traversed by a current.

When there is plunged into a bobbin wound with a long,
fine wire, whose coils are insulated, a second smaller bobbin,
wound with a short, thick wire, and traversed by a current
(Fig. 134), there is instantly produced in the wire of the first
bobbin an energetic current, going in the opposite direction to
that of the small bobbin: it is called the *inverse current;* this
current ceases with the movement, and, as long as the small
bobbin, always receiving a current, remains immovable in the
large one, no current is produced ; but, at the moment it is
withdrawn, there is produced in the wire of the large bobbin
another current, this time in the same direction as the current
of the small one, and named for this reason the *direct current.*

Fig. 134.—Experiment of Faraday with two bobbins.

The current of the small bobbin is called the *inducing*
current; those which are produced in the large bobbin are
called *induced* currents, or currents of induction. By extension these qualities are often applied to the bobbins themselves. The intensity of the induced current increases with
the intensity of the inducing one and with the rapidity of the
movement ; it diminishes at the same time with these.

If, instead of bringing nearer and drawing away the small bobbin, it is held motionless within the large one, only interrupting the passage of the current through it, the same phenomena are produced. A reverse current is immediately started in the wire of the large bobbin at the moment when the inducing current is started in the wire of the small one; as soon as the current is established, and as long as the in-

Fig. 135.—Experiment of Faraday with a bobbin and magnet.

ducing current continues to pass through the wire, it will produce no induced current; but at the moment when the inducing current is stopped, a direct current will manifest itself in the large bobbin. We will see below how each of these two modes of induction has been utilized.

The same phenomena are produced when the small bobbin is replaced by a magnetized bar (Fig. 135), either when the bar is displaced under the same conditions, or when its magnetization is made to vary by the approach or removal of a second magnet.

The phenomena of induction, as well as those of electrical attraction and repulsion, show clearly that the influence of a body charged with electricity or magnetism extends to a considerable distance around it. For magnets and electromagnets the space within which this influence can be perceived is called the *magnetic field;* by analogy, the space under the influence of a current is called the *galvanic field.*

We can not here enter upon the consideration of the hypotheses by whose aid the action of this influence is explained. The theory of particular fluids, generally accepted formerly, is to-day abandoned, and it is rather believed that electric and magnetic action is due to vibrations or movements in the layers of ether which exist in all bodies, and by which they are surrounded.

If the cause is unknown, the effects can be represented materially by the aid of those curious figures which M. de Haldat has named *magnetic phantoms*, and which are obtained with very fine iron filings spread upon a piece of paper or glass placed above the poles of a magnet. The magnetic force orientates these filings in a series of lines converging from one pole to the other, and which repel each other when two poles of the same name are brought together. These lines, which Faraday has named *lines of magnetic force*, are very convenient to illustrate the effects of induction which accompany the movement of a conducting wire through a magnetic field.

Each of the lines of force which the wire intersects in passing starts an induced current, and the quantity of electricity developed is proportional to the number of lines intersected in a given time. The direction of the movement in relation to the direction of the lines of force determines that of the currents. It is equally apparent, on inspection of these magnetic phantoms, that the density of the lines of force diminishes in proportion as they are removed from the poles, and it is thus manifest why it is so important for the wire to move in the densest regions—that is to say, the nearest possible to the inductors. The farther it is removed, the more will it be necessary to augment the velocity of displacement, to obtain again the same intensity of induced current.

RUHMKORFF'S COIL.

We have seen that induction can exert itself in two ways : 1. The inducing and induced current circuits are immovable ; the induced currents are produced, either by variations in the intensity of the inducing current, or by variations in the magnetism of the magnet.

2. The intensity of the inducing current and the magnetism of the magnet are invariable ; the induced currents are

produced by the relative displacement of the inducing or induced circuit.

The first of these two modes of induction was employed in 1842 by MM. Masson and Bréguet in the construction of the induction-coil named after Ruhmkorff, in memory of the ingenious constructor who gave it such high power. This coil is formed of two copper wires, perfectly insulated, wound into coils, one on top of or beside the other. One wire, short and thick, conducts the inducing current, to which a small special apparatus communicates a series of interruptions. From this a succession of inverse and direct induced currents results, whose intensity is proportional to the square of the resistance of the wire of the induced circuit, to the intensity of the inducing current, and to the rapidity of the interruptions. Besides this, the coil contains a bundle of pieces of iron wire, whose successive magnetizations and demagnetizations, due to the interruptions of the inducing current, increase to a considerable extent the intensity of the induced currents. Fig. 136 represents one of the models adopted for demonstrations in courses of physics.

The quantities of electricity put in motion in each induced current are equal; but the direct current has a higher tension. This follows from the variations in the inducing current due to the induction it exercises upon itself in its own circuit. This induction of an intermittent current upon itself is very important; it is exercised every time a circuit is formed by a coiled wire, whose spires approach each other, and causes the production in the same wire of induced currents, called extra currents.

When the circuit is opened an extra current is produced, which, following the general law of induction, is inverse—that is to say, the reverse of the principal current, whose intensity it diminishes. When the circuit is closed, the extra current is direct, and adds itself to the principal current, whose intensity it increases and whose duration it prolongs. It increases the power of the spark at breaking, but at the same time it prolongs the duration and weakens the tension of the corresponding induced current.

To overcome the effects of these extra currents, M. Fizeau interposes in the inducing circuit a condenser of large surface, in which the electricity of the extra current accumulates, to subsequently react again in the opposite direction.

The Ruhmkorff coil produces very powerful calorific effects; it has had some practical applications in the ignition of mines and illumination by means of Geissler tubes. An attempt has also been made to utilize it for lighting by means of incandescence, and we must recall the curious experiments made by M. Jablochkoff in 1877 with a thin plate of kaolin placed between the extremities of the secondary wire of one of these coils. The surface of this plate was kept in fusion by the passage of the currents, and gave a very beautiful

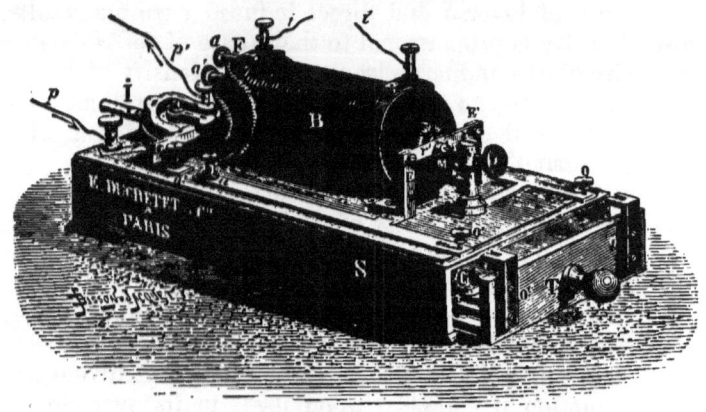

Fig. 136.—Ruhmkorff coil.

B, coil.
P, P', connecting wires of the inducing current.
i, reversing commutator of M. Bertin, permitting of controlling the current.
i, i', terminals of the induced circuit.
a, a, a, a', inducing current circuit wires.
S, base containing the condenser, kept in a movable drawer which may be drawn out, according to the current required, by unscrewing the screws o, o' and pulling it out a little.
M, bundle of iron wire.
E, E', vibrating commutator or interrupter.

light. By varying the dispositions and sizes of the coils, as well as the number of plates ignited by each of them, lights of different intensities can be obtained, from a half-carcel up to two carcels. M. Jablochkoff supplied his induction-coils from a machine with alternating currents, so that he could suppress in each of them the condenser and interrupter, and consequently increase considerably the intensity of the induced currents.

Analogous trials have been recently made in England, following out the experiments made by Mr. Spottiswoode, with

an induction-coil excited by alternating currents from a machine of M. de Meritens. These trials apply, above all, to
processes of incandescence which require a current of considerable tension, a tension which can hardly be derived directly from the machine. The Ruhmkorff coil is really an
apparatus for transformation ;: though it ordinarily is only employed to transform dynamic into static electricity, it can
also effect the opposite transformation, as M. Bichat has
shown, in passing into the fine wire of the coil a series of
sparks which caused in the large wire alternate induced currents, producing effects analogous to those of battery-currents.

The induction-coil with which Mr. Spottiswoode made his
experiments is the largest that has ever been constructed. Its
total weight is 762 kilogrammes, its length 1·22 metres, and its
external diameter ·508 metre. The primary wire is 2½ millimetres in diameter, and 445 metres long. The secondary coil
is wound with no less than 458 kilometres of fine wire, making 341,850 turns, divided into several bobbins in juxtaposition, according to the system of M. Poggendorff.

With 30 quart cells of Grove's battery, it gives sparks 1·08
metres (42½ inches) in length. With currents from the Meritens machine, the spark forms a true voltaic arc of 15 to 20
centimetres' length.

CHAPTER IV.

THEORETICAL PRINCIPLES OF MACHINES.

THE second mode of induction—that which results from
the relative displacement of the inducing or induced circuit—
has been much more fertile of application ; upon it depend
the construction and working of machines destined for the
production of dynamic electricity. Although presenting a
great variety of forms, these machines all contain the same
two elements—the inducing and induced circuits—repeated a
sufficient number of times ; one of the two, generally the induced circuit, has imparted to it a very rapid movement of
rotation in the magnetic field of the inductor, and it is the
mechanical work expended in moving it that is transformed
into electricity.

The former frictional machines also transformed mechanical work; but they only served to multiply charges of static electricity—that is to say, to raise the potential at the two ends of an open circuit, and not to maintain a continual flow of dynamic electricity in a closed circuit.

At first the inductors were composed of permanent magnets; as the power of these magnets is limited, and as their weight and dimensions increase in greater proportion than the power, to increase the power of these machines, electro-magnets were employed in which an electric current develops an enormously greater amount of magnetism than a permanent magnet of the same dimensions could contain. According to this difference in the inductors, the machines are ranged in two categories: *magneto-electric* machines, in which the inductors are permanent magnets; and *dynamo-electric*, in which electro-magnets are the inductors.

This classification, which is sanctioned by usage, is inexact, because magnetism and motion play the same *rôle* in both classes, and because there is no magneto-electric machine which may not become dynamo-electric by the simple change of inductors, and *vice versa.*

In the first machines of the dynamo-electric type, the current necessary to produce and sustain the magnetism of the inductors was furnished by a small auxiliary magneto-electric machine. This was the first application of exciting-machines. The system was soon simplified by the use of two separate circuits, the current in one of which excited the field magnets, while that in the other performed the external work. Eventually a third arrangement, yet more simple, was reached: the entire production of the machine was reduced to a single current, which was made to pass in its entirety through the field coils before passing into the external circuit; this last arrangement, generally adopted at the present day, gives us without complication the maximum magnetic power and the maximum intensity of current that can be derived from the organs of a machine of given dimensions; it has, however, the inconvenience of making the work of the machine inversely proportional to the variations in external resistance; if this increases, the intensity of the current diminishes, which weakens the inducing magnets, while, as a rule, the reverse is necessary. When the external resistance diminishes, the intensity of the current and power of the inducing

FIG. 187.   The ruins of the Coliseum at Rome illuminated by the electric light.

magnets increases ; from this results a useless expenditure of work, and often a production of heat dangerous to the struct-ure of the machine.   To overcome this trouble it suffices to send around the magnets a current shunted from the principal one, reducing, of course, the thickness of the wire with which they are wound.   The relation is then reversed.   If the ex-ternal resistance increases, the derived current increases also, and, along with it, the excitation of the inducing magnets and intensity of the current produced.   If this exterior re-sistance diminishes, the derived current also grows weaker, and the work absorbed is reduced in proportion.   It only re-mains necessary to see that the machine does not work with an open outer circuit ; for then the shunt circuit would alone remain closed, and work would be uselessly expended.

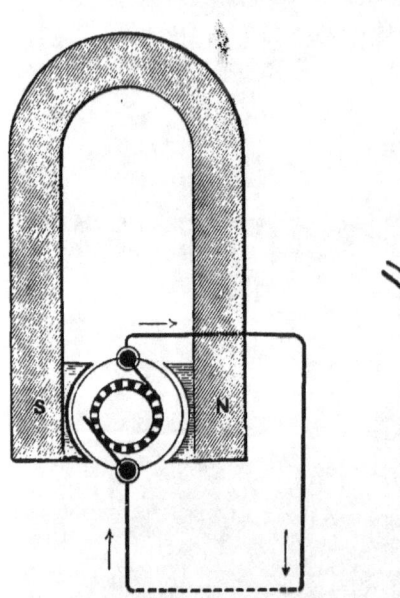
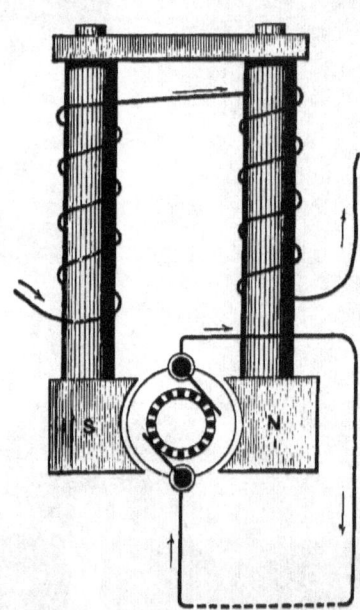

Fig. 138.—Magneto-electric machine.   Fig. 189.—Separately excited dynamo.

[The four ways in which the magnetism of the field of a machine may be maintained are shown in Figs. 138, 139, 140, and 141.*   The magneto machine, with a field formed of per-manent magnets, is shown in Fig. 138, and the dynamo, with

* From the journal of the Society of Arts.

its field magnets excited from an external source, in Fig. 139. It will be seen that in both of these cases the magnetization of the field is independent of the current flowing through the working circuit, which is not the case in the two remaining forms, in which a whole or part of the current generated by

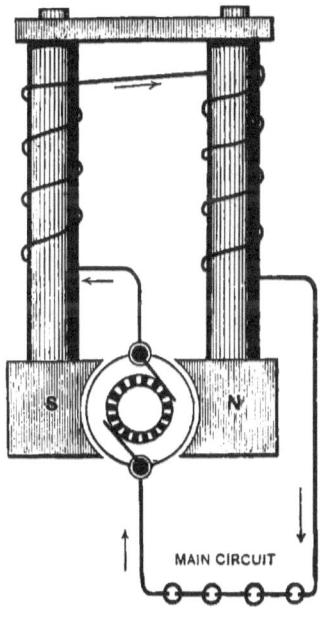

MAIN CIRCUIT

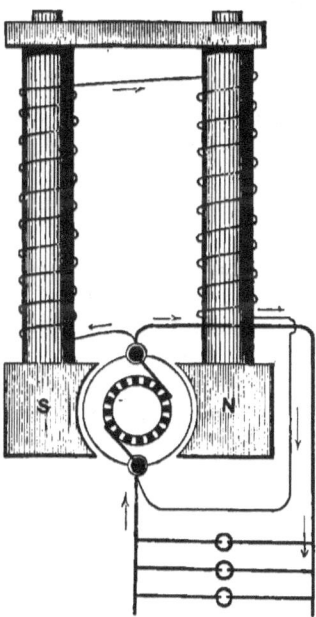

Fig. 140.—Series dynamo.   Fig. 141.—Shunt dynamo.

the machine is used to excite the field magnets. The type of dynamo in which the whole current of the machine passes through the field-magnet coils is represented in Fig. 140. It is known as the "series dynamo," and until recently was almost exclusively employed in arc-lighting. The dynamo in which but a portion of the current is used to energize the field· magnets, termed the "shunt dynamo," is shown in Fig. 141. Evidently in both of these types of machine the strength of the magnetic field will depend upon the resistance in the working circuit, since the magnetization depends upon the strength of the current circulating in the field coils. Various methods have been devised for keeping the strength of the magnetic field in the proper relation to the external circuit, which will be found described in Book V.

The two different methods of arranging electric lamps upon a circuit, "in series" or "in multiple arc," often spoken of as "in derivation," are also shown in Figs. 140 and 141. In the series method, used exclusively with arc-lamps and with open-air incandescent lamps, the lamps are strung one after another upon the same circuit. This is shown in Fig. 140. When placed in multiple arc, the method always adopted with incandescent lamps, the lamps are placed across the circuit, as shown in Fig. 141, so that one terminal is connected with the outgoing and the other with the return wire. In the series system the strength of the current is evidently the same, whatever the number of lamps, but the electro-motive must vary with them. In the multiple-arc system, on the contrary, the electro-motive force should remain constant, and the strength of the current be in proportion to the number of lamps.]

We see now that in this disposition of parts the inducing electro-magnets are excited by the passage of currents which they themselves induce. As the magnetization of the iron by these currents is only temporary, the magnetism of the inducing magnets disappears as soon as the machine stops, and the question arises as to what produces the induction when the machine is started again. This induction is simply produced by the traces of magnetism, extremely feeble, it is true, which the iron, soft as it may be, is certain to preserve after it has been once magnetized, and which is called residual magnetism. It is this residual magnetism, which is so hard to avoid in telegraphic apparatus, that becomes a most valuable auxiliary for charging the machine.

When the machine starts, this trace of magnetism starts at once an imperceptible induced current; this current passing into the coils of the inducing magnets increases a little their magnetism; at the second turn the current is a little stronger, and the magnetism increases a little more; the power of the inducing magnets thus successively increases until they are saturated. Residual magnetism generally exists even in new machines, and is attributed either to the operations which the inducing magnets go through in the process of construction, or to the influence of terrestrial magnetism. It is rarely necessary to charge a machine before starting it, and, at the most, a short application of a battery-current suffices.

The armature coils are generally wound with a wire or ribbon of copper, whose length and section are determined by the tension which the current is to possess.   The strength of the field and the speed being constant, the tension of the induced currents increases with the resistance of the wire, but only of that part of the wire that is active and contributes to the production of the currents ; the resistance of the inactive portion, although inevitable, has nothing to do with the tension to be finally produced.*   We must further observe that the co-efficient of resistance of copper is not the only factor to be taken into account, because the winding of the wire causes the wires that are close together to react upon each other, in proportion to the intensity of the currents that successively traverse them ; it follows that the real resistance of a coil is much greater than the theoretical resistance calculated for the same length of uncoiled copper wire.   Thus it appears that it is possible with the same parts, by the mere difference of dimensions of the armature coil, to produce from machines currents of tension or of quantity.

The copper used should be as pure as possible, because its conductivity is rapidly diminished by the presence of foreign bodies ; iron being a much inferior conductor, more of it must be employed, and the weight of the moving parts of the machine increased ; it also is susceptible of magnetization, and the mass of metal, formed by the coils of iron wire, would react upon the cores and weaken their magnetism.

The armature coils are generally wound in the form of helices or bobbins, upon one or more soft-iron cores which support them.   The alternations of magnetization and demagnetization which these cores experience on account of their movements in front of the inducing magnets, give a new electro-motive force, which further increases the charge of magnetism produced by each formation of current in the helices.   Unfortunately, the influence of the inductors is not limited to modifying the magnetic state of the cores ; it causes at the same time the production of induced currents which bring about the production of heat and increased

---

* [Resistance in any part of the circuit does not contribute to the tension of the induced current.   This depends upon the number of lines of force cut per second by the rotating conductor.   The total electro-motive force generated will be the sum of those set up in each turn of wire; hence, for the production of currents of high tension, many turns of wire are necessary, which increases the resistance.   In order to bring all parts of the coil within the inductive influence of the field, finer wire must be used, further increasing the resistance.]

16

resistance to movement. Faraday proved the existence of
these currents by reversing the experiment of Barlow's wheel.
The apparatus of Faraday (Fig. 142) suffices, on the other
hand, to demonstrate the two inverse actions of magnets
on currents, and the induction produced by these currents.
Faraday's apparatus was the first machine and the first magneto-electric motor. The parasitical currents of electricity
are often called Foucault currents, because it is to this physicist that the apparatus is due which serves to demonstrate
the transformation into heat of the work which they represent. To reduce as far as possible the formation of these

FIG. 142.—Faraday's apparatus.

A, inducing magnet.
D, induced disk.
B, binding-screw for entry or
exit of currents by the axis
of the disk.
B', binding-screw connecting
with a rubber *m*, for entrance or exit of currents
by the exterior circumference of the disk.
    If the galvanometer is
placed between the termi-
nals at B, B', and the disk
is turned by hand, the existence of a continuous current will be shown, whose
direction depends on the
direction of the rotation of
the disk.

If the galvanometer is replaced by a Bunsen cell, its terminals being connected to the
binding-screws B, B', the disk begins to turn, and the direction of rotation depends on
the direction of the current passing through the disk. To show the transformation into
heat, a very powerful magnet is needed, and a very rapid rotation of the disk. (Foucault's and M. Le Roux's apparatus).

currents, the cores are constructed of sheet-iron or of iron
wire; in some recent machines they are entirely suppressed;
in these the bobbins are supported by standards of wood or
other non-magnetic and non-conducting material.

    The wires used in the machines should be more perfectly
insulated, as the tension of the currents is greater. Silk cov-
erings are excellent; but, as they cost too much, cotton is
used, and the insulation is made complete by means of a
coating composed of bitumen of Judea, dissolved in turpen-
tine. A little wax and resin is sometimes added. Some machines owe a part of their superiority to the extreme care
exercised in insulating all their parts.

The arrangement of the armature coils with reference to the field magnets has given rise to many combinations, which can be grouped under four principal classes :

1. Machines in which the axes of the bobbins are parallel to the axis of rotation (Clarke, Alliance, Holmes, Niaudet, Wallace, etc.).

2. Those in which the axis of the single bobbin is perpendicular to the axis of rotation (Siemens, Wilde, Ladd).

3. Those in which the axes of the bobbins form a circle concentric with the axis of rotation (Gramme, Heffner, Von Alteneck, De Meritens, Brush, Schuckert, Burgin, etc.).

4. Those in which the bobbins have their axes radiating from the axis of rotation (Lontin).*

It may here be stated that it is the third type of machine that seems to utilize most perfectly the magnetic power of the field magnets.

The instantaneous currents produced in the induced bobbins are of opposite direction, as the movement always includes a period of approach to, and departure from, the field magnets. These two directions are themselves reversed according to the nature of the pole before which the movement takes place : thus, the approach to a north pole, and the departure from a south pole, give currents of certain directions ;

---

* [The common classification of armatures, according to their form, is : 1, disk armatures; 2, ring armatures; 3, drum armatures; 4, polar armatures. In the authors' classification, the ring and drum armatures are grouped together under 3 ; Class 1 refers to disk armatures; 2, to the double T-armature of Siemens; and 4, to polar armatures.

On the basis of the relation of the magnetic field to the moving coils, Professor Sylvanus P. Thompson has divided dynamos into the three following classes :

CLASS I.—" Dynamos in which there is rotation of a coil or coils in a uniform field of force."

Machines of this class are all continuous-current machines, and their armatures are usually of either the ring or drum form.

CLASS II.—" Dynamos in which there is translation of coils to different parts of a complex field of varying strength, or of opposite sign. Most, but by no means all, of the machines of this class furnish alternate currents."

CLASS III.—" Dynamos having a conductor rotating so as to produce a continuous increase in the number of lines of force cut, by the device of sliding one part of the conductor on or round the magnet, or on some other part of the circuit."

Faraday's disk machine is an example of a machine of this class. The first two classes comprise all the dynamos which have commercial value as generators, the remaining class being unimportant from this point of view.]

the approach to a south pole, and departure from a north pole, give currents of the opposite directions to those of the preceding currents.

These currents are collected just as they are produced, by the aid of metal rings, serving as intermediaries between the rotating circuit and the extremities of the stationary outer circuit, which are fixed. These rings are of brass, and fastened, with proper insulation, upon the shaft of the machine in the movement of which they partake; they are each connected with one of the extremities of the moving circuit, and convey the currents to the outer circuit by means of metallic rubbers, the pressure of which is regulated by springs. This is the arrangement adopted for alternating-current machines in which the armature is movable. In machines powerful enough to have the coils of their armatures divided into several groups, each giving a utilizable current, there must be as many pairs of rings as there are distinct circuits.

We shall see, further on, that in some recent machines, with alternating currents, this order of parts has been reversed—the inducers or field magnets moving, and the induced circuits being stationary; these last are then connected directly with the field magnets, and there is only one pair of rings for the entrance and exit of the magnetizing current.

It will be understood that in most applications of electricity alternating currents can not be used, because the work performed while the current passes in one direction will be destroyed by the next current which passes in the opposite direction. Thus they can only be used in the production of the electric light, where they have the advantage of causing equal consumption of the carbon electrodes, and we have seen that this condition is indispensable for parallel carbon-burners or for electric candles.

For all other applications it is indispensable to render the currents continuous—that is to say, to collect them—so that they shall succeed each other in the same direction; thus there is attained a current, which really is not continuous, like a battery-current, but which is almost the same thing, and produces the same effects, on account of the rapid succession of the partial currents which make it up, and which may be as many as fifty to sixty thousand in a single minute. These continuous currents are also used for the electric light with advantage; the plant is more simple, the machines do not produce the hissing which is telephonically transmitted to the lamps, and whose inconvenience we have already spoken of. These same currents are preferable for open-air incandescent lamps, and are used exclusively for vacuum incandescent lamps.

In the early machines, such as those of Clarke, whose bobbins are wound in opposite directions, and in machines whose induced circuit is formed of a Siemens armature (Siemens, Ladd, Wilde), there are only two changes of direction of the currents, and, to effect these, a very simple mechanism suffices, called a *commutator*. It is a ferule of ivory, on which are fastened two half-ferules of copper, insulated, and attached each one to the extremities of the moving circuit; they turn with it, and, at each reversal of the current, bring the terminals of this circuit before the corresponding terminals of the exterior circuit, terminating for this purpose in two rubbers.

As soon as the number of armature coils was increased so as to increase the power of the machine, the old commutator became insufficient. The commutator-plates needed to be increased in number, and it became the *collector*,* used universally to-day.

To understand how this commutator can gather the currents and give them all the same direction, we must examine the action which takes place in an induced coil in movement. To make this examination easier, we shall represent the machine by diagrametrical figures, and shall employ the signs + and − to indicate the polarity of the inductors and the direction of the currents.

Let us consider, first, a copper wire wound upon a drum turning between the poles of an electro-magnet: every time that the parts of a wire situated at the extremity of the same diametrical plane pass before the poles, induction will cause currents of opposite direction to be started, this direction depending on the nature of the pole and direction of the move-

---

* [The distinction made by the authors is not observed in English. The name *commutator* is given to the device by which the successive opposed currents are directed so as to follow one another continuously in the circuit, irrespective of whether it has few or many plates. The word *collector* is used only to denote the similar portion of an alternating-current machine, by which the currents are simply collected.]

ment, and it is in the plane passing through the poles and
through the axis of rotation that the action will be most
energetic ; it is there that the lines of force cut by the wires
are the most numerous. But as the wires form part of a circuit, the direction of the winding of this wire, referred to the
inductors before which it moves, must be taken into account:
if it presents itself in one relation in approaching the poles,
it will have the opposite relation in leaving them ; it is as if
the winding of the first period had been reversed for the
second ; it follows that in this last period the current, which
in an insulated wire should be of the opposite direction, according to Faraday's ·law, becomes redirected as far as this
branch of the helix is concerned, and takes the same direction
as that given during the first period of movement. In a word,
in this case the currents produced in the branches of the
helix under the influence of the same pole have the same
direction before and after their passage. As the respective
influences of each of the poles neutralize each other in a
second plane or section perpendicular to the first, and also
passing through the axis of rotation, the change of direction
of the currents induced will take place each time they pass
from one side to the other of this plane, which is termed
the *commutation plane.* The wire wound around the drum
will be divided into two halves, placed on each side of this
plane, and simultaneously traversed by equal currents but of
opposite direction.

If, in place of a drum, a cylindrical ring be employed as
a core on which to wind the wire (Fig. 143), the effects will be
the same; only the portions of the wire placed within the
ring will be the seat of currents opposed to those of the exterior wires, but of more feeble ones because farther removed
from the poles ; all that can ever be collected is the excess of
one set over the other. But if the ring is made of soft iron,
it will exercise a double influence upon the production of currents : on one hand it will answer as a screen for the interior
wires, whose induction will thereby be diminished, while at
the same time it will augment that of the exterior wires, because the magnetic field, concentrated between the poles and
the exterior surface of the ring will be much more powerful.
On the other hand, this ring will become magnetized ; the
two poles of contrary name will be produced in it, opposed
to those of the electro-magnet. These poles will be displaced

by the movement, which will start in the armature helices a second class of currents, which M. Du Moncel has termed *polar interversion currents*. These currents have the same direction during each period of the movement, because here again, during the second period, the action is produced on

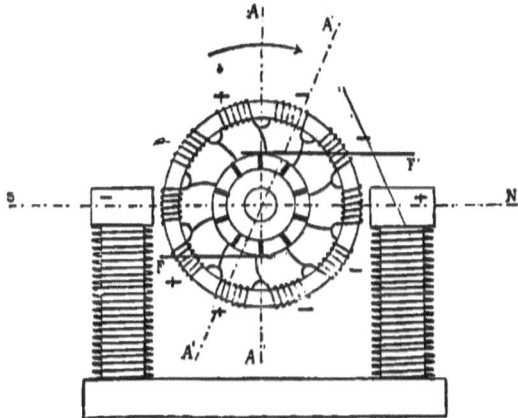

FIG. 143.—Direct induction in the ring armature.

the opposite side of the helices, which amounts to changing the direction of the winding. As this direction is the same as that of the currents produced at the same moment by the direct induction, the two currents are added to each other so as to form a single one of increased intensity.

Like the drum first spoken of, the ring is divided into two halves, in which the helices are traversed by equal and opposed currents, which are in equilibrium in the plane of commutation A A. By connecting all the helices in tension —that is to say, the entrance end of one with the exit end of the other—they can be considered as forming two batteries, composed of the same number of similar elements, connected by their like poles ; that is to say, two batteries in opposition. The two positive poles must then be put in communication by means of a rubber, F, with one of the extremities of an exterior circuit, and the two negative poles with the other extremity by a second rubber, F', for a current to be established ; this current will be formed by those of the two halves of the ring, which will thus be coupled for quantity.

On account of the movement of the induced helices, each one of them passes necessarily from one side to the other of the commutation plane, and consequently the currents, of which it is the seat, change their direction. The ring is always divided into two halves, but these do not always contain the same helices which originally constituted them, and the junctions with the exterior circuit must be changed. This is effected by arranging as many connecting wires as there are helices, and by terminating them by as many plates; these plates, perfectly insulated from each other, are united so as to form a little drum, which constitutes the commutator. It is mounted on the shaft of the machine and turns with it, so that it brings the brushes, F F′, necessarily in contact with the two plates which correspond to the helices reaching the commutation plane.

We have seen that the induced helices are subjected to a double effect of induction, one produced directly by the poles of the field magnet, the other by the change of magnetic

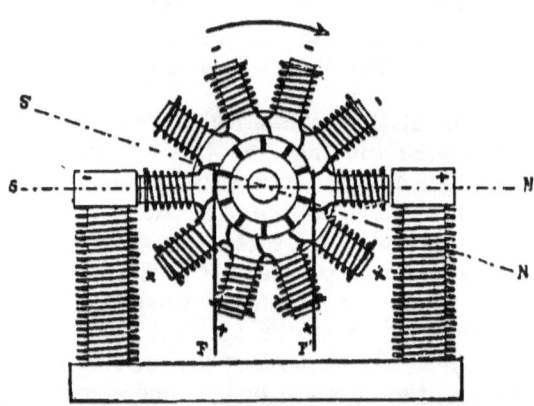

Fig. 144.—Indirect induction, or induction by magnetic reaction of the radiating armature-cores.

state of the core. What has just been said applies to cases where the first effect preponderates; it is different where the core reaction predominates (Fig. 144). Then the inversions take place at the moment of passage in front of the poles, because it is at this moment that the magnetization and demagnetization of the cores are produced. In this case the plane of commutation, and with it the points of contact of the brushes upon the collector, becomes one with the plane S N, passing through the poles.

The currents due to direct induction still exist, though they are much weaker, because the way in which the helices come before the magnet is much less favorable. As their commutation plane is not the same, they can not be collected, and they cause in the machine the production of heat, which increases that developed in the cores by the molecular movements due to change of polarity; thus machines of this class have their speed limited by the heating.

Up to this point we have not taken into account the galvanic field which results from the currents of induction, and which reacts upon the magnetic field of the inductors. In consequence of this reaction, the plane in which induction is most powerful is displaced; in the machines we are now discussing, and which are intended for the production of currents, the displacement is in the direction of the movement, as the reaction is dependent upon the existence of these currents, and increases in proportion as they attain their maximum intensity. It is, then, in a different position, A' A' or S' N', to be determined, that the real plane of commutation is situated, and consequently the contacts of the brushes on the commutator.

When the reversibility of these machines is utilized so as to transform them into motors—that is, when the armature receives an electric current from an external source—and when its movement is due to the reciprocal actions of the inducers and of the current, this displacement of the magnetic field takes place in a direction the reverse of the movement, as the galvanic field exists permanently, and can act before reaching the inducing poles. In both cases this displacement causes that of the plane of commutation, and consequently of the points of contact of the brushes upon the commutator. It will sometimes be found, on examining a machine at work, that the apparent points of contact do not correspond with the place that they should occupy theoretically; the requirements of construction making it necessary to seek a new position for them, by bending the wires which connect the plates of the commutator with the armature coils.

CHAPTER V.

THE FIRST MAGNETO-ELECTRIC MACHINES.

THE discoveries of Faraday were quickly utilized in the devising of apparatus to produce induced currents in a continuous manner.   In the year 1832 Pixii constructed in Paris an early machine (Fig. 145) in which a permanent magnet turned in front of the poles of an electro-magnet ; the soft-iron cores of this last one were thus magnetized and demagnetized successively, and created in the copper wire surrounding them alternating induced currents ; these currents, given the same direction by a commutator fixed on the axis of rotation, were so intense that, in Ampère's lectures at the Sorbonne, they could decompose the water in a voltameter, and redden a platinum wire. His first magneto-electric machine is preserved to-day in the cabinet of the Conservatoire des Arts et Métiers.

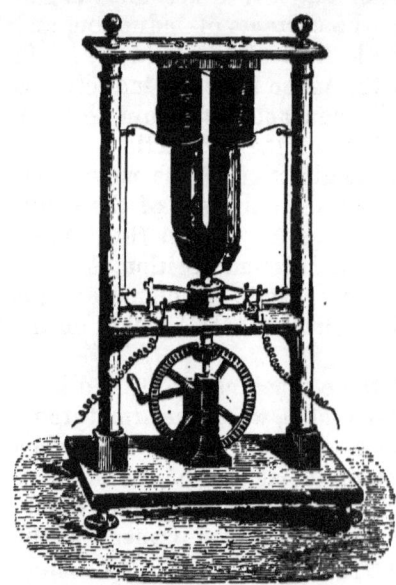

FIG. 145.—Magneto-electric machine of Pixii, 1832.

In 1833 an American named Saxton modified Pixii's machine by making the permanent magnet fixed, and having the much lighter electro-magnet rotate.   The following year Clarke put in practice the same idea, placing the magnet in a vertical position, and turning the electro-magnet laterally (Fig. 146).   In spite of the slight importance of this change, it is Clarke's name that is used to-day to designate this class of apparatus, employed now more particularly as illustrative of the science, in the lecture-room.

I. Nollet.—Van Malderen.—Holmes.

It seemed quite natural to increase the number of coils of Clarke's machine, for the purpose of obtaining stronger currents. This was done in 1849 by Nollet, Professor of Physics in the Military School of Brussels. He first doubled the number of coils; then he arranged eight upon a wooden cylinder, and turned them between the arms of four magnets opposite each other in pairs. He finally arranged sixteen on the same disk turning between the arms of eight magnets, and, placing

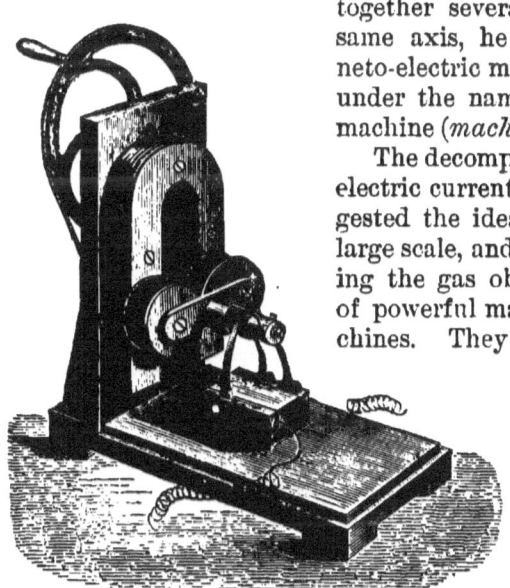

together several disks upon the same axis, he created the magneto-electric machine well known under the name of the *Alliance* machine (*machine de l'Alliance*). The decomposition of water by electric currents had already suggested the idea of doing it on a large scale, and of using for lighting the gas obtained by the aid of powerful magneto-electric machines. They were thus to indirectly produce light. It is not difficult to understand that the proposed speculation came to naught; the machine consumed too much power, and it was sim-

Fig. 146.—Magneto-electric machine of Clarke.

pler and cheaper to extract the illuminating gas directly from bituminous coal. Besides, it was necessary to render the currents continuous, and all the commutators tried were rapidly used up by the circuit-breaking sparks. It was after this, toward 1856, that M. Du Moncel advised the use of the machine for the production of the electric light, and, thanks to the idea suggested by M. Masson, the commutator was suppressed. It was then even by accident that for this use alternating currents were employed whose special advantages in certain systems of lighting we have already described. The success was as complete as was possible, and it is the first machine that was put to industrial use, principally the application of the electric light to light-houses, inaugurated in France in 1863.

In this machine the inductors, or field magnets, are stationary; they consist of two parallel rings of eight horseshoe magnets, placed radially around disks; these magnets are supported by wooden bars, and their poles, very regularly spaced, are alternated so that a north pole is opposed to a south pole, and so on; each of these magnets is composed of six steel plates, one centimetre thick, supplied by the Allevard Works; these plates are tempered, polished on a stone, and fastened together by screws; they are separately magnetized, and each set, weighing about twenty kilogrammes, can lift sixty.

The armature coils are movable; they are arranged around a brass disk by means of collars, and parallel to the axis of rotation; the spaces between them are regulated with the utmost precision, so that they all come at all times in the same relative positions with reference to the sixteen poles of the field magnets.

· The cores of Clarke's armature bobbins were made of soft-iron rods; but when they are caused to turn much faster in the presence of very powerful magnets, they need some modification to enable them to be magnetized and demagnetized more rapidly without heating.

We have already stated that the rapid changes of polarity cause molecular movements in the metal, accompanied by a production of heat; we have also seen that induced currents are produced in the cores like those whose existence was shown by Faraday, and that to diminish their strength, and facilitate the effects of the magnetic influence, the material of the cores had to be diminished and divided as much as possible.

This has been done with the Alliance machines by making the cores of iron tubes split longitudinally. The washers of brass, fastened at each end to keep the wire in place, are also split in a radial line. On this tube the wires are wound with proper insulation; at first too fine a wire was used, which became heated and developed a high resistance; it became necessary, for the sake of increasing the section, to wind several parallel to each other; instead of one, four were

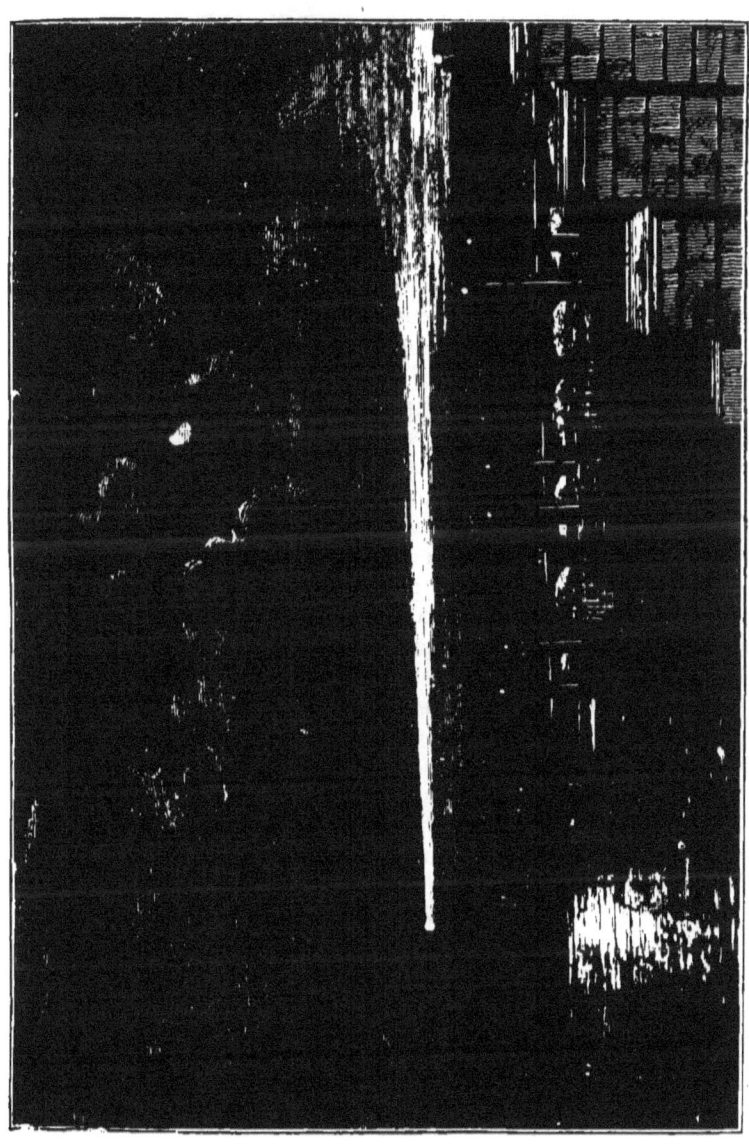

Fig. 147.—Experiments in the projection of the electric light at London, on the Thames, with a Brush lamp of six hundred carcels.

first substituted; to-day eight wires, of one millimetre diameter, are used.

There is no need, as we have already stated, to consider the production of electricity in these machines; it is clear that the currents change in direction every time the bobbins pass before the poles of the magnet: as there are sixteen magnet-poles, there are sixteen changes of current in each revolution, so that with a speed of four hundred revolutions per minute there are over one hundred reversals per second. Every time the currents change their direction the voltaic arc ceases to exist; the continuity of the light is due to the incandescence of the polar carbons; the duration of these interruptions is, moreover, so short—hardly the ten-thousandth of a second—that the arc easily starts anew through the air heated by the radiation from the incandescent carbons, and the more so as the reversals take place precisely when the currents attain their maximum of intensity.

Nollet died in the midst of his work, and it was Van Malderen, his collaborator, appointed engineer of the company, who gave the machines their last improvements; thanks are due to him for the success then obtained, whose promises were never destined to be realized; the hour of electric lighting had not yet come.

About the same period M. Holmes, who had assisted in the construction of Nollet's machines ordered from England for the production of illuminating gas, succeeded on his own part in utilizing them for the production of the electric light. The same appears to have happened to the *Compagnie l'Alliance*, and it is with one of these machines, which were built between 1858 and 1862, that the first experiments with electric light in the Dungeness light-house were conducted; the results were not very good, because the commutator for rendering the currents continuous was still in use.

II. SIEMENS.—WILDE.—LADD.

At this epoch it was principally from the changes in the magnetic state of the cores that the current was produced. To develop still more this method of induction, and obtain from it the most powerful effects, Mr. W. Siemens invented in 1854 the ingenious armature which bears his name (Fig. 148). It is formed of a cylindrical core of soft iron, with two longitudinal grooves cut in it, which gives it the section of a double T (Fig. 149). The wire that is subjected to induction is wound in the grooves which it fills so as to restore the cylindrical form ; binding-wires prevent the wire yielding to the centrifu-

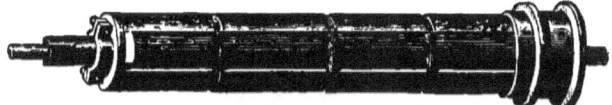

FIG. 148.—Siemens' armature.

gal force. The wings of the double T form poles extending along the core and reacting energetically on the wires.

This armature was first designed for a telegraphic induction apparatus. But in 1866 Mr. Siemens employed it in the construction of a small magneto-electric machine. The poles of the field magnets are united by a piece of brass ; the armature turns in a cylindrical cavity, between these three pieces, which completely surround it ; a commutator serves to render the currents continuous, whose commutation plane passes through the plane of the poles, subject, however, as before explained, to the displacement due to the working of the machine. In the Electrical Exhibition at Paris there could be seen Mr. Siemens's original model, as well as two more powerful machines of the same type which had been exhibited in 1873 at the Vienna Exhibition. This armature had then been discarded as an organ for development of currents, because of the enormous speed needed, and the great heat which was developed in it. Nevertheless, it is still employed with success in small electro-motors.

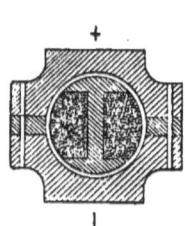

FIG. 149.—Cross-section of the Siemens armature.

It is with the Siemens armature that M. Wilde constructed one of the two machines which had such a success at the Paris Exhibition of 1867 ; the second was the machine of Mr. Ladd, of which we shall speak further on.

It is M. Wilde who, struck with the enormous superiority of electro-magnets over permanent magnets of the same weight, first conceived the idea of using them in the field as inductors. Wilde's machine, then, was the first dynamo-electric machine ; it was composed (Fig. 150) of a large Siemens armature, turning between the poles of a powerful vertical electro-magnet, arranged as we have seen in explaining the employment of this armature. The magnetizing or exciting current of the field was furnished by a small Siemens magneto-electric machine, placed above the first named; the

Fig. 150.—Wilde's first dynamo-electric machine, with Siemens' magneto-electric exciter.

movement was transmitted separately by pulleys to each of two bobbins, whose speed reached 2,400 turns per minute for the small bobbin and 1,500 turns for the large one. At the same time (1867) Mr. Ladd constructed a similar machine, but with an improvement; the small special exciting machine was suppressed in part, and the inducers or field magnets of the large machine were utilized to influence both bobbins at once. To this end the field magnets were formed of two large, flat, horizontal bobbins, placed one above the other and connected so as to have their opposite poles facing each other. The cores terminated at each extremity in polar masses, shaped so as to receive the armatures. In a second model Mr. Ladd suppressed the special exciting armature, only preserving a single one with two distinct circuits—one furnishing the exciting current, the other supplying the exterior circuit.

This method of utilizing the reaction on the field magnets of the currents which they themselves produced had also been applied some time before by M. Wilde to another type of machine resembling Nollet's. In this machine the field magnets are formed by thirty-two straight electro-magnets. arranged in a circle on a frame and forming two parallel series whose alternate poles are placed in front of each other. In the space between them a plate carrying sixteen armature coils on each side rotates.

The field magnets are excited by a current taken from four of these coils and rendered continuous by means of a commutator. The current of the other induced bobbins is collected on two friction-rings and sent into the lamp circuit. This machine, which received several applications in England, had been long abandoned in France by the company that had bought it in 1867. It was taken up again last year (1879), in spite of the inconveniences of its commutator, and quite satisfactory results obtained with it.

These different improvements were merely the application of principles which Mr. Varley had embodied in a machine patented by him in 1866, and which Messrs. Werner Siemens and Wheatstone had explained in two communications presented in that year to the Academy of Sciences of Berlin and to the Royal Society of London.* The first memoir showed that electric energy could be converted into magnetic energy without the need of permanent magnets; the second memoir showed that the power of an electro-magnet, which retained a trace of residual magnetism, could be developed up to saturation by the progressive increase of the induction currents produced by itself.

This succession of discoveries was the starting-point of the

---

* The principle of "self-excitation" was first enunciated by a Dane, Sóren Hjorth, who patented in England in 1854 a machine in which it was carried out.

17

rapid progress witnessed by our own eyes, and, thanks to which, we have succeeded in effecting at pleasure all those wonderful transformations of an agent which, always invisible and elusive, only manifests itself in its prodigious effects of heat, work, and electricity.

CHAPTER VI.

THE GRAMME MACHINES.

M. GRAMME is the first inventor who succeeded in practically developing these discoveries, and in making all the factors unite in producing electricity with the regularity and economy indispensable in industrial applications. It is in great part to the machine of this indefatigable worker that the development of electric lighting is due.

M. Gramme's improvements apply to all parts of the machine; the power of the field magnets has been brought to a maximum by the use of electro-magnets with consequent poles. The annular form given to the induced circuit has enabled us to utilize uninterruptedly the action of induction, and the currents have been collected and rendered continuous very successfully, thanks to the ingenious arrangement of the collector. These machines have received, besides, since their invention, numberless alterations; successively electro-magnetic machines (Fig. 151) and dynamo-electric machines have been constructed, something which is effected, as we have already seen, without difficulty. The field magnets were placed vertically in the first machines (Fig. 152), they are now horizontal, without other reason than the convenience of construction; finally the ring, after having been made duplex, so as to furnish separately the exciting and the working currents, has been reduced to a single circuit, whose entire current traverses the coils of the field magnets. We shall limit ourselves to the description of the latest model, designated workshop type (*type d'atelier*), which is the one most generally used (Fig. 153).

The inductor, or field magnet, is composed of two horizontal bars connected by bolts with the frame. The whole forms two electro-magnets with their two arms, united by similar poles, producing in the middle of the system two double or consequent poles of great energy, between which the ring turns. The cast-iron upright frame serves at once as support

Fig. 151.—Gramme magneto-electric machine for the laboratory.

for the parts of the machine and as a yoke for the electro-magnets, whose magnetic circle they complete. Although the residual power of cast-iron is considerable, its use is attended with no inconvenience, provided the pieces have to under-go no change of polarity. It is only necessary to take into account the fact that the magnetic capacity of cast-iron is less than that of wrought-iron, and to increase the dimensions in constructing the machine.

Fig. 152.—First form of Gramme dynamo machine for lighting.

The armature is formed of a flat annular core, constructed of iron wire, rolled into a circular shape by a special mill; the use of iron wire is for the purpose of subdividing the mass of metal, the necessity of which we have already spoken of. On this core are wound transversely several layers of copper wire, of suitable diameter, most carefully insulated, and separated into sections of distinct helices, placed side by side. Fig. 154 shows it complete in one part only ; the other part has the half of the helices removed, and farther on the ring is cut so as to show the section of the iron wires composing it. All the coils are connected for tension, the inner end of one and the outer end of the other being attached to the same

Fig. 153.—Gramme machine (workshop type).

plate of copper. Thus there are as many plates as coils, and naturally the division is made with an even number, so that the two halves of the ring may always contain the same number of coils. All the plates, also insulated, are prolonged back of the ring, and there form a small drum which constitutes the commutator.

The two rubbers are a species of brush or broom made of wires of a good conducting metal; they are made to bear against the collector by springs, which can be regulated by hand. This kind of rubbers insures perfect contact, and weakens the destructive effects of the sparks by dividing them between a large number of points.*

The collecting apparatus is the delicate part of machines; the contact must be sufficient to insure the passage of the current with the least possible resistance, without being strong enough for the friction to wear away the commutator rapidly. Moreover, this friction can not be reduced by the use of oil, because the lubricator, quickly becoming charged with metallic dust, would fill up the intervals between the plates and destroy their insulation. The collector and brushes must therefore be watched closely, and the greatest care taken of them; the points of contact of the brushes with the collector should always be placed exactly in the line of the commutation plane, determined once for all at the normal running of the machine, and exactly at the extremities of the same diameter of the commutator, as otherwise one part of the opposing currents produced in the ring would be destroyed by a corresponding part of the other current; the intensity of the remaining current would be weakened in proportion.

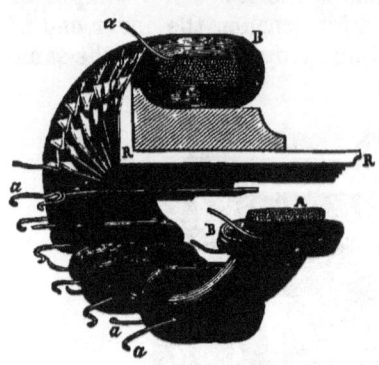

FIG. 154.—Gramme Ring.

We have seen that the currents of these machines were produced by the direct influence of the poles of the field magnets, and by the magnetic reactions of the ring; their intensity increases with the speed of the machine, as these effects are multiplied in proportion. There is, however, a limit which it would be dangerous to exceed, because the wire of the coils, being invariable, would finally be of insufficient section; the internal resistance would gradually increase, and would cause the development of a great deal of heat; the work expended would thus increase much quicker than the intensity of the current.

* [The brushes used on all machines in this country consist of a bundle of strips of sheet-copper.]

The following table, published by M. Fontaine, shows in what proportions the results vary with the speed of the machine, and with the distance between it and the lamps :

Influence of the Speed of the Machine.

NUMBER OF REVOLU-TIONS PER MINUTE.	Length of the conducting wire.	Distance between the points of the carbons.	LUMINOUS INTENSITY IN CARCELS.		WORK EXPENDED IN KILOGRAMMETRES.		Number of carcels per horse-power.
			Measured horizontally.	Mean intensity.	Total.	Per 100 carcels of mean intensity.	
	m.	mm.					
700	100	3	160	320	185	57·81	130
725	100	3	243	486	165	33·95	220
750	100	3	295	590	192	32·54	230
800	100	4	365	730	230	31·05	235
850	100	5	488	976	282	28·89	270
900	100	6	576	1,152	330	28·64	260
1,000	100	10	646	1,292	338	26·16	285

The mean luminous intensities are here the mean of intensities observed at different angles :

Influence of Distance of the Lamp from the Machine.

NUMBER OF REVOLU-TIONS PER MINUTE.	Length of conducting wire.	Distance between the points of the carbons.	ILLUMINATING POWER IN CARCELS.		WORK EXPENDED IN KILO-GRAMMETRES.		Number of carcels per horse-power.
			Measured horizontally.	Mean intensity.	Total.	Per 100 carcels of mean intensity.	
	m.	mm.					
750	100	4	321	690	186	28·9	267
800	150	5	345	642	230	33·3	225
825	200	5	315	630	232	36·8	178
850	300	5	275	550	225	40·9	183
900	400	5	260	520	241	46·3	162
950	500	5	245	490	230	46·1	160
1,000	750	5	236	472	243	51·4	145
1,100	1,000	5	215	430	256	59·5	126
1,350	2,000	5	160	320	230	71·8	104

In all the experiments the section of the conducting wire was ten square millimetres.

DIVISION MACHINES (*Machines à Division*).*

As soon as the improvements effected in regulators by the use of the derived current made possible the placing of sev-

* [This term, used to denote machines operating more than one lamp on one circuit, is quite erroneously applied, as it refers to no distinctive mode of construction. The number of devices which can be operated upon any circuit de-

eral lamps on the same circuit, M. Gramme devised new types
arranged to furnish the same results with continuous currents; the field magnets have received new polar extensions
of large section, and the power of their magnetic field is much

Fig. 155.—Five-light Gramme machine.

increased; the armature-wire is much finer and longer, consequently the electro-motive force is much greater for the same
speed, and the current possesses the necessary tension (Fig.
155). The field magnets are supplied by a special exciter; in

pends solely, so far as the machine is concerned, upon the quantity and electro-
motive force of the current furnished; but this is a matter of proportions of
parts and speed, and not of constructive differences. The term could be rightly
applied to denote machines feeding several distinct circuits, but these are better
described as "multiple-circuit machines."]

spite of its complication, this arrangement has the advantage of rendering the field magnets independent of variations in the resistance of the exterior circuit, and insures to the magnetic field a stability analogous to that of magneto-electric machines. These machines can supply from two to five, ten, and even twenty lights, by changing the speed of rotation and the resistance of the conducting wire, as is shown in the following figures, determined by M. Fontaine ("Revue Industrielle"):

NUMBER OF LIGHTS.	Number of revolutions per minute.	Resistance of conductor.	Normal length of the arc.	Distance of the carbons producing extinction.
		ohms.	mm.	mm.
1	500	1·00	2·5	6·0
2	700	2·00	2·5	5·7
3	975	3·00	2·5	5·5
4	1,125	4·10	2 5	5·5
5	1,300	5·30	2 5	5·5

The figures of the last two columns show that the current should always possess a tension superior to the effective resistance of the arcs used, so as to leave a sufficient margin for the action of the regulators.

The same types serve also for the production of the powerful lights in use in light-houses and in marine and war apparatus. MM. Sautter and Lemonnier, who construct so successfully this class of machine, have given a résumé of their conditions in the interesting figures in the following table:

TYPE OF MACHINE.	WIRE OF THE RING.		WIRES OF THE FIELD MAGNET.		Number of revolutions per minute.	Mean length of arc.	Diameter of carbons.	ILLUMINATING POWER.		Work expended in horse-power.
	Diameter.	Length.	Diameter.	Length.				Aver-age.	Maxi-mum.	
	mm.	m.	mm.	m.		mm.	mm.			
M (200 carcels)	1·2	340	1·8	440	1,600	3	9	226	625	1·25
AC (600 carcels)	1·8	264	3·4	565	820	4	13	490	1,200	2·75
CT (1,600 carcels)	2·8	336	3·4	1,280	675	4	18	1,015	2,500	5·25
CQ (2,500 carcels)	3·65	276	3·4	1,280	1,360	4·5	18	1,241	3,300	8·
DQ (4,000 carcels)	4·3	460	3·8	2,160	475	6	20	2,198	6,000	12·
2 AC machines coupled for quantity	1·8	264	3·4	565	880	4	13	1,185	2,600	5·50
2 CT machines coupled for quantity	2·8	336	3·8	1,280	675	5	18	2,200	4,000	10·5

The maximum intensities are those attained by using lamps inclined so as to expose the crater of the positive carbon to the surface to be illuminated.

The last two lines, compared with the second and third, show what an increase of light follows the coupling of two machines for quantity.

These powerful machines are sometimes constructed with a double ring—that is to say, the one hundred and twenty coils which it contains are divided into two series—sixty coils have their entrance ends on the right side and the others have them on the left. The machine is also supplied with two commutators, one on each side of the ring, and each of these serves to collect half of the sum total of electricity produced by the machine; these two halves can be connected for quantity or for tension, according to the exigencies of the work to be done; or, if it is desirable, one current may be used to excite the field magnets and the other for the working current.

OCTAGONAL MACHINES.

In all the preceding machines there are only the two field magnets or inducing poles; only two currents of opposite direction are produced, which, united in the external circuit, furnish only a single current. To increase the power of his machines in the proportions which the applications to the transmission of power necessitate, M. Gramme has increased the dimensions of his ring so as to exert upon it the influence of four electro-magnets simultaneously. The four successive poles are alternately of contrary name, and the commutations take place in planes passing through the axis of rotation, but forming with each other an angle of ninety degrees. The ring is thus divided into two parts, each working like a complete ring of the ordinary type. Four rubbers, pressing on a single commutator, gather the two currents, produced simultaneously, which can be connected for quantity or for tension. The large diameter of the ring makes it possible to obtain, with a moderate speed of rotation, a more rapid movement of the helices in front of the inducing poles. The particular form of the structure has given to these machines the name of *octagonal*. It will be understood that this system can be pushed still further, enabling us to construct machines of very high power.

ALTERNATING-CURRENT MACHINES.

Nothing remains for us now, to complete the review of the numerous inventions of M. Gramme, except to speak of his alternating-current machines. We have seen that on account of the improvements of regulators, several lights can be obtained from one machine, provided its tension is in proportion to the sum of the resistances of the exterior circuit. But this tension increases rapidly with the number of lights; it requires, besides the increased motive power necessary for its production, much greater precautions in the insulation of the wires of the machine and of the conducting or line wires; thus, at first, the practical number of lamps was limited to four or five per circuit, according to their intensity. With double-ring machines twelve lights on one circuit were attained. But it is easy to increase this, if currents of such high tension do not frighten us; and we shall see further on that Mr. Brush, an American, as might have been expected, made his machines produce a current that could support forty lights on a circuit ten or twelve kilometres long.

This is the only possible solution with direct-current machines, because of the difficulty of multiplying commutators; but with alternating currents, which are more easily collected, several of them can be taken from the same machine, each distinct and independent; thus a great number of lights is obtained by the use of multiple circuits; first, a division of the total production of the machine into several currents, and then a division of each of these among several lamps. We have shown how alternating-current machines, with movable field magnets and fixed armature coils, were thus reached, which arrangement Mr. Holmes patented in 1857. We shall see how M. Gramme transformed his machine in 1877 to adapt it to the Jablochkoff candles.

He preserved his original ring, but, making it stationary, he could increase its dimensions. The ring became a cylinder, within which turns an inductor formed of an electro-magnet with multiple alternate poles, whose arms radiate from the axis of rotation, and whose poles, considerably drawn out, leave only a small intervening space.

The wire which envelops this cylinder is divided into as many sections as there are arms to the field magnet, and each section contains the same number of coils, so that the corresponding coils of each of these sections are always placed in the same relation to the poles of the inductor. The currents which are thus produced at the same instant are of similar direction, and can be united. The diagram (Fig. 156) shows that the coils $a\,a$, $b\,b$, $c\,c$, $d\,d$, form as many distinct groups, each furnishing two currents of opposite direction, due to the approaching to and departure from the field-magnet poles. This annular arrangement of the armature coils is advantageous, as the inductor works with more continuity, and because, if the currents of different groups vary in intensity on account of the relative position which each of them occupies in succession, the minima are much less feeble than in other systems, where they are almost null in the center of the comparatively large space intervening between the armature coils.

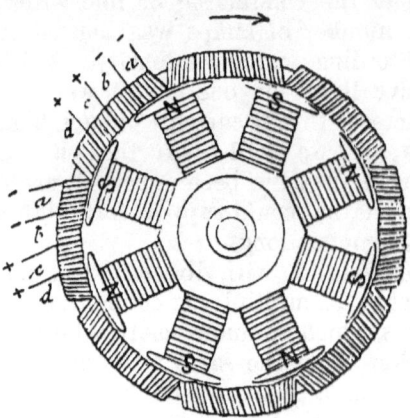

Fig. 156.—Diagram of alternating-current Gramme machine.

By using two rings, supplied with rubbers, the exciting current produced originally by a small machine with continuous current, called the *exciter*, and situated near it, can be passed into the rotating field magnet. This arrangement presents several inconveniences : in the first place, it increases the organs of transmission ; next, as the magnetization of the field is extremely sensitive to variations in the exciting current, it multiplies the chances of irregularity in the light.

SELF-EXCITING MACHINES.

To remedy these inconveniences, M. Gramme modified his exciter so as to make it possible to place both machines in the same framework, and use only one pulley to work both at the same time. These new machines, invented in 1870, have been named *self-exciting* (*auto-excitatrices*), (Fig. 157.)

The four arms of the inductor of the exciter are attached radially to the inner side of a ring, fastened to one of the ends of the frame, and cast in one piece with it ; their like poles are thus placed opposite each other in the apex of the two angles thus formed. The armature ring is fastened on the same shaft as the movable inductor of the alternating-current machine, which is not otherwise changed. The regu-

lating, which is done preliminarily by finding the best speed for the exciter when separate, is here obtained by means of a resistance interposed in the circuit of the exciting machine ; by making this resistance vary, the intensity of the current is changed, and consequently the magnetism of the field magnet as well as the intensity of the alternating currents is changed.

The most usual types are : one for eight candles of forty carcels, or twelve candles of twenty-five carcels ; another for

Fig. 157.—Self-exciting alternating-current Gramme machine.

sixteen candles of thirty-five carcels, or twenty-four candles of twenty carcels. A machine, with separate exciter, has even been constructed capable of supporting sixty candles at once.

We will only speak here, as a reminder, of the modifications introduced by M. Jamin in self-exciting machines ; they have principally borne upon the use of the exciting current, and the increase of tension of the alternating currents. The speed of the machine can be increased by them, as well as the expenditure of motive power; the increase of tension has made possible the lighting a number of lamps in the same

Fig. 158.—M. Gramme.

circuit, but their light "diminished because the heat regenerated in each of them is less."

This last expression recalls the fact that the heat of the voltaic arc is the result of that which is set free by the burning combustible under the boiler, or by the gas burned in the cylinder of the gas-engine; it still represents heat, even if a water-wheel be used, because it is the heat of the sun which transforms the water into vapor, and causes it to descend in the form of rain to supply our water-courses. All our sources of artificial heat are really the accumulated solar heat presented to us under three different forms:

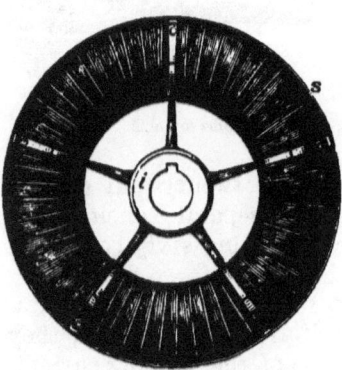

Fig. 159.—Armature of the Wood machine.

coal inclosed for centuries in the depths of the earth ; forests which slowly grow under our eyes ; and, finally the reservoirs of motive power, and consequently of the heat which the movement of water on the face of the earth create. When we shall have exhausted the first resource, which we waste, if the second does not de-velop with sufficient rap-idity for our needs, it will be electricity that will en-able us to utilize the last.

[The Gramme machine, as made in this country by the Fuller Electrical Company, after the de-signs of Mr. J. J. Wood, has several points of im-provement in its construc-tion. In the foreign ma-chine the central portion surrounded by the arma-ture ring is formed of a wooden block, driven into position, which operation not infrequently disar-ranges the wire and in-jures the insulation. It, moreover, prevents the cir-culation of air, which is useful in keeping the arm-ature cool. In the Amer-ican machine the armature ring is mounted upon a gun-metal frame, consist-ing of a central hub and radial bars or spokes. In its revolution this arma-ture has a fan-like action, and the wire is consequent-ly kept cool. This construction is clearly shown in Figs. 159 and 160. The general appearance of the machine, which does not differ greatly from the foreign form, is shown in Fig. 161. The regulation of the machine, in accordance with the num-

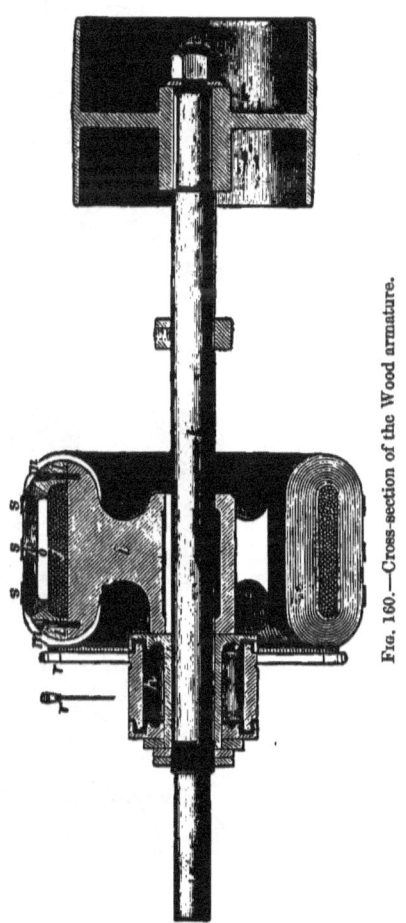

Fig. 160.—Cross-section of the Wood armature.

ber of arc-lamps in circuit, is effected by moving the brushes
to or from the maximum position.   This is done by the

FIG. 161.—Gramme machine as modified by Mr. Wood.

attendant when the necessity for it is shown by an electro-
magnetic indicator.]

PRECURSORS OF GRAMME.

As is often the case with important discoveries, M. Gramme's labors had been, unknown to him, preceded by analogous studies, carried on in 1860 by an Italian student, M. Pacinotti, to-day professor at the University of Cagliari. The original model of this inventor (Fig. 162), which was shown at the International Electrical Exhibition at Paris in 1881, present so surprising a resemblance to M. Gramme's machine, that we are obliged to ask why M. Pacinotti's machine remained completely forgotten until the extraordinary success of M. Gramme's machines made known its value. It is without doubt because, at the time when the learned Italian made his researches, the principal direction of such work was to produce motive power by means of electricity, and his apparatus was intended to be an electro-motor ; under this form they were necessarily doomed to impotence as long as they were obliged to use batteries for the production of the electricity.

Furthermore, the inventor, then only a student, was very soon engaged as assistant to Donati in the Astronomical Observatory of Florence, and obliged, by the requirements of this position, to direct his attention to other studies.

M. Pacinotti shows clearly, in the description of his machines, published in 1864 by a scientific Italian journal, "Il Nuovo Cimento," that it was doubtless possible to transform his electro-motor into an electro-magnetic generator of continuous currents ; but he did not appreciate the vast importance of this transformation, and, the circumstances not tending in such a direction, he gave up his experiments on the subject. We must add here that the jury of the Exhibition has recognized the merit of M. Pacinotti's inventions, and has decreed him, at the same time with M. Gramme, the highest award at its disposal, the diploma of honor.

In M. Pacinotti's machine the field magnet is an electro-magnet, whose poles spread out into the arc of a circle, within which the armature ring rotates, which the inventor calls the *transversal* electro-magnet ; it is a ring of iron provided with exterior projections, between which the coils of copper wire are wound. These coils are all wound the same way, and the ends of the wires are soldered to as many pieces of copper imbedded in a wooden drum, which form a commutator, against

18

which two metallic rubbers press; the passage of the current
through the coils magnetizes the annular iron ring, which can
be considered, in the words of M. Pacinotti, as formed of two
semicircular magnets connected by their similar poles. The
magnetic poles of the ring being attracted and repelled by those
of the fixed electro-magnet, the ring acquires a movement of
rotation. The same current circulates successively in the wire
of the ring and in the magnetizing coils of the field magnets.

By showing how his motor could be transformed into a
generator of electricity, M. Pacinotti explains the method of
producing currents of the same direction and the rules to be

Fig. 162.—Original model of the Pancinotti machine, exhibited at the Exposition of Electricity at Paris, 1881.

followed in placing the rubbers in position. Here was the
germ, as early as 1860, of all that constitutes the best actual
machines; and we should add, furthermore, that M. Pacinotti
himself had been preceded eight years by an American savant, Mr. Page, well known among electricians. In 1852 Mr.
Page had constructed in Washington a motor, with circular
electro-magnets, with which he succeeded in driving a small
locomotive.

Among the predecessors, not yet generally known, of the
Gramme machine, we must cite the one patented and con-

structed in 1866 by M. Worms de Romilly, on a theory far different from that which guided M. Gramme. He also wound his sectional bobbins in reverse directions, which forced him to redirect the currents. We have already explained that this redirection was impracticable.

The Electrical Exhibition in Paris has also shown us a model of much older date, as it goes back to 1842. It is a motor invented by M. Elias, which was exhibited in the Dutch section. All the elements of modern machines are found here in principle—windings, commutation, etc.; all this, it is true, in the function of motor, as with M. Pacinotti. Thus a quarter of a century was lost, because the question had been wrongly put, and because the world had never dreamed of perfecting the apparatus for production before the one destined to utilize the current.

CHAPTER VII.

THE SIEMENS MACHINES.

THE two firms of Messrs. Siemens Brothers and Siemens and Halske use for their actual lighting two types of machines, whose construction is due to M. Heffner von Alteneck : one is of the continuous-current type and dates back to 1872 ; the other, of alternate currents, dates from 1878. We shall study both at once, for they generally work together, one serving as exciter for the other.

The continuous-current machine (Fig. 163) has for a field two electro-magnets with consequent poles ; these poles, instead of being massive like those of M. Gramme, are formed of bars of soft iron, bent in the arc of a circle, and arranged one alongside of the other without touching, so that air circulates in the intervals, and contributes to the prevention of the heating of the machine.

The secondary coil or armature differs essentially from that of M. Gramme ; it is a cylinder of iron, which is nearly three times as long as its diameter ; the copper wire is wound exclusively around this cylinder, parallel to the axis of rotation ; it does not return through the interior. It is, then, the branches diametrically opposed to each other of one and the same helix, which are simultaneously subjected to induction, while in the ring of M. Gramme it is the two helices situated at the extremities of the same diameter which are subjected at the same time to the action of the field magnets; it follows that in the latter system it is the wires situated in the interior of the ring that can be considered inactive, if it be admitted that the iron core serves as a sort of magnetic screen; in the drum of Heffner von Alteneck it is the portion of the wires which cross each other on the extremities of the cylinder that are inactive. It can be deduced, then, that, under equal

Fig. 163.—Siemens continuous-current machine—vertical model.

conditions, the superiority of one system over the other can be estimated from the relative proportion of the active to the inactive wire.

To construct this drum wooden disks, which constitute a primary core, are arranged on the shaft of the machine, one beside the other, on which several layers of annealed iron wire are circularly wound. This first envelope is designed to charge the magnetic field of the inducing poles. The drum thus formed is covered again with taffeta, varnished with an insulating compound, and it is terminated by winding the

Fig. 164.—Mansion-House Square, London, lighted by Siemens' lamps.

copper wire longitudinally, as has been said above. This wire
is divided into an equal number of bundles, or coils, placed
one beside the other, and connected by their inlet and outlet
wires ; the whole forms an endless circuit, which can be understood from an inspection of the characters of Fig. 165, in
which the coils are supposed to be reduced each one to a
single wire.

The junctions of the coils are connected to plates of a commutator analogous to that of M. Gramme, and fastened upon
the same shaft as the drum. Fig. 166 shows the diagram of
these connections ; it will be seen that they are so arranged
that the total circuit of the coils is always divided into two
halves, in which the currents go in opposite directions and
unite at the two diametrically opposite plates of the commutator.

Thus from c to g and from g to c the circuits are :

$$c\,5\,5'\quad d\,7\,7'\quad e\,1'\,1\quad f\,4'\,4\quad g$$
$$-\ +\ -\ +\ -\ +\ -\ +$$
$$c\,3\,3'\quad b\,2'\,2\quad a\,8\,8'\quad h\,6\,6'\quad g$$
$$-\ +\ -\ +\ -\ +\ -\ +$$

If the drum and the commutator, whose movements coincide, continue to turn in the direction of the arrow, it is the
plates b and f which come opposite the rubbers, and the circuits become :

$$b\,3\,3'\quad c\,5\,5'\quad d\,7\,7'\quad e\,1'\,1\quad f$$
$$-\ +\ -\ +\ -\ +\ -\ +$$
$$b\,2\,2'\quad a\,8\,8'\quad h\,6\,6'\quad g\,4\,4'\quad f$$
$$-\ +\ -\ +\ -\ +\ -\ +$$

These machines are built of two types, that only differ
in the position of the field magnets, which are sometimes
placed vertically and sometimes horizontally. They serve not
only as exciters for alternate-current machines, but are also
employed for the production of the more intense of the electric lights, such as those of light-house, war, and marine apparatus. There are four models, designated by the letter D,
whose respective conditions are as follows :

MACHINES.	Horse-power.	Number of revolutions per minute.	Light produced in carcels.
D₂............	3¼	650	From 650 to 850
D₃............	2¼	850	300
D₄............	2	1,100	200

The machine D' is a very small machine, which makes about 1,300 revolutions, and is only employed as exciter.

The alternating-current machines of Mr. Siemens have one peculiarity which must not be passed over ; the iron cores of the armature are entirely suppressed, and the only induction utilized is that which is produced directly in the wires compos- ing it (Fig. 167). The moving part is light- er, and the principal cause of heating is done away with.

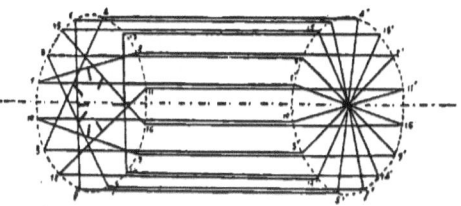

Fig. 165.—Diagram of the winding of the Heffner von Alteneck drum.

The inductors are straight electro-mag- nets, divided into two parallel series placed facing each other; they are fastened in a circle on the inner sides of two cast-iron frames bolted vertically on a cast-iron base and solidly cross-braced ; the cores terminate in polar plates, formed into sectors. The consecutive poles of each series are of opposite polarity, and unlike poles are placed op- posite each other. All the magnetizing coils of these electro-magnets are wound in the same direction, and it is by changing, by the way of fastening the inlet and outlet wires, the direc- tion of current traversing them that their polarities are reversed.

The armature is com- posed of non-magnetic bob- bins, whose wires are wound around wooden cores, fast-

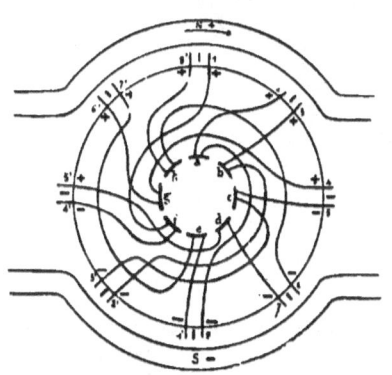

Fig. 166.—Diagram of the connection of the coils.

ened between copper disks ; holes pierced in these permit the air to carry off the small amount of heat which can be developed in the wires. These bobbins are equally elongated in the form of sectors, and are fastened by their disks around a bronze wheel; the whole arrangement presents the appear- ance of a flat disk, which rotates between the two circles of

inductors, or field magnets, whose influence it receives laterally, while the preceding systems are influenced cylindrically.

The central part of the brass wheel is supplied with a
wooden disk to which the wires from the bobbins are attached,
either directly together or by means of friction-rings. The
armature bobbins are connected either in tension or in quantity, as may be required; they form thus one or more series
whose currents are separately collected; each of these currents leaves the machine by a special ring; but all return to a
common ring, a little larger than the others.

Fig. 167.—Alternating-current machine of Heffner von Altenock.

There are three types of these machines, designated by the
letter W, having the capacity of supplying one, two, or four
circuits.

W¹, with 16 bobbins, running at the rate of 500 revolutions
per minute, and of sufficient capacity to supply 16 to 32 of
Siemens's differential lamps, with the machine D⁶ as exciter.

W², with 12 bobbins, making 600 revolutions, and of capacity to supply 12, 16, and 20 lamps, with the machine D⁶ as
exciter.

W³, with 8 bobbins, making 700 revolutions, and of capa-

city to supply 4, 6, 8, or 10 lamps, with the machine D⁵ as
exciter.

M. Heffner von Alteneck has succeeded, by several very
ingenious modifications, in transforming this alternate-current
machine into a continuous current, one which only contains
one commutator and two brushes, whatever be the number of
field magnets. This opens a new way for the construction of
generators yet more powerful than the machines with four
field magnets already existing, such as the octagonal machine
of M. Gramme, of which we have already spoken, and the
magneto-electric machine of the same kind constructed by M.
de Méritens, a machine which we shall examine further on.

Here we shall not enter upon this very interesting study,
one that at the same time is very complicated; we refer to
the study of the course of the currents in this class of machine, and the method of collecting them; such of our readers

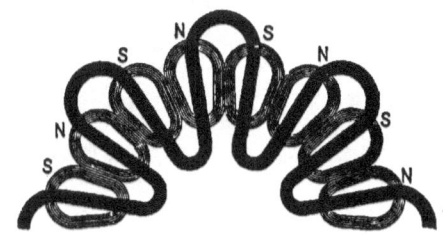

FIG. 168.—Diagram of armature and field coils of Ferranti machine.

as are interested in these special questions will find them
treated in the review of the machines of the Paris Electrical
Exhibition, published by "The Génie Civil" (November 1,
1881).

· [An alternating-current machine, of the same general appearance as the Siemens, but which differs materially from it
in the construction of its armature, has been designed by Sir
William Thomson and M. Ferranti. The field, like the Siemens, consists of two circular sets of bobbins with iron cores,
between which the armature revolves. The armature wire,
instead of being wound in coils, however, is in the form of a
zigzag, as shown in Fig. 168 by the dark band. One end of
this is attached to a ring on the axle, and the other to a similar ring insulated from both, and the current is taken off by
two rubbers bearing upon the rings. The field magnets are

excited by a separate continuous-current machine. An armature of this form has the advantages of little liability of over-
heating and low cost of manufacture.

The largest dynamo which has yet been constructed is an
alternating-current one designed by Mr. J. E. H. Gordon, and
shown in Fig. 169. It consists essentially of a central disk
carrying electro-magnets, and revolving between sets of similar electro-magnets on each side of it. The rotating portion
is the field, and the stationary electro-magnets the armature.

Fig. 169.—Gordon alternating-current dynamo.

This latter contains 128 coils, 64 on each side, this being twice
as many as in the rotating part. The coils of the revolving
magnets are excited by a separate continuous-current machine, as is the field of the Ferranti. The machine has a total
weight of eighteen tons, that of the revolving part being seven
tons. Its diameter is eight feet nine inches, and it is designed, when the machine is giving its maximum current, to
be driven at 200 revolutions per minute, and supply 7,000 sixteen-candle incandescent lamps.]

Fig. 170.—Weston dynamo.

CHAPTER VIII.

RECENT DYNAMO-ELECTRIC MACHINES.

THE systems of Messrs. Siemens and M. Gramme have given rise to two or three others of the same kind, whose inventors were content to combine in different ways organs and parts borrowed from the preceding machines, with slight modifications. The machines of Mr. Weston and Mr. Maxim, and even that of Mr. Edison, are of this number.

I. WESTON MACHINE.

Mr. Weston had exhibited in Paris, in 1878, a dynamo-electric machine constructed for electro-plating, which does not concern us ; it was, moreover, described in 1879, in the journal "La Lumière Électrique." We shall only examine the new continuous-current machine.

As Fig. 170 shows, this machine resembles in the form of its field magnets the machine of M. Gramme, and in its form of armature the machine of Mr. Siemens ; it only differs

Fig. 171.—Weston armature.

from these in some details. Thus the poles of the field magnets are divided by open slots, designed to prevent the production of Foucault currents, and to facilitate the circulation of air. The slots thus cut out are shorter in the middle than at the extremities, which, according to the inventor, insures more regularity in the production of the currents.

[The armature, wound with its wire, is shown in Fig. 171, and the core in Fig. 172. This latter is composed of a number of toothed disks of sheet-iron (Fig. 173), which are strung on the shaft and separated from each other by insulating washers. These disks and the washers are perforated to

allow the circulation of air.   The wire is wound lengthwise in
the grooves between the projecting teeth.   The commutator is
clearly shown in Fig. 170.   The plates were formerly arranged
spirally, but they are now constructed like those of the
Gramme and other machines.   The brushes are formed of a

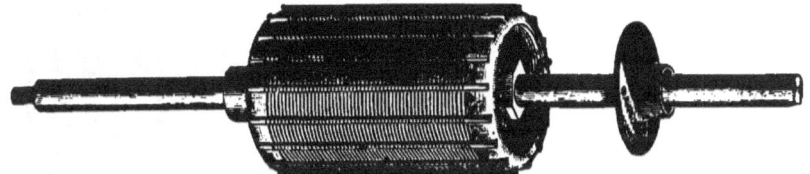

FIG. 172.—Core of Weston armature.

number of strips of sheet-copper, and are mounted in such a
manner that their position on the commutator can be readily
charged by means of the handle shown.   The field magnets
are placed in a shunt circuit in both the arc and incandescent
machine.]
   At the Palais de l'Industrie two Weston machines supplied eighteen lamps of the same inventor with an expenditure of eighteen horse-power.

II. Maxim Machine.

   Hiram S. Maxim's machine presents the reverse combination of the one just described ; the field magnets are identical
with those of the Siemens continuous-cur-
rent machines, and the armature is a Pacinotti and Gramme ring a little elongated ;
but what is most interesting is the general
arrangement adopted to obtain with these
machines a combination suited for lighting
by incandescence, and the current-regulator,
invented by Mr. Maxim to maintain the pro-
duction of a lighting current in exact pro-
portion to the demand made upon it.   It
forms, with the lamp of the same inventor,

FIG. 173. — Toothed
iron disk used in
Weston armature.

a complete system in which all the conditions of the problem
seem fulfilled, and which it appears has successfully worked
for some time in New York.
   This system comprises one or more machines for supply-

ing the lamps, and an exciting-machine for supplying the field magnets of the first-named.

It is to the exciting-machine that the regulator is adapted— by the aid of which the current supplying the lamps auto-

Fig. 174.—Maxim dynamo-electric machine for lighting, with double ring and two commutators.

matically regulates the intensity of the exciting current—in consequence, it (the lighting current) increases or diminishes, according to necessity, the power of the field magnets which produce it.

The elements of the two machines are the same: the field magnets are, as we have said, electro-magnets identical with those of Mr. Siemens. The annular armature is arranged like Pacinotti's ring and Weston's drum ; it is formed of a series of sheet-iron washers, cut out by means of a die, with fifteen projections distributed on their exterior circumference. A sufficient number of these washers are placed together, separated by sheets of paper, so as to form a hollow cylinder whose interior surface is smooth, and whose exterior surface has fifteen longitudinal projections or ribs, between which the wire is wound. The wire is wound transversely (longitudinally along the outside and inside of the cylinder, as in the Gramme ring), and is divided into sections whose incoming and outgoing ends are fastened, two by two, to the plates of a commutator analogous to that of M. Gramme. The brushes are double, and one is longer than the other, so that there is always one at least in contact with the plates of the commutator. This arrangement had already been adopted by Mr. Siemens. The openings which the ribs of the ring form between the wires, have for object, as in Weston's drum, the facilitating the cooling by the circulation of air caused by the rotation.

In the large machines which supply lamps (Fig. 174), the armature ring is doubled, of which we have seen an example in certain machines of M. Gramme. The coils of wire are wound half to the right and half to the left, and connected to two commutators placed at each end. The two currents thus collected can be used separately ; but for incandescent lamps they are preferably connected in quantity, a single circuit only being formed, on which the lamps are placed in multiple arc. Again, mixed lighting can be done, half of the ring being used for incandescent lamps, and the other half for one or two voltaic-arc regulators. All these groupings are made very easily by means of a plug commutator, shown on the top of the machine.

The exciting-machine (Figs. 175, 176) is generally less powerful ; the ring is not duplex, and there is only one commutator with one pair of brushes ; but the plates of this commutator are brought together, two and two, at their ends, so as to form a series of very prolonged V's. This differs a little from the arrangement in helices of the commutator plates of Mr. Weston, but leads to the same result.

The field magnets of the exciting-machine are placed in the same circuit as those of the lighting-machine, and a single exciter is enough for several machines. It is on this field-magnet circuit that Mr. Maxim's regulator acts. To under-

Fig. 175.—Maxim exciting-machine with automatic current regulator.   Front view.

stand its mechanism it must
be remembered that the intensity of the lighting current is proportional to the
power of the field magnets,
and that this depends in its
turn on the intensity of the
exciting current, and that, if
this last is made to vary, the
two other elements are at the
same time modified.

To vary, according to the
needs of the case, the intensity of the exciting current,
Mr. Maxim had recourse to
displacing the brushes on the
commutator; we have seen
that the currents are completely collected when the
brushes are placed so that
the two halves of the armature contain each one an
equal number of helices,
traversed by the currents in
the same direction, only opposed one half to the other.
If the brushes are removed
from this position the current which they collect diminishes, because each of the
two halves of the armature
contains at the same time
helices traversed by currents
of opposite direction, which
neutralize each other in part,
and whose difference or excess alone is collected. If
the displacement is carried
out until an angle of ninety
degrees is reached, the helices traversed by the currents
of opposite direction will be

Fig. 176.—Maxim exciting-machine with current regulator. Side view.

10

divided into equal numbers in each of the halves of the ring; the neutralization will be complete, and no current will be collected. Thus the displacement of the armature brushes can reduce the exciting current from its maximum to zero; at the same time it governs the power of the field, and in consequence the production of the lighting current.

The brushes are mounted on an independent support, which can receive a rotary movement by the action of a toothed sector and a series of cog-wheels, which is shown at the right of the first figure; the system comprises two ratchet-wheels, placed vertically one over the other. These wheels can be actuated by a horizontal lever, to which the main shaft of the machine communicates, by light gearing, an oscillatory movement. This lever has on both faces a small tooth, by which it turns one or the other of the two ratchet-wheels, according to whether it is raised or lowered; but when it is horizontal, the separation between the two wheels lets it pass freely.

The magnetic part of the regulator comprises two distinct electro-magnets, having each one different and successive functions, the second only acting as a safety apparatus, if the first is insufficient, and to give it time for acting. Both are wound with fine wire, forming shunts to the lamp circuit; the second has a slightly greater resistance.

The horizontal lever is connected with the armature of the first electro-magnet; an opposing spring, regulated by hand, pulls this armature, whose course is limited by two abutting screws. When one or more lamps are extinguished, the current becomes too intense for the lamps that remain; but now the derived current increases, the electro-magnet attracts its armature, the lever drops down, and one of its teeth engages with the lower ratchet-wheel. The oscillatory movement of the lever determines the rotation of the system, and consequently that of the brush-carriers. These approach the neutral point; the exciting current diminishes, which diminution is followed by all the consequences we have already indicated. This displacement of the brushes continues to be effected as long as the lighting current has not attained the degree of intensity corresponding to the number of lamps in use; at this moment of equilibrium the derived circuit grows weaker, the electro-magnet relaxes a little its attraction for its armature, and the toothed lever takes the horizontal position; the ratchet-wheels remain motionless. If new lamps are lighted again, the current in the shunt circuit grows still weaker; the opposing spring draws the armature entirely away, and lifts up completely the toothed lever, which acts then upon the upper ratchet-wheel. A reverse movement of the brushes is the result, which approach the points where the current collected will attain its maximum. The power of the field magnets is increased, and the intensity of the lighting current again becomes of the necessary strength.

It will be seen that the whole regulation depends upon the opposing spring, and that it suffices, to increase or diminish its tension, to raise or lower the intensity of all the lamps; they can be reduced to simple tapers.

To insure the absolute regularity of the light, the regulator must be made very sensitive; from this the inconvenience follows that it acts very slowly, so that if a large number of lamps are suddenly extinguished the intensity of the current does not diminish rapidly enough for the preservation of the remaining lamps; here the second electro-magnet plays its part, being excited by the considerable increase in the derived current. It acts by placing the two brushes in communication by a cross circuit of no resistance; the field magnets receive no longer any exciting current, and in consequence the lighting current immediately weakens; sometimes even all the lamps go out, which is an excess in the way of preservation which must be avoided. The weakening, however, is only of very short duration, because the derived current ceases at the same time, and all the armatures of the electro-magnets take again immediately their respective positions.

This system of regulating is very ingenious, although complicated; it appeared to have worked very well in America and in England; there was no way of trying it at the Paris Exhibition, doubtless on account of the conditions of the installation.*

III. EDISON MACHINE.

[The Edison machine is of the Siemens continuous-current type, though it differs from it in constructive details. Being designed to work on a circuit of low resistance, it was neces-

---

* [This method of regulation has been abandoned in this country by the company using the Maxim incandescent lamp, in favor of a special winding of the machine supplying the lamp circuit, described in the next book.]

Fig. 177.—Edison machine.

sary to make the resistance of the armature as small as possible, and, to do this and yet get sufficient electro-motive
force, Mr. Edison sought to make the magnetic field of great
strength.   To this end he has constructed his field magnets
much more massive than those of other machines, and has
greatly increased the length of the cores and the wire wound
on them.   In the smaller machines these cores are usually
placed upright, but in the large steam dynamos used at central stations they are arranged horizontally.   Fig. 177 shows a
machine of the former kind, and the large central station ma-

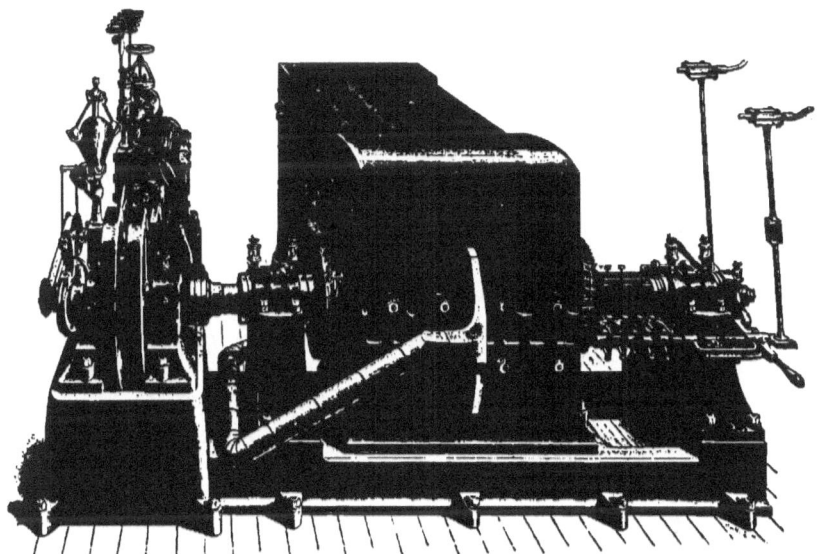

Fig. 178.—Edison steam dynamo.

chine such as is being used in the first district in New York,
and on the Holborn Viaduct, London, is illustrated in Fig. 178.
Besides giving a stronger field, large field magnets have the
advantage of greatly increased magnetic stability, an extremely important condition in securing steadiness of the lights.
The armature is drum-shaped, and is wound and connected
with the commutator in a similar manner to the Siemens.   It,
however, differs from it in an important particular.   In the
Siemens armature the wire starts from a commutator-plate,
and is carried a number of times around the cylindrical core
to form a coil of many strands.   It is then brought to the next

commutator-plate, and from this same plate another wire is
taken and likewise coiled around the drum, and then brought
up to the next plate, and so on. In the Edison, instead of
the wire being coiled over the drum a number of times, each
loop is brought to the successive commutator-plates, so that,
starting from one plate, the wire passes lengthwise along
one side of the drum
across the farther end,
back along the other
side of the drum, up
across the end, and is

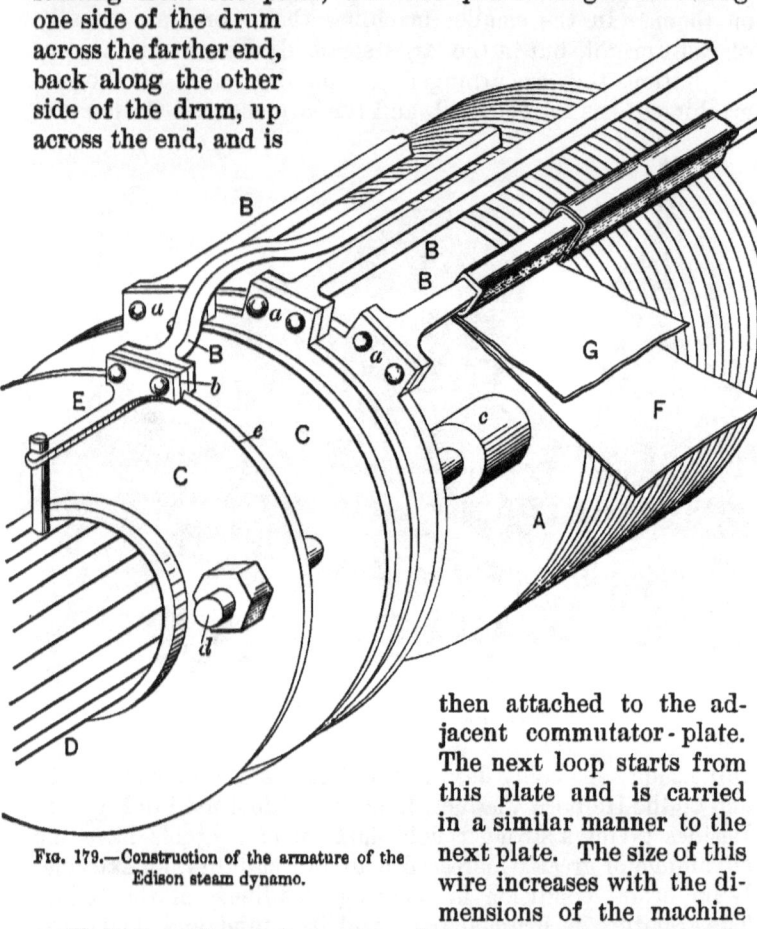

then attached to the ad-
jacent commutator-plate.
The next loop starts from
this plate and is carried
in a similar manner to the
next plate. The size of this

Fig. 179.—Construction of the armature of the
Edison steam dynamo.

wire increases with the dimensions of the machine
until it is replaced by copper bars connected at the ends
with copper disks. This construction is adopted in the larger
of the machines designed for isolated lighting and in the cen-
tral-station dynamos. The inductive portion of the armature
of this latter machine (Fig. 178) is composed of one hundred

and eight of these bars, arranged at equal distances around a cylindrical core, from which they are insulated. These bars are connected at each end with copper disks in such a way as to form a metallic circuit along one bar, across the end-disk, along the diametrically opposite bar, across a disk at the other end, then along the bar next to the first one, and so on. As stated, connections with the commutator-plates are made at the ends of each bar adjacent to the commutator. The armature core is made up of a great number of sheet-iron washers strung upon a central wooden cylinder and insulated from each other by disks of tissue-paper. The details of construction are shown in Fig. 179, in which C C are the copper disks, and B B the bars attached to them by means of bolts. The sheet-iron disks forming the magnetic core are shown at A, and one of the bolts by which the parts of the armature are securely bound together, at d. The commutator is shown at D. The complete armature has a length of five feet and a diameter of twenty-eight inches, and weighs over four tons. It is driven at a speed of three hundred and fifty revolutions a minute in the cylindrical cavity formed by the curved faces of the field-magnet poles. It has a resistance of only ·00049 ohm. The field magnets consist of twelve cylindrical cores, wound with insulated copper wire, which terminate in the massive pole-pieces seen in the front of the illustration, and are connected at the back by a heavy iron plate or yoke. They are placed in a shunt circuit—that is, a circuit arranged so that the current divides at the brushes, a part going into the external circuit to feed the lamps, and the rest circulating in the coils of the field magnet. The magnet coils are connected together so as to form two circuits having a total resistance of twenty-one ohms. The machine is driven by a Porter-Allen horizontal engine of one hundred and thirty horse-power. It is connected directly with the armature-shaft without the intervention of belts. The whole apparatus, including the bed-plate, weighs about thirty tons. Quite recently Mr. Edison has modified the construction somewhat, so as to be able to obtain about twenty per cent more current without any increase of the cost of construction. The present machine furnishes a current of eight hundred ampères under an electrical pressure of one hundred and fifteen volts, while the new one gives one thousand ampères with a pressure of one hundred and twenty volts.]

FIG. 180.—Art-gallery in New York lighted by Edison incandescent lamps.

We shall terminate this review of the machines, adopted
from M. Gramme's system, by indicating two modifications
invented for better utilizing the portions of the induced wire
which are included in the interior of the ring, so that the interior wires are equally subjected to induction, and contribute
to the production of currents instead of opposing thereto a
useless resistance. M. Jurgensen has gone further ; he causes
the ring to move between two field magnets—one interior, the
other exterior. The exterior magnet is composed of an electro-magnet with two arms, whose semicircular poles embrace
the ring almost completely, in the ordinary manner. The
wire of the magnetizing coils is accumulated behind the poles
in more numerous layers, to re-enforce their power.

The interior magnet, which recalls that of the alternate-
current machines of Gramme, is formed by two straight
electro-magnets, whose poles are spread out in the form of a
cylinder, concentric with the ring. This inner magnet is stationary, and supported so that the ring turns freely between
these double poles.

IV. Transformations of the Preceding Machines.

One of the first means invented for diminishing as much
as possible the quantity of inactive wire, was to transform the
cylindrical ring into a flattened disk, on whose faces the field
magnets acted laterally. It was thus that were formed a new
series of machines, based on the same principles, and differing only in the form of armature ; such are, among others, the
machines of Messrs. Schuckert, Ball, Gülcher, and Brush.
We shall examine this last, which is interesting from the results which it gives, and from the particular character of the
system of lighting of which it forms a part.

The field magnets of the Brush machine (Fig. 181) are
composed of two very powerful electro-magnets, whose arms
are terminated by polar plates in the form of sectors, sufficiently extended for three of the armature coils to be contained at once within each polar space. Here it is the similar
poles which face each other. It follows from this, on account
of the form and thickness of the armature disk, that there
are four magnetic fields, alternated two by two.

The armature has for core a cast-iron ring, of rectangular
section, in which are formed on each side as many grooves as

there are coils to be received; the projections that are left, and which separate the coils, form a series of polar projections designed to react laterally; the division is made in even numbers, so that the coils are diametrically opposite.

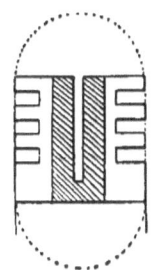

Four concentric grooves are cut in each lateral face of this ring, and a circular groove separates it almost completely into two disks, which play the rôle of two juxtaposed magnetic screens (Fig. 182 and 183); thus the formation of local currents is diminished, and a large cooling surface is obtained.

The armature wire is wound in the grooves, which it fills completely, so that the lateral faces of the ring and of the coils are in the same plane (Fig. 184); all the coils are wound in the same direction. The induction currents produced by the passage of the radial wires through the two opposite magnetic fields are of contrary direction, not only on each of the faces of the ring, but also in the coils situated at the extremities of the same diameter, so that if the incoming wire of one of them has a + sign, the incoming wire of the other will have the − sign; the coils are coupled, two by two, by connecting their incoming wires, and the outgoing wires, left free, represent poles of contrary name of each of the circuits thus formed, and are led to the commutators.

Instead of a single commutator, Mr. Brush uses as many commutator rings as there are pairs of induced coils; and each of these commutators is divided into three insulated segments (Fig. 185): one (C) represents only one eighth of

Fig. 182.—Cross-section of the Brush ring.

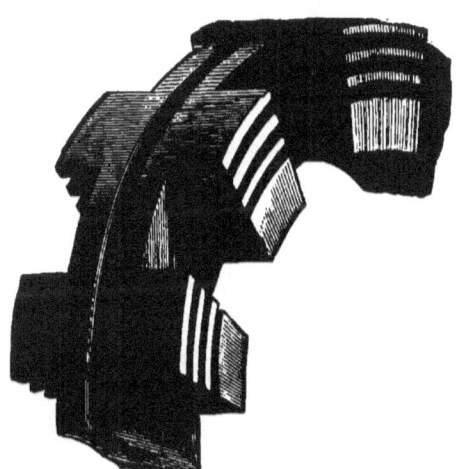

Fig. 183.—Construction of the Brush ring.

the circumference, the remainder of which is divided between the two others (A B); besides, the commutators are connected in two pairs, on each of which two elastic brushes rest to collect the currents.

For a ring containing eight coils, there are four commutators, whose eight large segments are connected with the out-

Fio. 184.—Brush armature, with its coils in position.

going wires of four pairs of coils; each of the segments of the same ring receives a wire of opposite sign. The small segments receive no wire, and are completely insulated.

We have seen that there were three coils induced at once

in each of the interpolar spaces; there remain, then, two in the neutral spaces, in which the currents produced are insignificant, and do not compensate for the loss due to the resistance of their wires. Mr. Brush has pre-ferred to cut them out of the circuit at the moment they traverse the neu-tral spaces, which is when one of the small completely insulated segments passes before the brushes.

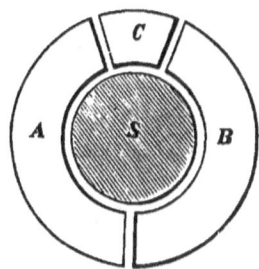

Fig. 185.—Cross-section of Brush commutator.

In the three pairs of active coils, two are associated in quantity by the simultaneous passage under the brushes of the segments representing them, and supply the working current of the outer circuit. The third pair form a special circuit devoted to the exciting of the field; this disposition has the advantage of rendering the exciting current independent of variations in the exterior circuit. In consequence of the movements of the ring, these change their *rôles* alternately; but the division of functions remains the same.

[Though so widely used, the Brush dynamo appears to be but little understood. It seems desirable, therefore, to sup-plement the description above given with the following clear and concise explanation of its mode of operation by Professor Sylvanus P. Thompson, in his lectures on "Dynamo-Electric Machinery," before the Society of Arts.

"Its armature—a ring in form, not entirely overwound with coils, but having projecting teeth between the coils like the Pacinotti ring—is unique. Though it thus resembles Paci-notti's ring, it differs more from the Pacinotti armature than that armature differs from those of Siemens, Gramme, Edison, Bürgin, etc.; for in all those the successive sections are united in series all the way round, and constitute, in one sense, one continuous bobbin. But in the Brush armature there is no such continuity. The coils are connected in pairs, each to that diametrically opposite it, and carefully isolated from those adjacent to them. For each pair of coils there is a sepa-rate commutator, so that, for the ordinary ring of eight coils, there are four distinct commutators side by side upon the axis—one for each pair of coils. The brushes are arranged so as to touch at the same time the commutators of two pairs

of coils, but never of two adjacent pairs; the adjacent commutators being always connected to two pairs of coils that
lie at right angles to one another in the ring. The arrangement is best studied graphically from the diagram given in
Fig. 186. In this figure the eight coils are numbered as four

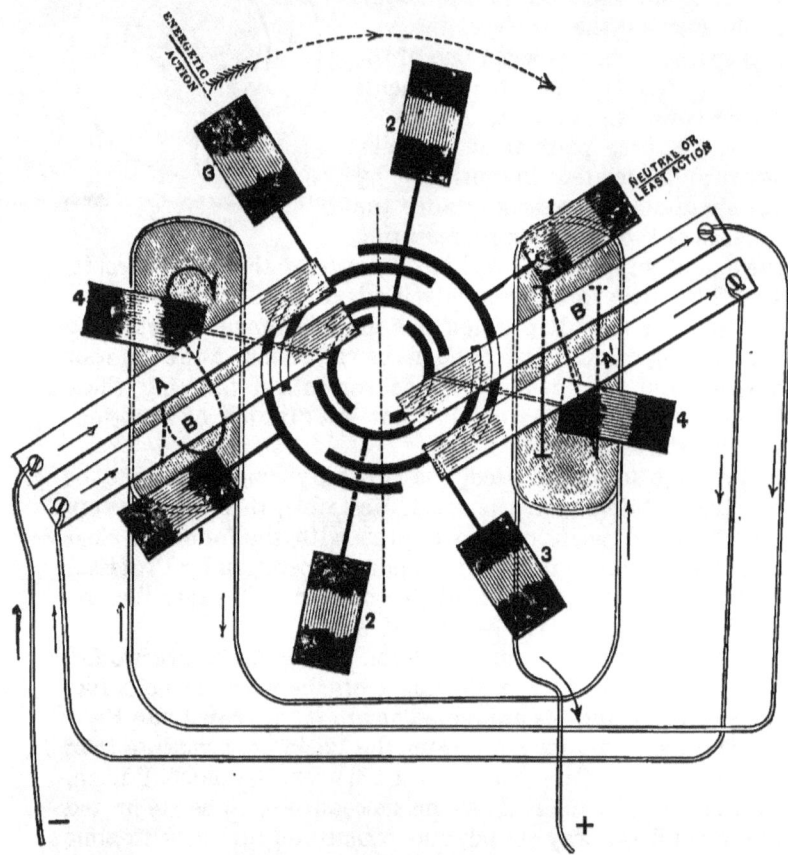

Fig. 186.—Diagram of Brush dynamo.

pairs, and each pair has its own commutator, to which pass
the outer ends of the wire of each coil, the inner ends of
the two coils being united across to each other (not shown in
the diagram). In the actual machine, each pair of coils, as
it passes through the position of least action (i. e., when its
plane is at right angles to the direction of the lines of force

in the field, and when the number of lines of force passing through it is a *maximum*, and the rate of change of these lines of force a *minimum*) is cut out of connection. This is accomplished by causing the two halves of the commutator to be separated from one another by about one eighth of the circumference at each side. In the figure it will be seen that the coils marked 1, 1, are 'cut out.' Neither of the two halves of the commutator touches the brushes. In this position, however, the coils 3, 3, at right angles to 1, 1, are in the position of best action, and the current powerfully induced in them flows out of the brush marked A (which is, therefore, the negative brush), into that marked A'. This brush is connected across to the brush marked B, where the current re-enters the armature. Now, the coils 2, 2, have just left the position of best action, and the coils 4, 4, are beginning to approach that position. Through both these pairs of coils, therefore, there will be a partial induction going on. Accordingly, it is arranged that the current, on passing into B, splits, part going through coils 2, 2, and part through 4, 4, and re-uniting at the brush B', whence the current flows round the coils of the field magnets to excite them, and then round the external circuit, and back to the brush A. (In some machines it is arranged that the current shall go round the field magnets after leaving brush A', and before entering brush B; in which case the action of the machine is sometimes, though not correctly, described as causing its coils, as they rotate, to feed the field magnets and the external circuit alternately). The rotation of the armature will then bring coil 2, 2, into the position of least action, when they will be cut out, and the same action is renewed with only a slight change in the order of operation. The following table summarizes the successive order of connections during a half-revolution:

First position.   (Coils 1 cut out.)

$$A - 3 - A; \ B < {}^{4}_{2} > B; \ \text{Field magnets} - \text{External circuit} - A.$$

Second position.   (Coils 2 cut out.)

$$A < {}^{1}_{3} > A; \ B - 4 - B; \ \text{Field magnets} - \text{External circuit} - A.$$

Third position.   (Coils 3 cut out.)

$$A - 1 - A; \ B < {}^{2}_{4} > B; \ \text{Field magnets} - \text{External circuit} - A.$$

Fourth position.   (Coils 4 cut out.)

$$A < {}^{3}_{1} > A; \ B - 2 - B; \ \text{Field magnets} - \text{External circuits} - A.$$

"From this it will be seen that whichever pair of coils is in the position of best action is delivering its current direct into the circuit ; while the two pairs of coils which occupy the secondary positions are always joined in parallel, the same pair of brushes touching the respective commutators of both."]

There are three types of these machines that can supply respectively six, sixteen, and forty lamps. In the sixteen-lamp machine the cores of the field magnets are wound each one with about 900 metres of wire of four millimetres diameter ; each of the armature coils contains about 270 metres of wire of about two millimetres thickness. The speed is 750 revolutions per minute, and the power expended about sixteen horse-power.

The Brush machines are made to supply currents of very high tension, which admit of placing all the lamps in a single series, whose length of circuit may attain ten to twelve kilometres. In the experiments in lighting made in Paris in the Théâtre de l'Opéra, the lamps of this system, which lighted the grand staircase, were supplied by a machine placed in the Palais de l'Exposition in the Champs-Élysées. There was evidently a great economy in the arrangement ; but the use of such currents requires very careful insulation, and involves serious dangers, which must also be taken into account.

The description of the other machines of this category would exceed the limits of this work ; they present hardly any peculiarities of interest, with the exception of M. Gülcher's machine, in which the field-magnet poles, that face each other, are connected by an intermediary piece of iron, so as to subject to induction those portions of the wire which come upon the outside surface of the disk.

V. Machines in which the Cores of the Armature Coils play a Preponderating Rôle.

We now have only to examine those machines in which the changes of magnetic state of the iron cores of the armature coil play a preponderating *rôle*, as was the case in the machines of Clarke and Nollet, with which we commenced. The machines of Messrs. Niaudet, Wallace and Farmer, and Lontin, come in this category ; the machines of Messrs. Bürgin and De Méritens occupy an intermediate position between the two systems.

We here speak of the machine invented by M. Niaudet in 1872, although it was never extensively introduced, because it was the first of this category which furnished continuous currents; for armature it had a series of bobbins wound on iron cores; these were arranged circularly on a wooden disk, and turned between the poles of two parallel magnets. The currents were collected by aid of a commutator like that of M. Gramme.

The machine of Messrs. Wallace and Farmer (Fig. 187), of which much has been said during the last two years, and which, nevertheless, did not figure at the Electrical Exhibition, is a machine analogous to that of M. Niaudet. There are

Fig. 187.—Wallace-Farmer machine.

two disks of iron in juxtaposition, and two rows of bobbins; the cores are flattened, and pierced with a hole to increase the cooling surface and diminish the production of Foucault currents. In these machines the commutation plane is coincident with that passing through the poles.

M. Lontin had constructed, in 1874, a machine in the same category, but with the armature bobbins differently arranged. In place of having their axes parallel to the axis of rotation, they radiate from this axis, which made their inventor call them pinion-machines.

In the first apparatus of this system the armature bobbins were flat, and were arranged parallel to the axis of rotation.

20

As now constructed (Fig. 188) the cores have a conical form, designed to prevent the throwing off of their coils under the effect of centrifugal force, and on account of their step-like arrangement on the axis, their polar extremities are successively presented at equal but more frequent intervals, to the action of the field-magnet poles. These are better utilized and the currents are more regular.

Fig. 188.—Armature of the Lontin continuous-current machine.

The copper-wire coils which envelop these cores are wound all in the same direction, and each of them has its incoming wire connected to the outgoing wire of the next helix, but from one ring to another and in the order in which they follow each other before the poles, so that the whole forms a continuous circuit.

Wires are taken from these junctions to the plates of a commutator similar to that of M. Gramme, but the brushes are prisms of an anti-friction alloy; these prisms slide in brass grooves, well insulated, and are pressed on the commutator by weights or springs.

The field is an ordinary electro-magnet with two arms, excited by the current of the machine; the poles are sometimes supplied with movable extensions, which can be prolonged or withdrawn at will, to regulate their action on the armature. It is a mode of regulation different from that which we have hitherto seen; for hand regulating it seems more simple to change the length of the magnetizing coils; on the other hand, the powerful attractions which are exerted between these pieces and the cores of the field magnets would render it difficult to make them self-regulating.

In 1876 M. Lontin constructed on the same plan a machine for alternating and divided currents, with a movable field magnet turning in the middle of a crown of fixed armature bobbins, whose currents were directly collected.

In these machines the movable field magnet is composed of a magnetic pinion of the same inventor, and consists, like the preceding, of an electro-magnet of multiple poles with radiating cores, having as common connector the cylinder to which these cores are fastened. With this system it is necessary, to obtain the maximum useful effect of the exciting current on the entire mass of iron of the field magnets, that the cores should present in equal numbers alternately poles of the opposite kind; which amounts to the establishment of an equal number of two-branch electro-magnets with a common base, so as to mutually re-enforce each other. This result is obtained in changing the direction followed by the current that circulates in the helices, either by the direction of the winding or by the mode of connecting the extremities of the different coils with each other.

The armature is composed of a fixed ring, supplied on its inner surface with cores evenly spaced in the form of radii, giving it the appearance of an interiorly-toothed wheel.

The field-magnet poles being alternately of different kind, the polarity of the armature coils also alternates, and the currents created at the same instant in their coils have directions opposite to each other. It is necessary, therefore, in order to obtain them of similar direction and to be able to couple them, to connect together the wires of the helices, having regard to the direction in which the currents go—that is to say, to unite alternately the incoming ends of the one and the outgoing ends of the others. The successive currents are not the less reversed, on account of the effect due to the removing and approaching of the field magnets. The exciting current of the field is furnished by a continuous-current machine of the same inventor.

It is with such machines that the first trial was made in 1877 of electric lighting at the station of the Paris, Lyons, and Mediterranean Railway, and it is these which are to-day in use in the experiments in lighting the Place du Carrousel in Paris.

The machine invented by M. Bürgin, and adopted by M. Crompton for his system of lighting, resembles rather the ring machines in its form of armature; but it comes in the category of the preceding machines in its method of induction. The magnetic core is of hexagonal form, and is composed of annealed iron wire; the copper wire is wound transversely on each of the sides of the hexagon, which is thus fitted with six distinct bobbins, a little thicker in the center; the portions of the core forming the summits of the hexagon are exposed, and pass very close to the field-magnet poles : it follows that there are in the core very energetic changes of magnetic state, which play the principal rôle in the production of currents.

As each of the rings thus constructed would be too feeble, a certain number are united on the same axis, by arranging them so that they assume the form of a drum with the rows of bobbins arranged spirally on it (Fig. 189). It is a similar disposition to that of the radiating bobbins of M. Lontin, to obtain the same result. The method of connection is the same, that is, the connections from bobbin to bobbin follow each other from the first bobbin of the first ring to the first bobbin of the last ring, which in its turn is connected with the second bobbin of the second ring, and so on. It is the sixth bobbin of the last ring which communicates with the

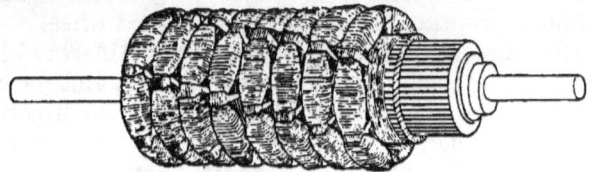

FIG. 189.—Drum-armature of the·Bürgin machine.

second wire of the first bobbin of the first ring, and thus completes the circuit ; from each of these junctions a wire is carried to the commutator, which contains as many plates as there are bobbins in the drum.

The field magnet is composed of two electro-magnets with flattened cores and consequent poles ; the cores and poles are of cast-iron, and in one piece. The machine can excite itself ; but in large electric lighting plants, using a number of machines, it is preferable to employ separate exciters.

The speed of the ring is usually 1,500 to 1,600 revolutions per minute ; a machine of forty-eight bobbins can supply three or four Crompton lamps arranged in series ; the expenditure of power varies with the intensity of the light.

CHAPTER IX.

RECENT MAGNETO-ELECTRIC MACHINES.

WE have already explained that it is the character of the inductors which has divided machines into the two classes of dynamo-electric and magneto-electric machines. This last system, which, as we have seen, was employed in Nollet's machines (Alliance), has long been abandoned, because of the size and weight of the apparatus; it is only used for small laboratory machines, and all the other machines that we have so far examined are dynamo-electric.

Magneto-electric machines, nevertheless, possess the advantages of increased simplicity, and of great regularity in the production of currents, resulting from the stability of the magnetic field. There is no need of fearing the reversal of polarity of the inductors, which may cause the passage through their magnetizing coils of reversed currents, which sometimes happens in electro-chemical operations, and in the charging of secondary batteries, Planté's or others. In some applications of electric light, especially in light-houses, this simplification of machines, and this certainty of a greater steadiness of light, have such importance that magneto-electric machines have really been given the preference. It is, without doubt, for the same reasons that M. de Méritens has taken up again the study of this system, and has obtained remarkable results. He not only has improved the construction of the permanent magnets, and has given them a much greater power, but, what is more important, he has invented a new arrangement of armature which, by its annular form, utilizes more completely the power of the field magnets.

M. de Méritens constructs his machines of three different types : a large alternating-current machine for powerful effects —it is the type actually employed in light-houses ; a smaller alternating-current machine for factory-lighting ; and, finally, a machine, also magneto-electric, producing continuous currents.

The light-house model (Fig. 190) is composed of five series of field magnets and five armature rings ; each series with its ring constitutes a complete machine, and the whole can be considered as formed of five machines in juxtaposition. Each of the series of field magnets contains eight compound horseshoe magnets arranged in star-shape, so that their poles form a circular crown, in whose interior the armature ring rotates. It is the well-known form of the old Alliance machines, but here the action of the magnets, instead of being lateral, is exercised endwise, directly on the armature, with full power.

Each magnet is composed of eight plates of Allevard steel, of ten millimetres thickness, bolted together and strung upon brass cross-bars fastened to the side-frames; adjusting-screws admit of exact regulation of the position of the cross-bars, and facilitate the putting together of the machine. Each

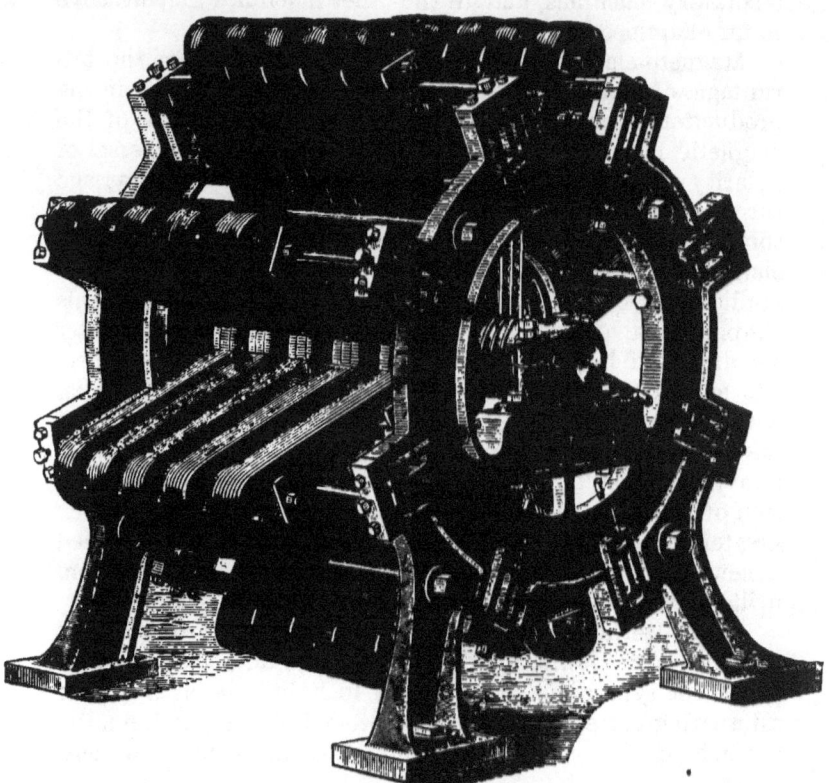

Fig. 190.—Magneto-electric machine of M. de Méritens. Lighthouse type.

group of horseshoe magnets weighs about twenty-seven kilo-grammes, and can sustain one hundred and fifty. The forty weigh altogether 1,080 kilogrammes.

The annular armature is composed of a series of flattened electro-magnets arranged in the arc of a circle, of the form shown in Fig. 191. These are united end to end by their poles, and fastened between the projections on a brass wheel. They are separated one from the other by small copper plates.

To facilitate the changes of the magnetic state of the cores and diminish their heating, these are formed of plates of soft

sheet-iron, a millimetre in thickness, cut out with a punch.
The armature wire is wound transversely on these cores, and
particular care is taken to obtain a perfect insulation, as well
between the wire and core, as between the individual coils or
turns. The spacing of the bob-
bins and magnets is laid out with
the greatest care; the distances
between the consecutive poles of
two neighboring magnets, and between the poles of a corresponding magnet, are exactly equal,
and each distance corresponds to
the length of two complete bobbins.

Each ring contains sixteen bobbins wound with wire one millimetre and nine tenths in diameter. The total weight of the wire
of the eighty bobbins is from
fifty-five to sixty kilogrammes.

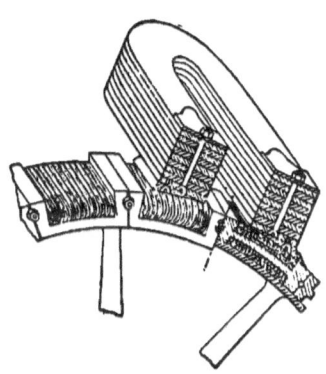

Fig. 191.—Details of the De Méritens armature.

All the coils are connected in a single circuit; but since,
from the arrangement of the field magnets, the armature bobbins pass successively in front of poles of different name, and
since the currents produced are in opposite directions in consecutive bobbins at the same instant, they are coupled two
and two by their positive and negative wires. The diagram
given in Fig. 192 shows how this coupling is done, which admits of their being united in a single circuit, whose extreme
ends are separately connected with friction-rings, mounted on
the shaft of the machine and properly insulated. We have
seen that the currents are alter-
nating, because each passage in
front of the poles is composed
of two periods, one of approach,
the other of recession.

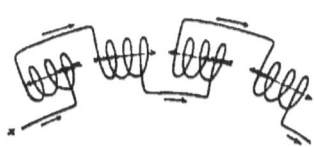

Fig. 192.—Diagram of the De Méritens armature coils.

The five rings are coupled so
as to furnish two distinct currents, which can be combined at
pleasure. These currents are collected on four rings; brushes, carried by long springs, bear against these rings and connect them with the four binding-screws whence the current
is taken.

According to experiments made in Paris by M. Allard, director in the light-house service, this machine furnished, with M. Serrin's regulator, an average luminous intensity of 636

Fig. 193.—Magneto-electric machine of M. de Méritens.   Workshop type.

carcels, with a speed of 790 revolutions per minute, and an expenditure of eight horse-power, or nearly eighty-five carcels per horse-power.

The machine called factory-machine (Fig. 193) is constructed on the same principles. The eight compound field magnets are placed horizontal, and arranged around a hollow cylinder; the alternate poles are joined together, and form a circular crown within whose interior the armature ring turns. Each magnet is composed of twelve plates of steel, each one 4·5 millimetres in thickness. The total weight of the field magnets is about 160 kilogrammes. The armature ring is identical with that of the large machine.

This factory-machine is supplied with an arrangement which has been called the permutator-plate (*plateau permutateur*), and which is capable, by the simple changing of metallic pins, of grouping the armature bobbins so as to vary the conditions of the current. The sixteen bobbins can be connected in tension, and in this case the machine can supply four Jablochkoff candles, or five Berjot regulators, of eighteen to twenty carcels each; the speed is 1,000 revolutions per minute, and the motive power expended is about three horsepower.

Two currents, from eight bobbins in tension, can also be associated in quantity, and two regulators of forty to fifty carcels each can thus be supplied. Finally, connecting the bobbins four in quantity and four in tension, the machine supplies a regulator of one hundred carcels.

Reducing the number of magnetic fields to four, M. de Méritens has constructed a magneto-electric machine for continuous currents which possesses all the advantages belonging to this class of generators (Fig. 194). The permanent magnets form four groups, composed each one of sixty-four

Fig. 194.—M. de Méritens's continuous-current magneto-electric machine.

steel plates one millimetre in thickness, arranged around a cylindrical brass frame. Their extremities, projecting from this frame, form four cylindrical surfaces within which the ring turns.

The ring also contains sixteen armature bobbins, but the core-plates are cut so as to form four projections, between which the wire, as wound, forms four distinct helices (Fig. 195). These bobbins are mounted in the same fashion around

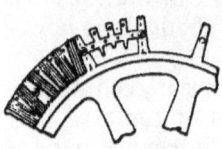

a brass wheel; they are connected in series, like those of a Gramme ring, and wires are arranged at each junction so as to connect them with the sixty-four commutator-plates.

Fig. 195.—Details of the ring of continuous-current machine of M. de Méritens.

The use of four magnetic fields involves two commutation planes, placed like those we have already seen in the octagonal machine of M. Gramme. There are then four brushes, two for each of the currents collected at the same instant—currents which can be utilized separately or combined at will.

The collector, or commutator, is mounted within the brass cylindrical frame, which prevents all displacement of the wires, short of dismountings. A movable brass ring serves as support for the axes of the brush-carriers, and facilitates the exact regulation of the points of contact of the brushes on the commutator. This arrangement also makes it possible to reverse the brushes when the machine is to be used as an electro-motor.

This machine is preferable to the dynamo-electric machines for charging secondary batteries. Under ordinary circumstances, when the battery is receiving its charge, there comes a time when the accumulated power of the battery is sufficient to overcome that of the machine furnishing the current.

With a dynamo-electric machine, unless a special safety apparatus is used, the direction of the current may become reversed, and the battery discharge itself through the machine. But the current, thus reversed, changes the polarity of the field magnets, and the machine, continuing to revolve, undoes all the work previously accomplished in the battery. With permanent magnets in the field, this trouble can not occur.

Besides the machines which we have passed in review, there are a very great number which work just as well, but whose description would take up too much space. The explanations which we have given will make their working easily understood, the differences only being in the form and rela-

tive positions of their constituent elements. It will be understood that we can not assign them their relative values ; in
general, each machine is part of a system for which it is
specially devised, and the results of experiments represent
rather the value of the whole than that of the particular
machine.

We shall summarize briefly only the chief conditions that
have to be observed. The machines should heat as little as
possible, because the heat thus disengaged is a loss of work, and
may become a cause of destruction of the insulation. This
production of heat can not be completely avoided, but it can
be reduced by diminishing useless resistances, such as those
of wires that do not participate in the production of currents.
The movable metallic cores should be constructed so as to
diminish the production of local or Foucault currents, and so
as to prevent the circulation of those which can not be entirely
suppressed.

The armature wire should be divided into as great a number of coils as possible, so that the partial currents shall be
weaker, which reduces the power of the sparks on the commutators ; it is true that the number of these currents must
then be increased, and consequently the speed of the moving
parts ; but these being lighter and easier to balance, can revolve without inconvenience at enormous speed, before the
contemplation of which electricians
would have recoiled some years ago.

Finally, the field magnets should
be so placed as to utilize well their
magnetic power. The mechanical
construction should be such as to
insure the stability and durability
of the moving parts, which ought to
revolve very close to each other, and
under the influence of high attraction.

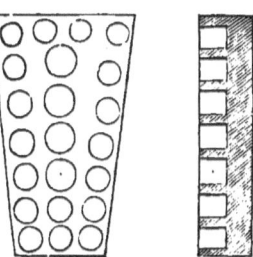

Fig. 196. — Gravier's plumbago
commutator-brushes.

The rubbing surfaces should have
dimensions larger than those used for the same speed in
ordinary machines ; their lubrication must be insured with
absolute certainty. We may recall on this subject a new
arrangement due to M. Gravier. The bearings are full of
holes, which are filled with plugs of graphite ; no other lubrication is required—it must, on the contrary, be absolutely

forbidden—nor is any repairing needed, and no heating need be feared.

M. Gravier uses the same plan for his commutator-brushes, which he constructs as shown in Fig. 196, and which press against a disk turning vertically. This disk carries pieces of copper arranged like the plates of ordinary commutators.

CHAPTER X.

EFFICIENCY OF THE DYNAMO.

[PERHAPS no term is commonly used more loosely, in its application to the dynamo and the electric system of which it forms a part, than efficiency. As is well known, this term indicates the completeness with which any machine or apparatus utilizes the work expended upon it, but it does not always seem to be remembered that it may have very different values, depending upon the quantities between which it expresses the relation.

A brief consideration of the efficiency of machines in general may perhaps be of service in helping us to a clear conception of its proper use in its application to electric apparatus.

Machines may be broadly divided into two classes—transmitters and transformers. Wind-mills, water-wheels, and pumps belong to the first class ; heat-engines, electric batteries, dynamos, and electro-motors to the second. The former do not convert energy in one form into some other form, but simply serve to redirect, in such a way as to be serviceable, the original mechanical energy. For instance, in a waterwheel the energy of the moving mass of water is in part transferred to the wheel, the motion of which we can utilize ; or, in the case of a pump, the mechanical energy spent in operating it is utilized in giving motion or position to water. In either case there is no transformation of energy, but simply a transference of motion from one mass to another. We start with energy in the mechanical form and end with it in the same form, without any intermediate transformation.

In the second class of machines there is always, on the other hand, a transformation of energy. In the steam and other heat engines the original work is in the form of heat, and in the final result, in that of mechanical energy. In the dynamo we have the conversion of mechanical energy into that of electric currents, and in the electro-motor the reverse operation; while in the electric battery we have the direct transformation of the work of chemical combination into electrical energy.

In the water-wheel and similar machines, we may distinguish two efficiencies: one the ratio of the gross return of the wheel to the total work of the falling water, the other the ratio of the utilizable work to this latter. A portion of the work done by the wheel is expended in overcoming friction, etc., and only the work above this is disposable. The ratio of this, which may be measured by a dynamometer, to the total work of the falling water, expresses the net or commercial efficiency as distinguished from what may be termed the gross efficiency. The former efficiency is the one which alone concerns the user of the machine, and which is always meant in tests of such wheels. In the water-wheel, or a well-designed steam-engine, the difference between these two efficiencies is not great, but it may in some instances—in the hot-air engine, for example—be very considerable.

A heat-engine of any form—steam, gas, or hot air—operates by taking into the cylinder a working-fluid at one temperature and discharging it at another, the proportion of the heat utilized depending upon the difference of these temperatures. We know from thermo-dynamics just how large a portion this can be in a perfect engine. This theoretical maximum is expressed by the formula $\frac{T - T'}{T}$, in which T is the temperature of the working-fluid on admission to the cylinder, and T' the temperature at discharge, both temperatures being reckoned from the absolute zero ($-461°$ F. and $-273°$ C.). Between the limits of temperature practicable in the steam-engine, this maximum efficiency does not exceed twenty per cent. The work done by the expanding fluid in moving the piston is measured by the product of the mean pressure upon it, and the distance through which it is moved. The ratio of this work to the work in the steam which was necessary to yield it, gives the efficiency of the engine as a *transformer* of heat into mechanical energy. In the best of modern engines this efficiency is from sixty to seventy per cent of the theoretical maximum, or twelve to fourteen per cent of the work in the steam.

The efficiency of a steam-engine is not, however, usually reckoned in this manner. It is commonly expressed by the ratio of the work performed by it to that of the fuel burned in the furnace. This, of course, does not give simply the efficiency of the engine, but the combined efficiency of the engine and boiler. But as in practice these two constitute one machine, it is the efficiency of this with which the consumer is concerned. In this case the efficiency of transformation is expressed by the relation of the work done upon the piston to that to which the fuel burned to produce it is equivalent. As stated above, the former work is obtained by multiplying the mean pressure upon the piston by the distance through which it is moved. In ordinary units, the power is therefore expressed by the total mean pressure on the piston in pounds, multiplied by the piston travel per minute in feet. This divided by 33,000 gives the horse-power exerted by the engine, generally known as the *indicated* horse-power, on account of the manner in which the mean steam-pressure is obtained. Taking the fuel-consumption as two pounds of coal an hour per indicated horse-power, we have the efficiency of transformation, regarding a pound of coal as equivalent to 10,000,000 foot-pounds, equal to $\left(\dfrac{1,980,000}{20,000,000}\right)$ one tenth nearly. The actual or available horse-power of the engine will evidently be the difference between the indicated horse-power and that required to move the engine simply, and the net or commercial efficiency the ratio of this actual horse-power to that of the fuel expended. In a good modern engine, the actual is eighty-eight per cent of the indicated horse-power.

We are now in a position to better understand the various efficiencies of the dynamo, and of an electric system. There is first the efficiency of transformation of mechanical into electric energy, usually termed the "generative efficiency." The relation here is that between the power required to turn the armature in the magnetic field at a given rate, and the electrical power. From this first power that required to overcome the friction of the moving armature must be deducted, as this friction does not contribute to the electrical result. This net power is obtained by measuring, by means of a dynamometer, the power required to revolve the armature when electrical work is being done, and subtracting from this the power required to drive it when no electrical work is performed. The electrical power in watts is the product of the current flowing through the circuit, by the electro-motive force. In the "series dynamo" there is but one circuit, and the current in it is of course the total current flowing; but in the "shunt dynamo" the total current is the sum of those in the main and field circuits. The difference of potential to be measured is that between the binding-posts of the machine, when the shunt is taken directly from the brushes, as is usually the case. Denoting the net power by P, and the electrical power by p, we have—

$$\text{Generative efficiency} = \frac{P}{P} \tag{1}$$

As no machine can be made frictionless, the practical generative efficiency will be expressed by the relation between the electrical power and the total power applied to the pulley of the dynamo, which we may distinguish as the gross or dynamometrical power. Denoting this by P′, we have—

$$\text{Practical generative efficiency} = \frac{p}{P'} \tag{2}$$

The amount of work done by an electric current in any part of its circuit depends upon the resistance encountered. As the machine has resistance, this work can not be performed entirely in that part of the circuit external to it, but its amount will depend upon the relative resistance of this circuit and the machine. The ratio of this portion to the total electrical work expresses the electrical efficiency. For a long time it was supposed that the law of Jacobi—stating that the maximum electrical work was obtained from a generator when its resistance was equal to that of the external circuit—was a law of efficiency, but we now know that this is not the case.

Instead of being limited to a maximum of only one half of the electrical work in the external circuit, we can get a much larger portion of it if the relative resistances of this circuit and the generator are rightly proportioned. Sir William Thomson has shown * what these relations should be in

* "British Association Report," 1881.

each of the two types of machine—the series and shunt
dynamo. In the series machine, denoting the resistance of
the external circuit by R, that of the field-magnet coils by R',
and of the armature by R", we shall have—

$$\frac{\text{internal work}}{\text{total work}} = \frac{R' + R''}{R + R' + R''}, \text{ and}$$

$$\frac{\text{external work}}{\text{total work}} = \frac{R}{R + R' + R''}.$$

He also showed that for the most economical working R"
should be slightly greater than R'.

In the shunt dynamo, these resistances should be related
to each other so that $R = \sqrt{R' \times R''}$, and the maximum work
is available in the external circuit when

$$\frac{\text{external work}}{\text{total work}} = \frac{1}{1 + 2\sqrt{\dfrac{R''}{R'}}}$$

Denoting the external electrical power by p', we have—

$$\text{Electrical efficiency} = \frac{p'}{p} \qquad (3)$$

The relation of the external electrical to the dynamometrical power is the one upon which the commercial excellence
of a dynamo depends. This may be termed the commercial
efficiency. We have, then, as a last efficiency for the dynamo—

$$\text{Commercial efficiency} = \frac{p'}{p'} \qquad (4)$$

There are, then, four efficiencies properly attributable to
the dynamo, the first two of which determine the comparative
merits of different machines as generators, but only the last
of which enables us to judge of their value as commercial apparatus. But even with this efficiency given, additional data
are necessary to determine the economy of different sets of
apparatus. Of the electrical energy in the external circuit
only a part is available, as some portion is expended in overcoming the resistance of the conductors. With currents of
small quantity and high tension this portion may be small,
but it may be very considerable in the case of currents of
large volume and low tension. Depending upon the character
of the currents used in any system, there will therefore be a
further efficiency expressing the relation between the gross
power applied to the pulley of the dynamo, and that in the
external circuit which may be used. This may be properly

termed the efficiency of the system. Denoting this utilizable power by p'', we have—

$$\text{Efficiency of system} = \frac{p''}{p'} \qquad (5)$$

While this last efficiency enables us to judge of the electrical excellence of a system, it does not necessarily inform us of the comparative merits of different systems in furnishing light. In this estimate another factor—the economy of the lamp—comes in as an element in determining the relation between the light yielded and power applied to the pulley of the dynamo. In the case of a plant consisting of a dynamo and arc-lamps, this relation may be termed the "lighting economy," but it must not be confounded with an efficiency, for it must be remembered that we can not speak of the efficiency of an arc or incandescent lamp in the same way as that of a dynamo-machine or an electrical system. In the latter we have an ascertained limit beyond which we can not go, and our efficiency simply expresses the nearness of approach to this limit. We know that for every foot-pound of work done upon the pulley of a dynamo we can not get more than a foot-pound of work in the electrical circuit; we know, in fact, that we can get but a portion of it. In the case of a lamp, on the other hand, we have not a well-defined limit to the light obtainable with a given amount of power. There is certainly a limit, but the data to enable us to determine it are at present wanting. In discussing the conditions of efficiency in incandescent lamps it was pointed out that the maximum economy was attained when the rate of the generation of heat per unit surface was as great as possible. The same condition applies to the arc-light, though here it is not so evident just what relations the various factors which have to be considered—strength of current, electro-motive force, and size of electrodes—should bear toward each other to realize it. Given a definite-current strength, it seems very probable that there is a particular electro-motive force and size of carbons which will make the light a maximum. If the carbons be too large, there will be undue cooling by conduction ; and if the arc be too short, the incandescent surface will be increased and its temperature lowered, both on account of increased cooling by the air, and a less rate of heat generation per unit of area. This latter consideration would lead us to expect that a long arc would be the more economical, and experience appears to justify this conclusion, though

21

it can not be said that the tests made of lamps of short and long arc have as yet settled the matter. So far as I am aware, no experiments have been made to determine this question solely, though it would naturally seem to be one to which attention would have been early given by those engaged in the commercial development of the arc-lamp.

The practical limit to the amount of light which a given heat-expenditure can be made to yield in the arc-lamp is dependent upon the consumption of the carbons. As the carbon particles are dissipated—both by combustion and by being thrown off from the electrodes—it is clear that it is no longer possible to impart heat to them, and therefore raise their temperature. Were it possible to obtain electrodes which would remain unchanged, their temperature could be carried up indefinitely, and the amount of light would then reach the theoretic limit. This limit, it has been previously suggested, is to be found at the point where an additional increment of temperature ceases to produce a proportional increase of light. Though we find that as the temperature is raised an increasing portion of the total radiation is luminous, we are not warranted in assuming that it would all become so with an indefinite augmentation of temperature. For it must be remembered that while there goes on at one end of the spectrum a transformation of heat-vibrations into luminous ones of shorter period, there goes on at the other end the transformation of the most rapid light-vibrations into others still more rapid, which are as incapable of exciting vision as are the longer-period ones at the red end. It would seem, therefore, that there is a maximum point beyond which in either direction there would be a less amount of light yielded per unit of heat.]

CHAPTER XI.

MEASUREMENTS OF DYNAMOS AND ARC-LAMPS.

[THE foregoing considerations enable us to understand clearly what factors must be determined in measuring dynamos and arc-lamps in order to judge of the comparative merits of different sets of apparatus. The final relation to be ar-

rived at is of course that between the gross power applied to
the pulley of the dynamo and the light yielded, and for commercial purposes this is ordinarily enough. But to form an
intelligent opinion of the inherent excellence of a system—to
know wherein it is good and wherein bad—it is necessary to
have all of the data indicated above.

It would seem, at first sight, a comparatively easy matter
to measure accurately a dynamo and set of arc-lamps, but
the numerous measurements made by different observers present very few points of agreement, while in the same set of
experiments there are often great discrepancies. The measurements most difficult to make with accuracy are those of the
horse-power applied to the machine, and the determination
of the luminous intensity. This latter, in the case of the arc-
lamp, is a very uncertain matter, as the arc is constantly
shifting, and the intensity of the light varies with every
change of angle under which it is observed. In order to get
a measurement which would give the average illumination
afforded by the lamp, the plan has been adopted of measuring the light in all directions and taking their mean. This
method was first employed by the Paris committee of 1881,
and has since been generally used in similar tests. It has
been termed the *moyenne sphérique* intensity, as it corresponds to the strength of the light at every point of a sphere
of which the arc is the center. It has the disadvantage of
giving a lower candle-power than the lamp actually yields, as
in all arc-lights but a comparatively small portion of the rays
are directed upward, but this does not detract from its merits
in comparative measurements.

Of the many tests made of arc-lamps and dynamos in the
past few years, it will be sufficient to give here those of the
committee of the Paris Exposition of 1881, as these are very
complete and include the better known and more successful
of this class of apparatus. The table is sufficiently clear to
render explanation unnecessary, though one or two points
require mention. The horse-power is given in French measure, which, as has been before stated, is equal to 75 kilogrammetres per second, or 735·75 watts. It will be seen that the
first of the percentages corresponds to efficiency (2), and the
second to efficiency (5), as given in the previous chapter.
The third gives the relation between the total electrical work
and that which is available in the arcs. The number of car-

Table of Experiments made with Con-

BY THE COMMITTEE APPOINTED AT

	Formulæ.	1 Gramme. 1 lamp.	2 Jur- gensen. 1 lamp.
MECHANICAL MEASUREMENTS.			
Speed of generator, revolutions per minute		475	800
Effective power applied, horse-power	T	16·13	21·68
ELECTRICAL MEASUREMENTS.			
Resistance of generator, in ohms	r	0·33	0·45
Resistance of mains (circuit without lamps), in ohms	r′	0·10	0·82
Resistance of mains and generator	R	0·43	1·27
Strength of current, in ampères	I	109·2	90·0
Fall of potential at each lamp, in volts	E	53·0	58·0
ELECTRICAL CALCULATIONS.			
Energy in generator and mains, horse-power	$\dfrac{RI^2}{75g}$	6 97	13·99
Energy in one lamp, horse-power	$\dfrac{EI}{75g}$	7·87	7·09
Energy in all the lamps, horse-power	t	7·87	6·97
Total electrical energy, horse-power	T′	14·84	20·96
Mean electro-motive force	nE + RI	102	172
MEASUREMENTS OF LIGHT.			
Diameter of carbons, in millimetres		20	23
Horizontal intensity, each lamp, carcels		952	607
Maximum intensity, each lamp, carcels		1,960	....
Mean spherical intensity, each lamp, carcels	l	966	688
Total mean spherical intensity, all lamps, carcels	L= nl	966	688
RESULTS.			
Percentage of applied power converted into electrical energy	$\dfrac{T'}{T}$	0·92	0·97
Percentage of applied power appearing in the arcs	$\dfrac{t}{T}$	0·43	0·32
Percentage of total electrical energy appearing in the arcs	$\dfrac{t}{T'}$	0·53	0 33
Carcels per horse-power applied to generator	$\dfrac{L}{T}$	60·0	31·7
Carcels per horse-power of electrical energy	$\dfrac{L}{T'}$	65·1	32·8
Carcels per horse-power of energy appearing in the arcs	$\dfrac{L}{t}$	128·8	98·7
Carcels per ampère	$\dfrac{l}{I}$	8·85	7·64

tinuous-Current Generators and Lamps.

THE PARIS EXPOSITION OF 1881.

3	4	5	6	7	8	9	10	11	12	13
Maxim.	Siemens.	Siemens.	Bürgin.	Gramme.	Gramme.	Siemens.	Weston.	Brush.	Brush.	Brush.
1 lamp.	1 lamp.	2 lamps.	3 lamps.	3 lamps.	5 lamps.	5 lamps.	10 lamps	16 lamps	40 lamps	88 lamps
1,017	737	1,330	1,535	1,695	1,496	826	1,003	770	700	705
4·07	4·44	5·31	5·32	8·11	8·00	5·05	13·01	13·39	29·96	33·35
0·70	0·66	1·68	2·80	0·52	4·57	7·05	1·88	10·55	22·38	22·38
0·25	0·12	0·13	1·50	1·25	0·62	4·50	1·50	2·56	2·60	7·90
0·95	0·78	1·81	4·30	1·77	5·19	11·55	3·38	13·11	24·98	30·28
33·0	35·0	26·2	18·5	19·0	15·3	10·0	23·0	10·00	9·5	9·5
53·0	53·0	44·5	41·0	53·0	49·8	47·4	32·0	44·3	44·3	44·3
1·41	1·29	1·69	2·00	0·87	1·65	1·57	2·43	1·79	3·07	3·72
2·37	2·52	1·59	1·027	1·369	1·04	0·64	1·00	0·60	0·573	0·573
2·31	2·52	3·18	3·03	4·11	5·20	3·20	10·00	9·60	21·88	20·79
3·72	3·81	4·87	5·08	4·98	6·85	4·77	12·43	11·39	24·95	24·51
84	80	136	203	193	328	353	398	840	2,009	1,971
12	18	14	13	14	12	10	9 & 10	11	11	11
246	210	142	50	155	112	67	92	37	63	63
465	805	537	227	357	184	72	154	76	78	78
239	306	205	82	167	102	52	85	38	39	39
239	306	410	246	501	510	260	850	608	1,560	1,482
0·91	0·86	0·92	0·95	0·62	0·86	0·94	0·95	0·85	0·83	0·73
0·57	0·57	0·60	0·58	0·51	0·65	0·63	0·77	0·72	0·73	0·62
0·62	0·66	0·65	0·61	0·83	0·76	0·67	0·80	0·84	0·87	0·85
53·7	68·9	77·2	46·2	61·8	63·8	51·5	65·3	45·4	52·1	44·4
64·2	80·3	84·2	48·4	100·4	74·5	54·6	68·4	53·4	62·6	60·5
103·5	121·4	129·3	79·9	121·6	98·1	81·3	85·0	63·3	71·7	71·4
7·24	8·74	7·82	4·43	8·79	6·67	5·20	3·70	3·80	4·11	4·11

cels per horse-power applied to the generator shows the commercial value of the different sets of apparatus as a whole for lighting, while the economy of the lamps by themselves is given by the "carcels per horse-power of energy appearing in the arcs." Aside from showing in a general way that the economy of a lamp is greater in large than in small lights, there is not much to be learned from these figures of the relative importance of the various factors upon which the light depends. The Siemens (9) and the Brush (11, 12, 13), which are the only long-arc lamps, appear to indicate a superior economy for such lamps, as the former gives 81·3 carcels per electrical horse-power appearing in the arc, in lights of 52 carcels, while the Brush yields 71 carcels in lights of but 39 carcels. The best of the short-arc lights shows 85 carcels per electrical horse-power in the arc, in lights of this candle-power (85 carcels). Such a comparison to be of value, however, should be made between lights of the same candle-power, or on the basis of the same expenditure of energy in the arcs.

The Edison machine has been very frequently measured, but it will be sufficient to give here two tests—one made by Mr. John W. Howell at the Stevens Institute, and the other by the committee of the Munich Exhibition of 1882.

In the former the electric energy developed in the circuit was determined by three methods. In the first, the current flowing was measured by means of a voltameter, or copper depositing-cell. This test is made by determining the amount of copper carried over from one plate of the cell to the other in a given time, from which the current is readily determined, as a current of one ampère deposits ·32456 milligramme per second. The electric energy in the circuit is then given by the product of the square of the current by the resistance ($C^2 R$). The second method consisted in determining the current by means of the calorimeter—that is, by finding the heat generated by the current in a coil of wire of known resistance in a given time. This heat is measured by immersing the coil in a definite weight of water and noting its increase of temperature. The energy in the circuit is then found as in the first method. The voltameter and calorimeter were each placed in the circuit, so that the whole current passed through them. This was accomplished by taking the shunt field-circuit, not directly from the brushes, but from the main circuit beyond the point at which the measuring-cells were placed. The third method consisted in measuring the electro-motive force and the resistance, the energy in the circuit then being $\frac{E^2}{R}$, which is equivalent to C E, since $C = \frac{E}{R}$. The external circuit consisted of iron wire of the normal resistance of the number of lamps for which the machine was designed, together with the copper leads to be used with them. The mechanical energy applied to the pulley of the dynamo was measured by a pendulum dynamometer built at the Institute, and every care was taken to have its indications correct. With a dynamometer of this kind, the power transmitted is proportional to the angle through which the pendulum—which hangs perpendicular in its normal position—is lifted. The instrument was standardized by determining the force which, acting at the circumference of the dynamometer-pulley (one foot radius), would hold the pendulum horizontal. This was found to be 171·2 pounds; the intensity of any other force would therefore be given by multiplying this by the sine of the angle through which the pendulum was raised. To get the work done per minute, or the power, it is necessary to multiply this force by the distance traveled by the pulley. This is, of course, the product of the number of revolutions by the length of the circumference in feet. As the radius of the pulley is one foot, the travel is equal to the number of revolutions multiplied by 6·2832. The total power transmitted by the dynamometer included that required to overcome the friction of both the dynamometer and the armature of the dynamo. These combined frictions were found to equal 13¼ per cent of the power transmitted, while that of the dynamometer was equivalent to 10·9 per cent. The net power applied to the armature is obtained, therefore, by multiplying the total power transmitted by ·865, and the gross applied power by multiplying the transmitted power by ·891. The data and the results obtained by these tests are given below:

DATA OBTAINED FROM VOLTAMETER TEST.

Weight of copper gained by negative plates = 24,465 milligrammes.

Time of test = fifteen minutes.

Weight gained per second = 27·183 milligrammes.

Average speed of dynamometer = 400·5 revolutions per minute.

Average deflection of pendulum = 42° 20'. (sine = ·67344)

Resistance of iron wire = ·76 ohm.

Resistance of iron wires and magnet coils in multiple arc = ·744 ohm.

Total resistance of circuit = ·744 + .029 = .773 ohm.

Internal resistance of armature = ·016 ohm.

RESULTS OBTAINED FROM DATA.

Value of current in ampères = $\dfrac{27·183}{·32456}$ = 83·753.

Electrical energy = $(83·753)^2$ × ·773 × 44·24 * = 239880·726 foot-pounds per minute.

Energy indicated by dynamometer = 171·2 × ·67344 × 400·5 × 6·2832 = 290125·54 foot-pounds per minute.

Friction of dynamometer and generator = 290125·54 × ·135 = 39166·9479 foot-pounds per minute.

Energy used in turning armature in field of force = 290125·54 × ·865 = 250958·59 foot-pounds per minute.

Friction of dynamometer alone = 290125·5 × ·109 = 31623·68 foot-pounds per minute.

Energy actually applied to armature pulley = 290125·54 × ·891 = 258501·96 foot-pounds per minute.

Of the total electrical energy, 239880·7$\dfrac{·016}{·773}$ = 4965·189 appeared in the armature, $\dfrac{·744}{·773 × 49·68}$ × 239880·726 = 4647·39 in the magnet coils, and 230268·176 foot-pounds per minute in the external circuit.

The efficiency of the generator is the ratio of the energy required to turn the armature in the magnetic field, to the total electrical energy developed = $\dfrac{239880·726}{250958·59}$ = ·955.

The commercial efficiency is the ratio of the energy required to drive the machine (including friction) to the

---

* This is the factor for converting watts into foot-pounds per minute: a watt = $\dfrac{1}{746}$ horse-power, = $\dfrac{33000}{746}$, = 44·24 foot-pounds per minute.

electrical energy which appears in the external circuit $=$
$$\frac{230268 \cdot 169}{258501 \cdot 96} = \cdot 8608.$$

DATA OBTAINED FROM CALORIMETER TEST.

Water in calorimeter $= 77$ pounds.
Correction for waste heat $= 1 \cdot 78$ pound.
Range of temperature $= 97° - 69 \cdot 8° = 9 \cdot 2°$ F.
Specific heat for this range $= 1 \cdot 0015$.
Average speed of dynamometer $= 394$ revolutions per minute.
Average deflection of pendulum $= 43° \, 24'$ (sine $= \cdot 68709$).
Time of test $=$ sixteen minutes.
Resistance of iron wires and calorimeter coil $= \cdot 68$ ohm.
This and magnet coil in multiple arc $= \cdot 667$ ohm.
Total resistance of circuit $= \cdot 667 + \cdot 029 = \cdot 696$ ohm.
Resistance of calorimeter coil $= \cdot 1$ ohm.

RESULTS OBTAINED FROM THESE DATA.

Energy developed in calorimeter $= \dfrac{78 \cdot 78 \times 1 \cdot 0015 \times 9 \cdot 2 \times 772}{16}$

$= 35022 \cdot 897$ foot-pounds per minute.

Total electrical energy $= 35022 \cdot 897 \times 6 \cdot 96 = 243759 \cdot 36$ foot-pounds per minute.

Energy indicated by dynamometer $= 171 \cdot 2 \times \cdot 68709 \times 394 \times 6 \cdot 2832 = 291201 \cdot 46$ foot-pounds per minute.

Energy used in turning armature in field of force $= 291201 \cdot 46 \times \cdot 865 = 251889 \cdot 265$ foot-pounds per minute.

Energy actually applied to armature pulley $= 291201 \cdot 46 \times \cdot 891 = 259460 \cdot 5$ foot-pounds per minute.

Of the electrical energy, $243759 \cdot 36 \times \dfrac{\cdot 016}{\cdot 696} = 5603.66$ appeared in the armature, $243759 \cdot 36 \times \dfrac{\cdot 667}{\cdot 669 \times 55 \cdot 41} = 4215 \cdot 89$ in the magnet coils, and $233039 \cdot 81$ foot-pounds per minute appeared outside.

Efficiency $= \dfrac{243759 \cdot 363}{251889 \cdot 265} = \cdot 967.$

Commercial efficiency $= \dfrac{233039 \cdot 81}{259460 \cdot 5} = \cdot 901.$

Data obtained from Measurement of Electro-motive Force and Resistance.

Electro-motive force = 53 volts.
Resistance of circuit (external) = ·64 ohm.
Resistance between binding-posts = ·029 ohm.
Average speed of dynamometer = 355 revolutions per minute.
Average deflection = 42° (nat. sine = ·66913).
Total resistance of circuit = ·658 ohm.

Results obtained from these Data.

Energy developed in external circuit $\dfrac{(53^2)}{·629} \times 44·24 =$ 197567·43 foot-pounds per minute.

Total electrical energy = $197567·43 \times \dfrac{·658}{·629} = 206673·0295$ foot-pounds per minute.

Energy in armature = $206673·029 \times \dfrac{·016}{·658} = 5025·5$ foot-pounds per minute.

Energy in magnet coils = $\dfrac{(53^2)}{37} \times 44·24 = 3358·6$ foot-pounds per minute.

Energy in external circuit = 198288·8 foot-pounds per minute.

Energy indicated by dynamometer 171·2 × ·66913 × 355 × 6·2832 = 255519·04 foot-pounds per minute.

Energy used in turning armature in field of force 255519·04 × ·865 = 221023·97 foot-pounds per minute.

Energy actually applied to armature pulley 255519·04 × ·891 = 227667·47 foot-pounds per minute.

Efficiency = $\dfrac{206673·0295}{221023·97} = ·935.$

Commercial efficiency = $\dfrac{198288·8}{227667·47} = ·87.$

Average efficiency, ·951.
Average commercial efficiency, ·887.

The Munich committee examined three sizes of the Edison machine—those for 250, 60, and 17 lamps—but it will be sufficient to give the tests of the 60-lamp machine. The experimenters explain that the low "practical generative efficiency" $\frac{L}{A}$, and the "commercial efficiency" $\frac{l}{A}$, are accounted for by the stiffness of the driving-belt, the power required to drive the machine when it was doing no electrical work being 2·19 horse-power. Subtracting this from the total power, A, applied to the dynamo, we have for the "generative efficiency" in the six cases in the table, $\frac{L}{A-2\cdot19} = 82\cdot3, 85\cdot5, 84\cdot9, 86\cdot2,$ 87·4, 87·4, and for the relation between the net horse-power and electrical energy in the external circuit, $\frac{l}{A-2\cdot19} = 71\cdot2,$ 74·4, 73·9, 75·4, 76·6, 76.6.

Examination of the Edison Dynamo

BY THE COMMITTEE OF THE MUNICH EXHIBITION OF 1882.

MACHINE USED.	RESISTANCE WARM (OHMS).		External circuit, r (ohms).	Intensity of current in the external circuit, I (ampères).	INTENSITY OF CURRENT (AMPÈRES).		Differences of potential between the ends of circuit, e (volts).	Total electro-motive force, E (volts).
	Armature, R₁.	Field, R₂.			Armature, I₁.	Field, I₂.		
Machine Z for 60 lamps. External circuit composed of a wire resistance.	·161	40·5	4·55	27·67	30·77	3·10	125·8	130·7
	·164	40·6	4·12	30·12	33·17	3·05	124·0	129·5
	·166	40·7	3·96	31·42	34·48	3·01	124·3	130·1
	·171	40·8	3·48	34·31	37·24	2·93	119·5	125·8
	·175	40·9	3·07	36·31	39·03	2·72	111·4	118·2
	·177	40·9	2·82	37·69	40·29	2·60	106·3	113·4

ELECTRICAL WORK.								Number of revolutions, n.	Power applied, A—horse-power.	RESULTS.		
EXTERIOR CIRCUIT, l.		ARMATURE.		FIELD.		TOTAL, L.				$\frac{1}{L}$	$\frac{1}{A}$	$\frac{L}{A}$
Watts.	Horse-power.	Watts.	Horse-power.	Watts.	Horse-power.	Watts.	Horse-power.					
3480·	4·73	152·2	·207	390·2	·530	4022·	5·47	1197·	8·83	86·5	53·5	61·9
3735·	5·08	180·8	·246	378·4	·514	4294·	5·84	1193·	9·01	87·0	56·3	64·7
3907·	5·31	197·9	·269	380·0	·516	4485·	6·10	1193·	9·37	87·1	56·7	65·0
4098·	5·57	237·4	·323	349·9	·475	4685·	6·37	1164·	9·58	87·5	58·1	66·5
4044·	5·49	266·1	·362	303·5	·412	4614·	6·26	1109·	9·36	87·7	58·7	67·0
4004·	5·44	287·8	·391	275·7	·375	4568·	6·20	1074·	9·29	87·7	58·6	66·8

BOOK V

DISTRIBUTION OF ELECTRICITY.

CHAPTER I.

FIRST MODE OF DISTRIBUTION.

IT is electric lighting which has had to solve the problem of the distribution of electricity. At first the most powerful center of light possible was sought for, by concentrating on one given point the highest intensity of current; when the first practical application of it came to be tried, it was evident that these concentrated masses of light did not meet all the necessities of the case ; that in the greater number of cases a light, weaker perhaps in total intensity, but better distributed, would be preferable ; finally, that it was necessary to increase the number of lights, even at the risk of reducing their brightness.

But all this was not unaccompanied by difficulties : as the question at this time was simply how a very limited number of lamps were to be made to work at the same time, attention was devoted to the lamp itself ; this first question was solved, as we have stated, by the derived-circuit lamps. Scarcely was this answer obtained, when it was found incomplete, and the endeavor was, not only to place several lamps upon the same circuit, but to derive even several circuits from one machine. Had this problem been attacked directly, it would have amounted to the very question of the division of the current. At the period alluded to, about 1872, it was far from ripe ; it was evaded, and, instead of dividing the electric current as it left the machine, the machine itself was divided.

I. Electric Conductors.

The first machine which had given a practical electric light, the Alliance machine, had already furnished an example of this method, and naturally pointed out this way; it is, as we have seen, composed of a series of bobbins placed circularly on wooden disks; each of these disks constitutes a complete machine, and can work independently. It was not long before it was known how to separate them so as to form independent circuits connected with different apparatus; the alternating-current machine of Lontin by different means attained the same result; the armature bobbins, fixed in place, were coupled in separate series, each devoted to supplying a circuit of its own; a similar arrangement was adopted in the Gramme alternating-current machine, where the sections of the armature ring were separated so as to work independently.

These methods did not amount to the true distribution of light; nevertheless, they are the only ones which have been employed in the last few years. Before the Exhibition of 1881 no other methods had been seen in genuine practical working, and it is with these very limited means that the important applications known to all the world have been made.

These works, however, have led to complete and interesting studies on conductors, and the method of arranging them; these results do not depend on the method of division employed, and are obtained from theory; it will be useful to devote a few lines to them.

All conductors hitherto employed are of copper; of all good conducting metals it is the only one whose price is reasonable; iron is cheaper, it is true, for equal conductivity, but, when currents of a certain intensity have to be passed, its use renders so large a conductor necessary that the wire ceases to be manageable, and necessitates repeated solderings, which would compensate, and more, for the low price of the iron.

There would be a certain advantage in using an uncovered wire suspended in the air: the cooling would be easier. But in practice this arrangement meets with many obstacles. A wire suspended in the open air is liable to many accidents; dampness occasions loss of current by the supports—losses which, annoying even with the weak telegraphic currents, would be intolerable with the strong currents used for the electric light. Thus, as a rule, the conductors are necessarily placed underground, and are properly insulated.

The section of the conductor varies naturally with the intensity of the current. It should be large enough to avoid all sensible heating; but as in reality the resistance of the conductor can not be reduced to zero, the passage of the current always causes heating. The question then arises of where the saving is to be: on one side are the interest and depreciation to be charged against the cost of putting up the conductor; on the other side the cost of the electricity which is wasted in heating the wire by its passage. This last expense is incurred only during the working periods of the system; the length of these periods of lighting must then be taken into account in these calculations. In cases where the conductor is of large diameter, instead of using a conductor formed of a single large rod of metal, a cable formed of several wires united and lightly twisted together is adopted. These cables are more flexible than a single heavy wire, are more easily placed, and are less liable to break, the wires rarely all breaking at one and the same place.

The conducting wires are covered with silk or cotton, braided by a machine; sometimes gutta-percha is employed. If a cable is in question, it is wrapped with silk bands impregnated with coal-tar, or with India-rubber bands; sometimes it is passed through a regular India-rubber tube; the cables used in the Jablochkoff system are thus insulated. If the conductors are placed in very wet situations, they are covered with leaden tubes; this, for example, has been done with the telephone wires that pass through the Parisian sewers; the cables running under the pavement of the Place du Carrousel were made in this manner also.

When a water or gas main is laid it is tested throughout its length for obstructions or leaks; in the same way, when one of these large conductors is laid, its good working has to be tested with exact instruments; not only must the current pass, but it must pass with the requisite intensity; for this reason the cable is tested to see if it has the normal resistance, and if there is no loss of electricity in its course through it.

Further on we shall see interesting systems of canalization for the most complete distribution; but so far they have not been applied. The means which we are about to briefly describe have, on the contrary, rendered great service; they have been used for important installations of light that were relatively quite different in their conditions.

The two extremes are, without doubt, on the one hand lighting with ordinary regulators, such as those established by M. Jaspar, in which each lamp has its machine; and, on the other hand the Brush system of lighting, where as many as thirty-four lamps have been placed on a circuit over six kilometres long. One can not help thinking that both systems have their weak points. The first, a very simple one, is very costly in its plant; the second, although it has generally given good results, evidently puts the apparatus in a condition of reciprocal dependence that is a source of danger. A medium course is probably the best, and, as in systems employing divided-current machines, distinct circuits may be adopted, each one carrying a reasonable number of lamps.

We will describe as an example the lighting of the port of Havre by means of the Jablochkoff candle, a plant recently put in place, and which comprises almost all the improvements which this method of dividing the light is susceptible of.

II. Disposition of Electric Wires for Lighting the Port of Havre.

The port of Havre, as is known, is a sea-port, and large vessels can only enter it at high tide. When both high tides come at day-time, vessels which miss the first can enter by the second tide, and consequently have only eleven hours to lay in the roads; but, when the tides come one in the day and one at night, the ship which missed the day-tide could not, up to the present time, enter the port before the following day; sometimes it had to remain twenty-four hours in the roads. The anchorage at Havre is excellent for vessels to lay at in calm weather, but, when it blows, the anchor must be lifted. The transatlantic steamers know something of this, and several steamers have been cited this winter that were forced to go to Cherbourg to land their passengers.

This was the source of the strong desire mariners had to be able to enter the port of Havre by night as by day, and it was at their request that the city authorities decided to light the port by electric light. This decision was reached in the

Fig. 197.—Plan of the electric-lighting system of the port of Havre.

year 1880, but it is only since the beginning of the year 1881 that the lighting has been in operation.

Whenever there is a night-tide the jetties, breakwater, and principal dock are lighted an hour before and two hours after the period of the full tide, and large ships can enter just as by daylight.

The installation comprises thirty-four lamps, thirty-two of which are shown on the plan in Fig. 197; two others were added after this plan was laid out, and the machines employed have capacity to supply forty.

These thirty-two lights are placed on six circuits. The first circuit of four lamps (1 to 4) lights the north jetty; it is 3,900 metres long, going and coming. The second circuit of five lamps (5 to 9) lights the large quay, it measures 2,900 metres; a sixth lamp has been added to it, placed in a red lantern and serving as a guide to steer by. The third circuit of six lamps (10 to 15) comprises the Notre-Dame and De la Barre docks; it is 1,900 metres long. The fourth circuit of six lamps (16 to 21) lights the lower end; it includes a red light, and measures 1,250 metres. The fifth circuit of six lights (22 to 27) lights the dock of the transatlantic and those of the Florida steamers; it is 1,400 metres long. The sixth circuit of five lamps (28 to 32) lights the south jetty; it measures 2,900 metres, and has a red light.

The machines are installed not far from the transatlantic dock. Two steam-engines of thirty-five horse-power each drive four self-exciting Gramme machines of type 2. One of these four Gramme machines works on open circuit; it is only intended for use when an accident happens to one of the three others. Each of the others supplies two circuits. As all the circuits are similarly arranged, we shall only consider the working of one of them.

It is shown in the annexed diagram (Fig. 198), in which the proportion of parts has not been preserved, but which is only designed to indicate their respective positions.

M is the self-exciting Gramme machine, supplying the two circuits C and C', of which we shall only consider the first.

The current of this machine is, to begin with, susceptible of a certain regulation by means of a resistance, R, connected with the terminals B and B'. This apparatus is placed between the exciting-machine and field of the generator, so that by changing the resistance the intensity of the magnetic field

22

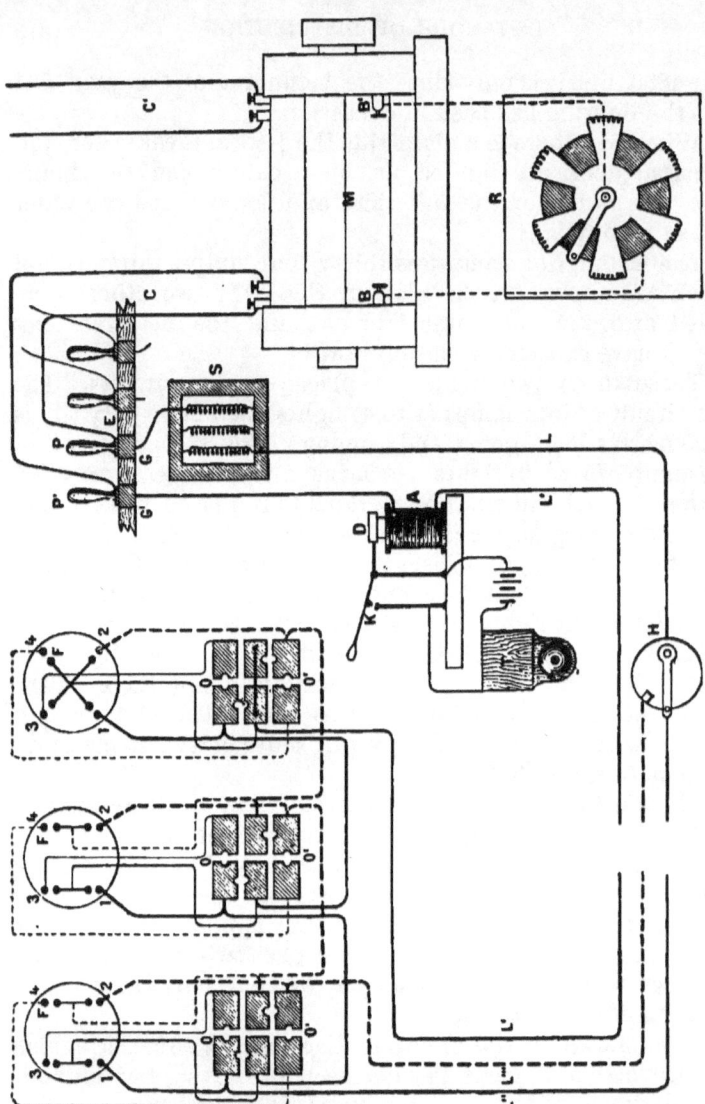

Fig. 198.—Diagram of one of the circuits in the electric-lighting of the port of Havre.

can be made to vary, and the current produced can thus be regulated.

The conductors forming the circuit C, under consideration, first reach two handles, P and P′, terminated by metallic pieces that go into metallic sockets, G and G′, fastened on the wooden base, E. The object of this arrangement is the following: If any accident happens to the machine, the handles, P P′, are lifted and replaced by two other similar ones that receive the wires from the reserve machine, so that the current will not be interrupted but for a very short period.

In the course of the conductor, L, as it leaves G, a resistance-frame is placed, designed to render the current through the circuit C equal to that through the other circuit C′ of the machine. The unequal intensity of these two currents is due to two causes: first, to the inequality of length of the circuits, and consequently of resistance, secondly, to this fact, proved by experience, that in the self-exciting machine the circuit C, that is nearest to the exciter, has a higher electromotive force produced in it than the other. The frame, S, makes both currents equal.

The conductor, L, next reaches at H a double-contact switch. The two conductors, L′ and L″, which leave H, run out of the engine-room, and carry the current to the lamps F, F, F; they return by the wire L′.

Before returning to G′, this return circuit passes through an electro-magnet, A, which, during the passage of the current, holds an armature, D, constantly attracted. If an extinction be produced in any lamp, the current ceases to pass; the armature, as it separates, closes the contact, K, and sounds an alarm-bell, T; this gives the warning, and, as we shall see, the relighting can be immediately effected.

As we have seen already, most of the circuits contain six lamps; in our diagram, for the sake of simplicity, we have only shown three. All these lamps hold four Jablochkoff candles, with six millimetre carbons; but the first ones contain each two candle-holders with two candles each, and have consequently two return wires; the last, on the contrary, contains a four candle-holder, of the ordinary form, with a single return wire. Finally, in the foot of each candelabrum is placed a switch-board, O O′, of six plates, through which the current passes before reaching the lamp.

This arrangement, apparently complicated, attains two results : first, in normal working, without leaving the engine-room, the superintendent can cause the current to pass from the candles 1 to the candles 2, by means of the switch H ; in the second place, in case of extinction, after having replaced the candles 1 by candles 2, he can prepare, by simple manipulation of the switches, O O', the candles 3 for a fresh passage of the current.

To understand how this is effected, let us first suppose the switch H so placed that the current follows the conductor L'' : it first reaches the upper left-hand piece of the switch-board O O' of the first lamp-post ; thence it goes to the candle 1 ; following then the return wire from the lamp 1–3, it reaches the middle piece on the same side, and leaves that for the switch of the second lamp-post. In this as in the rest the current takes the same course, and it is the same in the last, with this exception, that there is one return wire only ; finally, the current returns to the machine by the wire L', passing through the electro-magnet A.

In this course it will be seen that the current follows the full lines of the diagram. If, now, when the candles 1 are burned up, the switch H be changed, so that the current traverses L'', it will follow a course absolutely symmetrical with the first one, indicated by the dotted lines, and will supply the candles 2. The return will take place as before, through the wire L'. At present, suppose that the current coming through L'' (full lines) and lighting the candles 1, a sudden extinction takes place, notice of it, in the engine-room, will be given by the bell T; the first thing to be done will be to place the switch H upon L''', which will light all the candles 2, so that the lighting will have no interruption of any considerable length. Then each lamp-post must be visited, and the hole that separates the two upper pieces of its switch-board must be closed with a screw-plug ; the right-hand piece communicating, as we have seen in the drawing, with the candle 3, it follows that after this new arrangement of the switch-board O O', if, at the moment the candles 2 are burned, the switch of H be again pressed upon the conductor L'', the current will pass through all the candles 3.

If, then, following this out, the lower pieces of the switch-board at O' be connected, as the left hand is in relation to the candle 4, a new change of the switch H will light all the candles 4.

Thus, in a single evening all four candles of the same lamp

can be lighted. But in Havre this is never necessary; the illumination lasts only three hours, so that two candles are quite sufficient, and in normal operation the current is shifted from one candle to the other by the attendant in the engine-room. The arrangement we have just described is only of value in case of an accident.

In each of the switch-boards of the lamp-posts, the upper left-hand piece and the lower right-hand piece can be connected by a screw-plug each one with the corresponding middle piece. These two connections are for the purpose of cutting out the lamp from the circuit, whether the current passes through L'' or L'''.

The arrangement of the six circuits is similar to that which we have described : all the wires first reach the beam E which supports all the handles; the electro-magnets A and the switches H, marked with numerals in their order, are arranged side by side in the operating or engine-room, so that the manipulation is thus rendered very easy.

All the conductors go out together, and then diverge toward the different points where they are to be used.

At places where the cables must be fastened together underground it is desirable to avoid splicing and to provide a means of control and repair; for that purpose the special arrangement shown in section in Fig. 199 has been adopted.

A A is an earthenware cylinder about fifty centimetres high; it is placed underground, and the two ends of the cable to be united are passed into the box through its lower end and bent upward. The cylinder is then filled to about one third of its height with thin cement; above the layer of cement the cable is laid bare, and the two ends united by a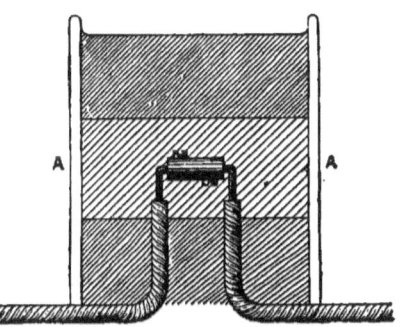

FIG. 199.—Junction-box.

screw-coupling; the whole is covered with a layer of paraffine; the cylinder is then closed with cement. Each cylinder of this kind contains several junctions; the number varying, according to the circumstances, from three to twelve. A sheet-iron cover with a hole through its middle, and laid flush with the soil, closes the cylinder. When the junctions are to be examined this plate is raised, the upper layer of cement is broken, and the paraffine is thus reached.

The engraving (Fig. 200) gives an idea of the effect produced, and enables a conception to be formed of the extent of this plant, one of the largest and most carefully laid out in existence.

CHAPTER II.

CONDITIONS OF A GENERAL DISTRIBUTION.

To tell the truth, in all the installations of a number of lamps which we are describing, the problem of the distribution of the light is more often studied than solved ; in practice, the generating machine is divided into several separate generators ; on each of the circuits thus obtained a restricted number of lamps, self-regulating within a certain range, is placed ; moreover, when the whole is once in position and adjusted, all remains in the same state during the period of action. In a genuine distribution, the power of adding or removing some lamps must exist, without disarranging those which are still working, the electrical generator furnishing always the exact quantity of current necessary for whatever number of lamps may be working at the time. Under these conditions variable quantities of work must be produced, according to the demand, and divided according to the needs, which may be variable. The problem is then infinitely more complicated.

The general conditions to which the solution must conform may be now understood. A generator being given, there are only two means of making it supply several electrical apparatus : the first is to place them in succession, one after the other, on a single circuit ; the second is to arrange them singly or in groups across the circuit: in the first case, the lamps are said to be either in series or in tension ; in the second case they are in derivation, quantity, or in multiple arc.

A comparison will render sensible the difference between the two arrangements. Suppose the problem is to utilize a waterfall by causing it to turn several water-wheels ; these can be placed one below the other, each of them receiving all

Fig. 200.—View of the port of

re lighted by Jablochkoff candles.

the water of the fall, but utilizing only a part of its height; or one can be placed beside the other, each of them utilizing all the height of the fall, but receiving only a part of its water-supply. In the first case the apparatus are in series, in the second they are in derivation.

This comparison shows us how the two systems of division can work. In the first case, the fall being already utilized, if we wish to introduce a new water-wheel, to find it a place, it will be necessary to increase the height of the fall, the volume of the river remaining the same; in the second case, it will be, on the contrary, the volume of the river which must be increased to actuate the new wheel, the height of the fall not needing to be changed. In an electric system it may be said that, with the arrangement in series the tension can be changed without changing the intensity, while with the arrangement in derivation the tension will remain constant, the intensity being made to vary.

In all cases there is an element which varies according to the expenditure of electrical energy which the lighting apparatus require. It will always be necessary, therefore, for variable conditions, to provide a system adapted for regulation of the generator, constantly keeping it in condition to furnish the quantity of electricity requisite for the work. This arrangement is indispensable; it can only be suppressed if the source of electricity could be reduced to a simple force without material organization; in this case, all the circuit being a useful circuit, the production would naturally become proportional to its chance of escape. But this result is impossible. The generator always forms a portion of the circuit, and indeed often an important part; its presence implies the necessity of a regulating organ, without which it is impossible to solve fully the problem of distribution.

The worth of the solution of the problem depends on the perfection of the regulating mechanism which it involves, and in the degree of perfection with which it fulfills the three following conditions :

1. All the apparatus placed on the circuit of the same electric generator must work independently of each other.

2. The regulation which should be exercised over the generator for attaining the preceding result should be performed automatically and by the current itself, no human surveillance being as quick and as exact as electricity.

3. The regulation should be managed so that the generator, while sufficing for variable expenditures, may never exact
work in excess of the expenditure, so that there is no loss.

I. REGULATORS OF THE INTENSITY OF CURRENTS.

We have said that the question of distribution had been
propounded after the serious study of electricity. As long
as regulators and candles only were used, the imperfect means
described above were sufficient. But with incandescent lamps,
illuminators of very reduced intensity, the number of pieces
of apparatus on the same generator must be considerably increased; the problem of distribution then presented itself,
and it had to be met and solved more or less completely.

As long as only light was under consideration, the apparatus all being equal, their consumption of electricity could
be known in advance, and the question was accordingly simplified. Thus, the Electrical Exposition of Paris contained a
certain number of distributions of light. But, to tell the
truth, none were seen actually at work; the lights of the Exhibition were regulated once for all; when they were in action they never changed, and the current-regulators had no
occasion for working. No special experiments seem to have
been made to determine their efficiency; nevertheless, they
are interesting to understand. We have described already,
in Book IV, the current-regulator of Maxim and Edison.*
We add to them that of Mr. Lane-Fox.

The regulator of current intensity of Mr. Lane-Fox, shown
in Fig. 201, has as principal organ a sort of vibrator actuated
by an electro-magnet, E, and designed to turn a ratchet-wheel,
N, whose axis carries a toothed pinion placed between two
beveled wheels, R R', mounted on a common axle. This axle
carries at its extremity a friction-lever, F, which moves in
front of a series of contact-pieces, C C, corresponding to regularly increasing resistances. According as one or the other of
the wheels, R R', moves the axle, and consequently the lever
in one or the other direction, it reduces or increases the
resistances introduced into the circuit.

The axle of the wheels, R, R', can be moved longitudinally

---

* [It was found necessary to substitute for the author's account a more complete one, and to place it after the description of Marcel Deprez's system, as the
reasons for its adoption could then be better appreciated.]

under the influence of the armature A, common to the two electro-magnets, E, E'. A relay with double-contact, E'', I, placed in a derived circuit, sends into one or the other of these electro-magnets a local current; the armature A attracted to the right or left moves the axle so as to make the pinion engage sometimes with one, sometimes with the other, of the two wheels R, R'.

It remains to examine briefly the extent to which these apparatus fulfill the conditions recited above.

Edison's method consists in the use, for exciting the generating machine, of a derivation of the prin-

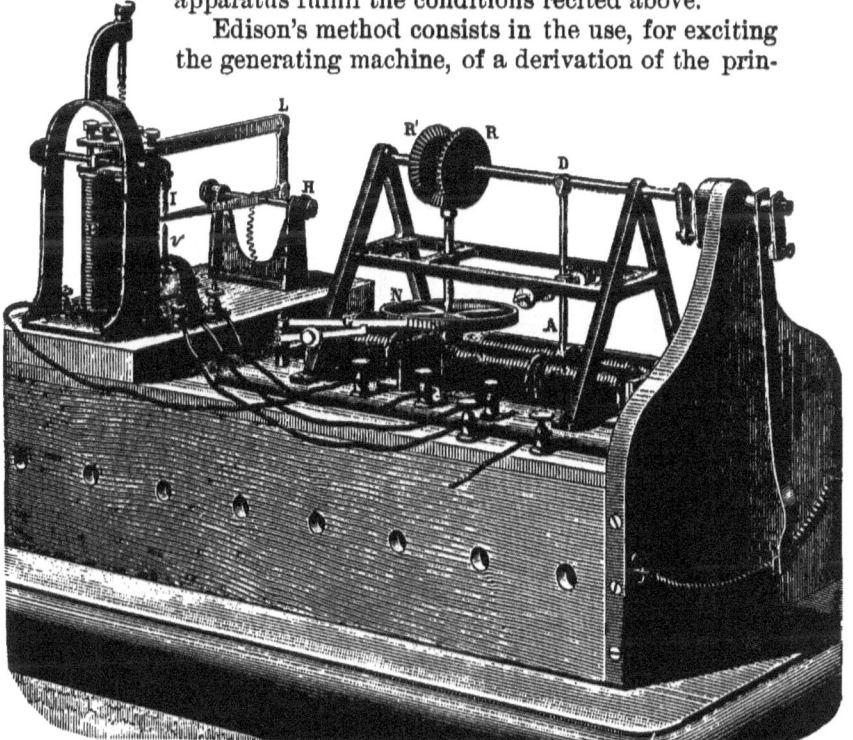

Fig. 201.—Lane-Fox's regulator of current intensity.

cipal circuit. In this derivation resistances are introduced by hand, according to the indications of a galvanometer, or more simply of a test-burner. What is lacking in this process is perfectly clear—it is not automatic, and only suffices for a preliminary regulation, or for slight and foreseen variations. It can not answer for the service of an extended and varied distribution in which sudden and considerable changes occur;

accidents would happen before the attendant could prevent them, admitting even that by sustained continuous attention he may be always ready to act. It is a practically useful method, sufficing perhaps for most systems of lighting ; but is not really a general solution of the problem of the distribution of light, nor, for a stronger reason, of the distribution of electricity for all the various uses to which it is adapted.

The methods suggested by Messrs. Lane-Fox and Hiram Maxim are theoretically more complete ; it is not certain that they are more efficacious. The regulators which they employ are very slow in action ; that of Maxim has also the defect of working by the displacement of rubbing-brushes, which

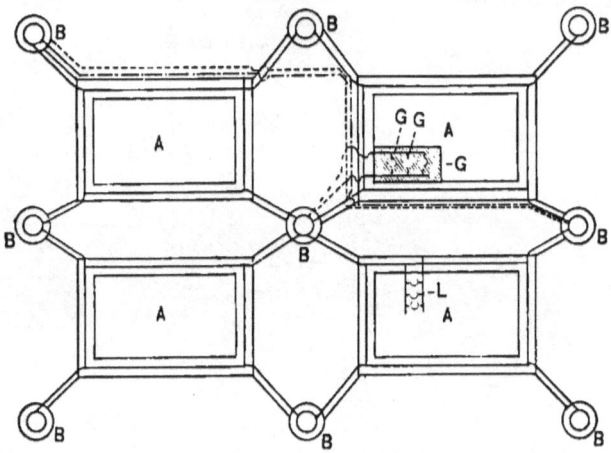

Fig. 202.—Diagram of Edison street-mains.

places the machine always under bad conditions of working. They have only been tried for the smaller class of distributions ; it does not appear that they can, on account of their slowness of action, suffice for a really complicated and very variable distribution.

They are, however, useful apparatus, and give a certain guarantee of security and good working for those apparatus to which they have been applied. It is true that incandescent lamps are not very difficult apparatus to employ in division ; they can support considerable variations in intensity of current, so that the regulation is less necessary with them than with large burners, such as regulators or candles.

II. Electric Canalization of Edison.

The Exhibition has shown us examples of notable division. The last plant of Mr. Edison supported about six hundred lamps, all placed on his large machine. It is necessary to repeat that this system was put in order once for all, and needed no regulating while working. His lamps were placed in groups of two in derivation, on a general circuit.

Mr. Edison has also arranged elsewhere much more extensive distributions of light, all of whose accessory arrangements he has studied out with remarkable care. At the Paris Exhibition of Electricity, plans in great detail were exhibited of the electric canalization which at this time [1882] is being completed in the First District of New York, and which is to supply fifteen thousand lamps in separate houses and in public places.

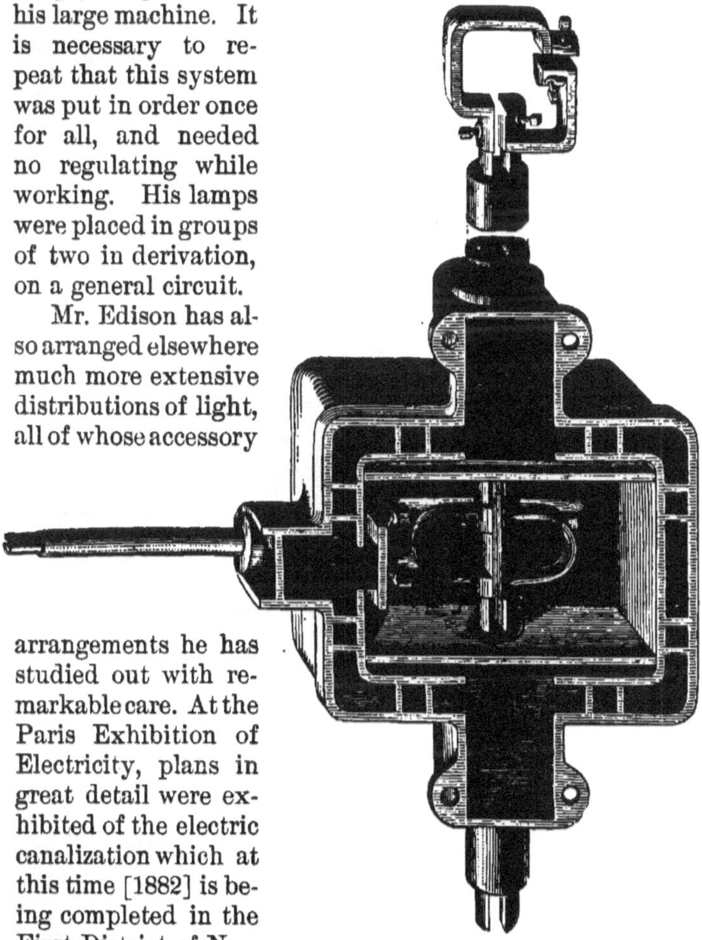

[In this installation the street-mains consist of small wrought-iron pipes, containing two half-round copper rods—the outgoing and return conductors—imbedded in a resinous

Fig. 203.—Edison junction-box, with fusible safety-catch, for street-mains.

insulator.   These mains are laid underground, about two feet
below the surface, and are arranged so that they form a net-
work throughout the entire district, constituting, in fact, a
gigantic sieve, of which the blocks are the meshes.   In actual
laying, a main is carried around each city block, and these
are joined together at the corners by means of junction-boxes.
The arrangement is shown in Fig. 202, where A represents the
city blocks, the full lines encircling them the conductors, and
B the junction-boxes.   These conductors are of successively
smaller diameter as they are removed from the central sta-

Fig. 204.—Edison junction-box, with safety-catch, for connection of service-wires with
mains.

tion.   Auxiliary mains, termed feeders, shown in the dotted
lines, serve to increase the conducting capacity to any desired
extent throughout any portion of the system.   The manner
in which the dynamos are connected with the mains is shown
at G, and the way in which the lamps are placed on the circuit
at L.   The main junction-boxes are constructed as shown in
Fig. 203, in which provision is made, by means of the curved
metal arms, for expansion and contraction.   Similar, though
smaller, boxes serve for the connection of the service or house
conductors with the mains.   The construction of these is
shown in Fig. 204.]

In these two boxes there will be observed a wire interposed in the branch circuit; it is a safety-catch of fusible metal, designed to cut off the current if, by accident, it should become strong enough to injure the lamps, or to cause in the conducting wires a dangerous heating. These boxes also enable the circuit, in case of accident, to be interrupted at the necessary point, so as to isolate parts of the circuit that may be inaccessible, while the remainder is still supplied.

As for the interior conductors for houses, these are copper wires, of proper size, wrapped in a casing of cotton rendered incombustible,

FIG. 205.—Safety-plate with fusible cut-off, placed at points where the wires enter a house.

and, if desirable, finally covered with silk. The placing of these wires does not differ from that already effected everywhere for electric bells.

In the path of these conducting wires Mr. Edison also places little safety-plates (Fig. 205).

Thanks to these multiplied precautions, a fire is not possible in case of irregularity in the strength of the current, from heating the conducting wires. The *cut-off* would, in fact, melt long before this heating would be sufficient to set on fire the most combustible materials, and would thus cut off all passage of a dangerous current. If electrical systems of other kinds have sometimes occasioned slight fires, it is precisely because they have neglected those multiplied precautions which are one of the characteristics of Edison's canalization.

The lamps are, moreover, as we know, provided with safety-pieces—either one for a group or one for each lamp—(Figs. 206, 207), and there is also one in the socket of each lamp, to arrest the current at the least irregularity in its behavior. Thus, no provision appears to have been neglected to reassure the most timid people.

The plants set up in the Paris Exhibition, of far vaster proportions than any preceding ones, have succeeded in proving that the division of electricity, like all other divisions, was not effected without loss, especially of light. As the burners became smaller, the quantity of light obtained by the expenditure of a horse-power in working the machine became less. The following figures may be accepted as at least proba-

ble : with a single-arc regulator on a machine, an average per
horse-power was obtained of the value of 100 carcels. M.
Fontaine estimates that with Gramme machines this value

may rise to as much
as 280 carcels. With
divided-current lamps
—differential lamps,
for instance—80 to 85
carcels are obtained for
the same expenditure
of work. The Jabloch-
koff candles, and the
Reynier-Werdermann
incandescent lamps,
give 30 to 50 carcels.
Finally, the small in-
candescent lamps with-

FIG. 206.—Lamp-socket with safety-catch.

out combustion—of the Edison, Swan, Maxim, and other systems—give hardly more than 10 to 16 carcels per horse-power
expended, varying with the system of lamps used.

It is clear that at this point the division becomes expensive ; but it then furnishes luminous centers analogous to our
oil-lamps, which cost us much more than gas, and can even
take the place of candles that are still more expensive.
Neither must we forget that lighting is not· the only field

for the application
of distributed elec-
tricity. It is, on
the contrary, only
a particular case of
a vast collection of
services to which
electricity is admi-
rably adapted, and
which make the
method of its gener-
al distribution one
of the most impor-
tant problems im-
aginable.

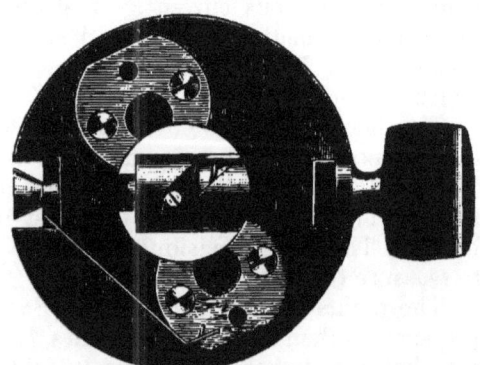

FIG. 207.—View from below of the lamp-base.

It is, in fact, an excellent means for the transmission and
distribution of motive power ; it enjoys the valuable property

of furnishing economically mechanical power in very small fractions, something which no motor now known to us can effect. From this point of view alone, a general distribution of electricity would be an immense advantage; its value appears still greater if we consider the multitude of different purposes to which electricity is so readily applicable, and which the Exhibition of 1881 showed with so much *éclat*.

This general problem does not differ on the whole from the narrower problem of the distribution of the light alone; the conditions to be fulfilled are the same. All that must be borne in mind is, that the apparatus to be supplied are very variable, very unequal; that the distances to be overcome will be greater, and the variations in service more considerable; so that for success to be attained all accessory conditions must be fulfilled with the greatest rigor, all approximate solutions, acceptable in minor proportions, inevitably failing as they are extended over wide areas.

This and other reasons, already given above, show that special methods, used for light, and which we have just described, will be entirely insufficient for a general distribution of electricity. For the rest, it must be said that their inventors never pretended to give them this destination.

At the Electrical Exhibition at Paris only two distributions striving for the full solution of the problem were to be seen : that of M. Gravier, and that of M. Marcel Deprez. We shall first study that of M. Gravier, which is far less complete than the other.

III. M. GRAVIER'S SYSTEM OF ELECTRICAL DISTRIBUTION.

We have said, it will be remembered, that the problem of distribution would disappear if the generator had no resistance. M. Gravier at once aims at this state of affairs in reducing the resistance of the generator. For this end he takes several machines and couples the armatures in quantity, which diminishes the resistance of the combined arrangement; he connects the field magnets in series, and produces their excitation either by a derived circuit or by a special machine. He uses an outgoing conductor that, according to him, acts as a reservoir. It is hard to understand what he means by this, as a conductor is not, and can not be, a reservoir. All that appears is that he makes it very large, which amounts to diminishing its resistance. Afterward he divides it into a certain number of circuits going to the separate pieces of apparatus.

The distribution of which we give here the plan (Fig. 208) is not that of the Paris Exhibition; it is a plant of the same

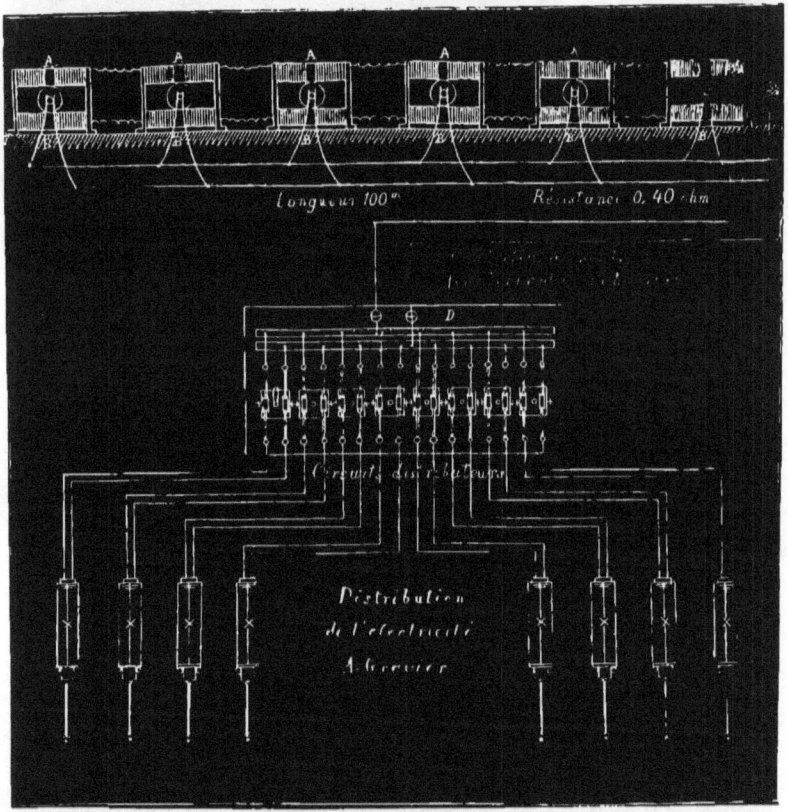

Fig. 208.—M. Gravier's system of electrical distribution at the Zawiercie works, Poland.

kind established in Zawiercie, in Poland; it gives an exact idea of the method.

It is perfectly clear that this system does not solve the problem of distribution; it does not even attack it. It is content, a restricted installation being given, to indicate the conditions most favorable to a good result, and that by the application of a well-known physical principle; there is nothing

in it constituting a special method.   It is easy to see its defects.   First, it does not satisfy any of the three conditions
specified above.   Finally, it requires the use of a very considerable amount of material, for, to diminish the resistance,
numerous machines must be employed instead of a single
powerful generator.   At Zawiercie, M. Gravier has four machines for eight lamps ; at the Exhibition he had six of them
for six circuits : such being the conditions, he might as well
not have divided his current at all.   Finally, it would be impossible with this system to obtain any extended capacity or
range ; the transmission of electricity can only be accomplished by giving the current a quite high tension, and this is
inseparable from a certain resistance in the generators.

M. Gravier has invented a very ingenious regulator (Fig.
200) which he calls either emission regulator or consummation
regulator (*regulateur d'émissions, regulateur de consomma-
tion*), and which serves to introduce suitable resistances into
the circuits or to withdraw them.   We have seen how costly
this method of regulating was.

Finally, to complete his system of regulation, M. Gravier
has proposed to adjust to the lamps a small apparatus which
he calls a rheometric regulator, and which is shown in Fig.
210.   It has for its object the rendering, by the intervention
of the derived current, the regulation of the machine more
rapid, an intervention which is not ordinarily produced except
when this derivation acquires a power sensibly greater than
that which balances the magnetic action.

This regulator is composed of a two-armed electro-magnet
(Fig. 210) placed in derivation, but whose circuit is opened
or closed instantaneously by the needle of a fine wire galvanometer of M. Marcel Deprez, a galvanometer which is itself
placed on another shunt from the principal circuit.   The
action of the electro-magnet on the releasing armature, shown
opposite the left-hand arm, is thus more complete and more
prompt ; the movement of the galvanometer-needle which determines the opening and closing of the circuit, and consequently the motion or stoppage of the mechanism, is effected
by a variation in distance scarcely exceeding a tenth of a millimetre ; the regulation thus becomes much more exact and
more rapid.   This arrangement was applied to the lamps
which M. Gravier had working at the Electrical Exhibition at
Paris.

23

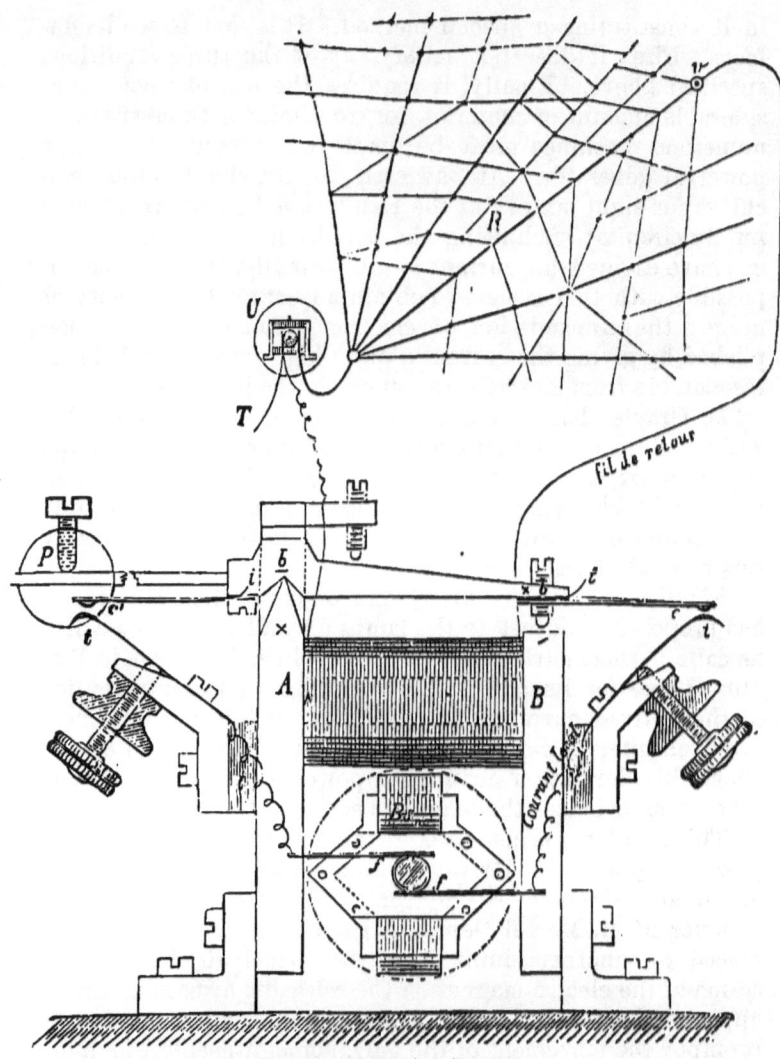

Fig. 209.—M. Gravier's Regulator.

U, electric generator, single or multiple, according to the works.

R, net-work of conductors.

v, point of distribution recognized as that most liable to be short of electricity; from this point the net-work communicates with the works by a special wire, which M. Gravier calls his return wire; and upon which is placed a fine wire galvanometer of M. Desprez, to indicate all the variations produced at the point *v*.

A B, horseshoe electro-magnet, whose wire is wound around the middle portion, and whose arms A and B are the expansions of the two poles.

b, b, vibrating armature of the electro-magnet A, B.   It carries on each side springs, c, c', arranged to come in contact with other springs, t, t, and to determine the passage of a local current, either in one or the other direction, through the bobbins B s.   The springs are insulated at i, i, i.

P, counterpoise serving to oppose the action of the electro-magnet on its armature.

B s, rotating armature (Siemens or other), turning from left to right, or from right to left, according to the direction of the local current traversing the magnet.

f, f, positive and negative brushes for entrance and departure of the local current in the bobbin, B s.

The variations of the return current cause the energy of the electro-magnet, A, B, to increase or diminish, and consequently the armature will touch the contact-pieces, sometimes at c, sometimes at c', thus determining the passage of the local current in the bobbin.   As long as the return current preserves the normal state for which its regulating mechanism has been adjusted, the armature remains in equilibrium, and the bobbin B s remains motionless; but if the return current changes in intensity, the strength of the electro-magnet, A, B, will be increased or diminished; the armature will yield either to the preponderating action of the weight P, or to the attraction of the electro-magnet; it will close one of the contacts c or c', and will determine the passage of the local current into the movable armature, which begins to turn in one or the other direction; it is this rotation which M. Gravier utilizes for making his electro-motive force vary, either by modifying the speed of the motor or by introducing resistances in the excitation circuit.

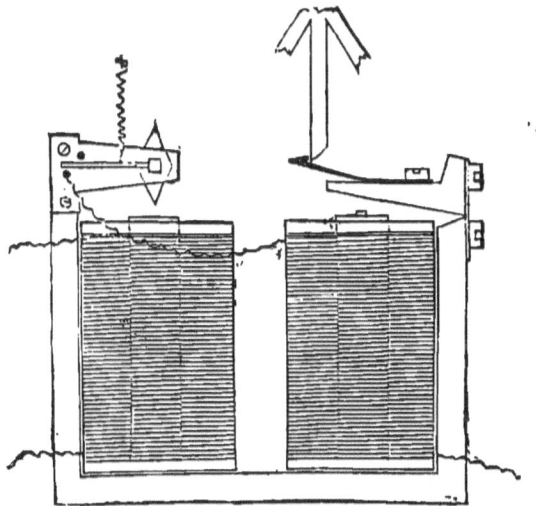

Fig. 210.—Rheometric regulator of M. Gravier.

The apparatus of M. Gravier have not yet been placed in practical working, and in questions of this sort, from our present point of view, those systems are, above all, worthy of confidence which have received the decisive test of experience. This guarantee is not wanting to the last solution which we have to examine, the important discovery of M. Marcel Deprez.

IV. System of Electrical Distribution of M. Marcel Deprez.

By a special study of the working of machines, M. Deprez found that the regulation necessary for distribution could be obtained from the machines themselves, using only their own proper action suitably combined, and without the intervention of mechanical organs.

To understand the system, it must first be remembered that the work produced by a steam-engine does not depend upon its speed, but on the quantity of steam which it expends and on the pressure. In large factories, where a central engine drives numbers of machines, its rate of speed does not change, whatever be the number of machines that are working; but it only admits each moment the quantity of steam that is necessary for it, thus regulating its work by the demand. It is the same with a gas-engine, which only admits gas in proportion to its needs, always preserving the same speed.

In like manner, dynamo-electric machines can expend more or less power without change of speed; it depends on the magnetization of their field magnets—a magnetization which determines the effort necessary to put them in motion; it is enough, in fact, to modify this magnetization, to cause to vary at the same time the work produced and work expended by a machine.

M. Marcel Deprez determines once for all the speed of his electric machine and of his engine: he varies the work by varying the magnetization.

When the apparatus to be supplied is placed in derivation, a single condition suffices to insure their independence; it is necessary that the electrical state at the two ends of the machine be always the same, whatever the exterior circuit. It is evident then, that if the machine be regulated so as to fulfill this condition, each circuit will be practically separate, and consequently have perfect independence.

Under the ordinary conditions of dynamo-electric machines, the electric state of the terminals of the machine, what is called the difference of potential of these points, is determined, for a given speed, by the excitation of the field; this is produced by the current of the machine itself, and consequently varies with the conditions of the circuit. The difference of potential varies at the same time. To keep constant

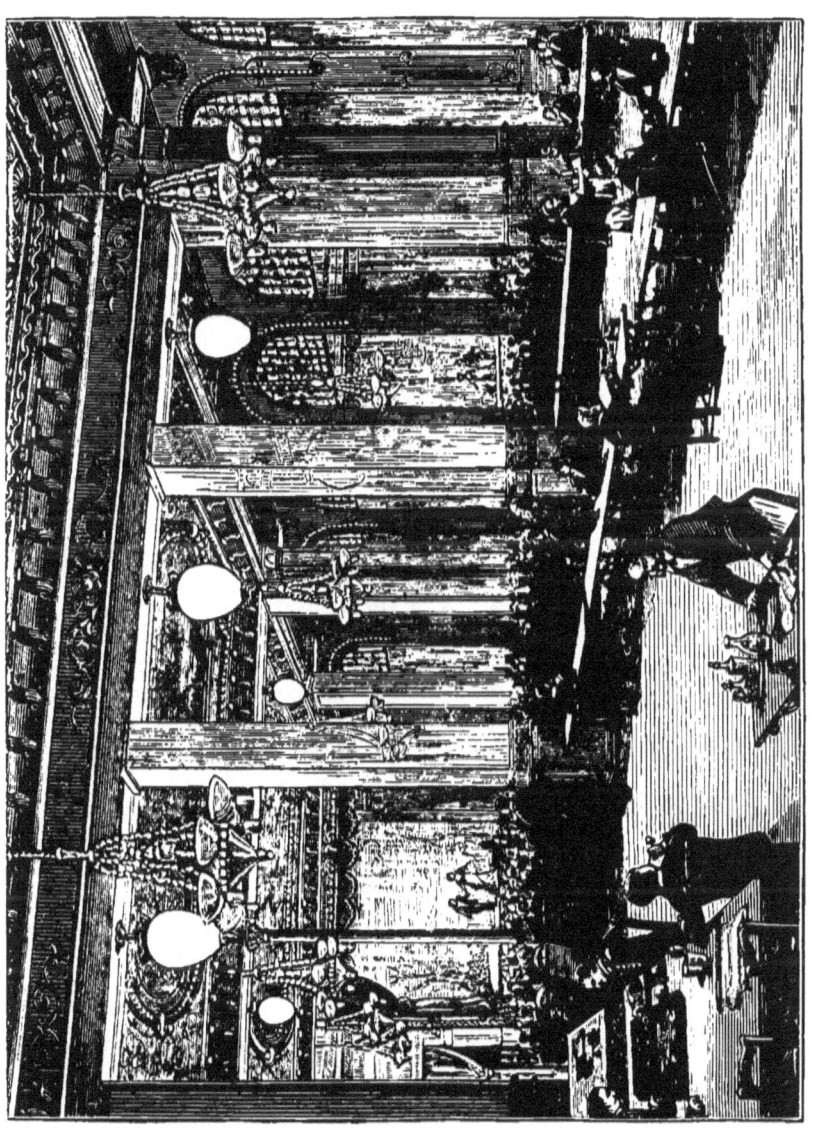

Fig. 211.—Music-hall on the Place du Château-d'Eau, in Paris, lighted by Jablochkoff candles.

this difference of potential, M. Marcel Deprez obtains the excitation of the field from two distinct currents, whose effects are added to each other; one of them is a constant current furnished by an independent source of electricity, either a battery or a second machine. The other is the current produced by the machine itself, and utilized in the exterior circuit. These two currents traverse two distinct sets of coils, formed of wires wound side by side, so that adjacent wires are sensibly at the same distance from the magnetized core. The speed of the machine is regulated to a fixed value resulting from its construction.

With this construction, there will always be two electromotive forces in the machine; one invariable, produced by the special exciting current, and which corresponds to the interior resistance, also invariable, of the machine; the other, which is produced by the working current, and which increases or diminishes in inverse ratio to the resistance of the exterior circuit. It follows that, without changing the speed of the machine, the difference of potential produced by the exterior excitation is kept permanent and invariable. The machine regulates itself, without any other intervention, and furnishes each instant the total quantity of electricity necessary to the working of the different apparatus.

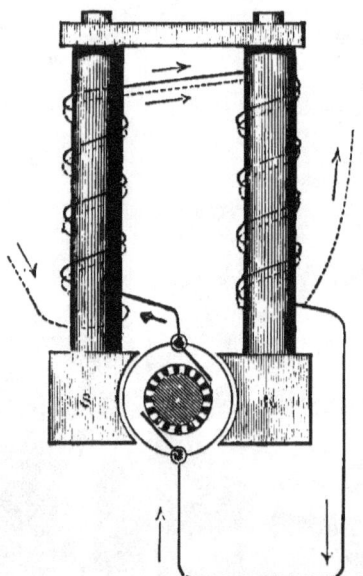

Fig. 212.—Marcel Deprez winding for constant electro-motive force.

It is evident that on long circuits and with numerous derivations the difference of potential will not remain the same over the entire length of the conductors; this is what happens in all cases of distribution, with water, gas, etc. But this presents no difficulty; it is enough to calculate the loss of the charge so as to know what pressure is to be used at each point of the circuit; this can be done equally and with great precision for electricity.

It is to be remarked that this method, based on rigorous mathematical theorems, gives us the solution of the question of distribution in the two systems—that is to say, in placing the apparatus either in series or in derivation. In practical working it is clear that the connections of the machines should be modified according to the system adopted, and, for distribution in series, the exciting of the magnets should be produced by a derived current from the main circuit. But a simple switch will suffice for this change, and the same machine can serve alternatively, without change of speed, for circuits arranged according to both systems.

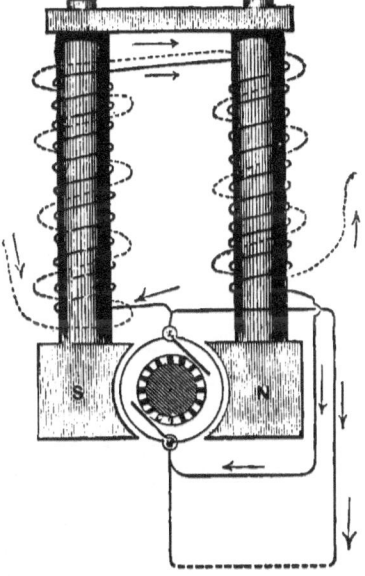

Fig. 213.—Marcel Deprez winding for constant current.

[The methods of winding adopted by M. Marcel Deprez in these two different cases are shown very clearly in Figs. 212, 213. When the apparatus to be operated are in multiple arc—as is always the case with incandescent lamps—the dynamo is required to give a current varying in compliance with varying demands of the circuit, but always of the same electro-motive force. The winding to accomplish this is shown in Fig. 212. The coils traversed by the constant current from an external generator are shown by the dotted lines, and those traversed by the main current produced by the machine by the full lines. The field magnets, it will be seen, are placed in the main circuit—that is, the winding is that known as the "series dynamo." To adapt this mode of regulation to apparatus arranged in series it is necessary to place the field in shunt, as shown in Fig. 213. That these methods of winding dynamos should accomplish their purpose—the preservation of a constant electro-motive force in one case and of a constant current in the other—the magnetization of the field magnets must be far from the point of saturation, and the machine must be driven at a certain velocity, to be determined in each case.]

As will be easily understood, this solution, reposing on the play of electric forces, and not on a material organ, is abso-

lutely general. It corresponds in the most complete way to
the requisite conditions; it admits all tensions, and nothing
limits its applicability; finally, it has been confirmed by a
decisive experiment that lasted during the whole duration of
the Paris Exhibition of 1881.

The electric generator (Fig. 214) was composed of a Gramme
machine, taking a part of its exciting current, according to
the method already described, from the constant current of
another small machine. The speeds were, two thousand revolutions for the generator, eight hundred for the exciter, and

Fig. 214.—Arrangement of dynamos for the distribution of electricity on the system of M.
Marcel Deprez.

one hundred and sixty for the gas engine. From the poles
of the generator two cables issued, forming the principal circuit; at all useful points there was taken from these cables,
by means of two wires, a derived current, which was conducted
to any given receptor, electric motor, lamp, electroplating
trough, etc.

Of the two arrangements of the working apparatus, in
series or in derivation, this last is the most practical, and
should be preferred in the great majority of cases. All the
systems we are describing have adopted it. It requires a

less extensive regulation, and leaves the individual apparatus more independent of each other; it is more reliable than the arrangement in series, with which a fault in a single point, wherever it is, influences seriously all the rest of the system.

We need not add that the distribution of M. Marcel Deprez requires no special construction of the conductors; it accommodates itself to all methods, and admits of the employment of all useful arrangements that practical experience may dictate. Following the course of logic, M. Marcel Deprez seems to have desired to establish his solution on solid bases, before devoting himself to accessory points.

The circuit went all around the Exhibition buildings ; the entire number of apparatus which it kept in action varied from twenty to twenty-seven ; these apparatus, on the other hand, worked with complete independence; they were far apart, and the workmen in charge of their operation worked without regard to what was going on in other parts of the system. In the circuit there were placed machines for making metallic braid, sewing-machines, saws, metal working-lathes, voltaic-arc lamps, incandescent lamps ; in private exhibitions, ventilators, electroplating troughs, the *"melographe repetiteur"* of M. Carpentier. Finally, at the end there was placed a Marinari printing-press, on which were printed the numbers of the journal "La Lumière Électrique," and various circulars. For the smaller class of apparatus the motor employed was the small magneto-electric motor of Marcel Deprez; for the printing-press it was a small Siemens machine. All this collection moved with perfect regularity and an absolute independence. As all can testify, the gas-engine driving the electric generator showed, by the variation in its consumption of gas, that the work expended was in exact proportion to the work utilized throughout the extent of the circuit. The experiment thus combined all necessary conditions, and should be considered absolutely conclusive. Furthermore, the considerations upon which M. Marcel Deprez bases his system are so clear and rigorous that its first success never seemed doubtful. It will be the same with experiments on the large scale, which will soon be tried, and which will complete the practical demonstration of the system.

From now on, this elegant solution of a problem as difficult as important can be considered as achieved. It is complete in other ways, because, independently of his studies on distribution, M. Deprez has completed experiments on the transmission of power by electricity, which have elucidated this question, still somewhat obscure, and have shown its true conditions. It will not be impossible, then, soon to try the utilization of natural forces hitherto lost, such as waterfalls that are inaccessible or too remote from working centers. Then the extreme division of light, so costly under other conditions, will become economically possible, the power employed being of low cost. But this would only be an insignificant part of the advantages that would be obtained, and every one can see the measure of consequences indicated by the expression "electricity in the home": it is at once light, power, chemical work, placed within the reach of every one, in as small fractions as can be wished for, with no trouble beyond turning a key. From this time the fact can be considered accomplished, and we can await with confidence the vast and impending development.

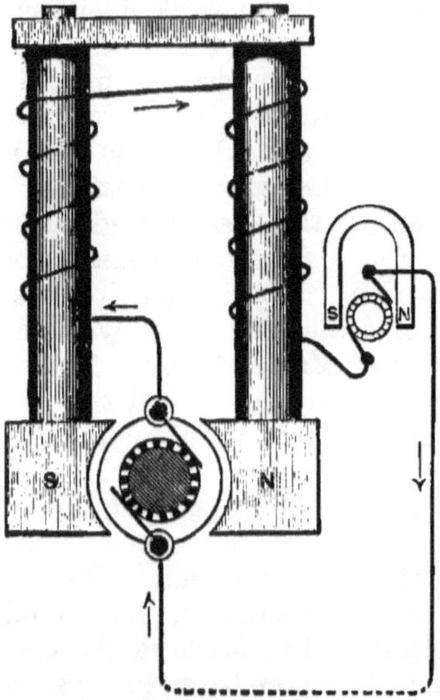

[A method of making a dynamo self-regulating, analogous to that of M. Deprez, has been devised by Professor John Perry. As the purpose of the current from an external source in the Deprez arrangement is simply to maintain an initial and independent magnetic field, any other means that will accomplish this can be employed. In Professor Perry's machine for maintaining a constant electro-motive force, shown in Fig. 215, a separate magneto machine is included in the circuit of a series dynamo, and is driven at such a speed as will maintain the desired electro-motive force between the terminals of the dynamo. In the machine for constant current, the magneto is placed in the shunt circuit (Fig. 216)].

FIG. 215.—Professor Perry's machine for constant electro-motive force.

V. Edison's Method of Regulation.

[The Deprez method of regulation for machines with constant electro-motive force was devised by Mr. Edison some time previous to any public exhibition by M. Deprez, and was patented in this country in September, 1882. The illustration (Fig. 217) is a reproduction of the drawing from this patent. The circuit 3, 4, serving to maintain an initial magnetism in the field, is here shown as a shunt to the main circuit, but Mr. Edison states in his specification that the current through it may be supplied from an external source. When this circuit is a shunt, it is made of high resistance, so that the amount of current flowing through it will not vary much within the limits of probable variation of resistance in the main circuit. As previously stated, in order that this method of regulation should work satisfactorily, the dynamo must be driven at a constant velocity.

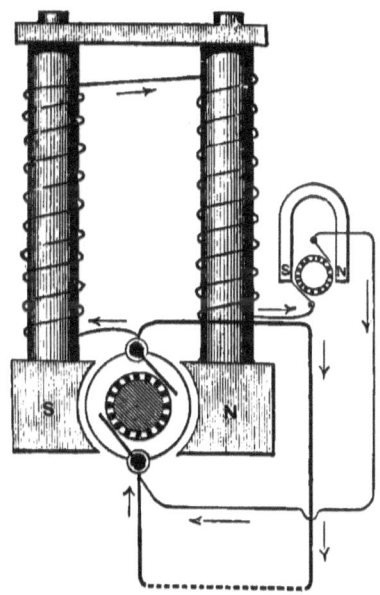

Fig. 216.—Professor Perry's machine for constant current.

The maintaining of a constant velocity is, however, much more difficult than would be imagined. Mr. Edison was, in fact, compelled to abandon this construction on this account, as he found that the variation in the speed of his driving-engine produced greater variations in his circuit than that due to the turning on and off of the lamps under normal conditions of lighting.

He has therefore adopted a mode of regulation which will enable the variation from both of these causes to be met. The method consists in interposing in the shunt circuit, in which the field magnets are placed, an adjustable resistance. When the number of lamps in circuit is increased, resistance

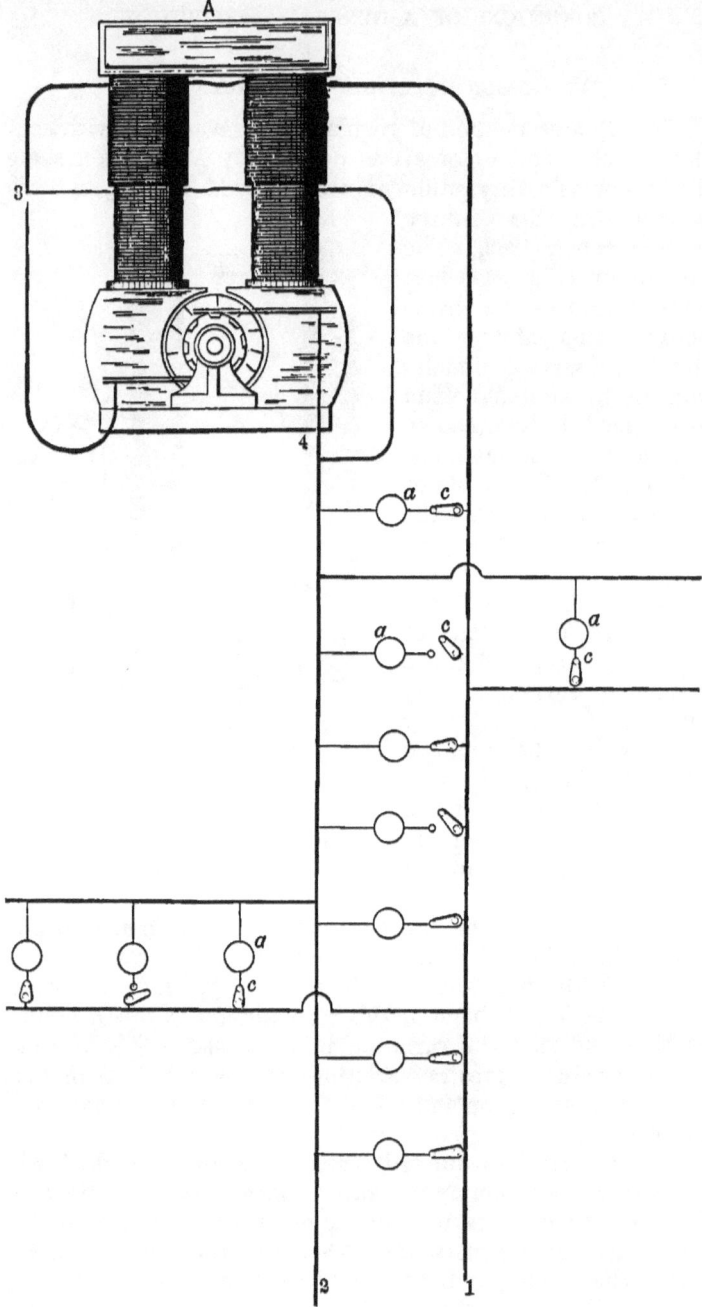

Fɪɢ. 217.—Edison dynamo with compound winding, for constant electro-motive force.

is thrown out of the field circuit, and, when they are diminished, it is introduced. Similarly, when the speed increases, resistance is thrown into the field circuit, and taken out when this diminishes. The electro-motive force of the current can thus be kept practically constant, whatever the changes in the working circuit. At central stations the shifting of these resistances is done by hand, but their manipulation is effected automatically in separate plants of moderate size, such as those designed for lighting workshops, large buildings, etc. The difficulties in the way of an automatic regulation of very large plants, such as those operated from a central station, are considerable, and Mr. Edison has always preferred to have a mode of regulation as free as possible from mishaps. The Deprez method of regulation he only intended to use with isolated plants.

The regulation, as carried out at the central station of the first district in New York city, consists in varying the field resistance in accordance with the indications of a galvanometer placed in a Wheatstone bridge. An incandescent lamp is placed on one side of the bridge, and the variable resistance of the bridge adjusted so that the galvanometer-needle stands at zero when the lamp is giving its normal light. As the resistance of the incandescent carbon filament varies with its temperature, any change in the current flowing through the lamp will immediately destroy the balance of the bridge and cause the needle to move in one direction or the other, according as the lamp rises or falls in candle-power. Resistance is then introduced into or thrown out of the field circuit until the needle returns to its normal position. These resistances, which consist of coils of German-silver wire, can be readily manipulated by the attendant by means of a switch. It might be supposed that this duty would require constant watchfulness on the part of the attendant, but this is far from being the case. In any extensive distribution the variation in the demand for light is a calculable one, and, the greater the number of consumers, the more easily the amount and time of these variations can be foreseen. When the station was first started there was little or no regularity in these variations, as consumers were constantly turning lights on and off to show friends how easily it could be done. With the attainment of normal conditions, however, these variations have assumed such a regularity that Mr. Edison asserts that it is possible to run the dynamos from a chart, in which the amounts of the resistances to be introduced into or withdrawn from the field circuit are indicated by the lengths of the ordinates of a curve, the time being denoted on the horizontal line.

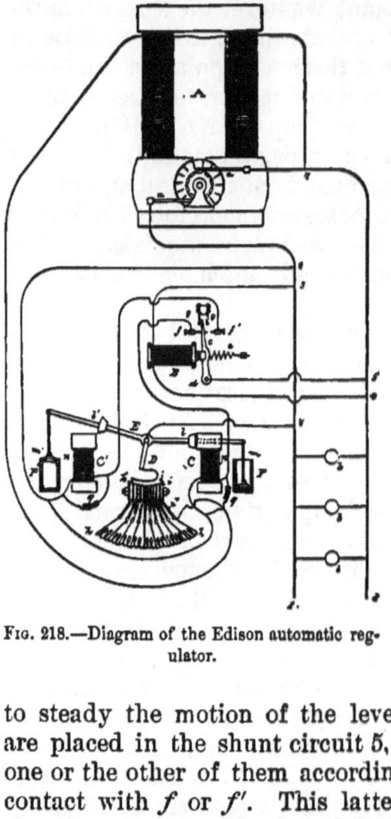

The automatic apparatus and its relation to the machine are shown in diagram in Fig. 218, and its external appearance in Fig. 219. The resistance coils h, h, which are included in the field circuit 7, 8, are connected with metallic plates i, separated from each other by mica. The upper edges of these plates form the arc of a circle, along which sweeps the elastic contact k, connected with the arm D. The movement of k is produced by the rocking-lever E, the armatures l and l' of which are attracted by the electro-magnets C and C'.

Fig. 218.—Diagram of the Edison automatic regulator.

Dash-pots F and F' serve to steady the motion of the lever. The magnets C and C' are placed in the shunt circuit 5, 6, which is closed through one or the other of them according as the armature c makes contact with f or f'. This latter armature is operated by the electro-magnet B, placed in another shunt circuit 3, 4. This magnet is thus connected with the main conductors in the same way as the lamps b, and will be affected in the same manner by variations in the line-current. When lamps are added, less current will flow momentarily through B, which will become weakened so as to allow its armature, c, to be drawn back by the spring e, and make contact with f'. The magnet C' will therefore draw down its armature l', and move k along the plates of the resistance coils, cutting resistance out of the field circuit. When lamps are removed, the mag-

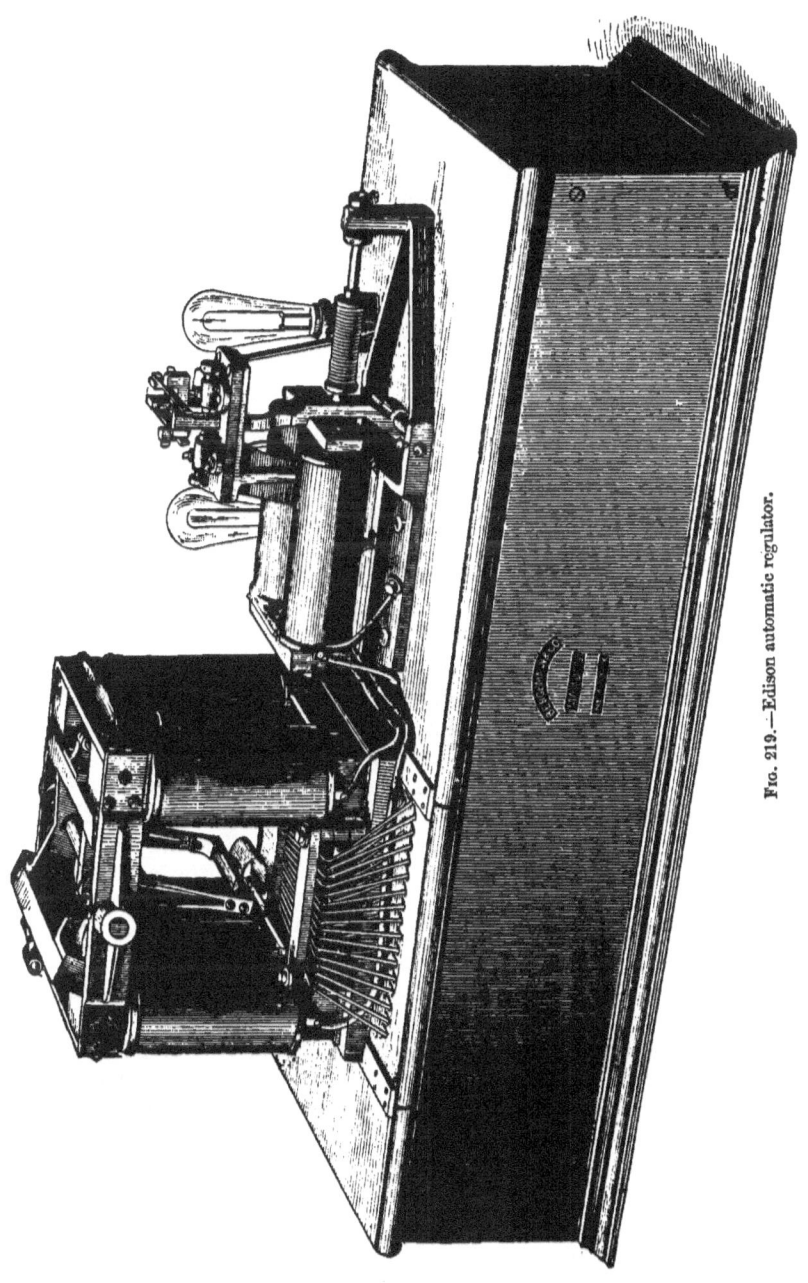

Fig. 219.—Edison automatic regulator.

net C will be energized and resistance thrown into the field circuit. A decrease of the speed of rotation of the armature will operate the same as an addition, and an increase of speed the same as a diminution of lamps. To prevent the burning out of the contact-points f and f', the magnets C and C' are provided with shunt-circuits, 9, for the currents due to the discharge of these magnets.]

VI. Weston's Method of Regulation.—Brush Regulator.

[Mr. Weston has sought to construct a machine of constant electro-motive force for incandescent lighting, by establishing a certain definite relation between the field of force and the rotating armature. The nature of this improvement is given by Mr. Weston, in his American patent, as follows :

"My improvements consist in so organizing the machine used for supplying current in the multiple-arc system of distribution that, by a law of operation of the machine, the electro-motive force is maintained practically uniform, whatever may be the quantity of current generated within the practical working limits of the machine. To accomplish this result I have found it necessary to so construct the machine that the inductive influence of the field magnets in determining the polarity of the armature-core shall so far preponderate over that of the induced currents circulating in and around the armature itself, that the effect of the latter is neutralized, at least to such an extent that the polar line of the armature and that of the field shall at all times during the normal operation of the machine practically coincide. . . . I also wind the armature in such manner that the requisite electro-motive force is obtained with comparatively few convolutions of conductors of large cross-section. It is important to use the smallest possible number of convolutions of conductor on the armature, in order to reduce to a minimum the magnetizing influence of the armature coils upon the core, and the resistance of the armature conductors is made as low as possible in order that the ratio of the external and internal resistances may not be greatly disturbed by variations in the external circuit. The purpose of this will be understood by a consideration of the magnetic condition of the armature-core of a machine having an ordinary cylindrical or annular armature, with the coils wound in a direction parallel to the axis of rotation. In such case the position of the polar line, or the points of maximum magnetic effect of the armature-core

Fɪɢ. 220.—Weston automatic regulator for arc lighting.

during the normal operation of the machine, is determined partly by the induced currents flowing in the armature coils

24

and circulating in the body of the armature itself, both of which tend to fix the polar line at right angles to that of the field, and partly by the magnetic induction of the field, which tends to cause the polar line of the armature to coincide with its own. As a result of the combined effect of these forces, the polar line of the armature will lie between the two points indicated. This is apparent from the fact that in all machines of this class, so far as my information extends, the maximum points of the commutator, or the line upon which the brushes are placed to take off the maximum amount of current, are in advance of the theoretical maximum points, which are on a line at right angles to the polar line of the field, and they are more or less advanced in proportion to the strength of the current induced in the armature-coils, and the consequent magnetizing influence exerted thereby. Probably the fluctuations in electromotive force observed in such machines are due largely to this angular displacement of the poles of the armature, acting substantially in the same manner to reduce the lines of force cut by the coils as would the removal of the field magnets to a greater distance from the armature. I have found that if the conditions which I have indicated above are properly observed in constructing the machine, the polar line of the armature may be made to coincide with the polar line of the field, and the real maximum points on the commutator be made to coincide so accurately with the theoretical points that the external resistance may be varied to any extent within the working limits of the machine ; or the machine may even be run in either direction without changing the adjustment of the brushes, and the electro-motive force will be practically constant for a given speed of rotation of the armature."

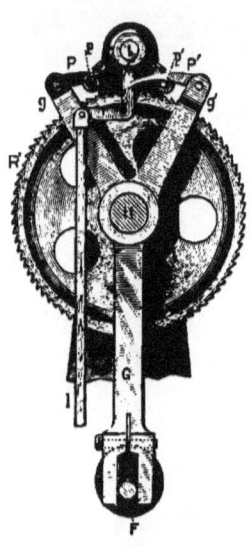

Fig. 221.—Details of the Weston automatic regulator.

The Weston method of regulation for arc-lamp circuits consists in introducing and withdrawing resistance from the field circuit, which is a shunt to the main circuit. The apparatus

for doing this is shown in Fig. 220, and the details of its
mechanism in Fig. 221. The resistances are cut in or out of
circuit by the movement of the arm J, which turns about J'
as a center, its upper end sweeping over a set of contacts arranged in a circle. Movement is given to it by the toothed-
wheels R, R', which are operated by the vibrating pawls P, P',
and are kept in motion by the pulley D. In normal position
these pawls are clear of the wheels R, R', but one or the other

Fig. 222.—Brush automatic regulator.

of them will be thrown into gear according as the electro-magnet M, to whose armature m the pawls are connected by the
lever l, or the opposing spring S is the stronger. This electro-
magnet is placed in the main circuit, so that it is affected by
variations in the lighting current, the same as the arc-lamp.

In the Brush machine for arc-lighting the field is in series with the lamps, and the regulation is affected by placing resistance in and out of a circuit forming a shunt across the field magnets. A carbon rheostat is used instead of wire coils, the resistance of which is varied by pressing the plates of which it is composed more strongly together. This pressure is applied by means of a lever operated by an electromagnet, the coils of which are in the lighting circuit. This magnet is also provided with coils included in the shunt circuit, in which the rheostat is placed, to increase its sensitiveness. The construction is shown in Fig. 222.]

CHAPTER III.

ECONOMY OF CONDUCTORS.

[As every electric conductor possesses resistance, a portion of the electric energy transmitted must always be expended in heating it, and therefore lost for any useful purpose. The resistance can, of course, be made as small as desired by simply enlarging the conductor, but the limit in this direction is soon reached, as account has to be taken, in practical construction, not only of the loss of power, but of the cost of the conductors. It is necessary, therefore, to choose the size of conductor with reference to both of these items, in order to obtain the maximum of economy. This condition is realized, Sir William Thomson has shown, when the yearly interest on the cost of the conductor equals the expense of the power lost in heating it.

How large a portion of the total power transmitted, this part lost in heating the conductor is, will depend upon the relation of the two factors—current-strength and electromotive force—which measure the amount of electric energy. Since the heat produced in a given resistance varies as the square of the current flowing through it, it is obvious that, to obtain the maximum economy in transmitting any given amount of electric energy, we must have a small current and high electro-motive force. A simple analysis will show the relation between the size and cost of conductor, and the strength of current, with the transmission of the same amount of energy.

Let C = current flowing through a circuit having a resistance, R, per unit of length. Then $C^2 R$ = loss by heating of the conductor per unit of length. In any other conductor of a resistance R_1 per unit of length, the loss by heating in conveying a current, C_1 will be $C^2_1 R_1$. Taking the loss the same in both cases—that is, $C^2 R = C_1^2 R_1$—we have $C^2 : C^2_1 = R_1 : R$, or $\dfrac{C^2}{C^2_1} = \dfrac{R_1}{R}$. But $\dfrac{R_1}{R} = \dfrac{d^2}{d^2_1}$, d and d_1 being the diameters of the conductors. Substituting the value of $\dfrac{R_1}{R}$, we have $\dfrac{C^2}{C^2_1} = \dfrac{d^2}{d^2_1}$, and $C : C_1 = d : d_1$, which shows that in order to have the same loss in the conductor in transmitting a given amount of energy, the diameters of the conductors must be directly as the currents flowing through them. But the weights of the wires, and hence their cost, depend upon their volumes, which in equal lengths are to each other as the squares of the diameters. If we call P and P_1 the prices of the conductors per unit length, we shall have $P : P_1 = d^2 : d^2_1$, and $P : P_1 = C^2 : C_1^2$; or the cost of conductors to transmit a given amount of energy with the same loss in each case will vary as the squares of the currents conveyed.

The importance of reducing the current through the circuit in order to obtain economy in distribution is very fully recognized by electricians. It is for this reason that arc-lamps are placed one after another, or "in series," upon a circuit, and that incandescent lamps are made of as high resistance as possible. Various other systems besides the two already described—the series and multiple-arc—have been proposed with a view of increasing the economy of distribution, but we will only notice two here: Mr. Edison's modification of the multiple-series system, and the induction-coil, or secondary generator system.

I. Edison's Multiple-Series System of Distribution.

As we have previously seen, in the simple multiple-arc system of distribution each lamp requires its own supply of current, so that, to maintain a hundred or a thousand lamps, one hundred or one thousand times the current requisite for one lamp must be transmitted through the conductors. If,

however, the lamps be arranged so that there are two or more
in each cross-circuit, or in multiple-series as it is termed, the
supply of current will depend not upon the individual lamp,
but upon the number of series cross-circuits, since the same
current goes through each of the lamps in series, in succession. Thus, if two lamps be placed in series, there will be
required but one half the current for a given number that
would have been requisite in the simple multiple-arc system.
If three lamps are placed in series, only one third the current
will be required, and so on. The electro-motive force must of
course be proportionately increased—that is, it must be
doubled for two lamps in series, trebled for three, etc. The
disadvantage of this arrangement is, that the lamps are not
independent of each other ; whenever one of a series is turned
out, all of that series must be, otherwise the remaining lamps
would be destroyed by the increased current which would

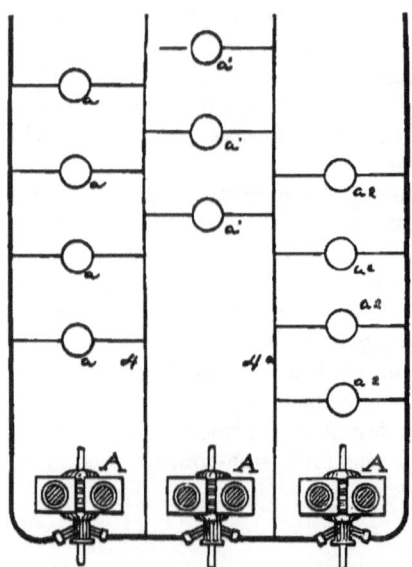

then flow through the
cross - circuit in which
they are placed. For in-
stance, with two lamps
in series, the turning out
of one of them would
reduce the resistance of
the cross-circuit to one
half. Double the current
would then flow through
it, since the electro-mo-
tive force is maintained
constant. With three
lamps in series, the cur-
rent would be trebled
when two are extin-
guished, etc. To render
this system of practical
value, therefore, it is
necessary to make each
lamp independent of the
others, as in the simple

FIG. 223.—Edison multiple-series distribution.

multiple-arc system. This Mr. Edison has succeeded in doing
in the manner shown in Fig. 223, which represents three lamps
arranged in series on each cross-circuit. The dynamos A, A,
A, are joined together in series, the two main conductors, P

and N, being attached, the one to the positive pole of the first machine, and the other to the negative pole of the last. Between each set of lamps, compensating conductors (as Mr. Edison terms them) are run to the generators, giving an arrangement similar to that of three simple multiple-arc circuits placed side by side.

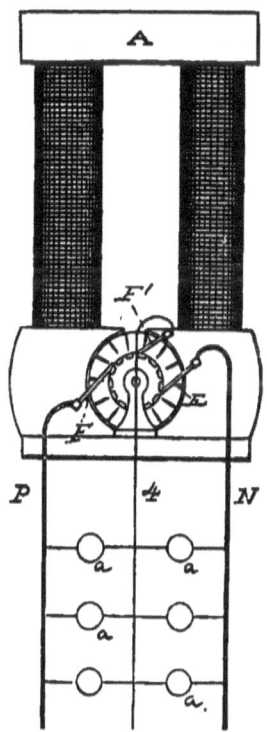

When the same number of lamps are in each multiple-arc circuit, no current will flow through the compensating conductors, but it will pass from the positive main conductor through each cross-circuit to the negative one. With, however, an unequal number of lamps in adjacent divisions, the excess of current above that necessary for the smaller number of lamps will flow through the compensating conductor between them. In actual construction the circuits will be arranged so that the number of lamps in adjacent divisions will be nearly the same at all times. The compensating conductors can therefore be made quite small and inexpensive. For two lamps in series Mr. Edison estimates that the conductors will need to be but thirty-eight per cent of the size required for the same number of lamps in simple

Fig. 224.—Edison multiple-series distribution applied to one generator.

multiple-arc, twenty-five per cent for the main, and thirteen per cent for the compensating, conductors. The application of this method of distribution to a single generator is shown in Fig. 224. In this case the compensating conductor is connected with an extra brush on the machine, placed between the other two.

II. THE SECONDARY-GENERATOR SYSTEM OF DISTRIBUTION.

In this system the lamps or other apparatus to be used are placed in the secondary circuit of an induction-coil, the pri-

mary wire of which is in the main circuit. As the tension
and intensity of the secondary-circuit current may be made
anything desired by a proper winding of the two coils, it is
possible to obtain with such an apparatus, from a high-tension
current in the main circuit, currents of low tension and considerable quantity in the secondary. Alternating currents are
preferably employed in operating the coils, as the circuit-
breaking apparatus may then be dispensed with. The induction system has been often proposed, and variously modified
by different inventors, but has been so far but very little used.
It was patented in England in 1857 by Harrison, and was employed by M. Jablochkoff in 1877 with his candles and his
kaolin incandescent lamp, already described. Mr. J. B. Fuller proposed the system in 1879, and arranged his secondary
coils so that they could be coupled in tension or quantity,
and made provision for varying the magnetic strength of the
iron core. The system was also used by Professors Thomson
and Houston for operating their vibratory arc-lamp, and an
induction system has been patented by Mr. Edison in which
a continuous high-tension current in the main circuit produces
a continuous current of low tension in the lamp circuit. None
of these attempts seem to have passed beyond an experimental
stage, but in the early part of last year the system was revived
in England by Messrs. Goulard and Gibbs, who have put it
into operation in the London underground railway. Their apparatus does not differ essentially from that previously used,
though they construct their induction-coils in a somewhat
different manner. Each circuit consists of cables containing
a number of wires, which cables are wound about a central
cylinder in the way in which the wires are usually wound.
The iron core is composed of a bundle of wires placed within
a brass cylinder by the withdrawal of which the secondary
current can be regulated, and consequently the amount of the
light. The secondary coil is divided into a number of bobbins, which can be connected in tension or quantity, so as to
furnish the kind of current desired. A number of these induction-coils are combined into one apparatus of sufficient
capacity to do the lighting at one point—that of a private
house, for example—and a number of these then arranged on
the circuit one after another, so that the main-line current
goes through each primary coil in succession.

The practical value of such a system of distribution depends, of course, upon its economy—whether the loss occasioned by the transformation of the high-tension line current into others of low tension is compensated for by the diminished cost of the conductors—in which, of course, must be included the cost of the induction apparatus. There appears to be no reason why the generative efficiency and the electrical efficiency should not be good. There is a difficulty in placing inductive apparatus in series on a circuit, as the work done in the secondary circuit of a coil directly influences the current ·flowing in the main circuit, and hence the electrical condition of all the coils on the same main line. This difficulty does not, however, appear to be insuperable. In long circuits the loss due to an alternating current would possibly be considerable, but there are no data on this point.]

CHAPTER IV.

DIVISIBILITY OF THE ELECTRIC LIGHT.

[At the time when attention was beginning to be directed to the incandescent light, some four or five years ago, a great deal was said about the loss of light resulting from division of the current, and the difference in this respect between gas and electricity. The production of economical burners of low candle-power was very generally spoken of as a solution of the problem of division, as if there was in some special sense a problem of this kind in the case of electricity quite different from that presented by any other agent. The observed fact was simply that a given amount of electric energy yielded much more light when utilized in a single lamp than when divided up among a number of smaller ones. But the inference which was apparently drawn from it was the very curious one that the power necessary to maintain a number of lamps was not directly proportional to their number, but increased at a greater rate. This inference was not distinctly stated, but was implied in much that was written on the subject, by the way in which the relation between small and large lights was presented. As the notion that there is a special difficulty in obtaining subdivision of light with electricity not expe-

rienced with other means of illumination has not yet wholly
disappeared, it may be worth while to consider the reasons of
the observed difference of the economy of large and small
lights, and the difference between gas and electricity in this
respect.

The rate at which energy is expended in an electric circuit
is measured, as we have already seen, by the product of the
strength of the current by the electro-motive force, or by the
square of the current by the resistance. Suppose we take a
wire—say ten inches long—and pass a current through it of
sufficient strength to bring it to a given incandescence. If
this current be denoted by C, and the resistance per inch of
the wire by R, the expenditure of electric energy in the wire
per second will obviously be $10\,C^2\,R$. Now, if this wire be
divided into ten parts, and these be arranged on a circuit one
after another, the expenditure of energy will evidently be the
same. If, instead of placing them one after another, or "in
series," they are arranged side by side, or in "multiple arc,"
there will still be the same expenditure, though in this case
the relation of the resistance and current will be different.
Each of the inch-pieces will require the same strength of current, C, to bring it to its previous incandescence, and, as its
resistance is R, the expenditure of energy will be $C^2\,R$, and
that for the ten wires, $10\,C^2\,R$. Whichever way, then, these
ten pieces of wire are arranged, they require precisely the
same amount of power to maintain them at a given incandescence, and it is quite immaterial (the resistance of distributing conductors being neglected) whether they are inclosed in one globe or each in a separate one, and thus form
ten small lamps or one large one.*

It appears from this that there is no loss whatever by subdividing the current, which is quite true so long as the other
conditions remain unaltered. The amount of heat generated
by a given expenditure of electrical energy is a definite quantity depending only on the current and the resistance, and is
wholly independent of the number of centers at which it appears, just as the quantity of heat generated by the burning
of a thousand feet of gas is independent of the number of
jets in which it is burned. The temperature to which a body

* There would be in practice a difference in the economy of the one long
filament and the ten short ones, due to the increased loss of heat by the latter
by conduction through the supports.

will be raised, however, by this amount of heat depends, as
we have already seen, upon the relation between the rate of
heat generation and the radiating surface, and the light depends upon the temperature. An amount of heat-energy sufficient to produce a powerful arc-light may be expended in
such a manner—in heating a long copper wire, for instance—
as to produce a hardly perceptible rise of temperature, and
consequently no light whatever. Or it may be expended in
a very small space, with the production of a high temperature
and a very intense light. If the whole of the energy expended in the ten-inch wire had been employed in heating
one of the small inch-pieces, the lighting effect would have
far surpassed that given by the entire wire when supplied
with the same amount of energy. So far from this fact being
an occasion for surprise, it would be very remarkable indeed
if there was a different result, for it would show that a long
wire could be raised to as high a temperature by a given heat-
expenditure as a short one of the same diameter. The loss,
then, experienced in passing from one powerful to many feeble
lights is a loss due, not to the mere fact of division, but to a
change in the conditions of the heat-supply by means of the
division—to a lowering of the rate of the generation of heat
per unit surface. If this rate be kept constant, we can divide
and subdivide indefinitely without any loss of light whatever.
This is the condition realized in incandescent lighting. The
unit burner may be multiplied indefinitely, and the power
will in all cases be directly proportional to the number of
lamps. In this respect there is no difference whatever between electric lighting and gas-lighting. The observed difference between the results obtainable in large and small lights
in the two cases is a difference due simply to the temperatures
which can be reached in the two cases.

   With electricity the limit of temperature is set by the resistance of the incandescent material to disintegration. Carbon is so refractory that this limit is far off, and, since the
light yielded by an incandescent body increases very rapidly
with the temperature, a given amount of electric energy expended in the production of heat in a small space is able to
produce a great amount of light. When this heat is expended over a larger space—a long wire, for instance—the temperature attainable rapidly decreases, and with it the light.

   The temperature attainable with gas is, on the other hand,

limited by the nature of the combustible and the point of dissociation—the point at which the chemical affinity of a combustible for oxygen begins to diminish, so that combination no longer takes place, and an increasing portion of the combustible gas passes off unconsumed. The heat generated by the combustion of a given amount of gas can not therefore be applied so as to raise the temperature of a body indefinitely, and the difference between the total lighting effect, when this gas is consumed in many small burners or in a few large ones, is consequently much less marked than in the case of electricity. This difference may, however, be considerable, as recent improvements in gas-burners have shown. A thousand feet of sixteen-candle gas burned in five-foot burners will give thirty-two hundred candles, while, if burned in fifty-foot Siemens burners, it will yield nine thousand candles.

From the above it will be seen that the ordinary way of presenting the relation between economy of large and small lights, and between electricity and gas, is extremely misleading. The electric light is represented as suffering a loss from which gas-lighting is free, while the fact is that electricity is able to attain an economy not realizable with gas. The proper statement of the relation of the two illuminants is that, with equal expenditures of heat-energy, you can get a much greater amount of light by means of electricity than by means of gas.

The electric light has labored under the disadvantage of an inversion of the natural order of development. The large light was produced first instead of last, and the results obtained with it have furnished the standards by which all others were judged. Had the small light been the first in the order of production, the significance of the superior economy of more powerful lights would have been readily seen, and incandescence would hardly have been given over for so many years as hopelessly uneconomical because it fell so far behind its more brilliant competitor. It would have been the more readily recognized that the problem of incandescence was concerned simply with the production of a lamp of moderate intensity which should be as economical as the gas-flame with which it would have to compete, and that the difficulties in the way, while great, were surmountable.]

CHAPTER V.

ELECTRIC METERS.

[IN any commercial electric distribution, by which the consumer is furnished with light and power in such amounts as he desires, some means of measurement must be provided. Though electrical quantities are capable of the most precise determination, and the instruments in use are among the most accurate which the physicist possesses, the devising of a practical electric meter is not without difficulties. The instruments of the physicist measure simply the amount of an electrical quantity at a time, but a meter is required to do more than this—it must measure the expenditure during a certain time. As that which the consumer is required to pay for is not electricity simply, but work, the meter must either measure the work done directly, or measure some quantity from which, under the conditions of the system of supply, the work can be determined. In instruments of the first kind, the work done during a certain time may be obtained by a summation of that performed at successive instants, and thus be given by a single measurement; or it may be obtained by means of two distinct ones—the one, the rate at which work is performed at each instant, and the other, the time during which it has continued. In instruments of the second class, the aim is to measure the quantity of electricity simply which has passed in a given time. This may be done, as in the other class of meters, by a summation process, or by a double measurement of the strength of the current flowing, and the time during which it flows. The summation method is evidently the more accurate, as there is but one measurement, and consequently a diminished chance of error.

One of the simplest instruments involving the use of this method for the measurement of the amount of electricity is the voltameter, or depositing-cell. As is well known, in such a cell a definite amount of metal—zinc or copper—is deposited upon the negative plate by a given current. If the current be doubled or trebled, or if the same current be continued twice or three times as long, there will be twice or three times the deposit. Each additional amount of electricity passing through the cell adds its own deposit to that already existing, so that at the end of any given time it is only necessary to determine the amount of the deposit in order to know the quantity of electricity which has passed through the cell.

This method is the one used by Mr. Edison in his first New

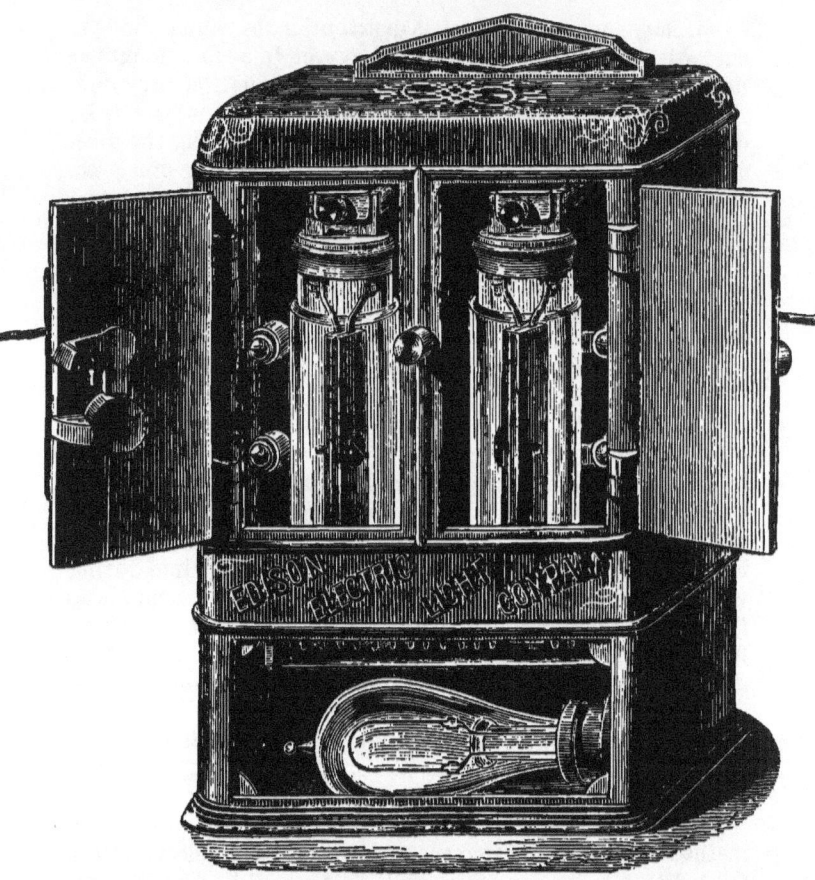

Fig. 225.—Edison meter.

York district. He at first employed copper, but these have been replaced by zinc, depositing-cells. The zinc plates are made of as pure zinc as possible, and are then coated with the same metal by electro-deposition, after which they are amalgamated. Two forms of meters have been devised by Mr. Edison, in one of which the amount of deposited metal is automatically registered, and in the other of which this is ascertained by weighing the electrodes at the works of the company, to which they are periodically taken by the meter inspectors. This latter, which is the one actually employed, is shown in Fig. 225. It contains two cells, the indications of one of which serve as a check upon those of the other. The latter cell is examined once a month, the zincs taken out and replaced by fresh ones. The indications of the former are taken but once in three months, the agreement of the two showing the accuracy of the meter. The cells are each placed in circuits, which form shunts to the main one, so that only a small portion of the total current passes through each, and this is different for each as the shunts are of unequal resistance. As the resistance of the cell varies with its temperature, provision is made for keeping this practically constant by means of a lamp inclosed in the chamber containing the cells, which is automatically lit when the temperature falls too low, and extinguished when it rises too high, by means of an expansion-bar closing and breaking the circuit of the lamp.

In the automatic registering meter, shown in Fig. 226, the weight of the deposited metal successively gained by the plates is caused to operate a counting mechanism. It consists of two cells placed side by side, constructed so that the cell itself forms one plate, the other being hung in the liquid from the scale beam. The electrical connections are made so that the current goes from the plate forming the jar to that suspended plate which is raised in one cell, and from the lowered suspended plate to the enclosing jar in the other cell. The raised plate is consequently gaining in weight, and the lowered losing. When the raised plate becomes the heavier of the two, it descends, and the current is reversed. There is therefore a successive gain and loss of weight by the suspended plates which causes the scale-beam to periodically oscillate, each movement of which acts upon the registering apparatus. The dials are constructed to show, not the amount of electricity in electrical measure, but the equivalent of the amount of gas necessary to give the light which has been furnished by the company.

Current meters, which record the amount of electricity by the employment of the summation method, have also been

designed by Mr. C. Vernon Boys and Dr. Hopkinson. In
Mr. Boys's meter, the current is applied so as to maintain a
pendulum in vibration. The impulses are given to the pendulum by means of the attraction of an electro-magnet, and,
since the force required to move a pendulum varies as the
square of the rate of vibration, and the attraction of a magnet varies as the square of the current flowing around it,

Fig. 226.—Edison meter, with registering apparatus.

the rate of vibration will be proportional to the current flowing. By means of simple mechanism, the number of vibrations can be registered, so that this arrangement can be readily made to record the amount of electricity which has passed
in a given time.

In Dr. Hopkinson's device, the measurement is effected by
overcoming the attraction of an electro-magnet by centrifugal
force, the parts being arranged so that the speed of a little

electro-motor is proportional to the current flowing. The electro-motor is placed in a shunt circuit, and drives a vertical shaft, upon which is mounted an ordinary ball-governor, which is connected with the armature of an electro-magnet, so that it raises this against the pull of the magnet as the balls are thrown out under the influence of centrifugal force. This electro-magnet is placed in the main circuit, and its strength therefore depends upon that of the current flowing through this circuit. With this arrangement it is evident that, when only a small current is circulating in the coils of the magnet, a low speed of the governor will be sufficient to overcome its attraction and draw away its armature. As the current increases, it takes a higher speed of the governor to do this, so that there is a definite relation between the speed at which the motor will rotate, when there is a balance between the magnetic attraction and the centrifugal force, and the current flowing. Since the centrifugal force varies as the square of the speed, and the magnetic attraction as the square of the current circulating in its coils, this speed of the motor will be directly proportional to the current. In order that the motor's speed should always be maintained against the opposing force of the electro-magnet, and therefore indicate the strength of the current, the motor circuit is interrupted when the centrifugal force overbalances the magnetic attraction. The speed of the motor therefore decreases until the armature descends and this circuit is again closed. The number of revolutions which have taken place in a given time evidently measure the quantity of electricity which has passed in this time.

A quite simple current-meter, of the class in which there is a measurement of both the current flowing and the time which it continues, has been designed by M. Cauderay. The needle of an ampère-meter (a special form of galvanometer) is placed so that it stands vertically in front of, and but a short distance from, a small roller, provided with projecting pins, similar to the barrel of a music-box. These pins are arranged in circles around the roller, the successive circles each way from the center containing a greater number. The central circle has no projection, so that when the needle is vertical the cylinder can rotate without touching it. If, however, the needle is deflected to one side or the other so as to incline from the vertical, its point, which is formed of a triangular

25

piece of brass, will be pressed out slightly by the projecting pins in the circle which it is opposite. Each movement of this kind causes, through appropriate mechanism, the motion of the hand of a dial similar to that used in gas-meters. As the extent to which the needle is drawn aside depends upon the strength of the current flowing through the ampère-meter, it is evident that, if the cylinder be turned at a constant rate, this arrangement will measure the amount of electricity which has passed in a given time. It will be perceived that the accuracy of this measurement depends on that of two distinct pieces of apparatus—the current indicator and the revolving drum—and that there is therefore a double chance of error. Both the speed of the drum and the accuracy of the ampère-meter can be very easily tested and regulated when found to be wrong, however, so that the instrument can be readily kept sufficiently accurate for all practical purposes. In the

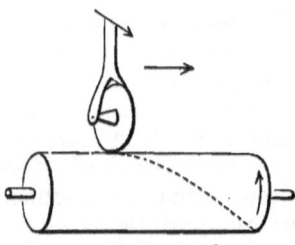

Fig. 227.—Mr. Boys' work-meter.

type designed for incandescent lighting, it is the intention to construct the meters to work with definite differences of potential between the terminals, the mechanism being so arranged that the meter ceases to register if the electro-motive force falls below a certain limit. The importance of this will be readily seen when it is remembered that by a slight decrease in the current through the lamp the light may be very greatly diminished, while the work done, for which the consumer would have to pay, would be but little less than when the lamp is giving its normal light.

Work-meters have been designed by Mr. Boys, whose current-meter has been described above, and by Professors Ayrton and Perry. Mr. Boys's meter belongs to the class above indicated, in which the total work done during a time is given by a process of summation or integration. The principle of its operation is shown in Fig. 227. A small wheel, mounted like a caster, so that it can swing around a vertical axis as well as revolve on its own, is pressed against a roller or cylinder free to turn on its axis. Under these conditions, if the wheel is inclined to the axis of the cylinder, and the cylinder be drawn under it in the direction of its length, the wheel will swing so as to stand lengthwise of the cylinder. But if the wheel be held in its inclined position, the cylinder will rotate, and the number of its revolutions, while being moved its own length, will depend upon the amount of the inclination. Now, it will require force to hold the wheel inclined while the cylinder is dragged under it, and this force will clearly be greater as the amount of inclination is increased. The cylinder will also pull the wheel around in the direction of its movement the more strongly as its movement is more rapid. The force required to incline the wheel, multiplied by the distance through which the cylinder turns, will evidently, therefore, be a measure of the work done, and, if we know the work represented by one turn of the cylinder, the number of revolutions will give the total work performed in a given time. It will be observed that it is not necessary to move the cylinder at any definite rate, since the same work will be done when the cylinder moves rapidly and the wheel is at a small inclination as when the wheel is at a great inclination and the cylinder moves more slowly. This apparatus may be readily adapted to measure the work done by an electric current, by inclining the wheel by magnetic attraction and moving the cylinder under it by means of clockwork. Work must be done by the current to maintain the wheel in its angular position, which work will be measured by the number of rotations of the cylinder. In Mr. Boys's arrangement, the cylinder is given a sort of mangle-motion, by which it travels forward in contact with one wheel and backward in contact with another on its opposite side, the object of this construction being to obtain a continuous revolution of the cylinder. The inclination of the wheels is obtained by means of an arrangement of solenoids traversed by the current to be measured.

In the work-meter of Professors Ayrton and Perry, the work is obtained, not by a direct measurement of it, but from the amount of deviation from the normal working of an apparatus produced by it. If we have a clock keeping time accurately, it may be made to gain or lose time by impulses given to its pendulum. To change the rate of vibration of a pendulum, however, requires work, and the total amount of work performed in a given time will evidently be measured by the amount of correction needed by the clock. In the instrument of Professors Ayrton and Perry, the control of the clock is effected very simply by means of two solenoids, one of fine and the other of coarse wire. The fine-wire coil takes the place of the ordinary pendulum-bob, and is placed in a shunt circuit, which forms a bridge between the mains when the arrangement of the lamps is in multiple arc, and is connected with the main wire, where it enters and leaves the house, when the devices are arranged in series. The current flowing through this coil, therefore, depends upon the difference of potential between its ends, and consequently indicates the potential of that furnished to the house. The coarse-wire coil is in the main circuit, and has, therefore, the current supplied to the house flowing through it. It is fixed to the frame of the clock directly behind the moving fine-wire coil. The attraction between these two, therefore, varies as the current and potential supplied to the house— that is, as the power—and the amount which the clock loses in a given time is proportional to the power supplied. The correctness of the indications of this meter evidently depend upon the accuracy of the clock, but, as clocks which are good time-keepers can be readily obtained, and at a comparatively small cost, this objection does not appear to be of much moment.]

BOOK VI

APPLICATIONS OF THE ELECTRIC LIGHT.

CHAPTER I.

ELECTRICITY IN LIGHT-HOUSES.

It is in light-houses that the electric light found its first important application. The luminous intensity that it could attain enabled the range of the light to be considerably increased, not only to that necessary for clear weather—this had already been attained for a long time by the powerful lamps in use—but to that required in times of storm. Against the storms there is, in fact, no other resource than to augment to its utmost the brightness of the focus, and this resource was often insufficient.

At the present day, when steam has rendered voyages so frequent and so easy, there are few persons who do not know what a light-house is, and who have not seen at night with interest those brilliant stars which mean lights upon the coast and on reefs to warn mariners at a distance, to indicate to them their position, and to guide them into ports. But this knowledge generally goes but little further, and we do not think it useless to add to it such explanations as will make better understood the progress which the use of the electric light in so important a service represents.

The origin of light-houses goes back to the beginning of navigation, of which they were indispensable auxiliaries. Homer described in the "Iliad" the use of fires lighted at night on the rocks to direct the galleys of the Greeks; but the first light-house properly so called is that which was built by a king of Egypt 300 years before the Christian era, opposite the port of Alexandria, on an island called Pharos, whence doubtless comes the name which has been given them, *phare*.

It was a tower of masonry seventy-five feet in height, on whose summit there was maintained an enormous bonfire. This primitive mode of lighting remained for a long time the only one employed ; sometimes large oil-lamps, with dipping wick—the only ones known at this epoch—were substituted for it.   In 1727, under Louis XV, it became necessary to re-place by an iron grate the ancient masonry fireplace of the tower of Cordouan, built at the mouth of the Gironde, to hold the fire when bituminous coal began to take the place of wood as a combustible.

Attempts had also been made to use lamps with reflectors, and an apparatus composed of eighty lamps had been estab-lished in 1782 upon this same tower of Cordouan ; but it was very imperfect, and the navigators had immediately demanded a return to the old coal-fire. The first real improvements date from the invention of the lamp with double air-draught by Argand, and from that of parabolic mirrors by a French en-gineer named Teulère.   In the year 1793 they were utilized in the construction of an apparatus formed of three groups of four lamps each ; these groups were spaced so as to divide the circumference into three equal parts, supported by a frame, which a machine, regulated by a pendulum, turned around every six minutes.   Thus, every two minutes, succes-sive flashes of extreme brightness, which lasted six seconds, were obtained.   This was a considerable progress, and all the marine powers hastened to adopt it.

These apparatus are called *catoptric*, because the concen-tration of the luminous rays emanating from the lamps is obtained by simple reflection.   Except in size and some few details of construction, those which are used to-day corre-spond with the apparatus of Teulère.

This solution was insufficient, because of the impossibility of giving to the mirrors suitable dimensions without rendering them much too difficult to construct, and too heavy to move. Recourse was therefore had to grouping together a large number with a lamp for each one, but then there was always a limit to the intensity of the lights.   In fact, and this is often lost sight of, it is elevation of temperature that increases the luminous radiation ; the concentration of a number of lights upon any one point only augments the illumination of this surface, without increasing in the same proportion the extent of the surface or the luminous range of the group thus constituted. Besides, the aberration inseparable from this mode of reflection renders useless the increasing of lights in the group beyond a comparatively restricted limit.

It was at this juncture that Augustin Fresnel thought of utilizing for light-house apparatus the property of convex lenses, refracting, parallel to their axis, rays of light emanating from their principal focus; he invented *dioptric* apparatus. On account of the difficulty which the manufacture of glass lenses thick enough for his needs would have presented, Fresnel first thought of making them of hollow blown glass, containing water or alcohol. Such lenses would not have been easy to construct and preserve. Fresnel thought of overcoming their excessive thickness by composing his lenses of a central part, surrounded by concentric rings, one projecting over the top of the other, and so to say representing a series of lenses of different radii, but with one common principal focus; it was the lens with ridges, of which Buffon seems to have had the conception in advance of him, and without his knowing it; but he could not construct it as he conceived of it as made in one piece, whereas Fresnel made it of separate pieces, molded and ground separately, and then accurately put together.

As there was no chance of placing several lamps in the center of such an apparatus, Fresnel and Arago, taking up again an idea of Rumford, succeeded in constructing lamps with several concentric wicks, quite close together, and separated by as many annular currents of air. The flames heating each other mutually, the general temperature is higher, and the light becomes white and brilliant. An excess of oil is caused to flow to the wicks, to retard their carbonization and cool the burners. In this manner lamps for vegetable oil are constructed that contain four wicks, and give three or four times the amount of light given by the largest parabolic reflectors; besides, the Fresnel lenses only absorb at most five per cent of the total light, while the best reflectors absorb fifty per cent of it. With this system it becomes easy to arrange all combinations of lenses necessary to give to the different lamp-flames the particular character that is necessary. Fresnel completed his invention by utilizing another property of glass rings of triangular cross-section—that is to say, refraction and total reflection—he thus constructed rings called *cata-dioptric*, which utilize the rays that could not be caught by the dioptric drum without unduly exaggerating its dimensions.

Once more it was on the light-house tower of Cordouan that the first apparatus of this sort was established in 1822, after the edifice had been increased in height so as to bring the lantern sixty metres above the level of the sea.

Since this epoch, thanks to the labors of Messrs. Doty and Dénéchaux, mineral oil can now be used without inconvenience of any sort, so that a fifth wick can be added to lamps of the first order, and so on. The light was increased without any great augmentation in the expense. Gas itself has been used, and with it most of the Scotch light-houses are illuminated.

For a long time the electric light was thought of for this use; but such a service must be characterized by absolute regularity and certainty; the electricity must be produced by sufficiently powerful machines, and as perfect an apparatus as possible must be used for regulating the voltaic arc. It is to the machine of Nollet, named the Alliance, and Serrin's regulator, that the honor belongs of having caused, in 1864, the adoption of the electric light in the light-houses of France, under the skillful direction of the inspector-general, Reynaud. It had in like manner been applied, in 1862, to the English light-house of Dungeness, with a Holmes machine (a copy of the Alliance machine), and a regulator identical with that of Serrin.

Although electricity had fulfilled all the promises it had ever given, its use did not extend very rapidly, and in 1881 there were only twelve light-houses thus lighted in the whole world—four in France, six in England, one in Russia, and the last at Port Said, at the entrance of the Suez Canal. The state of the case is, that the service of coast-lighting, obliged to follow the progress of navigation, could not wait for the last improvements in electricity, and that when the electricity at last was ready, all the light-houses that were necessary and possible were already supplied with optical apparatus constructed to receive the old oil-lamps. All these apparatus would have to be sacrificed, and after this a still greater expense would follow; for this reason the general use of it has been postponed to the time when these apparatus would be naturally replaced. In France, in consequence of the examinations and proposals presented in January, 1880, by the director of the light-house service, M. Allard, forty-two oil light-houses are to be transformed successively into electric light-houses. In England, the proposal is to establish one hundred. Similar examinations are being pursued in the United States, Australia, and even in Turkey.

It is important to remark that, in spite of the common expression, lighting the coasts (*éclairage des côtes*), light-houses do no lighting in the proper acceptation of the word. Their *rôle* is to be visible at the greatest possible distance, and this distance, which is called their range, depends on the height of the lantern above the horizon and on its luminous intensity. Thus *geographic range* should be distinguished from *luminous range*.

The first is limited by the roundness of the earth; it is equal to the length of a line carried from the lantern tangentially to the spherical surface of the sea, and prolonged until it reaches the eye of the observer; this last is naturally supposed to be at the greatest height attainable on the mast of the ship; by being elevated from three to twenty metres it is capable of increasing the distance some ten kilometres. Unfortunately, the height of the lantern is always limited by the difficulties of construction; the highest light-houses are those placed where the formation of the coast makes it possible to lay their foundations successfully in places already elevated high above the sea-level, such as those of Agde and Cape Camarat, in the Mediterranean, which are 126 and 130 metres above the sea-level, and whose geographic range attains the very unusual extent of 50 and 51 kilometres. When this advantage can not be had, they rarely exceed 60 metres in height and 30 to 36 kilometres of geographic range, like the Cordouan light-house in its present state.

With a powerful enough lamp, the luminous range can attain, and even exceed, the length of the geographic range, but, unfortunately, in clear weather only; it rapidly diminishes on many occasions with the transparency of the air, and, as we shall see, this diminution has to be taken into account in calculating the distances to be allowed between light-houses.

As a first service, light-houses are expected to indicate to the mariner his approach to coasts, and this at as great a distance as possible. Those used for this purpose should be of the highest luminous intensity; they are the light-houses of the *first order*, to which also is given the name of *phares de grande attenage*. If the navigator is deceived, or has deviated from his course in bad weather, he must be able to follow the coast-line, at a safe distance, until he reaches a point in front of his harbor. He must then be able to find an uninterrupted succession of lights of the same power, not losing sight of one before finding the next one ; in a word, the circles of luminous range of light-houses must reciprocally intersect at a good distance from shore, and, in order that this may take place as often as possible, there must be adopted for the radius of these circles the luminous range that corresponds to the mean degree of transparency of the atmosphere—that is to say, that which is reached or exceeded half the time. Rigorous observations carried on for years have established this factor for different parts of the coasts; it is greater in the Mediterranean than on the shores of the ocean or of the English Channel.

Having reached the desired spot, the mariner should be able to approach closer to the coast without danger, and it becomes necessary to indicate to him by a new system of lights the dangers he may meet in this second zone. Hence comes the necessity of employing, back of the first light-houses, other lights of various intensities corresponding to the second, third, fourth, and even fifth order. Finally, less powerful lights give him the. last ranges to follow to enter port at night ; these are the range-lights. In the sea-ports, lights of different colors show him at every hour of the night the depth of water in the port at each change of level of fifty centimetres.

Naturally, all light-houses do not have to distribute their rays around them in the same way: the large mainland lights, and sometimes light-houses of the second order, must light the whole horizon ; others only light a larger or smaller segment, and the light which would be useless on the landward side is reflected seaward. When the transparence of the air becomes so diminished that the circles of the luminous range of the mainland lights no longer intersect, the lights of the second line fill the void, and prevent, as far as possible, the danger which would result therefrom ; in practice this happens during about six months of the year ; during the other months the mariner only receives warning at a distance which is the smaller as the atmosphere is less transparent, and here will be one of the advantages of the electric light, in reducing this period to two months at the most on the Atlantic coast, and to one month on the Mediterranean, on account of the increase of luminous range.

In order that the indications they afford the mariner may be very clear, it is indispensable that all these successive lights present different and well-defined characteristic appearances. To attain this end, five varieties of lights are used: simple fixed light, double fixed light, eclipse-light, with flashes every thirty seconds; eclipse-light, with flashes every minute; fixed light, varied by four-minute flashes. As complete eclipses make it hard to again find the light, especially in bad weather, in the French light-houses a fixed light is maintained during the time of eclipse, so that the light-house can be kept in view. This fixed light is relatively weaker, and varies in value between one half and one seventh of the intensity of the regular light, according to whether it is composed of rays taken from the top and bottom of the apparatus, or of those taken from the bottom only.

These five characters not proving enough, they were supplemented by the color of the lights, in spite of the loss of intensity resulting therefrom, because a colored light is one that has lost a part of its luminous rays. Furthermore, only green and red can be used, and the last as seldom as possible. In this way there are obtained fixed lights varied by red and green flashes every four minutes, and lights composed of white and red flashes. These are the different characters used in actual light-houses using oil-lamps; their defect is too long a period of manifestation, forcing upon the mariner a long-sustained attention to recognize the character of the light he has sighted. A certain skill even is necessary to appreciate differences of only one half minute. They were adopted because of the difficulty of imparting to the old apparatus, large and clumsy, a somewhat rapid movement of rotation.

As the dimensions of optical apparatus depend upon the volume of the sources of light whose rays they concentrate, the great reduction in volume obtained by the use of the electric light makes it possible to reduce the size of the optical apparatus. The diameter of oil-lamp apparatus of the first order, which was 1·84 metre, can be reduced to ·5 or ·6 metre for electric lights of the same order. The extreme lightness of these new optical apparatus makes it possible to turn them much faster; thus, a new character of light, called *scintillating*, can be adopted. To produce it, a fixed-light apparatus is used which normally concentrates rays in a vertical plane; around this apparatus a drum of lenses, called *vertical-element lenses*, is caused to rotate. These lenses are plates of glass, having a lenticular section, the same throughout their length. Each of them concentrates rays in a horizontal plane, and consequently produces a flash. During the rotation, if all these lenses are equal, the navigator will see a series of equal white flashes succeeding each other; a simple scintillating light will be produced. If the vertical lenses are alternately red and white, red and white flashes will follow each other in alternation. So, in placing the red lenses two apart, three apart, or four apart, lights will be produced having two, three, or four flashes of white, followed by one red flash. It is necessary to remark in this case that, as red diminishes the luminous intensity, it is always necessary to give the red lens larger dimensions to compensate for this loss. Thus, by the form given to the lenses, the white and red flashes may be made equidistant in point of time, or else so that there may be, between the red flash and the next group of white flashes, a greater interval than that which separates these last from each other. But the red flashes cause a loss of light the greater as the number of white flashes is less. Thus, M. Allard prefers in many cases to separate the groups of white flashes simply by an interval of darkness. This effect is produced by a simple modification in the shape of the vertical lenses, and the eight following characters are obtained : scintillating lights with one, two, three, or four white flashes and one red flash ; white scintillating light ; scintillating light in groups of two, three, or four white flashes. These characters are the only ones permanently adopted. They possess the advantage of immediate and easy recognition without the use of any clock.

The regulator employed in light-houses for the electric light is that of M. Serrin. It is constructed after a special model, worked out with much care, and is made of larger dimensions than the ordinary model, and with rare skill. The apparatus rests upon a metal table, supplied with rails, between which are placed springs connected with the two poles of the circuit. It is enough to push the regulator into its place

Fig. 223.—Electric light-house of l'Planier, near Marseilles.

for its pressure upon these springs brings it into circuit, when the arc immediately forms. In the first light-houses, that only light a part of the horizon, a system of double rails crossing at an acute angle makes the rapid change of apparatus easy by allowing the extinguished one to be drawn out and the other to be pushed into its place.

In the new apparatus, such as that of Planier, which lights the whole horizon, it would have been necessary to have opened in the drums of lenses too large an entrance, and other arrangements had to be adopted. Perpendicular to the rail which enters the apparatus, and outside, is placed a second rail; at the point where they meet is a turn-table similar to those used on railways. The manœuvre is quite as easy and as rapid as with the other system, though the rotating drum has to be stopped, and two doors have to be opened.

A small lens projects the magnified image of the voltaic arc either on the wall of the machinery-room, as at La Hève, or down upon the working-table, by means of a rectangular prism, whose faces, forming the sides of a right angle, have received the necessary curvature. The keeper can then, without fatigue, observe the slightest variations in the position of the carbons by means of a curve traced in advance and corresponding to the exact location of the light; he regulates or adjusts them by means of a regulating-button with which the regulator is supplied, and which permits both carbon-holders to be raised or lowered without affecting the light.

The Alliance machines were the first employed. To-day those used are the magneto-electric machines of M. de Méritens, which we have already described. They are placed along with the steam-engine and shafting in a building near the light-house, and connected by perfectly insulated wire with the working-table. All the machines are in duplicate, which insures the certainty of service in case of accident to one of the machines, and, if necessary, on the occasions of severe storms, makes it possible to run both at once, so as to double the intensity of the light.

Experiments made with a Gramme machine, large size, prove that it can also give excellent results as far as its intensity and expense of running are concerned ; but the French Government prefers alternating currents, from considerations affecting the division of the light and the consumption of the carbons.

In England, after first employing Holmes's machines (Alliance system), Siemens's dynamo-electric machines, driven by Brown's hot-air engines, are to-day used, as well as the magneto-electric machines of M. de Méritens.

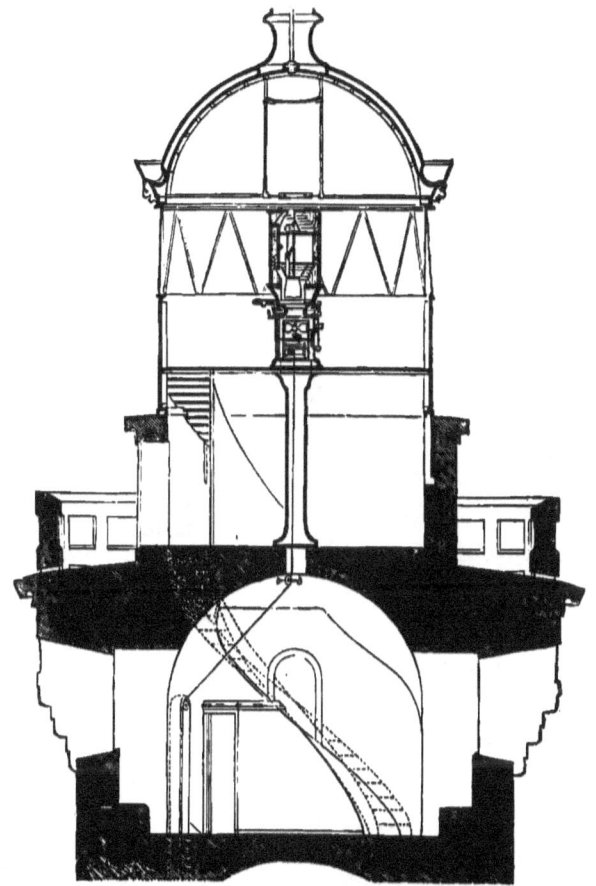

Fig. 229.—Arrangement of the Planier electric light-house.

To better illustrate the arrangements we are describing, we give here a plate illustrating the light-house recently erected on Planier Island, at the entrance to the port of Marseilles (Fig. 228). It is a cylindrical tower of masonry, 13·50 metres in diameter at the level of the foundation, and 6·70 metres in diameter at the top of the shaft; the center opening forming the stair-well is a cylinder four metres in diameter. The lantern is placed 57·60 metres above the foundation-level,

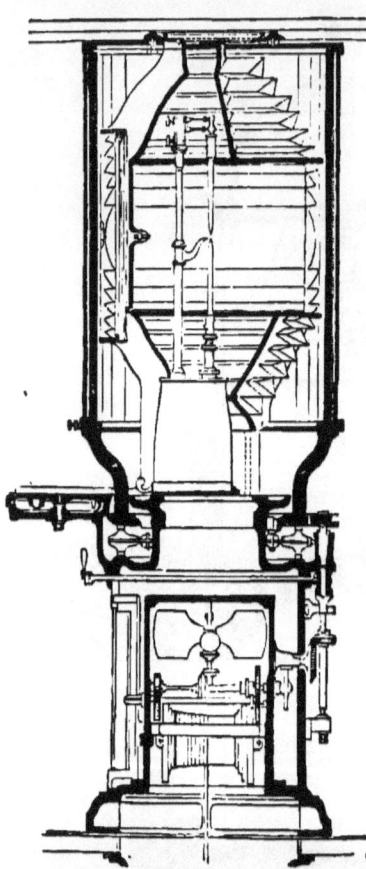

and 61·93 metres above high-water mark. It is composed of a scintillating electric light, with eclipses every five seconds, a red flash following three white flashes; the range should be about twenty-three geographical miles (over twenty-five and a half statute miles). It is the same apparatus that worked at the Champs de Mars during the whole time of the Universal Exposition of 1878; a similar apparatus worked also at the Palais de l'Industrie during the Electrical Exhibition.

Fig. 229 represents the section of the upper floors and of the lantern. The iron floor of this lantern-room is supported in its center by a hollow cast-iron column, through the center of which the cord descends that carries the weight which moves the outer drum of the optical apparatus. This cord is conducted around pulleys to a recess formed in the masonry. The bars between which the glasses of the lantern are fastened have inclined faces, so that they do not diminish the light sensibly in any direction.

Fig. 230.—Section of the upper story and lantern of the Planier light-house.

The optical apparatus is shown in Fig. 230; it is composed

of a stationary lantern of ·60 metre interior diameter, and of a movable outer drum, formed of vertical lenses. In spite of the bad economy of passing the light through two lenses successively, this combination has been adopted because by it the necessary duration can be given to the flashes by increasing the horizontal divergence of the lenses of the drum without modifying the vertical divergence due to the fixed lantern lenses.

The vertical drum is composed of six groups of four lenses, one red and three white. The lenses designed to produce red flashes include an angle three times greater than that of the lenses giving white flashes; this relation is necessary to insure the same range to it as to the others. It turns upon a circle of rollers by means of mechanism placed in the base; the regularity of movement is insured by a fan-regulator of Foucault.

Apparatus of this kind gives an intensity about fifty times greater than that of the electric light within it; the white vertical lenses nearly quadruple this intensity, so that the flashes are 200 times greater than the original light. If this latter be supposed equal to 500 carcels, each white flash will be equal to about 100,000 carcels. The lenses producing the red flash give three times this intensity, to compensate the diminution due to the coloration.

The adoption of the electric light in light-houses presents the following advantages: It makes possible the increasing at will of the luminous intensity, and, in consequence, the range of the light in stormy weather; the importance of this will be understood when it is stated that the unit light visible at a distance of nearly nine kilometres in clear weather, or seven in average weather, can not be discerned more than about five in stormy weather; beyond this comes foggy weather, when almost or quite nothing is discernible. Careful observations have proved the existence of the following differences per 100 observations:

At a distance of more than 37 kilometres,	Electric light is visible 69 times.
	Oil light " " 29 "
" " from 27 to 37 kilometres,	Electric light " " 12 "
	Oil light " " 43 "
" " less than 27 kilometres...	Electric light " " 19 "
	Oil light " " 28 "

This superiority at long ranges is due to the fact that the temperature of the arc is much higher, and its specific inten-

26

sity much more considerable. Thus the intensity per square centimetre of an electric light of 200 carcels is 550 times greater than that of the same surface of a mineral-oil lamp with five wicks. If now it be compared with the sunlight, it will be found, according to M. Allard, that the intensity of this latter light upon the earth is equal to a light of 6,000 carcels at a distance of one metre, and, taking into account the thickness of the atmosphere, estimated at nine kilometres, the luminous intensity of the solar surface per square centimetre is equal to 12,000 carcels, or 47 times as powerful as the electric light, and more than 2,600 times that of an oil lamp with five wicks.

The electric light also makes it possible, as we have seen, to prolong the duration of the flashes in rotating lanterns by the use of vertical lenses, which move in front of the fixed lantern, giving them six times their normal power.

It also makes it possible, on account of the lightness of the apparatus, to suppress, in the list of characteristic differences, the use of a stated period or duration in minutes and seconds. With the new characters which can be employed on account of it, every light-house declares its name more quickly and certainly, without the necessity of consulting a watch.

This same increase of power of the lights makes it practicable to add to the characters the use of red lights, in spite of the loss resulting from the coloration, the red light having only one quarter the range of white light; for green light it is still worse, only one eighth ; thus this last can only be employed for stationary range-lights and for signals at sea.

Finally, the intensity of the electric light being much greater than is necessary for an ordinary mainland light-house, MM. Sautter and Lemonnier have profited by it to cause it to produce a luminous plume, thrown vertically up from the light-house ; thanks to its height, this plume can be seen from ninety to one hundred kilometres, where the ordinary geographical range, limited by the curvature of the earth, rarely exceeds fifty-five kilometres. This will permit navigators to direct their course farther from the coast-line, and this is sometimes a condition of considerable importance. It is thus that in the Sea of Azof most vessels that enter this sea by the Straits of Yenikale to load with corn at Taganrog or at Berdiansk, wish naturally to follow the straightest possible line, traversing the sea where it is widest and far out of range

of the light-houses on the coast. A luminous indication of
the position of Berdiansk, as they enter the Sea of Azof,

Fig. 231.—Fixed light electric light-house.

would be most valuable to them, and to furnish such indication the Russian Government have engaged MM. Sautter and

Lemonnier to construct an electric light-house, surmounted by a vertical luminous plume, which will be visible at Yenikale.

The apparatus is that of a light flashing every five seconds, with eclipses three seconds in duration. The optic system consists of a fixed lantern one metre in diameter, in which the upper catadioptric part is replaced by a projection lens whose optical axis is vertical, and passes through the voltaic arc of the apparatus; it is this projector which produces the permanent beam or luminous plume.

Following out this principle, the same engineers have constructed a model of an electric light-house, shown in Fig. 231. It is supplied, like the preceding, with a projection lens, and the lower part has been enlarged so as to utilize the most intense rays of the voltaic arc produced by continuous-current machines.

A Gramme regulator is employed; it is supported from above, which does away with the tables and the supports; moreover, the lamp is double, and can burn all night without needing replacement. It is enough to turn the lamp through an arc of 180° around its pivot for a second pair of carbons to become lighted in the focus of the optical apparatus; the period of extinction is inappreciable.

The factory of MM. Sautter and Lemonnier, founded in 1825 under the direction of Augustin Fresnel, is one of the first in which the electric light was applied to the illumination of workshops. Fig. 232 illustrates this installation, of which we shall speak further on.

The latest improvements shown in the Electrical Exhibition of 1881, in the production and distribution of currents, gives room to hope that light-houses, even when far from the coast, and in situations which do not permit the use of machines, may profit by it, as we have seen that at the present day these latter can be placed at a considerable distance from the lamp. Perhaps the time will come when the most important buoys can be lighted at night, either directly or by projection.

Fig. 282.—Factory of MM. Sautter and Lemonnier lighted by the electric light.

CHAPTER II.

THE ELECTRIC LIGHT IN WAR AND NAVIGATION.

NIGHT does not put a stop to military operations, it only imposes different conditions, which the electric light can modify in more than one way by the intensity of the light which it produces. It can especially serve to direct night attacks, and at the same time render visible the outworks of a place or surroundings of a vessel threatened with a secret attack. At sea it can also furnish a sort of light-house carried by each vessel, to signal its approach to others and prevent collisions. Finally, without speaking for the moment of a number of other uses, it gives very powerful luminous signals, which have originated a system of optical telegraphy even more useful for military correspondence in the enemy's country than for communications between vessels, as it requires no intermediary wire.

I. MILITARY AND MARITIME APPLICATIONS FROM 1855 TO 1877.

The importance of this new element of action was appreciated at an early date by studious officers, perhaps even at an epoch when no practical means were known of employing it efficaciously. The French fleet tried it in 1855 at the siege of Kinburn, during the campaign of the Baltic. A parabolic reflector was used to project a beam of electric light upon the point attacked. A short time after, M. Martin de Brettes published an extensive work in which he enumerated all the services that the electric light could render to the art of war, either for the lighting up of siege-works and military operations, or as a means of telegraphic communication.

The war in Italy, in 1859, directed the attention of the French military authorities to this subject, who instituted experiments to fix the elements of construction of an apparatus fit for campaign use. These experiments, conducted at Paris, were performed with a Grenet battery and a parabolic reflector like that which had been used before Kinburn. But the peace of Villafranca interrupted them before long, and the Italians next took them up. In the short campaign of 1861,

against the King of Naples, General Menabrea used a lighting apparatus constructed upon similar principles, and capable of giving useful results at a distance of 1,500 metres.
This much at least was indicated by the test experiments, for
the apparatus, prepared for the attack of Gaeta, had no
chance to be tried in actual practice—that is to say, before
the enemy, in the midst of siege operations.

The military use of the electric light met a greater obstacle
in field use than elsewhere, due to the inconvenience of the
means of production.   Batteries were still the only available
source, and, to obtain an intense light, very many cells were
required.   These were not only cumbrous and fragile for
transportation, but they were difficult and slow to set to
work, which deprived them of much of their practical value
in a condition of things where promptitude is the first element of success.

Toward 1862 the Alliance magneto-electric machine, considerably improved, furnished a source of electricity less complicated and more powerful.   But it still was too heavy, so
that its transportation for an army in the field was almost
impossible.   The same obstacle did not exist in the case of
ships, which placed it in position as a part of their equip-
ment.   Thus the Alliance machine was first used on the sea.
Its first application is due principally to the initiative of M.
Georgette Dubuisson, commandant of the yacht of Prince
Napoleon, the Reine Hortense.   In 1867 this yacht was provided with an electric beacon, with regulator, which lighted
the pathway in advance of it, and enabled it to enter at night
into several Mediterranean ports of most dangerous approach
with as much ease as if it had been full day.

This minor triumph of electricity inevitably attracted attention.   M. Eugène Pereire, engineer of the Compagnie Transatlantique, immediately introduced similar apparatus on the
Sainte-Laurent, then on other ships of the same company,
where it was fully appreciated.   Soon after the Parfait, the
d'Estrées, the Coligny, the Héroïne, and finally the France,
were supplied also with an electric light maintained by an
Alliance machine.

In 1870 the Emperor's new yacht, Hirondelle, received in
its turn a similar plant, which thereupon, as a matter of
course, chose the entrance into Cherbourg for its trial trip,
where the ship broke its cutwater and demolished its stem to

a considerable extent against the Grande Douane wharf. More important events prevented the perfecting of this defective installation. But, during the same year, electricity made a greater success upon another imperial yacht, the Greif, belonging to the Emperor of Austria. This yacht entered Villafranca and several ports of the Mediterranean by night, as the Reine Hortense had already done, and by night went through the Suez Canal, lighting marvelously the shores. In 1871 the Russian navy also introduced upon several ships electric lights with lenticular projectors, which gave them the power of passing by night the narrow straits of the Baltic, of entering the port of St. Petersburg, and of performing fortunate rescues.

What was then sought in the electric light was a means of perceiving the obstacles which could menace the ship on her course. It played the rôle of lantern that every peasant carries with him at night to keep him in the streets of the village when there is no moon. The same necessity becomes more pronounced when a narrow river is to be navigated at night.

In this connection we must not pass over the part taken by M. Menier (Fig. 233). By an electric light operated by a Gramme machine, driven by a Brotherhood engine, his yacht easily passed at night through the windings of the Marne and the Seine, between Paris and his large chocolate factory at Noisiel.

This, it is true, is an exceptional case, and if such lights should be employed to facilitate the course of vessels in the darkness, the dazzling produced by them might render them more annoying than useful. It would be necessary to find a means of utilizing this light while avoiding the trouble. It would be doubtless more practicable to light up difficult passages as a boulevard is lighted up for the travel of vehicles.

On land, the weight of the Alliance machine made its use in really active military operations difficult. But this did not destroy all hopes of utilizing the electric light in war. The Universal Exposition of 1867 had already proved this. The Austrian Government sent to it large parabolic mirrors, in silvered metal, designed to project the light of an electric lamp placed in the focus of the parabola. A number of designs showed the military applications that were contemplated. In 1869 Russia had similar plans in contemplation, whose existence is only known to us by the purchase of a

FIG. 283.—M. Menier's yacht, with electric projector, navigating the Marne by night.

certain number of Alliance machines, and of lenticular projectors. It is entirely probable that other powers did the same in secret.

A short while after, the Franco-German War of 1870-'71 gave the electric light a chance to make its *début* upon the field of battle, under precisely those circumstances where its use was best understood—in a great siege.

The defenders of Paris used it both as a source of light and as a means of telegraphic communication by optical signals. The lamps were those of Foucault and Serrin; the source of electricity was Bunsen batteries, of not more than fifty elements, placed in the *postes d'octroi* all around the city. Upon one point, nevertheless, near Montmartre, an Alliance machine had been placed, which naturally furnished a much more energetic current and consequently a more intense light. The forts had also electric lamps, supplied from Bunsen batteries. But the reflectors which were used to direct the luminous beam were quite insufficient, and the lights themselves were not sufficiently powerful to light all expected localities.

The electric light, nevertheless, rendered considerable service; it prevented several nocturnal surprises, and revealed several movements of the enemy which would, without it, have escaped notice. The Montmartre light, supplied by the magneto-electric machine, bathed with its rays the plateau of Argenteuil.

The Germans used the electric light very skillfully to direct their battery practice and keep track of our night operations. They had machines at their disposal, and hence obtained much more powerful lights than were given by our lamps supplied from Bunsen batteries.

The dynamo-electric machine of M. Gramme, invented and presented to the Academy of Sciences at Paris in 1870, could only be known industrially after the Franco-German war. More powerful and much lighter than the Alliance machine, it was a source of electricity much better adapted to the necessities of war. Soon after, the first Siemens machine appeared in Germany, which presented analogous advantages. The attention of military engineers was then again directed to the electric light. The Germans first studied it. At the Universal Exposition of Vienna in 1873, they sent large projection apparatus, with an electric lamp, supplied by the first

Siemens machine, designed by M. Heffner von Alteneck. In the French section a new electric projector was to be seen, specially destined for use at sea; but it belonged to the domain of individual industry; it was the work of MM. Sautter and Lemonnier, the great light-house builders of Paris.

The Russian navy was the first to substitute the Gramme for the Alliance machines. In 1873 and 1874, the Peter the Great and the Livadia tried the new apparatus, with lenticular projectors analogous to those of light-houses. This apparatus, constructed by MM. Sautter and Lemonnier, gave a light of about five hundred carcels, and showed edifices in the darkest of nights three kilometres distant. It will be seen how great was the progress since 1870. The Livadia in particular found it useful on more than one occasion, and was able to follow at night a buoyed channel not over twenty metres wide.

In France it is the commercial marine that leads the way for the national marine to follow. We have seen that in 1867 M. Eugène Pereire had placed upon one of the large transatlantic steamers, the Sainte-Laurent, electric projectors supplied by Alliance machines. After first having attracted numerous imitators, these attempts were gradually abandoned in face of the passive resistance of old habits. Most captains saw in the new apparatus only a cumbrous luxury, expensive, awkward in use, and of doubtful efficacy. The projectors had sought in it an argument for reducing the rates of insurance against the accidents of the sea, because the chances of collision were lessened. Naturally, the insurance companies did not care to yield too quickly, and the projectors, deceived in their hopes, soon ceased to impose upon the captains a costly encumbrance that was attended by no compensation.

The discovery of the Gramme machine diminished, however, the force of these objections, as it placed at the disposal of the marine less cumbrous, much more powerful, and at the same time cheaper, machines. M. Eugène Pereire again addressed himself to the question, and, in 1876, he ordered M. Fontaine to establish the electric light upon the transatlantic steamer Amérique.

The following year, in 1877, the navy took up the long interrupted experiments. MM. Sautter and Lemonnier placed upon the Richelieu and the Suffren electric lights with lenticular projectors like those which had been constructed four years before for the Russian navy. During this period the

army had been occupied also with this investigation, and at
the commencement of this same year (1877) M. Mangin, colonel of engineers, combined a new projector with a mirror of
a particular form, to which we should give a moment's attention, because it is the only one adopted to-day in this
country (France) for military or maritime operations. Germany has retained parabolic-mirror projectors, and lenticular projectors. As for the commercial marine, the latter are
the ones generally in use.

II. Electric Projectors of the French Army.

The principal defect of lenticular projectors was that they
occasioned a considerable loss of light. Though wasting less
light, the parabolic-mirror projectors presented serious difficulties of construction, and were easily bent out of shape.
The aplanatic-mirror projector of Colonel Mangin, invented
in the beginning of 1877, was designed specially to avoid this
double inconvenience.

Spherical-surface mirrors are much easier to construct and
keep intact than parabolic mirrors ; but they do not bring all
the luminous rays into parallelism, so that there is a considerable lateral dispersion of light in long-distance projections.
M. Mangin formed his mirror by superimposing two spherical
surfaces of different curvature. These two surfaces are represented in their relation to each other by the two faces of a
concavo-convex lens, whose second face—the convex face—is
silvered, and forms the back of the mirror—that is to say, the
reflecting surface. The luminous rays which fall upon the
mirror and are reflected from the silvered face, twice traverse
the glass, and are twice refracted in opposite directions. The
final result of these changes of direction depends upon the
ratio of the lengths of the radii of the two spherical surfaces.
By combining them in a suitable manner, Colonel Mangin has
completely abolished what physicists call spherical aberration, and has succeeded in bringing all the rays into the most
absolute parallelism.

The projector has the form of a cylindrical box, quite
short, of a diameter of ninety centimetres, whose back is
formed by the aplanetic mirror we are describing, a certain
distance in front of which the voltaic arc is placed. It is an
arc playing between two carbons that are brought together by

hand, by means of a thumb-screw worked from the outside. There is therefore no regulator. This rudimentary arrangement, which would be inadmissible in any other case, suits perfectly cases of lighting of short duration, and which need no particular steadiness. The carbons, instead of being vertical, are inclined at an angle of about thirty degrees ; the

Fig. 234.—Mangin projector.

experiments of MM. Sautter and Lemonnier, of which we have spoken in Chapter IV (Fig. 23), have shown that they thus give a greater quantity of useful light, on account of the position which the cup or crater of the positive carbon then occupies. Finally, an auxiliary lens, placed between the arc and the mirror, collects and projects upon it a part of the

light which would otherwise escape its action, and thus increases the intensity of the lighting; it makes possible, in
fact, the utilization of all the rays emitted in an angle of one
hundred degrees, while the mirror by itself would only utilize them within an angle of sixty-eight degrees (Fig. 234).

When the electric light is placed in the focus of the mirror, the projector throws out a very powerful cylindrical luminous beam, twenty times more powerful than with an ordinary spherical mirror, but whose area of lighting is very
limited. To rapidly reconnoitre a suspected ground, it is
necessary to enlarge this field of view by abandoning the
cylindrical beam, and by giving it a slightly conical form.
This result is obtained in the most simple manner, by removing the luminous center from the focus of the mirror and
placing it nearer to, or further from, this focus. The change
is quickly effected by a screw placed on the exterior. When
the voltaic arc is displaced four centimetres, the surface
lighted at one kilometre distance increases from fifteen square
metres to one hundred and fifteen, and at four kilometres distance the surface lighted increases to four hundred and sixty
square metres.

The divergence thus obtained is produced in the direction
of height, as well as in that of width. As it is the earth only
—that is to say, the horizon—which is usually to be inspected,
the light cast up in the sky is lost without benefit. To avoid
this trouble, a disk of glass is placed in front of the projector, which disk is formed of a series of divergent plano-
cylindrical lenses, which spread out horizontally the luminous
beam in such a manner as to give the field of illumination a
nearly rectangular form; the effect is the same as if the luminous cone had been flattened against the earth, as a paper
cornet might be. By this process divergences of twelve to
fifteen degrees can be attained with a beam that originally
had only two degrees divergence on leaving the mirror.

The projector is carried upon a small carriage (Fig. 235)
that one horse can easily draw about where it is to be used, as
its total weight is not over seven hundred and fifty kilogrammes. The apparatus is mounted upon trunnions, and
suspended so that it can easily be turned in all directions, and
be made to sweep the ground as easily as the eye itself.

It is true that this electric eye has to be animated by a
dynamo-electric machine, driven itself by a steam-engine

which draws its supply from a boiler. These three parts form a plant that must be movable so as to follow the projector, and they weigh nearly five thousand kilogrammes with the wagon carrying them.

Fig. 235.—Mangin projector, with its accessories, mounted upon the field-wagon.

MM. Sautter and Lemonnier, who construct all these apparatus, have combined them so as to diminish their weight without reducing their power. The machine is a Gramme

machine of the D. Q. type, which gives a light of 4,000 carcels
—almost the most powerful that can be produced under good
conditions. It is driven directly by a Brotherhood engine,
which has been chosen simply on account of its small volume,
and because it is adapted to drive the dynamo-electric machine
directly without the intervention of pulleys and belts, whose
working is interfered with by the least rain. Finally, the
field boiler has the advantage of rapidly getting up steam, and
of furnishing steam, as it were, as soon as the fire is started.

Thus arranged, the Mangin projector has a useful range of
five or six kilometres. The numerous experiments to which
it has been subjected since 1878, at the fortress of Mount Va-
lerien, show even a better result, because in full night all the
details of the towers of the Trocadero could be seen, situated
at a distance of nearly eight kilometres. At five kilometres
houses, carriages, and the movements of soldiers could be
well distinguished ; at three and a half kilometres it was possible to count the dispersed soldiers and to recognize their
occupations.

In all these experiments, the observer being placed near
the luminous source, the light had to pass twice over the
given space to return to him. In its passage away from the
observer, it weakened in proportion to the square of the distance, and, on its return, proportionally to the square of the
square—that is to say, to the fourth power of the distance.
For instance, when the object to be examined from a distance
is only lighted one hundredth as much as if it were near the
luminous focus, the observer, situated near this focus, will
only receive a light of one millionth this intensity. That
which diminishes the visibility of objects is especially their
distance from the observer. But in war this distance can be
shortened by advancing the observers near the enemy, while
the projector would remain behind under protection of the
cannon.

The large projectors of ninety centimetres are designed
especially for the defence of fortified places, and of the coasts.
They are relied on in following the movements and operations
of the enemy. Toward the middle of 1881, MM. Sautter and
Lemonnier sold forty to the French Government, of which
ten were in service in fortified places, and thirty on the coasts.
Each of these apparatus, with the machines attached to them
and their accessories, cost nearly 30,000 francs.

Fig. 236,—Portable apparatus, with Brotherhood

and Gramme machine, for use with Mangin projector.

For field service a somewhat lighter model was chosen, easier to transport but of somewhat less power. The projector has two thirds of the diameter of the other—only sixty centimetres—and has no auxiliary lens. Its range does not exceed four or five kilometres. It is supplied by a weaker Gramme machine, of the C. Q. type, producing a light of 2,500 carcels intensity. The Brotherhood engine and the Field boiler are also of smaller size, but the general arrangement is the same.

The projector-carriage can be drawn by men, and be removed from the engine and machinery-carriage, which supplies the current, by paying out the cable supplied to it. A dozen examples of this type are still in service, and are a little less expensive than the others.

Finally, there is a third model, much lighter, but also much weaker, as its range hardly attains three kilometres. It is a projector of forty centimetres diameter, with a Gramme machine of only 1,600 carcels power. The whole in this case is carried upon a single carriage. The projector is so light that two men can dismount it, carry it off some distance, and place it in position on a movable base instead of the special carriage, in this case dispensed with. This third model is designed for subsidiary lighting and for the small forts situated along our new frontier, to arrest the movements of an invading army. They can also be employed to project upon the clouds luminous jets, which would serve as signals, and would form a sort of special optical telegraph. At the present time the French army has only eight apparatus of this kind.

The Mangin projectors, only four years invented, have never had a chance to be tried on the battle-field or in sieges. They were used, however, at the beginning of the Tunis expedition. The frigate Surveillante used them in exploring the coast of the island of Tabarka, before disembarking our troops (Fig. 237), and possibly the effect produced upon the natives by this apparition, terrifying to their eyes, had something to do in facilitating the operation.

III. THE ELECTRIC LIGHT AT SEA.

As we have said before, it is to M. Eugène Pereire that, in France, is due the initiative in taking up again nautical lighting in March, 1876, after the abandonment of the long trials

27

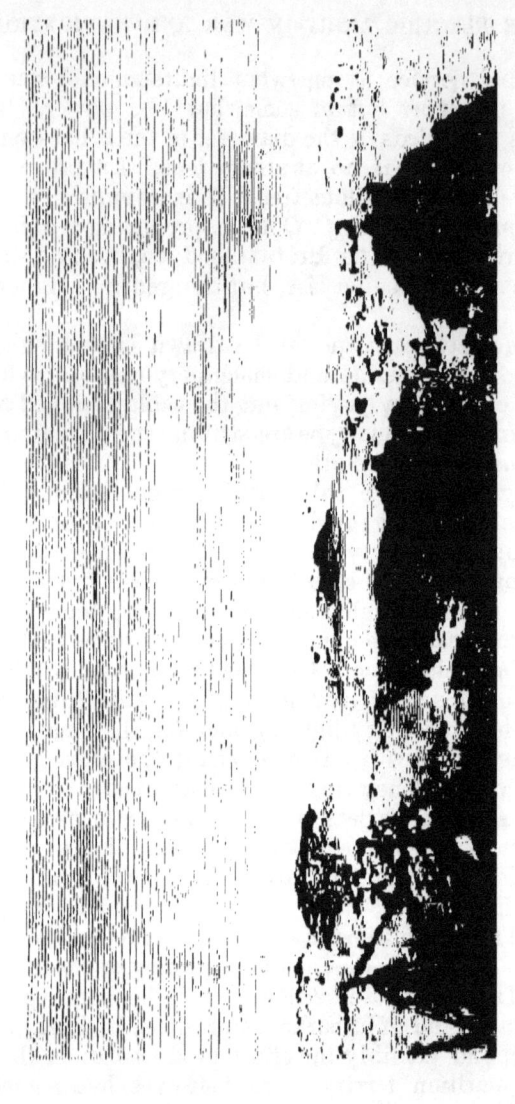

already gone through by the Compagnie Transatlantique, under his impulse, when the Alliance machine was their only generator. The new system was put into the steamer Amérique by M. H. Fontaine, with the assistance of the captain, M. Pouzalz. We give the description in the words of M. H. Fontaine himself :

"The light is placed at the top of a little tower, which is ascended by interior steps, without the necessity of going upon the deck, because the tower comes over one of the regular companion-ways. This arrangement is very advantageous, especially in bad weather, when the ship's bows are hard of access by the bridge. The tower was originally seven metres high, but M. Pouzalz made it two metres less, to give it more stability and lower the level of the beam of light, so that now this tower rises five metres above the deck. Its diameter is one metre, and it is placed forward on the ship, about fifteen metres from the bow.

"The lantern (properly so called) is made with glass prisms ; it can light an arc of 225°, leaving the ship almost entirely in shade. The regulator, on the Serrin system, is suspended from a dial-plate. A small seat placed in the top of the tower makes it easy for the watchman to regulate the lamp when in position. The beam of light is about ·80 metre across.

"The Gramme machine which supplies the light is of 200 carcels power ; it is driven directly by a three-cylinder Brotherhood engine, which reduces the space occupied by the two machines to 1·20 metre in length, and ·65 and ·60 metre in breadth and height respectively. These two machines are placed upon a false flooring in the engine-room, about 40 metres from the lantern.

"All the wires pass through the captain's state-room, who has under his hands switches which enable him to cut off at will the light from the lamp in the tower, or from a second movable lamp—of which we shall speak further on—and all this without interrupting the running of the Gramme machine.

"The novelty in the arrangements of the Amérique consists in the automatic intermittence of the light in the tower-lamp. This effect is obtained by a very simple commutator, placed on the extremity of the arbor of the Gramme machine, and which sends alternately the current into the lamp or into a closed metallic coil of the same resistance as the voltaic arc, which coil is heated and cooled alternately. This arrangement has been adopted to leave the Gramme machine, which always turns 850 times a minute, in the same conditions in relation to the exterior circuit. According to the calculations of M. Pouzalz, the best ratio between the eclipses and flashes of light is produced by a light of 20 seconds duration and an eclipse of 100 seconds.

"The light is ten metres above the sea-level, and the possible range of the light, with regard to the depression of the horizon, is ten geographical miles (18,520 metres) for an observer whose eye is six metres above the level of the water.

"For the purpose of lighting the topsails and top-gallant sails, leaving the lower sails in darkness, M. Pouzalz constructs a galvanized iron cone, and places it over a movable lamp, the large end being upward. In this way the Amérique could be seen a long distance off by ships and telegraph stations, when the commander chose to leave the light in action during the whole night."

This last described light, resembling the "plume" light-houses, can above all be of incontestable service, as no one can find any fault with it. As much could not be said for the horizontal projection, which was assailed with criticisms already made against the first electric lighting of 1867 to 1870. This enormous light, it was said, would be confounded with light-houses by other ships, and would be liable to take them from their course. Again, its glare caused the disappearance of the regulation green and red lights, placed on right and left of each ship to indicate its course in the darkness to other vessels, and new chances of collision would result therefrom. Finally, it was said that the electric light dazzled the ship's officers, and prevented them from seeing obstacles ahead as well as they would have seen them without it.

To these objections responses were not wanting. It was easy to give to the light of the ships an altogether different character from that of light-houses. By elevating them sufficiently above the deck, the starboard and port lights would not be interfered with. Finally, after having tried it, the captain of the ship, M. Pouzalz, formally declared in his report that the light produced by short flashes had never troubled the sight of any officer of the deck, nor of the watch-men on the bow, and that the glare of the side-lights, red and green, was not diminished by the use of the forward light-house.

Another captain, M. de Bacandé, was no less satisfied than M. Pouzalz, and a similar electrical plant was placed upon another transatlantic ship. In spite of all this, routine prevailed, and these two plants have disappeared after some years' service, as the others had done, under the indifference of the captains who were obliged to keep them in order.

But it was not thus in other countries, where a certain number of steamships possess to-day lighting apparatus supplied by Gramme machines; notably the packet-ships of the Austrian Lloyds, and a certain number of English, Danish, Russian, and other vessels. A great part of these lighting-apparatus are French in origin, and came from the factory of MM. Sautter and Lemonnier, in Paris. The Siemens establishment, in Berlin, has also furnished a considerable number.

In spite of the opposition encountered by electric apparatus in the commercial marine, it is probable that they will soon come into use, because of the increasing danger of collisions at night, so dreadful in the case of iron ships, that leave no floating wreck to serve as a life-preserver for the shipwrecked people. The sea, which seems so vast, is much smaller than it appears so far as navigation is concerned, as the whole of its expanse can not be used. It is furrowed by actual routes, which ships from various motives are obliged to follow exactly, and which become at last as crowded as a railroad when commerce is very active—for example, on the line between Liverpool and New York. It is absolutely necessary, in this case, that ships, continually increasing in speed, shall see each other from a distance to avoid colliding. It will soon be conceded that the electric light alone can give this result in stormy weather, so frequent in the North Atlantic.

Although more distrustful, and slower in taking up the electric light than the merchant marine, the French navy has been more faithful to it. The experiments made in 1877 on the Suffren and Richelieu quickly brought about the general introduction of projection-apparatus as a means at once of nautical lighting and of defense. But in the ensuing year Colonel Mangin's projectors, invented for army use, were substituted for the lenticular projectors hitherto employed, and the navy has nearly a hundred copies of this particular apparatus.

On board the Suffren and Richelieu, only one projector was introduced, placed upon the captain's bridge, and rolling from port to starboard upon special rails, so as to explore at will upon either side of the vessel. To-day the necessity is recognized of lighting when desired both sides of the vessel at the same time.

Large armored vessels and cruisers now require two projectors for each one, port and starboard, at the ends of the captain's bridge or a little below it. But there is only one electric generator, a Gramme machine, whose current can supply one or the other of the projectors by the movement of a switch placed under the hand of the captain or officer of the deck. Rapid as this movement may be, it is preferable to have two machines, so that the lighting of both sides of the ship shall be really simultaneous. This arrangement is adopted in the navy of other countries, especially of England, Austria, Denmark, and Italy; the two Gramme machines used are then connected so that both projectors can be lighted at once, or their whole power be concentrated upon a single apparatus.

When the ship has only a single projector, its proper place is well forward, as in the Russian ship, the Livadia. It would be still better to carry it upon a special platform running out over the bow, as M. Dalman arranged it upon the Spanish armored ships, Numancia and Vitoria.

Apparatus similar to those of the large ships have been established in the principal ports of France to light the courses on which an enemy's fleet would approach. When the channel is two kilometres wide, two projectors at once are used to light the whole of it. Most of the European nations have adopted similar arrangements, and exhaustive experiments were made in several countries between 1878 and 1881 to ascertain the range and efficacy of these new means of defense. We shall especially cite the experiments in the Gulf of Jouan, at Toulon, and Cherbourg in France, those at Chatham in England, Pola in Austria, and Cronstadt and the camp of Valkof in Russia, etc.

These experiments have shown that with a powerful and concentrated beam of light (4,000 carcels) persons placed near the projectors could distinguish, with opera-glasses, white houses seven kilometres distant. Under similar conditions, a fort or war-ship three kilometres distant could be lighted, by throwing upon it a beam of light three hundred metres wide, when the embrasures could be easily discerned. Finally, at this same distance of three kilometres, the red buoys which indicate a channel, or similar objects, could be made visible.

The new apparatus were also well tried in the North Sea during the Turco-Russian war. The ports of Odessa, Sebastopol, and Orchakow were thus secured against surprise by the enemy. The port of Odessa especially, supplied with a Mangin projector, operated by a Gramme machine, could with certainty show at night, four or five kilometres distant, large ships coming to attack it. Low-built vessels, painted in dark colors, escaped the sight for longer periods, but they even were seen two kilometres off. The German apparatus, placed in the other ports, had one third less range.

Great as their power may be, electric projectors would not suffice to protect armored ships against the attack of torpedo-boats. These are, in fact, very well concealed under a general black color, which covers even the figures of the sailors, as they are dressed in the universal black. In these conditions, the most that can be hoped for is to see the torpedo-boat five hundred metres away, and then it is too late to elude it. The best means of avoiding the danger is to protect the ships at a distance by steam launches, which patrol on all sides like the pickets of a camp.

But to keep up this surveillance on all sides, the launches need also electric projectors, and they can only carry small ones. For them very small ones (thirty centimetres in diameter) have been designed, which weigh only one hundred and sixty kilogrammes with their accessories. The Gramme machine which supplies them can be driven, on an emergency, by four men, without any steam motor; but it must be understood that they are also provided with a Brotherhood engine.

In spite of their reduced dimensions, these apparatus have still great power, for their range extends to two kilometres when the night is clear. It will be understood that we speak of the range for ordinary objects, of light colors and pretty large size. The torpedo-boats, painted black, would only be seen some hundreds of metres distant. Furthermore, the torpedo-boats themselves have a similar plant, which costs about six thousand francs.

The picket-boats and gunboats have a more powerful apparatus that costs nearly ten thousand francs, and sometimes they have two projectors, like the large armored ships, which brings up the expense to more than sixteen thousand francs.

The use of powerful electric lights in naval tactics is far too recent for it to be known, as yet, all the use that can be made of them, or all the manœuvres in which they can be employed. A number of very interesting features in their operations have, however, been observed. We give some examples :

When not too far off, the best method of discerning an object—a suspected embarkation, for instance—is not to light it directly. The light should rather be projected above it. The particles of water and of solid matter always present in the air reflect the luminous rays upon the suspected party, and make it very visible. If, on the other hand, the beam of light falls upon the sea in front of the object sought for, it will completely disappear from view. This is because the rays of light are reflected from the surface of the water, and form, as they rise again, a sort of luminous veil that conceals the object sought for. This is due to a general law. The eye can not penetrate a beam of intense light. In this may be found a means of hiding certain manœuvres from the enemy behind a curtain of light, just as the movements of troops are now hidden behind a curtain of cavalry.

The luminous ray can constitute for the enemy a very great embarrassment, and can even paralyze his movements. It has been remarked, in fact, that a party of men surprised suddenly by the projection upon them of the luminous beam, become incapable of manœuvring for some time at least. This is because men who have been some time in darkness are blinded by a sudden light.

The *rôle* of the electric light in optical telegraphy, on land or on sea, must now be spoken of. In this it plays no part except a source of intense light, and the mechanism used in optical telegraphy has no direct relation with the electric light. In principle, too, this mechanism is very simple. It is known to our readers that in ordinary telegraphy the Morse alphabet expresses all the letters of the alphabet by dots and dashes variously combined. The same signals are employed in optical telegraphy ; but, instead of tracing them upon paper, they are written in the air with flashes of light ; the dots are instantaneous flashes, the lines are flashes of light having a certain duration. Here it will be seen is a mechanism analogous to that producing the signals of light-houses. It works very well with petroleum lamps. But, when the source of light is more intense, the range naturally increases in proportion, which is of importance, especially in bad weather. It is in this regard that the electric light is particularly available in this application. As there is in these cases generally no need of a large quantity of light, in the army a very light Gramme machine, driven by four men who turn a crank like that of a rotary pump, is considered ample.

Thanks to the labors of Colonel Laussedat, to-day director of the Conservatoire des Arts et Métiers, in Paris—labors pursued subsequently by Colonel Mangin—optical telegraphy works very well at the present day in France. By means of it, it may be specially noted here, during the campaigns of Southern Oran and Tunis, the news of the entry of military forces into the heart of the Sahara was transmitted to Paris in a few hours, several hundred kilometres intervening between the nearest telegraph station and the scene of operations. Using this system, a besieged place, such as Paris in 1870, could often communicate over the heads of the assailants, without fearing any revelation of the dispatches to the enemy. In such a country as the Algerian Sahara, its importance is still greater, because it is enough, if a certain number of distant fortified places are occupied, to be almost instantly informed of what is passing at the extreme limit of our lines, without attempting the almost impossible task of guarding a telegraphic wire in the desert.

CHAPTER III.

THE ELECTRIC LIGHT IN THE THEATRE.

ALTHOUGH the electric light was first used industrially— to any extent, at least—in light-houses, it is in another field, in the theater, that it made its *début* into practical life, it may even be said into industrial life, as it does not work there for nothing. It appears to have been in a fairy piece, entitled "The Sick Potatoes," that it made its first appearance before the French public ; but we are ignorant of the *rôle* it there played.

A little later, in 1846, it was applied with great splendor in the famous opera, "The Prophet," where it had to represent the rising sun. The effect of the rising sun was obtained by the use of a parabolic mirror (Fig. 238), which brought all the rays into parallelism, and projected a cylindrical beam of light upon a silken screen, where it produced perfectly the

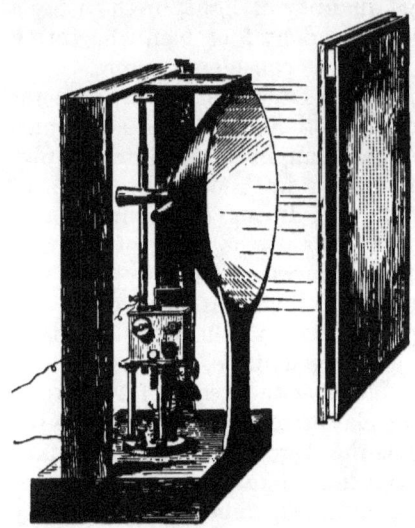

image of a disk. The apparatus was made to rise back of curtains so arranged as to hide its mechanism from the audience, and thus produced the complete illusion of the sunrise.

M. J. Duboscq, the co-laborer of Foucault, was the first who superintended the introduction of the electric light upon the stage of the Grand Opera of Paris. In 1855 he was finally put in permanent charge of a service, which is still in his care, and, five years later, on the occasion of the repro-

Fig. 238.—Apparatus used in "The Prophet," to represent the sun.

duction of the opera of "Moses," he produced for the first time a real rainbow.

It is known how important a part the rainbow plays in this opera, at the moment when the waves of the Red Sea are closing in behind the Hebrews to engulf the pursuing army of Pharaoh. Previous to this the rainbow had been represented by colored bands of paper stretched upon a large blue cloth, which represents in the background the sky of Egypt. To make it appear at the proper moment, large lamps are lighted behind it, which can hardly be made to supply a light sensibly greater than that of the scene. To make this rainbow come out, the general light has to be reduced, as if night was coming upon the scene. The miracle thus becomes a little too great, even for the remote epoch where it is placed, because the rainbow appears in full night before spectators well informed of the fact that it is due to decomposition of the rays of the sun.

The electric light furnished M. J. Duboscq the means of producing a rainbow bright enough to be seen with the scene fully lighted, and which is, moreover, a true rainbow, obtained by the identical processes of real nature. We give the description of the apparatus according to M. Saint-Edme:

The electrical apparatus, whose arc is supplied by one hundred Bunsen cups, is placed upon a scaffold of suitable height, five metres from the curtain, and perpendicular to the cloth which represents the sky upon which the rainbow is to appear. The whole optical apparatus is fitted for and kept in a blackened box, which permits no light to escape into the air (Fig. 239). The first lenses give a parallel system of rays,

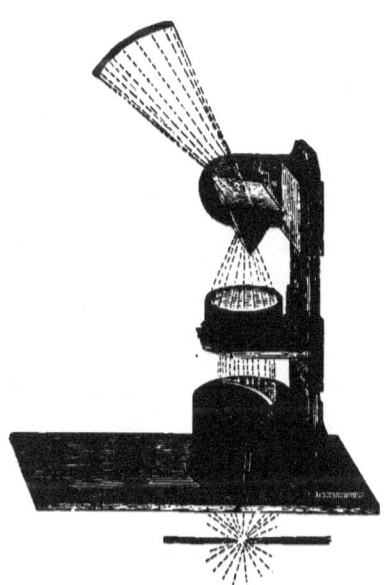

which passes next through a screen with an opening in the shape of an arc. This beam is received by a double-convex lens of very short focus, which plays the double *rôle* of increasing the curvature of the image and of giving it a greater extension. As they leave this last lens, the rays of light pass through the prism arranged to decompose them, and consequently produce the rainbow. The position of the prism is not a matter of indifference; its summit must be upward, referred to the incident beam, without which the colors of the arc would not be displayed upon the receiving screen in the same order which follow in the rainbow. By the use of this system the rainbow appears luminous even when the stage is brightly lighted. We have endeavored to reproduce its effect in Fig. 240.

Fig. 239.—Apparatus for the production of the rainbow on the stage.

The rainbow is not the only meteorological phenomena

which it is desirable to reproduce upon the stage. The storm, especially, appears so often in pieces of all classes that it is important to know how to accurately reproduce it.

The noise of thunder can easily be imitated in the theater; the "properties" comprise always a *tom-tom* and a sheet of elastic metal designed for this use; but what is not so easy is to produce upon the stage flashes of lightning having more resemblance to the real.

In early days, to imitate the phenomenon, the cloth of the back scene was lighted up from behind by a flame colored

Fig. 240.—The rainbow in the opera of " Moses."

red, a narrow, sinuous opening being made in the canvas. The art of scenery advancing with the progress of science, it became necessary to do better, and the choice of a source of light naturally fell upon the voltaic arc, whose origin is identical with that of lightning. But more was necessary; an optical arrangement was required which would give the power of emitting and extinguishing the luminous ray at short intervals, and at the same time of giving it the characteristic zig-zag movement of lightning. For this end M. J. Duboscq had recourse to a species of magic mirror (Fig. 241), in front of which was placed the electric light.

The mirror is concave, and the luminous point corresponds with its focus. The upper carbon electrode is stationary, but the lower carbon can receive at any given moment a movement of separation which lights the apparatus. This same effect can be produced by electro-magnetic attraction. As the mirror is held in the hand, it is easy, by shaking it, and using a switch, to imitate quite well the zig-zags of lightning and their sudden apparition.

The name of magic mirror has been given to this apparatus, because its small dimensions enable it to be held by one of the actors, who can produce many useful effects with it, especially in fairy scenes. It was for this particular end that it was invented, and it was shown for the first time in the theater of the Variétés, in Paris, in a play called "The Travels of Truth." Wires hidden in the sleeves of the actor conducted the electric current, and a small key placed under the

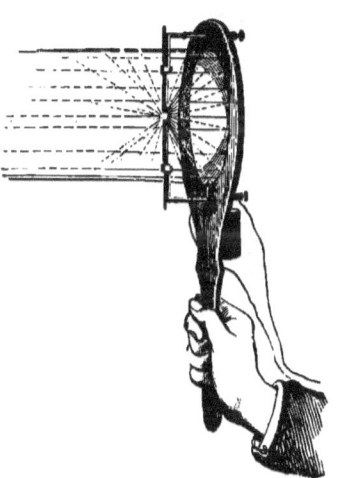

Fig. 241.—Magic mirror for the production of lightning in the theatre.

actor's finger lighted the apparatus. It is easy to imagine the varied scenic effects that could be thus produced.

The incidents of the action, especially in operas and fairy pieces, require sometimes a strong ray of light to follow a personage through all his movements. The ordinary apparatus are too bulky and hard to move for this purpose. M. J. Duboscq has invented lighter ones, provided with the necessary joints to direct the luminous rays in all directions, and which, moreover, can be hung upon the wall.

This apparatus (Fig. 242) is composed of a wooden or sheet-iron lantern containing the electric lamp, whose light emerges through lenses which make it possible to concentrate all the rays upon a single point. This point can be enlarged or contracted at pleasure by the movements of a special diaphragm which limits the field of lighting.

When larger surfaces have to be lighted, as a panel of a wall or the corner of a garden, another apparatus (Fig. 243) is used, also articulated in all directions, but whose light is concentrated by a large enough mirror of silvered glass instead of a lens.

We could cite numerous instances of such applications in well-known operas. It will be enough to reproduce one of the scenes in the opera of " Moses," where the principal personage is thus lighted by the luminous rays (Fig. 244).

FIG. 242.—Electric lamp for illuminating an actor in the play.

Among the other applications of the electric light in the theater, one of the most used and most applauded is the luminous fountain.

When a liquid escapes from a vessel by a circular orifice, the jet takes the form of a parabola ; moreover, the liquid vein is not absolutely cylindrical ; it is contracted at a point whose distance from the orifice is mathematically determinable. In consequence of this, if a ray of light is directed upon the orifice of escape, it seems drawn along by the liquid, and follows it in all parts of its course.

The phenomenon is designated in optics by the name of total reflection; on account of the curvature of the liquid vein, the beam is reflected at each point of its course by

FIG. 243.—Electric lamp, with mirror, for lighting a particular point of the scene.

the molecules which it meets, and, instead of escaping from it into space, it is reflected onward by the molecules in the direction of the jet, which takes the appearance of a jet of fire. If the liquid curve be broken, the phenomenon of reflection ceases, and flashes of light play around the point of interruption.

The water is placed in a cylindrical prismatic vase of considerable height. The electric lamp, supplied for this purpose with a system of lighting lenses, is placed in front of an

Fig. 244.—Scene in the opera of " Moses."

orifice closed by a pane of transparent glass, so directed that the luminous ray shall enter the arc of curvature formed by the water as it escapes. By placing colored glasses in front of the electrical apparatus, the color of the jet is changed at will.

In 1853 the first luminous fountain was shown in the opera at Paris, in the ballet of " Elia and Mysis." Every one has seen, in the second act of "Faust," the fountain which Mephistopheles causes to play, and whose nature he subsequently changes. It works upon this principle. It is one of the first ever used, and it has been followed by many others,

in all kinds of theaters. They now make them much stronger
and more beautiful. In grand spectacular pieces immense
cascades are often illuminated which sometimes fall almost in

Fig. 245.—Luminous fountain.

a semicircle. When fountains are alone to be used, fountains
playing in the air and falling back like those in our public
parks (Fig. 245) are generally used.

We could cite many other applications of the electric light
to theatrical machinery. Whenever an extremely intense
light is required to obtain a certain effect, the electric light is
called upon.

This happens especially in the case of apparitions of spec-
ters in the midst of the characters upon the stage—apparitions that always produce a good effect when they are well
managed. These spectres are living people, placed below the
level of the stage, generally near the prompter's box. Their
image is reflected on a piece of plate-glass, placed on the
stage and inclined at an angle of 45°. The clear glass can
not produce images except by receiving upon one of its faces
a much more powerful light than on the other. This is

effected by lighting with a strong electric light the characters who are to become spectres in the glass.

Besides the uses of the electric light which we have pointed out as accessory in theatrical representations, there is another much more important, and to which the terrible accidents which have recently occurred in Nice and Vienna give the greatest importance; we speak of the substitution of electric lighting for gas-lighting. The chances of fires, the insupportable production of heat and foul air, finally, the rapid deterioration of all the decorations, are serious faults of the latter, from which its rival is exempt.

Its advantages are so great, that it would doubtless have been everywhere adopted already, if this were as easy as supposed. This we must briefly examine, if only to indicate the way to follow in pursuing experiments upon this subject.

The principal parts of a theatre to be lighted are the vestibule and main stairway, the auditorium, the stage, and the lobby. From the point of view of lighting, these places are not as independent as might be supposed; a fixed relation between them must be maintained, a skillful graduation, and for this end a single system, too feeble for the one and too strong for the other, would not answer. The lighting of the lobby seems easy, and yet we have seen that at the Opera two different systems are needed for the lobby: a moderate light for the people promenading there; powerful lights of warm colors to reach the ceiling and bring out the paintings, which are its principal ornament.

The vestibule and stairs are easily lighted, and if advantage be taken of this to waste the light, the other places near it will seem obscure. If the auditorium be lighted as brilliantly as this place, what will become of the stage? In the auditorium, the chandelier can not well be dispensed with, not only as a matter of decoration, but also because it is really the necessary and natural radiating point of the luminous rays, which have to diffuse the necessary light under all the ceilings of the different galleries. The bad effect of luminous ceilings on which many hopes were founded has not been forgotten; at the Opera, the luminous circle formed by cut-glass globes, placed in the cornices and lighted with electric candles, has shown that the chandelier could be assisted by the formation, at this height, of a network of powerful light which

28

is effectively reflected by the ceiling. It is at the same time very decorative.

But, assuming all this to be settled, the stage remains to be provided for, and it is enough to have examined it near at hand to understand the difficulty. Here the electric light must be more pliant and obedient than elsewhere. The actual gas apparatus are the fruit of long study, and electricity can only replace it light by light, on the condition that it can accommodate itself to the graduations on which all possible effects depend.

To all this must be added the necessity of generating the electricity, by the aid of machines, at a distance from the theatre, which has already without this enough other causes of fire and accidents; the absolute necessity of organizing the service so as to avoid all possible chance of extinctions, accidental or premeditated, or at the least to make them of little account by confining them to a restricted range; and all this without speaking of the expense, which can be supported by national, subsidized theatres, but which would be beyond the resources of others.

The conclusion must be that the electric light and gas-light have to be introduced under the same conditions. When works of large capacity distribute electricity, and when the consumer can have a constant and regular supply and lights of all degrees of intensity without extinctions or inconveniences, it can, in the natural course of things, be introduced into our theatres, which can not be expected to generate their lighting current any more than it would be supposed practicable to annex a special gasworks to them.

To realize this improvement, whose urgency admits of no debate, a vast amount of study and experimentation has to be gone through with. As for employing the electric light as an auxiliary of gas, this is a half solution, which adds the difficulties of the one to the inconveniences of the other. It can only be tolerated as a means of arriving gradually at the complete solution of the varied conditions of this difficult programme, which must be solved and applied by the management itself.

Outside of regular theatres properly so called, on whose account experiments are still being prosecuted, there are some of a much simpler kind, and for which the electric light can furnish at the present time a light superior to and much cheaper than that of gas. We shall cite, as example, the plant which has worked for two years at the Hippodrome of Paris (Fig. 57). This immense hall, whose area is 6,300 square metres, and which holds 8,000 spectators, is lighted by the aid of two systems, twenty voltaic arc-lamps, and one hundred and twenty Jablochkoff candles. The first light the ring ; the others are arranged in two lines on the circumference of the hall, and in four groups around the columns that sustain the edifice. Two steam-engines of one hundred horse-power drive four gramme machines of twenty Jablochkoff candles, twenty gramme machines of the factory type, and one sixty-candle machine, the most powerful of this kind that has ever been built. The cost of the plant has been put at 200,000 francs in round figures, and the expense per night at 320 francs for a light equivalent to 12,000 carcels. Gas would cost for the same light 1,200 to 1,500 francs.

CHAPTER IV.

INDUSTRIAL APPLICATIONS.

I.

WE have now reached the most important question—as much from our point of view as consumers as from that of the development of this new application of science, to which so much energy and money have been devoted—its use in general lighting, concurrently with the other methods of lighting of which we have already spoken, and which, we must not cease asserting, have much more to gain than to lose by its general introduction.

We are, fortunately, not obliged to speak of its good qualities. The Electrical Exhibition at Paris has succeeded beyond doubt in proving to the most incredulous what marvelous resources it places in our hands, and what a varying amount of candle-power we can obtain from it, ranging from two or three candles to several thousands of carcels if necessary. Steadiness, coloration, division of the lights, all has been realized ; it is easy to select lights the most appropriate for the conditions to be filled, and only the question of expense has to be thought of. It is true that this last consideration is a most important one, and, without regard to the special qualities of the electric light, we might say of its superiority over other systems, it is desirable that economy should be added thereto—it is necessary, in a word, that it should be both better and cheaper.

Unfortunately, the electric light does not come within ordinary conditions; we have not got electricity at our disposal like gas, which presents itself at our hand without our needing to give a thought to its production. This may be in the near future—it will come eventually; on that day electricity will have to be used; all discussion will cease. Meanwhile, to have the light, the electricity must be generated by the consumer; the expense of establishment, of maintenance, and the sinking fund, must be advanced. All this becomes an element of much importance in computing the cost of supply —an element which, in the case of gas, is comprised in the selling price, and which does not weigh heavily on the consumer, as it is spread over an enormous total of sales. The importance of this element is naturally proportional to the number of hours of lighting. This is not much for cases where it is needed by day and by night, as in certain factories and some departments of railroad work; it is a burden upon a business that only needs artificial light during the evenings. In spite of this, the electric light, judiciously used, is even now, in many circumstances, more economical than gas, not only at the high price paid for it in Paris, but even at the reduced price given to the municipalities and railroad companies, and even at the still lower price that gas is sold at in coal-producing regions.

Since the year 1856, when experiments with the electric light were first begun—on the one hand, with the old batteries, and on the other hand with the Alliance machine, then making its *début*—the price of this light has continually diminished.

In the experiments made in Lyons, in 1857, by MM. Lacassagne and Thiers, a light of about fifty carcels, produced by sixty Bunsen cups, cost, according to M. Becquerel, three francs fifty-five centimes per hour; this is about what it would cost to-day with this mode of production. According to experiments made in the Conservatoire des Arts et Métiers with the Alliance machine, in 1856, M. Leroux found as the cost of 100 carcels light, the figure four francs thirty centimes; this cost refers to a lighting of 500 hours per annum, and we can see now the influence of the number of hours in the figures found by M. Reynaud for a machine of the same system used in light-houses. The cost of maintaining a light of 230 carcels is reduced to one franc ten centimes per hour.

With the Gramme machine the price falls still lower. A light of 150 carcels, used for a lighting of 500 hours per annum, does not cost more, according to figures obtained by M. Fontaine from its first applications to use, than one franc ninety-two centimes. In the factory of M. Manchon, this cost descends to one franc twenty-three centimes, and, according to M. Picou, in another plant to ninety-two centimes.

The division of the light was not yet perfected, and a special machine was needed for each light; nevertheless, remarkable results were obtained by a plant set up in 1876 by the Northern Railroad Company for lighting its freight depot, and the principal figures of which have been published by M. Sartiaux.

A room seventy metres square and eight metres high, a shed seventy by fifteen metres, of the same height, and a court twenty metres square, separating the room from the shed, had to be lighted. A complete small plant was erected, including the house and motor, with counter-shafting, six Gramme machines, five working and one in reserve. The cost of establishment was as follows:

Shed area, forty square metres (430 square feet). 2,200 francs ($440)
Structure upon which to mount the six dynamo
  machines, counter-shafting, etc............... 8,400 francs ($1,680)
Conductors, material, and labor, for a mean dis-
  tance of eighty metres (262·4 feet) from dyna-
  mos to lamps................................. 700 francs ($140)
Engine and boiler of ten horse-power, with a ca-
  pacity of fifteen at need, including setting in
  place.. 9,800 francs ($1,960)
Six Gramme machines at 1,500 francs each..... 9,000 francs ($1,800)
Six Serrin regulators at 450 francs each........ 2,700 francs ($540)
Five lanterns, with pulleys and chains......... 500 francs ($100)
Various other items........................... 2,200 francs ($440)

Total............... 35,500 francs ($7,100)

The interest for this amount and depreciation, at ten per cent, for 365 days, and an average ten hours daily operation of the plant, represent ·243 franc (4·86 cents) per lamp per hour.

The first trials began with four machines and four lamps only. Under these conditions, the daily expense was as follows:

Coal, 400 kilogrammes (880 pounds) at 25 francs ($5) per ton..............	10	francs	00	centimes	($2.00)
Kindling wood......................	00	"	15	"	(.03)
Mechanic at 50 centimes (10¢) per hour,	05	"	00	"	(1.00)
Lubricating-oil......................	00	"	80	"	(.16)
Carbon electrodes, at 1 franc 50 centimes (30 cents) per metre (3·28 feet), 4 lamps burning 10 hours at 10 centimetres per lamp per hour.	06	"	00	"	(1.20)

(These were retort carbons, 9 millimetres ($\frac{9}{25}$ inch) thick and 33 centimetres (13 inches) long. They lasted 8½ hours, waste included.)

Gas for lighting the machine-room....	00	"	30	"	(.06)
Total per day........	22	francs	25	centimes	($4.45)
Or per lamp per hour........................			55.6	"	(.11)
Interest and depreciation, as above............			24.3	"	(.05)
Cost of light per lamp per hour..............			79.9	centimes	($0.16)

The lights are placed four and a half metres high, and the lighting is sufficient within a radius of thirty-five to forty metres; the lanterns are one metre in height and ·50 metre wide; to avoid the dazzling, the glasses are partly painted over with zinc-white. The lantern placed in the court is provided with double glasses to prevent breakage by cold or rain. The ceiling and walls of the room are whitewashed, so as to reflect the light.

This light takes the place of twenty-one gas-burners, burning 120 litres (4·2 cubic feet) each, and the hand-lamps which the baggage-agents had to carry to find the packages, decipher the addresses, and read the address labels. It has reduced considerably the errors in direction and delays resulting therefrom, the damages caused by the loading of goods, and the consequent indemnities of all kinds that the company were obliged to pay.

The weight of baggage moved during the day per man per hour was 850 kilogrammes; at night it was only 530 kilogrammes with gaslight; with the electric light it came to 680 kilogrammes. Fifty-five gas-burners would have been required to attain the same result.

If in this example the price of plant is a little high, on the other hand fuel costs the Northern Company much less than it does individual consumers. Assuming that a five-light Gramme machine was used, costing 2,800 francs, Gramme regulators costing only 400 francs each, and Carré's carbons ; and also assuming that fuel cost forty francs a ton, the workman sixty centimes per hour, the result attained is about 18,000 francs for the plant, and twelve centimes for interest and depreciation. The expense per hour comes to 67·5 centimes, which, with the preceding figure of twelve centimes, gives 79·5 centimes for the price per lamp per hour that such a system of lighting would cost an ordinary factory. It is clear that a special building need not always be constructed, and that the motive power can often be taken from a more powerful engine already driving other machines in a factory. This will diminish the expense greatly.

The Paris, Lyons, and Mediterranean Railroad, which in September, 1879, experimented with electric lighting with the Lontin Company's apparatus, also decided to adopt this system for the baggage-room of the fast-freight department. But, instead of undertaking to produce the electricity itself, it made an arrangement with the Lontin Company to furnish it light at a fixed price of fifty centimes per hour and per lamp. The company has published the following report of this lighting (Fig. 246):

The plant comprises eighteen lamps, forming six series of three regulators each, of which six are unused during such times as the service is most restricted, and lighted at the moment when it again becomes active. A perceptible economy results, but its amount has not yet been accurately determined.

The cost of plant is thus given :

Steam-engine of 15 horse-power, with capacity of 20 at need	10,000 francs	($2,000)
Shafting, pulleys, belting, water-pipes, etc.	1,500 "	(300)
Dynamo-electric machines (Lontin system)	15,000 "	(3,000)
Cables, about	7,500 "	(1,500)
Nineteen Mersanne regulators (one for interchange)	7,600 "	(1,520)
Lanterns, suspending apparatus, and other accessories	5,400 "	(1,080)
Total	47,000 "	($9,400)

FIG. 246.—Electric lighting of the fast-freight room of the Paris depot of the Paris, Lyons, and Mediterranean Railroad. (Lontin System.)

The interest and depreciation on this amount, at ten per cent for 4,000 hours lighting per annum, come to 1·175 franc per hour.

The items of cost of running per hour are:

Coal for the boilers, kindling included, 40 kilogrammes (88 pounds), at 40 francs ($8) per ton	1 franc 60	centimes	($0.32)
Carbons for the lamps, 1·7 metres	1 "	55 "	(.31)
Oil and minor expenses	0 "	80 "	(.16)
Wages of two workmen for running the machines, taking care of and watching the lamps, and, in winter, the wages of a third workman in the daytime	1 "	50 "	(.30)
	5 "	45 "	($1.09)
Interest and depreciation, as above	1 "	17½ "	(.23½)
Total	6 "	62½ "	($1.32½)

Or per hour and per lamp, 34·6 centimes. Something must be added for general expenses and maintenance; but, as the fuel is furnished by the railroad company at a lower price than that given above, a compensating saving will be found in it. The interest on the cost of plant and depreciation represent, in this most favorable case, more than one fifth of the working expenses.

This system is also used in the Marseilles passenger depot and baggage departments. The lighting of the Paris depot has just been extended to all the departments of the depot; the number of lights has been increased to fifty-four, and the high-power gas-burners, which had been experimented with, have been abandoned.

Lighting-plants of the same character have been established abroad, always with voltaic arc lamps, which the height of the buildings required to be placed at a sufficient elevation, so that a single lamp can light from 1,000 to 1,500 square metres.

At the King's-Cross Station of the Great Northern Railroad, in England, two covered sheds, 265 metres long by 32 metres wide, and a cab-stand near the quay, are lighted by fourteen Crompton lamps, supplied by five Bürgin dynamo-electric machines. The expenditure of motive-power is reckoned at twenty-nine horse-power; the twelve interior lamps require a horse-power and a half each; the lamps are

9½ metres high, and about 30 metres apart; the three strong lamps, placed on the outer *façade*, use three horse-power each; they are placed at a height of 20 metres, and their illuminating power is equal to six hundred carcels.

At St. Enoch Station six Crompton lamps are used, supplied by six Gramme machines.

The cost of working is about forty centimes (eight cents) per hour and per lamp, exclusive of the interest on the investment and depreciation, which items we are not in possession of. We only know that the eight-light Bürgin machine costs about ten thousand francs.

II.

For lighting large areas, then, the voltaic arc lamps are the most economical, and in this category must be put open yards, workshops, and even the quays and docks.

In the workshops of MM. Sautter and Lemonnier, which we have already cited, Fig. 232, three electric lights of one hundred and fifty carcels, supplied each one by a Gramme machine, give a far superior light to that of the gas which they have replaced. Each machine uses two horse-power, taken from the steam-engine of the works. The consumption of carbons is seven centimetres per hour and per lamp.

M. Menier has had the electric light since 1875 in all his factories. He uses fourteen lamps of one hundred and fifty carcels. Each regulator is suspended by means of a single special cable and windlass, which very happily solves the problem of access to the lamps, and permits them to be placed at the suitable height. The cable contains two conductors, one annular and enveloping the other, with the necessary insulation; this cable is, nevertheless, sufficiently pliable to wind up without difficulty on the drum of the windlass.

The setting-up shop of the machine works of MM. Thomas and Powell, at Rouen, 40 by 13 meters, is lighted with two Gramme machines and two Serrin regulators, placed 8 metres high, representing 260 square metres per lamp. The plant cost 5,000 francs, and the daily expense is ·98 franc. The motive power expended, reckoned at five horse-power, is derived from a large engine, only using 1·50 kilometre per horse-power per hour; thus it only costs ·18 franc per hour.

It is clear what services the electric light can render in the

Fig. 248.—Farm-work carried

by means of the electric light.

case of out-door building operations; it has been thus employed from the beginning, even when there was no other
source than batteries. It was first used at the bridge of
Notre-Dame. A little later, the Northern Spanish Railroad
used, in the Guadarrama excavations, twenty electric lights
during 9,417 hours. They were supplied by batteries, and
the expense per hour and per lamp rose as high as 2·90 francs.
Since this epoch, on account of the introduction of machines,
it has met with numerous applications. It was by the assist-

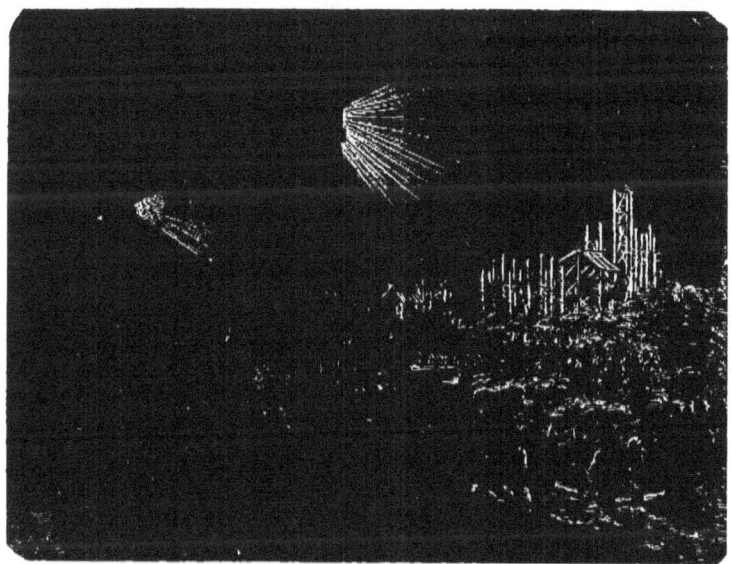

FIG. 247.—Electric lighting of an open space.

ance of the electric light that the buildings of the Universal
Exhibition of 1878 were completed by the date assigned.

Figs. 247 and 248 show how these applications are generally arranged.

The operations of M. Jeanne Deslandes for the improvement of the outer harbor of Havre received sufficient light
from two voltaic arc lamps of five hundred carcels each, to
enable one hundred and fifty workmen to work without difficulty, and, more recently in Paris, the foundations of the
Crédit Lyonnais building were laid by the light of eighteen
electric lamps.

The house of Sautter and Lemonnier construct for this out-door illumination special movable apparatus, consisting of a steam boiler, a Brotherhood engine, and a Gramme machine. The price is six thousand five hundred francs for a single-lamp apparatus, and nine thousand francs for a two-lamp one.

Other analogous systems have been arranged by M. Albaret, of Liancourt, for the employment of the electric light

Fig. 249.—Electric lighting of the work on the Kehl bridge.

in agricultural operations (Fig. 248). In this case, a single lamp may be considered sufficient for working in a radius of one hundred metres.

In January, 1880, when the city of Havre decided to introduce the electric light with Jablochkoff candles, as described in a preceding chapter, the chamber of commerce of Rouen carried on a more complete series of experiments; they desired to have a light powerful enough to permit ships to discharge, load, and equip at night-time; it also was to facilitate the watching at night of the merchandise on the quays.

Three systems were tried simultaneously—the Jablochkoff candles, the high candle-power lamps of Siemens, and of Sautter and Lemonnier. The "Bulletin de la Société Industrielle" of Rouen published, in 1881, very interesting figures on the result of this trial.

Thus, taking as the minimum illumination at the limit of the area of action of each lamp that given by a carcel lamp at a distance of three and a half metres, and assuming the lamps to be placed on a single line three thousand two hundred and fifty metres long, the following comparative figures were obtained :

SYSTEM.	Number of lamps.	Radius of action of each lamp. METRES.	Total surface lighted in hectares. (1 hectare = 2·47 acres.)	Illuminating power of a lamp in carcels	Total number of carcels.	Carcels per hectare.	Consumption of carbons per hour. METRES.	Total work in actual horse-power. HORSE-POWER	Per hectare lighted, and per hour.	
									Work of the motor. HORSE-POWER	Carbons consumed. METRES.
Jablochkoff.........	65·25	16·25	86	5,590	344	6·17	102·97	6·34	0·879	
Sautter & Lemonnier..	26	62·50	40·62	472	12,272	302	1·33	87·75	2·16	0·0327
Siemens............	25	65	42·25	476·5	11,912·5	281·9	2·50	112	2·65	0·0597

If the Jablochkoff candle be reckoned at 1·5 franc per metre, polar carbons at 2·10 francs per metre, and a horse-power at ·1 franc per hour, the following figures, per hour and per hectare, lighted under the conditions given above, are obtained :

SYSTEM.	EXPENSE OF CARBONS.			EXPENSE OF POWER.			Total expense. Francs.
	Metres.	Price per metre.	Francs.	Horse-power.	Price per horse-p'w'r	Francs.	
Jablochkoff.......	0·3796	1·50	0·5694	6·34	0·10	0·634	1·2034
Siemens..........	0·0597	2·10	0·1253	2·65	0·10	0·265	0·3903
Sautter & Lemonnier	0·0327	2·10	0·0686	2·16	0·10	0·216	0·2846

The end which it was proposed to attain in these experiments placed them under different conditions from those of ordinary lighting of public streets, of which we shall soon see other examples.

III.

The Siemens lamps used in the Rouen experiments are of a special large-lamp model, called "clock-lamps." We have seen that, for ordinary lighting, MM. Siemens use differential lamps, giving intensities of twenty-eight to fifty carcels, according to the number of lamps placed in each circuit. We give here the figures which have been obtained for the expense of a plant of this system of lighting :

Expense of Plant.

TYPE OF MACHINE. (Described in Book IV.)	NUMBER OF DIFFERENTIAL LAMPS.						
	4	6	8	10	12	16	20
	Francs.	Francs.	Francs.	Francs.	Francs.	Francs.	Francs.
Machines W³ and D⁵............	2,500	2,500	2,500	2,500			
" W⁴ " D²............					3,700	3,700	3,700
Lamps, each......... 300 francs							
Accessories.......... 25 "							
323 "	1,300	1,950	2,600	3,250	3,900	5,200	6,500
Cable at 1·5 franc per metre .... { 150 metres	225	225					
200 "			300	300			
300 "					450		
500 "						750	
600 "				-			900
	4,025	4,675	5,400	6,050	8,050	9,650	11,100
Cost of placing and incidentals, about 5%....................	200	230	270	300	400	480	550
Price of Installation... { Total...	4,225	4,905	5,670	6,350	8,450	10,130	11,650
Per lamp	1,056	817	709	635	704	633	582

Cost of Maintaining the Light.

	NUMBER OF LAMPS.						
	4	6	8	10	12	16	20
	Francs.	Francs.	Francs.	Francs.	Francs.	Francs.	Francs.
Cost of installation.............	4,225	4,905	5,670	6,350	8,450	10,130	11,650
Depreciation for ten years, and interest at 5%, or a mean of 12·75% per annum..................	538	625	723	810	1,077	1,291	1,485
Depreciation and interest per hour for 600 hours of lighting per annum........................	·89	·104	1·20	1·35	1·79	2·15	2·47
Coal for engine, 2 kilogrammes per horse-power per hour, at 30 francs per ton........ { 4 horse-pow'r	·24						
5 " "		·30					
6 " "			·36				
7 " "				·42			
8 " "					·48		
9 " "						·54	
10 " "							·60
Carbons, ·1 franc per lamp per hour	·40	·60	·80	1·00	1·20	1·60	2·00
Surveillance and oil.............	·30	·30	·30	·30	·50	·50	·50
Total price per hour........	1·83	2·24	2·66	3·07	3·97	4·79	5·57
Price per lamp per hour......	·457	·373	·333	·307	·332	·300	·278

IV.

From the point of view of economy, the arrangements adopted for best utilizing the light of electric lamps are of the greatest importance. One of the great advantages of powerful lights is that they can be placed very high, and then not require the use of ground or opal globes. It is enough in such a case, to obtain the most effective results, to reflect toward the surface to be lighted the rays sent up above the lamp. Very large flat reflectors, or slightly concave ones, placed above the lamps, as was done in the Lyons Railway depot in 1877, and as M. Jaspar used them with much success in the Electrical Exhibition in Paris, are at once the simplest and the best. When it is possible, as in this last case, to hide completely the luminous arc, using only the reflection, the most satisfactory results are obtained.

The luminous ceiling, introduced in 1877 by M. Fontaine, in one of the halls of the Louvre stores in Paris, is an interesting example of this mode of lighting by reflection. The central part of the ceiling was replaced by a large, unsilvered glass, above which was placed the regulator and its reflector. This last was formed of an inverted frustum of a pyramid, whose four faces were coated with tin, with a suitable arrangement for introducing and removing the regulator.

When the ceiling can be employed as reflector, there are no difficulties, and M. Fontaine has already used it with success in the thread-mill of Mme. Dieu, of Daours (Somme), and at M. Menier's establishment at Noisiel. But, when there is no ceiling, as in many workshops, or when the ceiling is of glass and serves for daylight to pass through, other means must be adopted.

The flat, circular reflectors, of which we have spoken, are limited in their dimensions, and they lose a great part of the rays sent up above the lamp. M. Boulard thought of substituting for them a reflector with a series of round plates, whose width and distance between the plates are so graduated that all the rays are reflected yet none of them are intercepted. These plates, or blinds as they may be called, only descend to the level of the lamp ; below it they would be use-' less, because the luminous rays naturally distribute themselves. It is, moreover, important for all reflectors to only use for reflection their lower surfaces, which are not exposed to obscuration by dust. They must not, either, be so inclined as to present dazzling surfaces, insupportable to the eye.

In ordinary lighting, the plates are of metal. Fig. 250 shows the arrangement of one of these reflectors with a horizontal Mersanne regulator.

When it is desired to avoid the line of shadow produced at the limit of action of the reflector upon the neighboring surfaces, such as the façades of houses or monuments, the plates are formed of opaline glass, and so adjusted as to per-

Fig. 250.—Plate reflector.

mit a part of the light to pass through. The useful effect of a city lantern thus provided has been found far superior to that of all other systems of diffusion. The loss of light does not exceed ten per cent.

V.

In addition to these regulator systems, powerful centers of light can be obtained with the sun lamp; in this system, more facility for increasing or diminishing the light at will is found, in changing the intensity of the current supplying them.

In estimating the cost of installation, allowance has only to be made for the difference of cost between these lamps and regulators. This difference may acquire considerable importance, because their extreme simplicity makes it possible to obtain them at a very low price. The cost of the blocks and of the carbons will be slight; the inventors estimate it at 2·5 centimes per hour for the block, costing originally 40 centimes and lasting fifteen hours. The expense of carbons is reckoned at 3 centimes. These two items give a total of 5·5 centimes per hour and per lamp.

We have no reports upon the exact total expenses of existing plants, as they have not yet worked long enough; but we have succeeded in gathering the following figures from a report made of a series of experiments conducted in Belgium by MM. Bède, Desguin, Dumont, and Rousseau, engineers and professors of physics, assisted by M. Wauters, manager of the Gas Inspection Department of Brussels:

Number of lamps.	Length of blocks in milli-metres.	Intensity of each lamp in carcels.	Total motive power expend-ed in horse-power.	Total quantity of light ob-tained in car-cels.	Number of carcels per horse-power.	Number of horse-powers per lamp.
2	35	587	18·0	1,174	65	9·00
2	30	280	16·5	560	34	8·25
3	30	186	17·0	558	33	5·65
3	22	256	12·0	868	64	4·00
6	22	234	22·8	1,404	61	3·80
8	22	126	20·9	1,008	47	2·60
12	11	107	24·7	1,284	51	2·00
16	11	83	23·8	1,328	55	1·50

All the experiments were performed with a self-exciting Gramme machine of model No. 1, constructed to supply four, six, or eight Jablochkoff candles.

The motive power was furnished by a steam-engine of 25 nominal horse power.

The power was taken by a Richards indicator and measured

29

by an Amsler planimeter. The photometric measurements were taken with a Bunsen photometer. We need not recall the particular qualities of this system, which had much success at the Paris Exhibition, where it lighted a gallery of pictures.

VI.

We have seen, in the experiments at Rouen, the Jablochkoff candles contrasting with the voltaic arc regulators. Such conditions must be disadvantageous to them, because the last-named are much more economical when the power of the burners can be increased, the number diminished, and themselves placed at a proper height. But in proportion as these favorable conditions disappear, the economic difference between the two systems grows less, and often the candles come to be preferred on account of their simplicity.

The extra expense due to them does not only come from the increased motive power required in the production of currents; it comes also from the inevitable loss of light from the use of globes, which they absolutely require, as they must burn protected from strong currents of air; it must be remembered that once extinguished the candle does not relight.

This loss of light can be estimated for globes ordinarily used, of ·4 metre diameter, at twenty-five per cent for Baccarat-glass globes, at thirty-three per cent for roughened globes and ordinary light-milky globes, and at forty-two per cent for opal globes; in calculating lighting projects with these candles, a mean of forty-one carcels for the exposed candle only can be reckoned on, which reduces to thirty carcels for the glass globes, twenty-seven for the milky globes, and only twenty-four for ordinary opal globes. On the other hand, the mean cost of establishing them hardly exceeds one thousand francs per light; it varies again with the number of lamps, the extent of the circuit of the conductors, and the greater or less elegance of the apparatus.

One of the principal running expenses, the cost of the candle itself, has diminished considerably since its beginning, on account of the reduced price of the carbon rods, and by the successive improvements introduced into the manufacture of the candles; it has been reduced from ·75 franc since July 1, 1881, to ·30 franc. The length has been slightly increased, so that their practical duration, which at first was only one hour thirty-five minutes, can reach two hours ten minutes. The motive power required is an average of one and a half horse-power per lamp. It nevertheless decreases as the number of lamps increases, and the engineers of the Metropolitan Board of Works in London, Sir Joseph Bazalgette and Mr. T. W. Keates, proved in 1879 that :

To produce 5 lights, 1·59 horse-power per lamp was required.
"   10 "   1·27   "   "   "
"   15 "   1·03   "   "   "
"   20 "   ·9   "   "   "

These figures express the motive power in indicated horse-power—that is to say, the power deduced from the indicator record. The co-efficient of reduction that they employed to transfer, indicated into actual horse-power, was about ·85.

The report of the same engineers contains interesting figures relating to the first installation of this kind in London, between Westminster and Waterloo bridges, upon a length of 2,150 meters.

The cost of plant for forty lights is estimated as follows :

One steam-engine of 20 horse-power, nominal,
   including boiler .... 12,474 francs ($2,495)
Two Gramme machines................... 9,072 " (1,814)
Shafting, belting, etc..................... 882 " (176)
Conducting cables and accessories.......... 9,828 " (1,965.60)
                                         ————
   Total..................... 32,256 " ($6,451)

As the experiments only referred to the first twenty lamps, the interest and depreciation were calculated for 25,000 francs only, say 4·9 centimes per hour per lamp for twenty lights, and 3,600 hours' service per annum.

The average daily expense is :

Coal for boilers, about 226 kilogrammes (497
   pounds), at 21 francs per ton................ 4.70 francs ($0.94)
Coal and wood for kindling.... .... 1.20 " (.24)
Oil and incidental expenses of the engine........ 1.95 " (.39)
Wages of mechanics, firemen, and inspectors..... 16.85 " (3.37)
Salaries of assistants......................... 12.50 " (2.50)
                                         ————
   Total....................... 37.20 " ($7.40)

Or per lamp and per hour ·338 franc.

Adding to this the cost of candles reduced to ·20 franc per hour per lamp we find :

Daily expense.......	.338 francs	(6.76 cents)
Interest and depreciation..................	.049 "	(.98 cents)
Electric candles	.200 "	(4.00 cents)
Total.....................	.587 "	(11.74 cents)

The price allowed for the candles in this case seems less than the real expense. M. Th. Levy, engineer of the Municipal Service of Paris, had demonstrated in 1878 the cost of maintenance per hour for the sixty-two lamps of the Avenue de l'Opéra in the following manner :

Coal for boilers..........................	6.64 francs	($1.328)
Oil and minor expenses....................	1.23 "	(.246)
Motive power.............................	3.20 "	(.64)
Salary of inspectors........	3.20 "	(.64)
Sixty-two candles at ·50 franc..............	31.00 "	(6.20)
Total.....................	45.27 "	($9.054)

Or per lamp per hour ·73 franc.

The cost may have been greatly reduced since this period, but it is still far above the sum appropriated by the city, ·30 franc per hour per lamp ; for this reason the electric lighting has to be stopped after midnight and the gas has to be lighted. This mixed system is only an incomplete solution.

If the city of Paris had the honor of the initiative in electric lighting, it must not be forgotten that the trials were pursued in England, in London notably, on a much larger scale. Thus, in the beginning of 1881, three districts were allotted and conceded, one to the Brush Company, the second to MM. Siemens Brothers, the third to the English Electric Lighting Company.

The Brush Company support thirty-three lamps on a single circuit of about 6,600 metres. The cables are composed of seven wires of 1·65 millimetres diameter, enveloped in India rubber and with a wrapping of tarred ribbon ; they are placed in cast-iron pipes underground. The lights are five metres high and provided with reflectors. The electricity is supplied by two Brush machines, driven directly by a Brotherhood engine of thirty-two horse-power. The cost as stated is about 18,750 francs for the installation and 16,500 francs per annum for lighting.

MM. Siemens use twenty-eight ordinary lamps, supplied by two alternate-current machines, eighty-six powerful lamps at an elevation of twenty-four metres, and each one supplied by a continuous-current machine. The cables are also placed in cast-iron pipes. The cost for this district is 36,375 francs for the plant, and 56,750 for the lighting, per annum.

The third installation comprises ten very powerful lamps, supplied by two continuous-current Gramme machines. These are driven by a twenty-five horse-power steam-engine. The lamps of the Brockie system present this peculiarity, that the movement of the polar carbons, instead of being regulated by variations in the intensity of the current, is produced periodically by an interrupter of the derived current actuated by the motor of the dynamo-electric machine.

This installation was ready for work much later, the price —33,750 francs for the plant and 39,500 francs for the lighting—not having seemed enough to the first company who had the allotment.

In France we have had the very interesting trial which has been going on since the National Fête of July 14, 1881, on the Boulevard des Italiens in Paris. Four lamps of Million (system using horizontal carbons, analogous to those of M. de Mersanne) were suspended over the center of the roadway of the boulevard ; they were supplied by one of M. de Mériten's machines. Fig. 251 gives an idea of this installation, which seemed well adapted for lighting the boulevards—something hard to accomplish because of the trees bordering the roadway on each side. Unfortunately, these trials were of too short duration. Finally, since November 3, 1881, the Place du Carrousel has been lighted with fourteen Mersanne lamps supplied by Lontin machines ; twelve of these lamps are suspended from lamp-posts placed on the sidewalk curbs ; two more intense lights are suspended, at a height of twenty metres, from the arms of a column of iron lattice-work.

The Lyonnaise Mechanical Construction and Electric Lighting Company, which put in this installation, also lights fifty-four Brush lamps in the temporary offices of the Post-Office department. Four other Brush lamps will be lighted in the Court of the Louvre, called the Court of Francis I, where the lamp-posts are already erected.

As for the electric lighting of the Place de la Bastille, it has ceased working since the month of February, 1880.

FIG. 251.—Lighting of the Boulevard des Italiens by the Million lamp.

It is far different in the United States, where the use of the electric light seems to have acquired a considerable development. In New York there are six powerful companies, representing together a capital of thirty millions of francs. They prosper very well, in spite of the severe competition existing between them.

VII.

For the Werdermann lamps we have only the data relating to the installation effected in 1879 in the Kensington Museum. Two halls were lighted, each one by four lamps of this system placed 2·44 metres above the ground, with opal globes. They were placed by fours in derivation upon the circuit of a Gramme machine, old model. The motive power was supplied by a gas-engine, the Otto silent, of eight horse-power, and the gas used came to eight and one half cubic metres (297½ cubic feet) per hour.

In an experiment made in Paris in 1879 a special Gramme machine, driven by a six horse-power gas-engine, was found capable of supplying ten Werdermann lamps of fifteen carcels, or twelve lamps of twelve carcels. The carbons were four and one half millimetres in diameter, and the consumption came to ten centimetres (four inches) per hour for each lamp.

We do not know the exact running expenses of the Werdermann-Reynier-Napoli lamps—we only know that the twenty-four lamps of this system that worked at the Electrical Exhibition in Paris were supplied by a self-exciting twenty-light Gramme machine, requiring about twenty horse-power. The expense per hour and per lamp may be put at about ·30 franc. We are in possession of somewhat more exact figures relative to the lighting of the bleachery of M. P. Duchesne-Fouret, in the Valley of Auge, the work being executed by M. Reynier, and the figures established by M. E. Dupuy, engineer and director of this establishment.

This lighting comprises eleven Reynier lamps, distributed as follows :

Four in the soaping and washing rooms. 46·20 × 16·60 metres = 766·92 sq. metres.
One in the wringing-room .... 19·70 × 16·60   "   = 327·02   "
Two in the first drying-room......... 66·20 × 11·50   "   = 761·30   "
Two in the second drying-room...... 66·20 × 11·50   "   = 761·30   "
One in the engine-room..... .... 10·70 × 6·60   "   = 69·62   "
One in the boiler-room.............. 11·50 × 6·80   "   = 78·20   "

The expense of installation comprises :

One Gramme machine (factory type).............	1,500	francs	($300)
Eleven Reynier lamps.........................	1,100	"	(220)
Eleven Reynier automatic lighters.............	275	"	(55)
One interrupter..............................	30	"	(6)
One galvanometer........	30	"	(6)
Five two-way switches, special model...........	150	"	(30)
Twenty white-glass globes................	40	"	(8)
Ten tin reflectors............................	50	"	(10)
Two hundred and eighty-five metres of cables and different wires........	240	"	(48)
Total......................	3,415	"	($683)

The interest and depreciation on which amount, at the rate of ten per cent and for seven hundred hours of lighting, come to ·488 franc per hour.

The Gramme machine makes 1,275 revolutions per minute ; the motive power taken from the factory engine is reckoned at three horse-powers, which seems rather too little. The running cost per hour is :

Carbon rod for the lamps at the rate of 17 centimetres per hour per lamp, 1·87 metre, at ·35 franc.................................	0.655	francs	($0.131)
Motive power, 3 horse-power, at 0 06 franc....	0.180	"	(.036)
Total......................	0.835	"	($0.167)
Interest and depreciation....................	0.488	"	(.0976)
Together....................	1.323	"	($0.2646)

Or about ·12 franc per hour per lamp, whose photometric value is equal to eight to twelve carcels. It is a very advantageous result for a factory obliged to manufacture its own lighting gas.

This class of applications will certainly multiply, if all the companies which exploit the different lighting systems will publish the necessary data to establish comparative exact and complete figures.

VIII.

We have not believed it necessary, as it often is thought, to compare the economic results of electric lighting with those of gas lighting. In general, when it is decided to use electric light, it is for the object of obtaining a sum total of light far greater than that which existed before, and which proved insufficient. For the comparison to be just, it must be made with the gas necessary for the production of the same degree of light, and in this case the advantage is with electricity.

It is far otherwise with incandescent lighting by the Edison, Swan, and other systems, whose light has almost the actual value of our gas-jets. In spite of their superiority, the small electric lights can not hope to be adopted unless they cost no more ; Edison hopes to reach this point with the installation he is preparing in New York, and all the plans of which he has exhibited in Paris ; it is enough ·in fact to distribute the cost of plant and exploitation among a considerable number of lamps and hours of lighting. There is nothing impracticable in this. Allowing for an installation of only five hundred horse-power, supplying ten thousand lamps * in a net-work of twenty-five or thirty kilometres, an annual revenue of 450,000 francs is reached on the basis of a price of *three centimes* per hour and per lamp, and for 1,500 hours lighting per annum. Estimating this first installation at 2,000,000 of francs or 100,000 francs interest per annum, and the motive power at 30,000 francs, there is left for other expenses and profits 320,000 francs. We have already seen that this price of three centimes is lower than the net cost.

But if, instead of confining the work to lighting, electricity is furnished, as M. Marcel Deprez suggests, at once for light and for power at home, the number of hours of activity may exceed four thousand per annum. Success does not seem doubtful.

It must not be concluded from this that the use of the electric light is dependent on the formation of such immense plants. It is already utilized with advantage on the condition of producing at the lowest possible price the power required. This is difficult because, as we know, the smaller the power the greater the relative cost of producing it.

Up to the present time, for electric lighting, portable engines or those of an analogous type have generally been used, and it is on the work of such engines that the cost of electricity must be calculated.

In a conference held at the Congress of Electricians in 1881, Professor Ayrton recalled that, in a recent exhibition

---

* [In the first Edison district in New York, six lamps are maintained per indicated horse-power. This figure is therefore much too high.]

in England, where several of the best machines of this type were running, the consumption of coal ran as high as two kilogrammes — exactly 1·800 kilogrammes — (four pounds) per horse-power per hour.

As all this took place at an exhibition, where the cost was to be determined, nothing was neglected to obtain the most favorable conditions ; the fires were managed by experienced firemen, the boilers were new and clean.   This does not represent the daily condition of such things in ordinary work, where 2·5 to 3 kilogrammes (5½ to 6·6 pounds) represent more nearly the usual consumption, especially when the boilers have worked several months ; it is a return of only one thirtieth of the calorific power of the carbon.

It is hardly necessary to add that all those who employ portable engines in different localities agree that the practical consumption is much higher, that it goes up to five or six kilogrammes per horse-power per hour, and even higher in many operations where the wasting of the coal is unavoidable.

It becomes absolutely necessary to find a motor that is more economical to drive the dynamo-electric machine if the cost of electricity is to be diminished.   We have also the hotair engine, whose use in English light-houses we have alluded to.   Its return of power is governed by the same law as that of steam-engines—the fall of temperature during its work upon the piston.   For it, also, the initial temperature must be increased to obtain good results, because the pressure of hot air increases more slowly than that of steam.   It can be raised, then, without danger, to temperatures where the latter would be capable of breaking all inclosures.

Unfortunately, this advantage is accompanied with a trouble that quite annuls it; lubricating oils burn very easily, and the bearings soon begin to rub.   These engines are also very large and heavy ; the slowness of their motions does not correspond to the high speeds of dynamo-electric machines, and brings on complicated problems of transmission.

The gas-engine remains, in which the power is produced by the explosion of a mixture of air and gas introduced into the interior of a cylinder at each movement of the piston.

There is a great difference between the hot-air engine and the gas-engine.   It is that in this last class of motors the elevation of heat is produced within the interior of the cylinder, so that, in spite of the high temperature of the gas, the cylinder and piston can be cooled, and the lubricators kept from drying, by means of a current of cold water. This useful cooling is impossible in the hot-air engine, the air being heated outside of the cylinder. Again the mixture of air and gas enters the cylinder at a low temperature. After the explosion there is a sudden lowering of the high temperature developed, because the piston moves before the gases have time to communicate much of their heat to the cylinder or piston.

Superheated steam can not, either, be employed without recourse to apparatus of extreme strength; account must also be taken of the great loss of heat, in the passage of this highly-heated vapor through the pipes and distributing apparatus, which would also be rapidly deteriorated by an excessive heat. It is clear, then, that with a gas-motor the high temperature necessary for an economical result can be used without encountering the practical difficulties which have prevented the use of steam or hot air under the same conditions.

In actual steam-engines the steam hardly ever exceeds 180° C. at its entrance into the cylinder, and the fall of temperature during the period of work may reach 120° C., which will furnish, according to thermo-dynamic laws, a theoretical return of twenty per cent, or one fifth.* In a gas-engine the initial temperature at the moment of explosion is estimated at 2,500° C., and it falls to about 300° C. when the piston has completed its movement, which gives a fall of temperature of 2,200° C., corresponding to a theoretical return of three quarters, or of seventy-five per cent instead of twenty per cent.†

Thus the gas-engine works under much more favorable conditions than a steam or hot-air engine—that is to say, it transforms into mechanical work a much greater quantity of the heat produced. But it does not follow from this that it works more cheaply. This depends on the price of combus-

---

* [With these extremes of temperature this would be 26·5 per cent, nearly, as follows: Efficiency $= \dfrac{T - T'}{T} = \dfrac{(180 + 273) - (60 + 273)}{180 + 273} = \dfrac{120}{453} = \cdot265.$]

† [These figures are much too high. Mr. Dugald Clerk gives 1537° C. as the maximum temperature, and 648° C. as the temperature of exhaust in the most economical type of the gas-engine. This would make the theoretical efficiency $\dfrac{(1537 + 273) - (648 + 273)}{1537 + 273} = \dfrac{889}{1810} = \cdot49.$]

tibles used, and on the other greatly varying items of cost necessarily incurred in the running of any machine.

To make the comparison with some approach to exactness, Professor Ayrton has arranged detailed tables of the expenses of all sorts required by two motors of thirty horse-power, one a steam-engine of the portable type, the other a gas-engine of the Otto type, running three hundred days, ten hours a day— that is to say, for three thousand hours of effective work. The final result came to 9,500 francs for the steam-engine, and 11,100 francs, or 1,600 francs more, for the gas-engine. It is a difference of sixteen per cent. It must be stated here that in the calculation gas is charged at fifteen centimes a cubic metre (eighty-six cents per thousand feet), which is one half the price charged in Paris to small consumers. If it be calculated on the basis of its selling price, the total expense of the gas-engine will exceed 21,500 francs—that is to say, more than double that of the steam-engine doing the same work.

Such a result does not seem encouraging. But coal to-day is manufactured for the production of light, and not of heat; it must, to be adapted for this purpose, undergo costly purifying operations, which diminish rather than increase its calorific power. When it is used for heating it is turned aside entirely from its original destination, and it should occasion no surprise if bad results are obtained.

In spite of this feature, the enormous calorific power of gas is so inefficiently utilized in the production of ordinary lights that there is an advantage in transforming it into motive power, and in converting this into electricity and into light. A cubic metre of gas burned in ordinary burners does not give over eight or nine carcels of light; it is true that here we experience the bad economy of division, because, with Siemens regenerating burners, a cubic metre of gas can give as much as thirty-five carcels. Used in a gas-engine, it represents a horse-power, that is to say, an average light of one hundred to one hundred and twenty carcels; but this advantage disappears if, in its turn, the electricity be divided into small lights—and, with incandescent lamps, scarcely twice the light produced by direct combustion in burners will be obtained.

On the other hand, gas-engines are without danger; they can be placed anywhere without permission from the authorities; no special workmen are required to run them; they work without noise; the expenditure of gas governs itself automatically in proportion to the work done, and ceases as soon as the work ceases; all that has to be added to the expense are the items of oiling and of about fifty litres of water per horse-power per hour to be used in cooling the cylinder.* These machines are an excellent resource whenever more powerful lights or more beautiful illumination is required. They are made of all sizes, and at the Electrical Exhibition in Paris they contributed largely to the production of the motive power necessary for the evening illumination. They represented one hundred and fifty-two horse-powers distributed in the following manner:

One engine of fifty horse-power, driving sixteen Gramme machines, factory type, divided into two groups.

One engine of twenty-five horse-power, driving a Kremenetzki machine, and the six Gramme machines of the Gravier distribution system.

One engine of twenty - five horse - power, driving seven Gramme machines, factory type, and one two-light Gramme machine, of the Sautter-Lemonnier Company.

One engine of twenty horse-power, driving the Schuckert (six lights) and Gülcher (six to twelve lights) machines.

One engine of twelve horse-power, driving one Gramme machine, factory type, and one Gramme self-exciter for eight Jablochkoff candles.

One engine of eight horse-power, driving one Gramme electroplating machine (Christofle), two Gramme machines, factory type (two light), and one Gramme self-exciter for four Jablochkoff candles.

One engine of eight horse-power, driving two Gramme machines, supplying the two lights in the green-house.

One engine of four horse-power, driving the two Gramme machines on M. Deprez's circuit.

The machines used for lighting the green-house (showing the influence of the light upon vegetation) worked night and day without cessation during the whole time of the Exhibition.

The speed of these machines was one hundred and forty revolutions for the five first, and one hundred and sixty revolutions for the others.

To reduce the expense of gas-engines it has even been pro-

* [No expenditure is necessary on this account, as the same water is used over and over again.]

posed to manufacture a special gas, and Mr. E. Dowson, of London, showed at the Electrical Exhibition a new apparatus producing very cheaply excellent gas for the motors.

Using just such means as those' alluded to above, for a Dowson gas-motor of thirty horse-power, running three hundred days, during a period of ten hours each day, Professor Ayrton reached a total cost of 5,240 francs. This new engine, then, will cost forty-five per cent less than a steam-engine and fifty-three per cent less than an ordinary gas-engine supplied by illuminating gas at a rate of fifteen centimes—that is to say, one half the cost of Paris gas.

Unfortunately, the establishment under our public streets of a new system of gas-mains is at present almost impossible of realization, and could not pay except by a greater development of the uses of the new gas than could be counted upon, especially with the resources now offered us by electricity in the distribution of motive power.

This is, moreover, much more advantageous, because it admits of a division which can never be attained with other motors. But nothing will prevent the realization of the economy presented by the use of the Dowson gas, in employing for the production of electricity powerful gas-engines in place of steam-engines. This new way, opened up for the utilization of combustibles, may bring about an industrial revolution in the production of motive power.

IX.

Some have thought of developing the use of vacuum incandescent burners, with accumulators that could be charged during the daytime, either by Reynier or Thompson batteries, or by a dynamo-electric machine driven by a gas-engine. But, besides the fact that the plant would be too complicated for an unimportant lighting, we do not know yet whether the incandescent lamps of different systems which were seen at the Electrical Exhibition can be procured, and, if they could be found, they would cost too much ; they speak of twenty-five francs per Swan lamp for the first purchase, and 12·50 francs for the lamps that replace the first, whose duration is only guaranteed to be three hundred hours burning. It would probably be just as difficult to obtain improved accumulators. All this has not passed the experimental stage, although a very interesting application of it has been recently made in England. On the London and Brighton line a car is lighted by twelve Swan lamps supplied by thirty-two Faure accumulators. These same lamps are also on trial in lighting the interior of armored vessels, and in mine galleries.

Assuming an approximate estimate for the installation of fifty of these lamps, at a probable cost of five francs per lamp (Edison system), the lighting will come to the following : For five hundred hours per annum, 8·2 centimes per hour and per lamp ; for fifteen hundred hours, a term which may be applied to domestic lighting, 1·8 centime ; for four thousand hours' lighting, the cost descends to 1·4 centime.

While waiting for industrial lighting to be instituted, very interesting applications have been made in England, which show well how the electric light can be made use of in domestic economy.

The late Mr. Spottiswoode, president of the Royal Society of London, used, for his country-house and laboratory at Coombe Bank, a large magneto-electric machine of M. de Méritens, two Gramme ,machines, factory type, one small continuous-current Siemens machine, and one large Burgin machine. Besides the experiments for which they are destined, these machines give a very remarkable illumination, which comprises twelve Jablochkoff candles, four powerful Crompton lamps, and ninety Swan incandescent lamps ; of these last, thirty light the grand saloon, twenty are in the dining-hall, and the rest are distributed through the other parts of the château.

Elsewhere, Sir W. G. Armstrong uses the incandescent light for lighting his residence in the country, and that almost without expense, the motive power coming from a neighboring water-fall. A six horse-power turbine drives a Siemens dynamo-electric machine ; the distance of the turbine from the house is about four and a half kilometres, the conductors are formed of copper wire seven millimetres thick. The number of Swan lamps is forty-five, but, as a rule, only thirty-seven are lighted at the same time.

The library, which is ten metres by six, is perfectly lighted by eight lamps ; the dining-room, also by eight lamps, six of which form a lustre over the table ; the two others are in brackets. A picture-gallery, serving as a study, is lighted by twelve suspended lamps, to which are added eight others when the dining-room is darkened ; the gallery is well lighted by the twelve lamps, but, with all twenty lamps in operation, the pictures show to as much advantage as in daylight.

The other lamps are distributed through the other rooms of the house.

Each lamp is estimated at twenty-five candles, so that the six horse-power gives a total light of about two hundred and twenty-five candles.

In conclusion, it must be said that the electric light has won for itself an important position among the resources of our civilization ; its defects will vanish one by one, and each new improvement is followed immediately by numerous applications; its qualities were demonstrated at the Exhibition of 1881, so as to convince most of its adversaries. Its general use is only a question of time ; it always was the same with inventions that disarrange our habits, and force us to learn new things. It is probable that our grandchildren will pity us who depended on gas and steam-engines, as we pity our ancestors who only had candles and stage-coaches.

INDEX.

THE END.

Important Works on

ELECTRICITY

A PHYSICAL TREATISE ON ELECTRI-
CITY AND MAGNETISM.

By J. E. H. GORDON, B. A., Assistant Secretary of the British Association. 2 vols., 8vo., with about 200 full-page and other Illustrations. Cloth, $7.00.

" There is certainly no book in English—we think there is none in any other language—which covers quite the same ground. It records the most recent advances in the experimental treatment of electrical problems, it describes with minute carefulness the instruments and methods in use in physical laboratories, and is prodigal of beautifully executed diagrams and drawings made to scale."— *London Times.*

" The fundamental point in the whole work is its perfect reflection of all that is best in the modern modes of regarding electric and magnetic forces, and in the modern methods of constructing electrical instruments."—*Engineering.*

ELECTRICITY AND THE ELECTRIC
TELEGRAPH.

By GEORGE B. PRESCOTT. With Illustrations. Fifth edition. 8vo. Cloth, $5.00.

" The object which has been aimed at in the preparation of the present work has been to furnish a treatise on the subject of Electricity and the Telegraph, which should present a comprehensive and accurate summary of the present advanced state of the science and art, both in this country and abroad, and at the same time serve a useful purpose as a manual for the information and guidance of those engaged in the different branches of the telegraphic service. Especial attention has been paid to the voluminous contributions of Germany, a nation whose electricians unquestionably occupy the foremost rank among discoverers and inventors, but whose labors have heretofore remained for the most part unknown to the English reader. The discoveries, inventions, and practical improvements of the past few years, especially those relating to the duplex and quadruplex methods of transmission, and to the improved type-printing apparatus, which in America have almost revolutionized the telegraphic service, are now described and illustrated for the first time with a completeness commensurate with the great importance of the subject."—*From the Preface.*

The MODERN APPLICATIONS of ELECTRICITY.

By E. HOSPITALIER. New edition, revised, with many Additions.
Translated by JULIUS MAIER, Ph. D.
Vol. I. ELECTRIC GENERATORS, ELECTRIC LIGHT.
Vol. II. TELEPHONE: Various Applications, Electrical Transmission of Energy.
Two vols. 8vo. With numerous Illustrations. $8.00.

" M. Hospitalier distinguishes three sources of electricity, namely, the decomposition of metals or other decomposable bodies in acid or alkaline solutions, the transformation of heat into electrical energy, and lastly the conversion of work into current—giving rise to the three specific modes of force styled respectively galvanism, thermo-electricity, and dynamic electricity. He gives a history of the progress of each, from the first crude constructions of the pioneer to the latest and most perfect form of battery, thus furnishing the student of science with a sufficiently copious text-book of the subject, while at the same time affording to the electrical engineer a valuable encyclopædia of his profession. The work presents a most useful and thorough compendium of the principles and practice of electrical engineering, written as only an expert can write, to whom the abstruse by long study has become simple. The translator has acted the part of an editor also, and has added considerable material of value to the original text. His account of the Edison, Fox, and Brush systems of lighting, for example, is more complete than that of M. Hospitalier in his second edition. He has also added full descriptions of the fire-damp indicators of Liveling, Sourzée, and Mounier; of Bright's fire-alarm and district telegraph, and of Dolbear's telephone, and Kelway's electric log, together with other recent inventions not mentioned in Hospitalier's treatise, exhaustive and excellent as it is."—*New York Times.*

THE SPEAKING TELEPHONE, ELECTRIC LIGHT, AND OTHER RECENT ELECTRICAL INVENTIONS.

By GEORGE B. PRESCOTT. New edition, with 200 additional pages, including Illustrated Description of all of Edison's Inventions. 214 Illustrations. 8vo. Cloth, $4.00.

" Mr. Prescott's work on recent electrical inventions being American, is naturally largely occupied with the results of Mr. Edison's researches and the work of other distinguished Americans, though it is by no means limited to the results obtained on the other side of the Atlantic. It is a magnificently illustrated volume, and is the most complete history and discussion of telephones and allied instruments and the electric light which has come under our notice. It will probably remain a standard work until the progress of discovery leaves it behind, for every instrument of which it treats is explained so fully and illustrated so well that there is but little room left for improvement. For the student and all who have sufficient knowledge or interest in the subject, it will be a valuable magazine of information."—*Westminster Review.*

ELECTRICITY AND MAGNETISM.

By FLEEMING JENKIN, Professor of Engineering in the University of Edinburgh. Illustrated, and Index. With Appendix on the Telephone and Microphone. 12mo. Cloth, $1.50.

"The plan followed in this book is as follows: First, a general synthetical view of the science has been given, in which the main phenomena are described and the terms employed explained. This general view of the science can not be made very easy reading, although it will probably be found easier by those who have no preconceived notions about tension, intensity, and so forth, than by students of old text-books. If this portion of the work can be mastered, the student will then be readily able to understand what follows, viz., the description of the apparatus used to measure electrical magnitudes and to produce electricity under various conditions. The general theory of electricity is permanent, depending on no hypothesis, and it has been the author's aim to state this general theory in a connected manner, and in such simple form that it might be readily understood by practical men."—*From the Introduction.*

THE ART OF ELECTRO-METALLURGY, INCLUDING ALL KNOWN PRO-CESSES OF ELECTRO-DEPOSITION.

By G. GORE, LL. D., F. R. S. Illustrated, and with Index. 12mo. Cloth, $2.50.

"I have endeavored to produce such a book as would be useful to scientific students, to practical workers in the art of electro metallurgy, gilders, platers, etc., and to all persons who wish to obtain in a compact form an explanation of the principles and facts upon which the art is based, the circumstances under which nearly every known metal is deposited, and the special details of technical workshop manipulation in the galvano-plastic art. I have also given an historical sketch of the development of the subject, arranged in chronological order. I have endeavored not only to make the book a treatise on the practical art of electro-metallurgy, but also to include an outline of the science of electro-chemistry, upon which that art is based ; and I have spared no trouble to make the book as perfect as I could. The most complete portions are those which treat of the common methods of silvering, gilding, molding; the deposition of copper, nickel, brass, iron, and tin; the special details of the art; and the accounts of such experiments and processes with the less common metals as scientific investigators and practical inventors may be likely to further examine, or practically apply. Numerous experiments of my own on the subject (many of them through want of previous opportunity being now for the first time published) are scattered through the first part of the practical section of the book; a few of them being made to fill up missing links, while the book was in progress."—*From the Introduction.*

LIGHT AND ELECTRICITY:

NOTES OF TWO COURSES OF LECTURES BEFORE THE ROYAL INSTITUTION OF GREAT BRITAIN.

By Professor JOHN TYNDALL.   12mo.   Cloth, $1.25.

" In thus clearly and sharply stating the fundamental principles of electrical and optical science, Professor Tyndall has earned the cordial thanks of all interested in education."—*From the American Editor's Preface.*

LESSONS IN ELECTRICITY, AT THE ROYAL INSTITUTION, 1875-'76.

By Professor JOHN TYNDALL.   12mo.   Cloth, $1.00.

ELEMENTARY TREATISE ON NATURAL PHILOSOPHY.

By A. PRIVAT DESCHANEL, formerly Professor of Physics in the Lycée Louis-le-Grand, Inspector of the Academy of Paris.

Translated and edited, with Extensive Modifications, by J. D. EVERETT, Professor of Natural Philosophy in the Queen's College, Belfast.

Sixth edition, revised, complete in Four Parts.   8vo.   Illustrated by 783 Engravings on Wood, and Three Colored Plates.

Part I. MECHANICS, HYDROSTATICS, AND PNEUMATICS. Cloth, $1.50.

Part II. HEAT. Cloth, $1.50.

Part III. ELECTRICITY AND MAGNETISM. Cloth, $1.50.

Part IV. SOUND AND LIGHT. Cloth, $1.50.

Complete in one volume, 8vo, with Problems and Index.   Cloth, $5.70.

"Systematically arranged, clearly written, and admirably illustrated, showing no less than 783 engravings on wood and three colored plates, it forms a model work for a class of experimental physics. Far from losing in its English dress any of the qualities of matter or style which distinguished it in its original form, it may be said to have gained in the able hands of Professor Everett, both by way of arrangement and of incorporation of fresh matter, without parting in the translation with any of the freshness or force of the author's text."—*Saturday Review.*

These books are sold by all booksellers; or will be sent by mail, post-paid, on receipt of price, by

D. APPLETON & CO., Publishers,

1, 3, & 5 BOND STREET, NEW YORK.